INTERNATIONAL COMMERCIAL ARBITRATION

Arbitration clauses in international commercial contracts are often reused from existing contracts. By so doing, the parties choose to apply, for example, either ad hoc or institutional arbitration and the UNCITRAL, ICC, LCIA, SCC, Swiss or other arbitration rules without necessarily being aware of the consequences. Moreover, parties often assume that an arbitration clause has the effect of excluding any kind of interference from a court of law and of rendering any but the chosen law redundant.

This book highlights the specific features of various forms of arbitration and enables lawyers to make informed choices when drafting arbitration clauses. Chapters explain the framework for arbitration, its relationship with national law, and the features of the main arbitration institutions in Europe. Attention is also paid to new trends in other parts of the world that may have repercussions on the theory of international arbitration.

GIUDITTA CORDERO-MOSS is a professor at the Department for Private Law at the University of Oslo, where she is in charge of International Commercial Law, International Commercial Arbitration and Private International Law.

INTERNATIONAL COMMERCIAL ARBITRATION

Different Forms and their Features

Edited by

GIUDITTA CORDERO-MOSS

CAMBRIDGE
UNIVERSITY PRESS

CAMBRIDGE
UNIVERSITY PRESS

University Printing House, Cambridge CB2 8BS, United Kingdom

Published in the United States of America by Cambridge University Press, New York

Cambridge University Press is part of the University of Cambridge.

It furthers the University's mission by disseminating knowledge in the pursuit of education, learning and research at the highest international levels of excellence.

www.cambridge.org
Information on this title: www.cambridge.org/9781107033481

First published 2013
3rd printing 2013

Printed in the United Kingdom by the CPI Group Ltd, Croydon CR0 4YY

A catalogue record for this publication is available from the British Library

Library of Congress Cataloguing in Publication data
International commercial arbitration : different forms and their features / Edited by Giuditta Cordero-Moss.
p. cm.
Includes index.
ISBN 978-1-107-03348-1
1. International commercial arbitration. I. Cordero-Moss, Giuditta.
K2400.I5926 2013
346.07–dc23
2012032733

ISBN 978-1-107-03348-1 Hardback

CONTENTS

CONTRIBUTORS

DIEGO P. FERNÁNDEZ ARROYO is professor at Complutense University, Madrid, and School of Law of Sciences Po, Paris. He is member of The Curatorium of The Hague Academy of International Law, former President of the American Association of Private International Law (2007/2010) and member of the International Arbitration Institute (IAI).

STEFANO AZZALI is active in the area of international arbitration and is a frequent speaker internationally within this area. He is Secretary General of the Milan Chamber of Arbitration and Secretary Treasurer of the International Federation of Commercial Arbitration Institutions (IFCAI).

GEORGE A. BERMANN is Jean Monnet Professor of EU Law, Walter Gellhorn Professor of Law and Director of the European Studies Centre, Columbia University, New York. He is a leading figure in the study of International and European law, both within the United States and abroad. He is Chief Reporter on the ALI Restatement of the US Law on International Commercial Arbitration.

JENS BREDOW, Rechtsanwalt (Cologne) is Secretary General of the *Deutsche Institution für Schiedsgerichtsbarkeit*. He publishes and lectures internationally within the area of international arbitration.

GIUDITTA CORDERO-MOSS, is a professor and Director of the Department for Private Law at the University of Oslo, and Head of Private International Law, International Commercial Law and International Commercial Arbitration. Founder and manager of the research project 'Arbitration and Party Autonomy', she is a former international corporate lawyer and is active as an international arbitrator.

DORINE FARAH is an associate in the international dispute resolution group of Baker Botts and is based in London, her practice focusing exclusively on international arbitration work, both public and private, with a particular emphasis on contractual disputes governed by English law and LCIA arbitration.

HENRIK FIEBER is a partner in the Stockholm office of the law firm Roschier. He regularly acts as counsel in domestic and international arbitrations under the ICC, SCC, and CCCF rules as well as in *ad hoc* arbitrations – in disputes spanning a range of sectors. His previous experience includes working for the Swedish court system, as a judge in the District Court and the Court of Appeal.

SIMON GREENBERG is counsel with the international arbitration team of Clifford Chance, Paris, where he advises clients and acts as arbitrator in international arbitrations. From January 2008 to January 2011 he served as Deputy Secretary General of the ICC International Court of Arbitration. He previously practised international arbitration with another leading law firm in Paris, and before that with a leading firm in Australia. He is the author or co-author of numerous articles on international arbitration, a lecturer at Sciences Po in Paris and at Hong Kong University, and a co-author of two books: *International Commercial Arbitration: An Asia Pacific Perspective* (2010) and *The Secretariat's Guide to ICC Arbitration* (2012).

STEPHEN KNUDTZON is a partner in the Thommessen law firm, Oslo. He is active in arbitration, particularly in the fields of insurance, shipping and construction. He is also the chairman of the Arbitration Institute of the Oslo Chamber of Commerce.

JOHANNES KOEPP is a partner in Baker Botts, London. He is qualified in the jurisdictions of England and Wales and of Germany. He has extensive experience in the substantive and procedural laws of both common and other civil law jurisdictions and has published numerous works in the field of international arbitration. He sits as an arbitrator and was recently selected by *Global Arbitration Review* as one of their '45 under 45' leading international arbitration practitioners.

ALEXANDER S. KOMAROV is a leading expert in international arbitration in Russia and a member of numerous international arbitration institutions and international commissions. He is Professor and Head of International Private Law at the Russian Academy of Foreign Trade, a member of the Presidium of the International Commercial Arbitration

Court at the Chamber of Commerce and Industry of the Russian Federation and acted as its president from 1993 to 2010.

GEORG LETT is a partner in the Lett law firm, Copenhagen. He is active in arbitration, particularly in the fields of insurance, finance and EU law, and has various publications in his fields of expertise. He is a member of the ICC Court of Arbitration.

WERNER MELIS was President of the International Arbitral Centre of the Austrian Federal Economic Chamber, Vienna (VIAC) and has been a Vice-President of the London Court of International Arbitration (LCIA). He is active as an international arbitrator and is the author of various contributions to professional journals and textbooks on international arbitration.

CORINNE MONTINERI is a legal officer in the International Trade Law Division of the United Nations Office of Legal Affairs, which also functions as the Secretariat of the United Nations Commission on International Trade Law (UNCITRAL). She is the secretary to the UNCITRAL Working Group II on Arbitration.

LUCA RADICATI DI BROZOLO is a professor at the Catholic University, Milan, where he is Head of Private International Law and International Arbitration Law. He is also a partner in the law firm Bonelli Erede Pappalardo, Milan, where he practises mainly in the fields of arbitration, international law and competition matters.

ANDERS RYSSDAL is a partner in the law firm of Wiersholm, Oslo. As head of its Litigation and Arbitration Law Practice Group, he practises within European law, international arbitration and litigation. He has had many appointments as counsel, chairman, sole arbitrator and co-arbitrator in domestic and international arbitrations. He is the Norwegian member of the ICC Court of Arbitration in Paris.

MARCO STACHER is a senior associate in the litigation team of the law firm Walder Wyss, Zurich. He practises mainly as counsel in international commercial arbitration seated in Switzerland or elsewhere.

EVA STORSKRUBB is a Senior Associate in the Stockholm office of the law firm Roschier. She practises in the field of international dispute resolution and has experience of multi-jurisdictional cases involving both court litigation and arbitration in several countries. She is also an internationally recognised specialist in EU procedural law.

CARITA WALLGREN-LINDHOLM is a partner in the Lindholm Wallgren law firm, Helsinki. She practises in the areas of arbitration, delivery contracts and as a corporate advisor. She is active internationally and has published in her field of expertise.

PETER WEBSTER is a member of Essex Court Chambers, London. He was previously a junior associate in Baker Botts' London office.

DANIEL WEHRLI† was a partner in the law firm of Gloor and Sieger, Zurich. He practised mainly within arbitration and commercial law. He was Vice President of the Swiss Arbitration Association.

Introduction

GIUDITTA CORDERO-MOSS

Arbitration is very common for disputes arising out of international commercial contracts. With an arbitration clause in the contract, disputes between the parties are solved by an arbitral tribunal chosen by the parties and outside of the ordinary courts.

Despite their obvious importance, arbitration clauses are not always given their deserved attention in international contract practice. Most commercial parties know that it is advisable to choose arbitration, but often they have little specific knowledge regarding the choice of arbitration type that an arbitration clause entails. The drafting of a dispute resolution clause may be reduced to a 'copy and paste' exercise using contracts that were used in the past; by so doing, the parties choose *ad hoc* arbitration or institutional arbitration, the UNCITRAL, ICC, LCIA, SCC, Swiss or other Arbitration Rules, without actually being aware of the differences between them.

In addition, parties do not always have a precise understanding of what consequences an arbitration clause has. Often parties assume that an arbitration clause choosing a foreign venue, coupled with the choice of a foreign law to govern the contract, has the effect of excluding any kind of interference from any court of law, and of rendering any other law but the chosen law fully redundant. Parties may feel that by choosing international arbitration, they enter an autonomous dimension completely detached from the systems of law to which their legal relationship is connected. The parties may even assume that the arbitration law of the place of arbitration is irrelevant.

In reality, arbitration is a complex system that deserves more thorough evaluation than an automatic reproduction of an arbitration clause found in an old contract.

Arbitration depends on international conventions as well as on the national law of the place where the arbitral tribunal has its seat.

Moreover, the enforceability of an arbitral award depends on international conventions as well as on the national law of the place of enforcement. The interaction between the national law and international arbitration may lead to results that come as a surprise to those parties who relied on the fully autonomous nature of arbitration.

In addition to the local arbitration law, other factors may influence an arbitral proceeding: the proceeding will be subject to the arbitration rules of the chosen institution, to harmonised arbitration rules referred to by the parties such as those issued by the UNCITRAL or to the discretion of the tribunal, depending on whether the arbitration clause provides for institutional or *ad hoc* arbitration. National arbitration laws may differ quite considerably from each other, and there is a variety of arbitration institutions to choose from.

This renders it highly advisable to make an informed decision when writing the arbitration clause in a contract. In turn, this assumes an understanding of the specific features that characterise the various arbitration forms, both in respect of the applicable arbitration rules and in respect of the applicable arbitration law.

This book highlights the specific features of various forms of arbitration, thus enabling an informed choice. The focus of the book is on the features of the main arbitration institutions in Europe as well as on *ad hoc* arbitration.

In addition, the book also presents new trends in other parts of the world that cannot be ignored when dealing with international arbitration because of the repercussions that they may have on the theory of international arbitration.

Part I gives an overview of the role played by national arbitration law in international arbitration. This part is intended to give an understanding of the extent to which national law is relevant in the context of international arbitration.

Part II discusses the main differences between *ad hoc* and institutional arbitration, and will analyse the UNCITRAL Arbitration Rules, often used in *ad hoc* arbitration. This part is intended to give an understanding of the legal sources regulating *ad hoc* arbitration, thus enabling to make an informed choice between *ad hoc* and institutional arbitration.

Part III examines the arbitration institutions in Europe that are more commonly used for international commercial disputes: the ICC, LCIA, Swiss Rules, Arbitration Institutes in the Chambers of Commerce in Austria, Denmark, France, Germany, Italy, Norway, Russia and Sweden.

The authors present their respective topic by highlighting the specific features in respect of the following (having regard both to the applicable arbitration rules and to the applicable arbitration law):

1. Time frame for the proceeding
2. Cost determination (including security)
3. Procedure for the appointment of the tribunal
4. Identity and role of the appointing authority
5. Form of the arbitration agreement
6. Interference/support by the courts (including the tribunal's powers to involve them)
7. Tribunal's powers *ex officio*
8. Possibility of interim measures and their enforceability
9. Multiparty arbitration (including joinder and consolidation)
10. Conduct of arbitration (terms of reference, number of briefs, disclosure, written or oral evidence, modality of hearings, applicable law)
11. Confidentiality
12. Institution's role
13. Possibility of excluding the courts' review of the award's validity
14. Grounds for invalidity of the award
15. Other specific features in the arbitration rules or the arbitration law.

Part IV examines trends in other parts of the world that should not be ignored when dealing with international arbitration irrespective of the geographical area. The American Law Institute's first Restatement of international commercial arbitration law is presented, an unprecedented work that is in the course of being issued and will certainly receive attention even in Europe. Moreover, trends in Latin America are presented. Latin America has often been considered as an arbitration-unfriendly environment and its doctrines are sometimes referred to in support of a restrictive understanding of party autonomy in arbitration. An overview of the trends will be relevant to the general discussion on arbitration.

There are numerous publications on international arbitration. Many of these are a presentation of, or guidelines for the procedure at a specific arbitration institution. There are also numerous detailed analyses of various legal aspects of arbitration. It is entirely possible, on the basis of the existing literature, to obtain the information necessary in order to make an informed choice of arbitration form.

However, it may be quite demanding under the time pressure of contract negotiations to identify from the wealth of information the specific features that under the given circumstances may justify preferring one form of arbitration to another.

The aim of this book is to present a reasoned comparison of various arbitration forms, so that it becomes apparent what distinguishes one from the other.

PART I

Arbitration law's significance for international disputes

1

International arbitration is not only international

GIUDITTA CORDERO-MOSS

Parties to international arbitration are sometimes under the impression that they may draft arbitration agreements and prepare arbitration proceedings without taking national laws into consideration. National laws may seem to be irrelevant if international arbitration is considered to be an autonomous system that depends on the will of the parties and on some international instruments that are uniformly applied all over the world. This, however, is an oversimplification.

To a large extent, arbitration's autonomy is confirmed by international instruments – primarily, the 1958 New York Convention on the Recognition and Enforcement of Foreign Arbitral Awards. If parties decide to submit a dispute to arbitration, according to article II of the Convention, the courts of the nearly 150 states which have ratified the Convention[1] must decline jurisdiction on that dispute. If the arbitral tribunal chosen by the parties renders an award based on the instructions given by the parties and applies the law chosen by the parties, according to article V of the Convention, the courts of all those states have to enforce that award, subject to a few exceptions. This is certainly enhancing the impression that arbitration is an autonomous system, where national laws are allowed to have an impact only to the extent that they have been chosen by the parties.

In addition, the UNCITRAL (United Nations Commission on International Trade Law) Model Law on International Commercial Arbitration has been adopted in more than sixty countries[2] and is widely used as a reference elsewhere. The Model Law was intended as a source of

[1] For an updated overview of the status of ratifications see the Convention's official site at www.uncitral.org/uncitral/en/uncitral_texts/arbitration/NYConvention_status.html

[2] Of the countries analysed in Part III of this book, the following have adopted the Model Law: Austria, Denmark, Germany, Norway and Russia. For an updated overview of the countries that have adopted the Model Law see www.uncitral.org/uncitral/en/uncitral_-texts/arbitration/1985Model_arbitration_status.html

harmonisation in international arbitration. To this end, and to ensure continuity, it was deliberately aligned with the New York Convention.[3] This contributes greatly to the harmonisation of national arbitration laws, thus enhancing the impression that arbitration law is standardised and that there is no need to pay attention to the peculiarities of national laws.

On this basis, sometimes arbitration is deemed to be detached from national laws. According to an opinion that was quite influential, especially some decades ago, arbitration is international, and as such it does not even have a *forum*.[4] In particular, no importance should be attached to the legal system of the place of arbitration; this opinion assumed that the mere circumstance that an international arbitration happens to have its seat in a certain state should not create any link with the legal system of that state. The choice of place of arbitration, according to this opinion, is based on considerations of practical convenience, such as the relative vicinity to the states of both parties, the possibility of having convenient flight connections or the availability of modern and efficient meeting facilities.

This chapter will show that the place of arbitration has a significant impact that may affect the validity and enforceability of the arbitral award, and that, therefore, the venue should be chosen first of all out of legal considerations (Section 1 below).

Also, this chapter will show that not only the law of the place of arbitration, but also other national laws may have an impact on arbitration, and that this is quite irrespective of whether the parties have chosen them to apply or have even decided that they shall not apply: the law of the place of enforcement (Section 2 below) and, to a certain extent, the law applicable to the substance of the dispute (Section 3 below).

[3] See the Explanatory Note by the UNCITRAL Secretariat on the Model Law on International Commercial Arbitration, available at www.uncitral.org/uncitral/en/uncitral_texts/arbitration/1985Model_arbitration.html

[4] See, for example, Marc Blessing, 'Choice of Substantive Law in International Arbitration', *Journal of International Arbitration*, 14(1997), 39ff.; Marc Blessing, 'Keynotes on Arbitral Decision-making: The New 1998 ICC Rules of Arbitration', *ICC International Court of Arbitration Bulletin*, (1997), 44ff.; Ole Lando, 'The New Lex Mercatoria in International Commercial Arbitration', *International and Comparative Law Quarterly*, 34(1985), 747, 765ff.; Jan Paulsson, 'Arbitration Unbound: Award Detached from the Law of its State of Origin', *International and Comparative Law Quarterly*, 30(1981), 358ff, 362ff and 381; Jan Paulsson, 'Delocalisation of International Commercial Arbitration: When and Why It Matters', *International and Comparative Law Quarterly* 32(1983), 53ff.

1 International arbitration and the state law of the place of arbitration

The law of the place of arbitration (also known as the *lex arbitri*) affects various aspects of an arbitral proceeding: the validity of the arbitration agreement, the procedure of the arbitration and the validity of the arbitral award.

1.1 The relevance of the lex arbitri *to the validity of the arbitration agreement*

The jurisdiction of an arbitral tribunal on a certain dispute and the consequent exclusion of jurisdiction by courts of law on the same dispute are based, for international arbitration, on the already mentioned New York Convention. In article II the Convention provides that: 'Each Contracting State shall recognize an agreement in writing under which the parties undertake to submit to arbitration all or any differences which have arisen or which may arise between them in respect of a defined legal relationship, whether contractual or not, concerning a subject matter capable of settlement by arbitration.' Article II does not make reference to any national law for the validity of the arbitration agreement, and seems, therefore, to be a provision that contains all applicable criteria for validity.

However, article V(1)(a) of the New York Convention, regulating the enforcement of an arbitral award, states that enforcement may be refused if '[t]he ... agreement referred to in article II ... is not valid under the law to which the parties have subjected it or, failing any indication thereon, under the law of the country where the award was made.' The latter – the *lex arbitri* – is more commonly used: it is rare to see an arbitration clause specifying which law governs the arbitration, and the general choice of law made by the parties to govern the contractual relationship does not extend to the arbitration agreement, not even if this latter takes the form of a clause in the contract that contains the choice of law.[5] Coordination of article II and article V of the Convention may create some challenges, as will be seen immediately below.

[5] As a result of the separability doctrine that receives large support internationally. See, for references to literature and case law, Gary Born, *International Commercial Arbitration* (Kluwer Law International, 2009), vol. 1, pp. 312–408.

1.1.1 The formal validity of the arbitration agreement

A large number of contracts contain arbitration clauses entered into electronically, by reference to other documents or even tacitly. This raises questions, particularly in relation to the requirement laid down in the New York Convention that arbitration agreements should be 'in writing'.

The UNCITRAL has recently recommended that the New York Convention be interpreted broadly so that arbitration agreements entered into by electronic means of communication may be considered to comply with the writing requirement.[6] Also, the UNCITRAL Model Law on International Commercial Arbitration, originally issued in 1985, has been amended in 2006 so as to exclude any doubt regarding the admissibility of arbitration agreements entered into electronically – emphasising, however, that the clarification resulting from the amendment did not modify the Model Law, but simply confirmed the liberal interpretation that was already adopted by various courts.[7]

National laws may vary considerably in the formal requirements they lay down for arbitration agreements. Thus, article 807 of the Italian Code of Civil Procedure, article 178(1) of the Swiss Private International Law Act, article 1031 of the German Code of Civil Procedure and section 5 of the English Arbitration Act all require the arbitration agreement to be in writing, albeit with small differences in the specification of how to meet this requirement: under German law, for example, it is sufficient that the arbitration agreement was contained in a document sent by one party to the other, if such a party had not raised objections in good time; under English law, the criteria are also met by agreements that are made other than in writing, so long as they refer to terms that are in writing, and agreements that have been recorded in writing only by one party. Some countries, however, have abolished the writing requirement altogether: article 1 of the Swedish Arbitration Act and article 3–10 of the Norwegian Arbitration Act recognise any arbitration agreement,

[6] UNCITRAL 'Recommendation regarding the interpretation of article II(2) and article VII,' paragraph 1, of the Convention on the Recognition and Enforcement of Foreign Arbitral Awards, done in New York, 10 June 1958, adopted by the United Nations Commission on International Trade Law on 7 July 2006 at its thirty-ninth session, A/RES/61/33, available at www.uncitral.org/pdf/english/texts/arbitration/NY-conv/A2E.pdf. For a more extensive comment see Giuditta Cordero-Moss, 'Form of Arbitration Agreements: Current Developments within UNCITRAL and the Writing Requirement of the New York Convention', *ICC International Court of Arbitration Bulletin*, 18(2007), 51.

[7] See A/CN.9/WG.II/WP.118, para.11.

without laying down any particular form for that agreement, provided that the parties have reached a consensus.

A similar proposal has been adopted for the UNCITRAL Model Law on International Commercial Arbitration in 2006, but only as one of two options that the states adopting the Model Law may choose.[8] As a consequence, states that adopt the UNCITRAL Model Law on International Commercial Arbitration will, in the future, have to choose between one option requiring that the arbitration agreement be in writing, which clarifies that electronic communication meets that requirement, and one where there are no formal requirements at all.

The abandoning of formal requirements for the arbitration clause raises various questions. In particular, is an arbitral award enforceable under the New York Convention if it has been rendered on the basis of an arbitration clause that, while valid under the applicable national law, is not in writing as required by article II of the New York Convention? Traditionally, despite the reference to national law contained in article V of the Convention, it was widely considered that the formal requirements of article II of the New York Convention prevail over any formal requirements also laid down by applicable national law in the phase of enforcement.[9] This is because the New York Convention was traditionally thought to embody an approach more favourable to arbitration than is found in national laws. However, now that some national laws and the amended UNCITRAL Model Law on International Commercial Arbitration have become more arbitration-friendly than the New York Convention in respect of formal requirements for the arbitration agreement, it may rightly be asked whether that view should change and national arbitration laws be given preference. This would be more in line with the wording of article V(1)(a) and with the spirit of the Convention.[10]

8 Article 7 has two versions in the Model Law as amended in 2006.

9 For a survey of the various approaches taken by courts of different states, see the UNCITRAL Secretariat note A/CN.9/WG.II/WP.139, available at http://daccess-ods.un.org/TMP/9440393.44787598.html, paras. 12–15. Only the Italian Supreme Court seems to have held that different parameters were applied at the two stages with article II not applying at the enforcement stage: Supreme Court decision No. 637, 20 Jan. 1995, *Rivista dell'Arbitrato* (1995) at 449 and *Yearbook Commercial Arbitration* XXI (1996) at 602f.

10 Article VII of the New York Convention permits applying national laws that are more arbitration-friendly than the Convention itself. For a more extensive analysis see Cordero-Moss, 'Form of Arbitration Agreements'.

1.1.2 The legal capacity of the parties to the arbitration agreement

According to article V(1)(a) of the New York Convention, one of the grounds for refusing recognition or enforcement of an award is that one of the parties of the arbitration agreement was under some incapacity under its own law. The UNCITRAL Model Law has used this article of the New York Convention as a basis for its own rules on annulment of awards and on the possibility of being able to refuse recognition or enforcement; respectively, articles 34(2)(a)(i) and 36(1)(a)(i). Similar references to the law of each of the parties may be found in the arbitration law of countries that have not adopted the Model Law. Thus, two recent court decisions rendered in countries that have not adopted the Model Law, one of the Swedish Court of Appeal[11] and one of the English Supreme Court,[12] have established the ineffectiveness of international arbitral awards on the basis that the arbitration agreement was not binding on one of the parties in accordance with the law applicable to that party. These decisions are a reminder that the law chosen by the parties to govern the contract does not cover all aspects of the legal relationship between the parties, and that other laws may become applicable in spite of the parties' choice. The general attitude among practitioners sometimes seems, on the contrary, to rely fully and solely on the law chosen by the parties and to disregard any other laws – on the basis that an international arbitral tribunal will be obliged to follow the will of the parties. Decisions like those mentioned here, therefore, may come as a surprise, although they simply give proper effect to the applicable sources of law.

1.1.3 The scope of the arbitration agreement

In the past, drafters of arbitration agreements devoted particular attention to the wording used in defining the scope of the arbitration

[11] *State of Ukraine* v. *Norsk Hydro ASA*, Svea Hovrätt, 17 December 2007, T 3108–06, see *ITA Monthly Report*, KluwerArbitration, 6(5) (2008). The losing party attempted to appeal the decision before the Supreme Court, but the Supreme Court denied leave to appeal: decision dated 2 June 2008, case no. T 339–08.

[12] *Dallah Real Estate & Tourism Holding Co* v. *Ministry of Religious Affairs, Government of Pakistan* [2010] UKSC 46. This decision was not based on the lack of legal capacity of one of the parties, but on the relevance that that party's law has to the criteria for being deemed bound by an agreement. For a more extensive analysis and a comparison between the Swedish and the English decision, see Giuditta Cordero-Moss, 'Legal Capacity, Arbitration and Private International Law', in K. Boele-Woelki *et al.* (eds.), *Convergence and Divergence in Private International Law: Liber Amicorum Kurt Siehr* (The Hague: Eleven International Publishing, 2010).

agreement. This seems to have been a reaction particularly to some English court decisions that placed considerable emphasis on the language of the arbitration clause and drew (out of words that actually were not intended to restrict the scope of the arbitration agreement) unexpected conclusions on which disputes could be deemed to have been referred to arbitration. To cite one example, a court found that a clause relating to arbitration of any disputes 'arising under' a certain contract covers only those disputes in terms of the rights and obligations created by the contract itself, whereas a clause referring to disputes 'in relation to' the contract or 'connected with' the contract has a wider scope.[13] This led to more and more detailed formulations aiming at clarifying that the arbitration agreement covers all possible disputes between the parties. These fine verbal distinctions have now been abandoned by English courts: in the words of the House of Lords, these distinctions 'reflect no credit upon English commercial law. It may be a great disappointment to the judges who explained so carefully the effects of the various linguistic nuances if they could learn that the draftsman [. . .] obviously regarded the expressions "arising under this charter" [. . .] and "arisen out of this charter" [. . .] as mutually interchangeable. [. . .][T]he time has come to draw a line under the authorities to date and make a fresh start.'[14] The House of Lords affirmed that the parties 'are unlikely to trouble themselves too much about [the clause's] precise language or to wish to explore the way it has been interpreted in the numerous authorities, not all of which speak with one voice. [. . .][I]f the parties wish to have issues as to the validity of their contract decided by one tribunal and issues as to its meaning or performance decided by another, they must say so expressly'.[15]

In spite of the new approach by the English courts, the London Court of International Arbitration still determines the scope of its model arbitration clause by reference to 'any dispute arising out of or in connection with this contract, including any question regarding its existence, validity or termination'.[16] This detailed formulation has spread even beyond the area of English law: the model arbitration clause

[13] *Overseas Union Insurance Ltd* v. *AA Mutual International Insurance Co Ltd* [1988] 2 Lloyd's Rep 63.

[14] *Fiona Trust & Holding Corporation and others* v. *Privalov and others* [2008] 1 Lloyd's L Rep 254 at 257.

[15] Ibid., at 259.

[16] Available at www.lcia.org/Dispute_Resolution_Services/LCIA_Recommended_Clauses.aspx.

recommended by the Arbitration Institute of the Swedish Chamber of Commerce refers to 'any dispute, controversy or claim arising out of or in connection with this contract, or the breach, termination or invalidity thereof'.[17] Similarly, the model clause of the Swiss rules refers to 'Any dispute, controversy or claim arising out of or in relation to this contract, including the validity, invalidity, breach or termination thereof',[18] and the model clause of the UNCITRAL Arbitration Rules to 'Any dispute, controversy or claim arising out of or relating to this contract, or the breach, termination or invalidity thereof'.[19] Along the same lines, although somewhat more succinctly, the model clause of the International Chamber of Commerce refers to 'All disputes arising out of or in connection with the present contract'.[20]

A detailed arbitration clause is meant to counteract restrictive interpretations that may be imposed by the applicable arbitration law. A simple clause may probably have the same effect in many jurisdictions, including those considered above. What a detailed arbitration clause may not achieve, however, no matter how clear and precise it is, is to extend the scope of what the applicable arbitration law considers to be arbitrable. The matter of arbitrability will be analysed in Section 1.3.1 below.

1.2 The relevance of the lex arbitri *to the procedure of the arbitral proceeding*

Generally, arbitration is governed by the arbitration law of the place where the tribunal has its venue (territoriality principle). The territoriality principle is affirmed, for example, in article 46 of the Swedish Arbitration Act, article 176 of the Swiss Private International Law Act, section 2 of the English Arbitration Act and article 1(2) of the UNCITRAL Model Law. The territoriality principle applies only to the law governing the arbitration procedure and does not extend to also cover the law governing the merits of the dispute (more on the law governing the merits of the dispute in Section 3 below).

[17] Available at http://sccinstitute.se/engelska-16.aspx.

[18] Available at www.sccam.org/sa/en/clause.php.

[19] Available at www.uncitral.org/pdf/english/texts/arbitration/arb-rules-revised/arb-rules-revised-2010-e.pdf.

[20] Available at www.iccwbo.org/court/english/arbitration/word_documents/model_clause/mc_arb_english.txt.

Some states have opened up for the parties to choose the law governing the arbitration procedure. Therefore, in these states the parties may derogate the territoriality principle: see, for example, article 182(1) of the Swiss Private International Law Act and article 1494 of the French Civil Procedure Code. That the parties have chosen a certain law to govern their contract, however, is not sufficient to make the chosen law applicable also to the procedure. If the parties wish the arbitral proceeding to be regulated by a law different from the law of the place where the arbitral tribunal is seated, they should make specific reference to the arbitration procedure (assuming that the arbitration law of the place of arbitration permits them to make such a choice).

It has been authoritatively commented that 'the choice of a foreign procedural law is extremely unusual (and often ill-advised), as well as subject to doubts as to its validity'.[21] In England, a High Court decision commented that, in theory, it would be possible to submit arbitration to a procedural law different from the law of the state where the arbitral tribunal has its venue, but the result would be highly unsatisfactory or absurd.[22]

Irrespective of whether the parties have chosen to submit their dispute to an *ad hoc* or an institutional arbitration, the arbitral proceeding will thus generally be subject to the arbitration law of the state where the arbitral tribunal has its venue. If the parties have provided for procedural rules (in an *ad hoc* arbitration, directly in the agreement or by reference to the UNCITRAL Arbitration Rules; in an institutional arbitration, via the choice of the institution), the rules provided by the parties will apply to their proceeding and will prevail over the rules contained in the national arbitration law, if the latter permits to be derogated from by agreement of the parties. In the case of mandatory provisions of the national arbitration law, however, the arbitration law will override the arbitration rules chosen by the parties. Examples of mandatory provisions are the rules on arbitrability and on due process, such as the necessity of giving both parties the chance to be heard. In addition, the law of the place of arbitration contains rules on the powers of the arbitrators to issue interim measures, to summon witnesses and to

[21] Born, *International Commercial Arbitration*, vol. 1, p. 1310. On the adequacy of considering that the law governing the arbitral agreement is the law of the state where the tribunal is seated, see Fritz Alexander Mann, 'Lex Facit Arbitrum', in Pieter Sanders (ed.), *International Arbitration: Liber Amicorum for Martin Domke* (The Hague: Martinus Nijhoff, 1967) at pp. 164ff.

[22] *Union of India* v. *McDonnell Douglas Corp.* [1993] 3 Lloyd's Rep, 48.

request assistance from the local courts in such operations. Also, this law contains rules on the role of courts; for example, in the case of a challenge to the impartiality of the arbitral tribunal.

Arbitration laws are, usually, quite liberal in their regulation of arbitration. The parties desire to have as much flexibility as possible in the organisation of a mechanism for dispute resolution that is chosen precisely because it leaves ample room for private determination. If state law started to regulate arbitration in detail, this method of dispute resolution would probably lose much of its appeal to commercial parties. However, if there were no regulation at all, the parties might fear that fundamental principles of due process might be neglected. Therefore, a successful arbitration law is an instrument that manages to ensure a high degree of flexibility, though providing certain rules to protect the principle of due process.

1.3 The relevance of the lex arbitri *to the challenge of an arbitral award*

The assumption that the legal system of the seat of arbitration (*lex arbitri*) has no link with the arbitration itself is not correct in other respects. The losing party may, in most jurisdictions, challenge, before national courts, the validity of an arbitral award that has been rendered in that state. This means that the courts of the state of arbitration have the chance of controlling the validity of the award; and this is definitely an important link between international arbitration and the *forum*. The judicial control on the arbitral award in the phase of the challenge is regulated by national arbitration law. This means that courts apply their own law when they determine whether the award is valid or not.

In some states, awards rendered in disputes without any contact with that state enjoy a certain detachment from the system of the *forum*. Swiss[23] and Belgian[24] law permit the parties to enter into an exclusion agreement, thus excluding the court's jurisdiction to challenge the validity of the award. Also, Swedish[25] law permits the parties to exclude the control by Swedish courts, but only in respect of the so-called relative invalidity grounds, i.e. grounds that have to be invoked by one of the parties. Exclusion agreements are not allowed by Swedish law in respect

[23] Article 192 of the Swiss Private International Law Act.
[24] Article 1717(4) of the Belgian Judicial Code.
[25] Article 51 of the Swedish Arbitration Act.

of absolute invalidity grounds, upon which the judge can act on his or her own motion. In most other states, as well as under the UNCITRAL Model Law, the control jurisdiction of the courts cannot be excluded.

The list of grounds upon which a court may declare an award invalid varies, as mentioned, from state to state. In some states, as in England, the judge has relatively wide powers. Among others, an English judge may verify the arbitral tribunal's application of law,[26] although the possibility of setting aside an award for error in law has been significantly restricted in the English Arbitration Act of 1996. In most other European states, the list of invalidity grounds can broadly be said to coincide with the list contained in article 34 of the UNCITRAL Model Law which, in turn, coincides with the list of grounds upon which an award may be refused enforcement under the New York Convention. These grounds may be summarised as referring to invalidity or irregularity in the following areas: the arbitration agreement (which is governed primarily by the law of the place of arbitration, as seen in Section 1.1 above); the composition of the arbitral tribunal (which may be considered as part of the arbitral procedure and is therefore governed by the agreement between the parties, the procedural rules chosen by the parties as well as by the law of the place of arbitration, as seen in Section 1.2 above); the procedure of the arbitration (also governed by the agreement between the parties, the procedural rules chosen by the parties as well as by the law of the place of arbitration, as seen in Section 1.2 above); and the scope of power exercised by the tribunal (which is determined primarily by the agreement of the parties, but also by the procedural rules chosen by the parties and by the law at the place of arbitration).[27] In addition, the award can be declared invalid if there is a contrast with that state's rule on arbitrability or with that state's public policy (*ordre public*), as will be seen more in detail in Sections 1.3.1 and 1.3.2 below.

1.3.1 Arbitrability

There are various rules of state law that restrict the parties' ability to submit to arbitration disputes between them. One of the main effects of

[26] Section 69 of the English Arbitration Act.

[27] More extensively on the arbitral tribunal's powers, see Giuditta Cordero-Moss, 'Tribunal's Powers versus Party Autonomy', in P. Muchlinski, F. Ortino and C. Schreuer (eds.), *Handbook of International Law on Foreign Investment* (Oxford University Press, 2008).

submitting a dispute to arbitration is, as is well known, that the parties exclude the jurisdiction of courts of law on the same dispute. The other important effect of arbitration is that the winning party can present the award for enforcement to any court in a state where the losing party has assets. Arbitration enjoys such a significant recognition as long as the disputed matters concern areas that national legal systems consider suitable for self-regulation by private parties. As soon as matters of public policy or of special economic or social interest are touched on, however, it can seem less appropriate for a state to waive jurisdiction or to lend its courts' authority to enforce private awards. In such areas with important policy implications, states wish to preserve the jurisdiction of their own courts of law: this preference is based on the assumption that an arbitral tribunal would not be able or willing to apply the law as accurately as a judicial court would.

In the past, a clear trend could be observed towards reducing the areas in which disputes are not deemed arbitrable. In the past decades, for example, the US legal system has undergone a clear shift from an expressed suspicion against arbitration, to an arbitration-friendly attitude;[28] the same evolution can be observed in other legal systems, such as, for example, the Swedish system.[29] Notwithstanding this trend in favour of arbitrability, however, various areas of law are still deemed to be exclusively in the hands of the courts of law. The areas where arbitrability is excluded vary from state to state: as a general rule, arbitration is usually permitted in all matters that fall within the boundaries of private law. This would exclude from the scope of arbitration matters such as taxation, import and export regulations, concession of rights by administrative authorities, bankruptcy or the protection of intellectual property. These matters are mostly regulated by mandatory rules from which the parties cannot derogate. Disputes concerning aspects of commercial transactions falling within the scope of the

[28] The first Supreme Court judgment recognising the arbitrability of matters that previously were deemed to be for the exclusive competence of courts of law, was *Scherk* v. *Alberto-Culver*, 417 US 506 (1974). See, for further references, Paul Carrington and Paul Haagen, 'Contract and Jurisdiction', *Supreme Court Review*, 8(1997), 331, 362f., and Jean Sternlight, 'Panacea or Corporate Tool? Debunking the Supreme Court's Preference for Binding Arbitration', *Washington University Law Quarterly*, 74(1996), 637, 652.

[29] See, for example, the evolution regarding the validity of arbitration clauses entered into in the framework of general conditions of contract, as appears from the comparison of three Swedish Supreme Court decisions rendered in 1949, 1969 and 1980: Lars Heuman, *Current Issues in Swedish Arbitration* (Stockholm: Juristforlaget, 1990), pp. 22ff.

freedom to contract, however, should be arbitrable, even if the solution of the dispute assumes that the tribunal takes into consideration these mandatory rules. As long as the tribunal is requested to decide upon the private-law consequences of these rules' existence and is not required to apply or enforce any of these rules, there should be no obstacles to arbitrability.

Recently, the arbitrability exception is being used more frequently, particularly in disputes involving mandatory regulation protecting the weaker party, when this regulation belongs to the system of the court where the dispute would be heard if it had not been for the arbitration clause.[30]

Since the arbitrability rule may have a different scope according to the law it belongs to, it is necessary to find out which law determines whether the subject of the dispute is arbitrable or not. As already mentioned, under the New York Convention and the UNCITRAL Model Law, a court always applies its own rules on arbitrability. Hence, the arbitrability of the dispute will be evaluated under the law of the seat of the tribunal if a court of that country is judging the validity of the award, and under the law of the place of enforcement if a court of another country is asked to enforce the award.

This may lead to a situation where a court applies its own rule on arbitrability in a dispute that has no connection with that legal system apart from it being the seat of the tribunal or where the presence of assets permits enforcement. In this context, it may be useful to remember the rationale of the arbitrability rule: the arbitrability rule is meant to preserve the jurisdiction of the courts of law in certain areas of law that are deemed to deserve a particularly accurate application of the law. This particularly affects areas of law with public policy implications, where the public interest is deemed to prevail over the freedom of the parties to regulate their own interests. The legal system does not consider private mechanisms of dispute resolution as sufficiently reliable in this context and wishes to maintain the jurisdiction of its own national courts of law. This rationale does not necessarily apply when the dispute has no connection with that court's legal system, because in the absence of an arbitration agreement the court would not have jurisdiction over the dispute.

[30] See *Accentuate Ltd* v. *Asigra Inc* [2009] EWHC 2655 (QB), regarding a distribution agreement. See also, in Belgium, Cass., 16.11.06; in Germany, OLG München, 17.5.06; in England, High Court 30.10.09.

If a dispute has no connection with the legal system of the arbitral seat, therefore, the arbitrability rule should be applicable to set aside an award or refuse enforcement only if the annulment of the award is necessary to avoid an unacceptable result reached by the arbitral tribunal.[31] In itself, the fact that the arbitral tribunal has resolved a dispute that is not arbitrable under the law of the arbitral seat or of the place of enforcement would not be unacceptable: the courts would have neither the interest nor the competence to apply their own law to that dispute. What would be unacceptable is a decision made in a specific case; for example, because it has given effect to an agreement that violated a UN embargo. In short, what should be an annulment ground or ground to refuse enforcement in this situation is not the fact that the tribunal has exercised jurisdiction on the dispute, but the fact that the result of the decision conflicts with the fundamental principles of the court's law. In situations where the dispute does not have any links with the legal system of the arbitral seat, therefore, the arbitrability clause would overlap with the public policy rule, which will be discussed below. The evaluation of the award's validity or enforceability, in other words, cannot be made in advance, automatically applying an abstract measure of arbitrability. The evaluation of the award's validity or enforceability has to be made on the basis of the specific decision rendered in the particular case, and by measuring the actual decision against fundamental principles of the court's law.

1.3.2 Public policy

The rule of public policy has the purpose of permitting the judge not to give effect to an award that would contradict the fundamental principles of the judge's social system. It is, in the context of international arbitration, universally interpreted in a very narrow manner.[32]

[31] For a more extensive analysis of the matter see Giuditta Cordero-Moss, 'National Rules on Arbitrability and the Validity of an International Arbitral Award: The Example of Disputes regarding Russian Petroleum Investments', *Stockholm Arbitration Report* (2001), 7.

[32] See Born, *International Commercial Arbitration*, vol. 2, pp. 2841 ff., with extensive references, and Alan Redfern, Martin Hunter, Nigel Blackaby and Constantine Partasides, *Redfern and Hunter on International Arbitration* (Oxford University Press, 2009), para. 11.110. See also, for a confirmation of this approach and further references, the International Commercial Arbitration Committee, 'International Law Association Final Report on Public Policy as a Bar to Enforcement of International Arbitral Awards' (paper presented at the International Law Association Conference, New Delhi, 2002). See also the International

In particular, it does not have the same function as ensuring full compliance with rules and principles of the judge's legal system; public policy is usually defined by reference not to the legal system, but to basic notions of morality and justice,[33] features essential to the moral, political or economic order of the country[34] or to fundamental notions of morality and justice.[35] In a similar vein, the European Court of Justice found, regarding the applicability of the public policy exception contained in the then applicable Brussels Convention on Jurisdiction and Enforcement of Judgments, that a court cannot refuse enforcement of a judgment 'solely on the ground that it considers that national or Community law was misapplied in that decision'.[36] The European Court of Justice found that the fact that an alleged error in applying the law concerns rules of Community law does not alter the conditions for being able to rely on the clause on public policy.[37] In particular, a court cannot review the accuracy of the findings of law made in the judgment when the enforcement of that judgment is being sought.[38] Moreover, the judgment must be at variance, to an unacceptable degree, with the legal order of the enforcing state in as much as it infringes a fundamental principle, and the infringement must constitute a manifest breach of a rule of law regarded as essential or of a right recognised as being fundamental.[39] This European Court of Justice decision was not rendered under the New York Convention, but there is no reason why the reasoning made in respect of public policy as a ground for refusing recognition and enforcement of judgments under the Brussels Convention (or its successor, the Brussels I Regulation) should not also apply to public policy as a ground for refusing recognition and

Commercial Arbitration Committee, 'International Law Association Interim Report on Public Policy as a Bar to Enforcement of International Arbitral Awards' (paper presented at the International Law Association Conference, London, 2000). This is often defined as the 'pro-enforcement bias' of the New York Convention, which, in turn, is considered to constitute a principle of public policy: see Redfern *et al.*, *Redfern and Hunter on International Arbitration*, para. 11.105.

33 Redfern *et al.*, *Redfern and Hunter on International Arbitration*, paras. 11.109, 11.111 and 11.112.

34 Dirk Otto and Omaia Elwan, 'Article V(2)', in Herbert Kronke and Patricia Nacimiento (eds.), *Recognition and Enforcement of Foreign Arbitral Awards: A Global Commentary on the New York Convention* (Kluwer Law International, 2010), p. 365.

35 Ibid., p. 366.

36 *Régie nationale des usines Renault SA* v. *Maxicar SpA and Orazio Formento*, C.38/98, para 33.

37 Ibid., para. 32. 38 Ibid., para. 29. 39 Ibid., para. 30.

enforcement of awards under the New York Convention or as a ground to set aside an award under the UNCITRAL Model Law.

We have established that it is not the national rules that must be applied through the public policy clause, but it is their inspiring principles that have to be given effect to. It remains to attempt to define what inspiring principles can be deemed to be those of public policy. Not every principle inspiring a mandatory rule can be considered a public policy principle. Not even every principle inspiring an overriding mandatory rule (i.e. one of those mandatory rules that is deemed to be so important that it requires to be applied even in international situations and without taking into consideration the general choice of law rules, also known as *lois de police*) can be considered as a public policy principle.[40] It is only the fundamental principles – those that constitute the basis of the society – that can be deemed as public policy. But how can these principles be identified?

There is no absolute rule to determine public policy: what is fundamental may vary from state to state, and, even within the same state, the conceptions develop, and what was deemed public policy a decade earlier, may not be deemed so any more.[41]

Court decisions in the various states annulling an award or refusing to enforce it because the award is in contrast with the court's public policy are reported in the ICCA Yearbook, Commercial Arbitration, also available at www.kluwerarbitration.com. A survey of these decisions, from the first volume in the mid-seventies to the present time, shows that such decisions are not numerous. A decision that originated a wide debate in legal literature was rendered by the EU Court of Justice in the *Eco Swiss* case:[42] here the Court affirmed that European rules of competition law

[40] Luca Radicati Di Brozolo, 'Arbitration and Competition Law: The Position of the Courts and of Arbitrators', *Arbitration International*, 27(2011), 1, 6. See also Born, *International Commercial Arbitration*, vol. 2, pp. 2843ff.

[41] The example of swap agreements and other financial derivate instruments is quite descriptive: this kind of contract developed into a recognised financial activity in the course of the 1980s, and is not considered as being against fundamental principles. However, up to as late as the 1980s, courts in Germany and in Austria were considering them against the basic moral principles of the system that forbid gambling (so-called *Differenzeinwand*). See, for example, the decision of the Austrian Supreme Court no. 3 Ob 30/83 of 1983, and of the German Supreme Court (*Bundesgerichtshof*) of 15 June 1987. Only a few years later, the *Bundesgerichtshof* did not consider these agreements as violating any fundamental principles of the German legal system, see the decision dated 26.2.1991, XI ZR 349/89.

[42] *Eco Swiss China Time Ltd* v. *Benetton International N.V.* C-126/97.

must be considered to belong to public policy. The wide debate that followed this decision related, among other things, to the scope and effects of the Court's findings.[43] In judicial practice, at least two approaches have been taken to the question of the courts' power regarding arbitral awards: the so-called maximalist and minimalist approaches. According to the former approach, the court has the power to make, in addition to the evaluation made by the arbitral tribunal, an independent evaluation of the application of the competition law in order to ensure accurate application of competition law. This approach is criticised and is deemed not to express the mainstream position on the subject.[44] The minimalist approach is held to prevail in court practice both in the USA[45] and in Europe, and legal literature affirms that the courts shall not make a full review of the arbitral tribunal's application of competition law but shall accept the arbitral tribunal's evaluation.[46] That the European Court of Justice has defined European competition law as part of public policy does not mean that any violation of every European competition rule will be a breach of public policy. It is only the most serious violations that qualify, and the breach must be concrete and effective, so that it truly jeopardises the goals of competition policy.[47]

Another situation where arbitral awards are traditionally deemed to conflict with public policy is where the award gives effect to an agreement that violates applicable rules on bribery.[48]

Arbitral awards rendered in commercial disputes may run the risk of conflicting with public policy where contracts are also legal under the law chosen by the parties, but violate, in certain areas, the law that would be applicable if the parties had not made a choice of law. If the violated rules were meant to protect third-parties' interests or to ensure the proper functioning of systems such as banking and financing, an award giving effect to those agreements may have implications in terms of public policy.

[43] For an overview and a summary of the debate so far, see Radicati Di Brozolo, 'Arbitration and Competition Law'.

[44] Ibid., p. 10.

[45] *Baxter Int'l* v. *Abbott Laboratories*, 315 F. 3rd 829 (7th Cir. 2003) and *American Central Eastern Texas Gas Co. v Union Pacific Resources Group*, 2004 U.S. App. LEXIS 1216 (5th Cir. 2004).

[46] Radicati Di Brozolo, 'Arbitration and Competition Law', pp. 9f.

[47] Ibid., pp. 6 and 11.

[48] For a recent critical review of the relationship between bribery and public policy in international arbitration see James Barratt and Hayley Ichilcik, 'Bribery', *European & Middle Eastern Arbitration Review* (2011).

Many commercial agreements have implications that may affect the interests of third parties: for example, an agreement creating a security interest on the assets of one party for the benefit of the other party has implications for the other creditors of that party, who may not count on those assets in the case of the insolvency of the debtor. In order to give full effect to the security interest, legal systems have various rules, such as imposing public registration of the security so that the potential creditors are aware of the patrimonial situation of the debtor. Let us assume that the parties created a security interest under a law of their choice that does not require public registration, and that the contract contained an arbitration clause. If a dispute arises and the secured creditor obtains an award in its favour, it will try to enforce it in the country where the assets are located and where the law actually requires registration. The enforcement court will thus be expected to enforce an award giving effect to a contract that violates rules ensuring the proper functioning of the economic system. Will that award be considered as violating public policy?

Another example is a shareholders' agreement with provisions that violate the applicable company law on the competence of corporate bodies, for example, with the purpose of favouring a group of shareholders against the interests of the minority shareholders. Assuming that an arbitral award gives effect to the agreement of the parties, thus violating the applicable company law, will the award be valid and enforceable in the country to which the applicable company law belongs?

The nature of the public policy principle prevents us making general assertions as to the quality of public policy for a whole area of the law: while some rules of property law or company law may protect interests that are deemed to be so fundamental that their disregard may contradict public policy, it will depend on the circumstances of the case as to what extent the result of a specific violation actually contrasts with such fundamental principles. On a general basis, however, it seems legitimate to affirm that the policy upon which various rules of property and company law are based may be deemed so strong, that a serious breach of those rules may represent a violation of public policy.[49]

[49] This matter is the object of research in a project that I run at the University of Oslo on Arbitration and Party Autonomy ('APA', www.jus.uio.no/ifp/english/research/projects/choice-of-law/). For a more extensive analysis see Giuditta Cordero-Moss, 'International Arbitration and the Quest for the Applicable Law', *Global Jurist (Advances)*, 8(2008), 1.

Thus, an award disregarding the applicable company law to give effect to the parties' agreement may run the risk of being ineffective if it is challenged or sought to be enforced before the courts of the place to which the disregarded company law belongs.[50] The same applies to fields such as insolvency[51] and, as seen above, competition law.[52]

1.4 *The relevance of the* lex arbitri *to the enforcement of an arbitral award*

The *lex arbitri* is also relevant in the context of the enforcement of an award. We have already seen above that the law of the place of arbitration determines the validity of the arbitration agreement, and that an invalid arbitration agreement renders the award unenforceable under article V(1)(a) of the New York Convention. Moreover, the law of the place of arbitration determines the regularity of the arbitral procedure and the criteria for the composition of the arbitral tribunal, which are also criteria for the enforceability of an award under article V(1)(d) of the New York Convention.

In addition, in article V(1)(e), the New York Convention considers it as a sufficient ground to refuse enforcement of an award if the award has been set aside by a competent authority in the state where the award was made. The New York Convention, however, does not specify on what grounds an award may be set aside; this is for the arbitration law of the court of challenge to determine. Therefore, even if enforcement is uniformly regulated by the New York Convention, reference to the annulment of an award opens a channel between the enforcement of an award and the unharmonised grounds for annulment of the *lex arbitri*. Usually,

[50] See, for example, the decision of 31 December 2006 by the Federal Commercial Court of West Siberia regarding an arbitral award on a shareholder agreement between, among others, *OAO Telecominvest, Sonera Holding B.V., Telia International AB, Avenue Ltd, Santel Ltd, Janao Properties Ltd and IPOC International Growth Fund Ltd.* The Court affirmed that the parties to a shareholders' agreement may not choose a foreign law (in that case, Swedish law) to govern the status of a legal entity, its legal capacity, the function of its corporate bodies or the relationship to and within its shareholders. These matters are, according to the court, governed by mandatory rules of the law of the place of registration (in that case, Russian law). Violation of these Russian rules was defined as a violation of Russian public policy.

[51] French Supreme Court, Civil Chamber, 6 May 2009, no. 08–10.281. *Salen Dry Cargo AB* v. *Victrix Steamship Co*, in *Yearbook Commercial Arbitration*, XV (1990), 534 ff., 825 F.2d 709 (2nd Cir. 1987).

[52] *Eco Swiss China Time Ltd* v. *Benetton International N.V.* C-126/97.

article V(1)(e) is applied so that an award that has been annulled in its state of origin is considered without any legal effect; however, French courts enforce awards that have been set aside,[53] and there are also some precedents – albeit not undisputed – in other countries, such as the USA.[54] Recently, a Dutch court[55] decided to enforce an award despite its annulment in the country of origin: Russia. This decision, however, cannot directly be compared to an enforcement decision in a usual commercial case, based as it was on considerations of impartiality and independence of the Russian courts in a case involving the interests of the Russian state. The award had been rendered in a dispute on investment protection regarding breaches by the Russian Federation of its public international law obligations following what the arbitral tribunal had found was an unlawful treatment of the oil company Yukos.

Disregarding an annulment made in the award's country of origin is, however, the exception rather than the rule, and it is certainly not uncontroversial.[56]

2 International arbitration and the state law of the place(s) of enforcement

If the losing party refuses to carry out the award, the winning party will have to seek enforcement through the courts of a state where the losing party has some assets. The enforcement of foreign arbitral awards is uniformly regulated by the New York Convention, which provides a simple and arbitration-friendly procedure. The only reasons that a court may invoke to refuse enforcement of an arbitral award are listed in article V of the New York Convention. These grounds correspond to those contained in the UNCITRAL Model Law in respect of a challenge of the validity (article 34) as well as in respect of enforcement (article 36). Therefore, the enforcement of an arbitral award can be refused in the case of invalidity or of irregularities relating to the arbitration agreement, the composition of the arbitral tribunal and the arbitral procedure, as

[53] The most well-known example is *Hilmarton*, reported in *Yearbook Commercial Arbitration*, vol. XX, 663–5 and vol. XXII, 696–8. See also the *Chromalloy* decision, reported in *Yearbook Commercial Arbitration*, volume XXXI, 629ff.

[54] For references, see Born, *International Commercial Arbitration*, vol. 2, pp. 2677–2691.

[55] Decision of the Amsterdam Court of Appeal of 28 April 2009.

[56] For an overview of literature on this matter see Born, *International Commercial Arbitration*, vol. 2, pp. 2672ff.

well as excess of power, conflict with the arbitrability rule of the state of enforcement or with the public policy of the state of enforcement. In addition, as seen above, an award may be refused enforcement if it has been set aside in the state of origin.

The law of the place of enforcement, hence, becomes relevant in a rather restricted respect: when the subject matter of the dispute may not be subject to arbitration according to the law of the court and when the award conflicts with fundamental principles of the court's system and, therefore, can be considered as violating the court's public policy.

What is worth noticing in respect of the invalidity grounds of arbitrability and public policy, is that they refer to the criteria set in the legal system of the court that is at any time competent. By contrast, the other grounds for invalidity relate to the rules of a specified law: the invalidity of the arbitration agreement is determined by the law of the place of arbitration; the legal capacity of the parties is determined by the law of each of the parties; and the regularity of the procedure is determined by the law of the place of arbitration. This means that those particular laws will be applicable irrespective of which court is competent; thus, the validity of the arbitration agreement, the legal capacity of the parties and the regularity of the procedure will be governed by the same law both in the case where the award is challenged before the courts of the place of arbitration, and where the award is sought to be enforced before the courts of another country. The rules on arbitrability and on public policy, however, relate to the law of the court that is dealing at any time with the award. This means that the award will be evaluated according to the criteria for arbitrability and public policy of the place of arbitration if it is challenged before the courts of that place, and according to the criteria of the place of enforcement if it is sought to be enforced before the courts of another state.

Sometimes legal doctrine uses the term 'international public policy', and sometimes it uses the term 'truly international public policy'. The former term does not designate a category of public policy different from the one just explained above, but is simply a different use of the terminology; the latter term, on the contrary, refers to a different concept. We can briefly analyse the two terms.

International public policy is usually deemed to refer to those principles in a legal system that are so fundamental that they should be respected even if the context of the dispute is international. In other words, the principles should have such an importance for that legal system that they should be considered as basic, irrespective of the existence of a close link between the legal system and the disputed matter. The judge who is to determine the validity or enforceability of an award cannot be expected to run counter to these principles, not even if the award has no link with the judge's legal system. This concept of international public policy does not differ considerably from the restrictive concept that has been described in Section 1.3.2 above, according to which it is only fundamental principles, and not rules (not even overriding mandatory rules) that constitute public policy. Then why is one category defined as 'international', whereas the other one is not? This is primarily a question of terminology. In some systems the term public policy is used in a domestic context and is deemed to have a wider scope than the one that we explained in the above section.[57] It is deemed to extend to also cover the overriding mandatory rules of that legal system. The extensive concept of public policy is also known as 'positive *ordre public*'. This is because public policy, in the extensive sense, has a wider function than that of excluding interference in the basic principles of the legal system (which is the function of public policy in the narrow sense). The wider public policy also has the function of ensuring the application of the legal system's overriding mandatory rules: positive public policy, therefore, is a vehicle for actively applying certain rules of the judge's legal system. Since this is in contrast with the policies underlying the recognition and enforcement of foreign awards, positive public policy has to be restricted when operating within an international concept. The extensive concept is restricted by adding the qualification of 'international'. The meaning of international is not, in this context, that the public policy stems from international sources: the meaning of international is that the (national) public policy is limited to those principles that are fundamental and that the judge cannot disregard even if the disputed matter has an international character.

If the concept of public policy is used with the narrow scope described in Section 1.3.2 above, it is not necessary to add the qualification 'international' to restrict it. The narrow concept, also known as negative public policy, enjoys wider recognition in international legal doctrine, judicial practice and legislation. It is defined as negative because its function is to prevent recognition or enforcement of an award (or application of a foreign law) if the result of such recognition, enforcement or application would violate fundamental principles of the judge's legal system.

[57] See ibid., pp. 2834ff. For further references see Giuditta Cordero-Moss, *International Commercial Arbitration: Party Autonomy and Mandatory Rules* (Oslo: Tano Aschehoug, 1999), fn 248 and accompanying text.

While the discrepancy between 'public policy' in its restrictive sense and 'international public policy' turns out to be simply a question of terminology with no significant difference in substance, the term 'truly international public policy' designates a different concept.

In this case, the qualification as 'international' does not refer to the context of the disputed matter, but to the sources from which the public policy stems. The idea is that truly international public policy does not originate from one single legal system; only if a principle is recognised as fundamental in a plurality of legal systems can it be considered to be the expression of a policy that is truly international. Truly international public policy is a concept primarily recognised in some academic circles,[58] where it is considered to be more adequate in terms of international transactions and international arbitration than national public policy, even in its restrictive sense.

However, the usefulness of this concept may be questioned. The concept aims at avoiding that a legal system uses its own fundamental principles to declare a foreign award invalid or to refuse its enforcement (or to restrict application of the governing foreign law) if such principles are particular to that specific legal system and do not enjoy recognition internationally. In such a situation, the peculiarity of that legal system undermines the ideals of international uniformity that inspire international commercial law and international arbitration. The aim of the theory underlying truly international public policy, therefore, is to disregard the fundamental principles that are proper only to one legal system, even if they represent the basic values upon which that society is based. Instead, that legal system should look at what basic principles are recognised on a more international level and prefer those principles to its own. It seems too ambitious to me, however, to expect that a state court waives application of its own fundamental principles in the name of an ideal of harmonisation in international commerce. As long as the validity of an arbitral award is regulated by national arbitration laws, and the enforceability of an award is regulated by the New York Convention, the standard of reference will be the fundamental principles of the *lex fori* (though in the narrow 'negative' sense described above).[59]

[58] For further references see Cordero-Moss, *International Commercial Arbitration: Party Autonomy*, fn 774 and accompanying text.

[59] See, confirming the position taken here, the Recommendation 1(b), particularly para. 11, Recommendation 1(c), particularly para. 20ff., Recommendations 2(a) and 2(b), particularly para. 43 in the International Commercial Arbitration Committee, 'International

In conclusion, the definition of public policy is relative; it may vary from state to state and, within the same state, with the lapse of time. What remains solid is that the exception of public policy has to be applied restrictively; in particular, the simple violation of a rule is in itself not sufficient to trigger applicability of the public policy clause, not even if the violated rule is mandatory or an overriding mandatory rule. Public policy can be considered as violated mainly if the result of that violation conflicts with the most fundamental principles of the society.

3 International arbitration and the law applicable to the substance of the dispute

The law applicable to the substance of the dispute is often chosen by the parties in the contract. To a large extent, the parties' choice excludes applicability of any other law. This does not mean, however, that the chosen law is the only one that has to be taken into consideration under all circumstances. In order to understand the restrictions to party autonomy in arbitration, it is necessary to look at the sources that regulate this matter.

3.1 Party autonomy as the main rule

An arbitral tribunal must comply with the series of rules that are applicable to it: (i) the arbitration agreement; (ii) the relevant arbitration rules (in the case of institutional arbitration, these are issued by the institution in the frame of which the process is organised; in the case of *ad hoc* arbitration, the parties may adopt the UNCITRAL Arbitration Rules that are written for the purpose of providing a legal framework for *ad hoc* arbitration, may agree on specific rules in an agreement between them, or may leave it to the arbitral tribunal to determine the procedural rules); (iii) the rules in the applicable arbitration law (usually, as seen above, the law of the place of arbitration); and (iv) the New York Convention. These sources stand with each other in a formal hierarchy:

Law Association Final Report on Public Policy as a Bar to Enforcement of International Arbitral Awards'. See also, with more details, the International Commercial Arbitration Committee, 'International Law Association Interim Report on Public Policy as a Bar to Enforcement of International Arbitral Awards'. See also Audley Sheppard, 'Public Policy and the Enforcement of Arbitral Awards: Should there be a Global Standard?', *Transnational Dispute Management*, 1(2004), 7, commenting on the work on public policy made in the frame of the International Law Association, International Commercial Arbitration Committee.

the arbitration agreement between the parties is at the lowest level of the hierarchy; the chosen arbitration rules are incorporated into the arbitration agreement and can therefore be regarded as taking the same hierarchical position as the arbitration agreement; the applicable arbitration law has a higher rank and, to the extent that it has mandatory provisions, it prevails over the arbitration agreement and the institutional arbitration rules; and the New York Convention can be considered to have the highest position prevailing over all the other mentioned sources, to the extent that it has mandatory provisions. The analysis below will show that, regarding the choice of the law applicable to the merits of the dispute, the effects of the parties' agreement on the applicable law are considerably enhanced by being confirmed by all applicable sources, even those with a formally higher rank. There are, however, some limitations.

3.1.1 The arbitration agreement

The arbitration agreement is the primary source of jurisdiction for the arbitral tribunal. Without the arbitration agreement, or beyond the scope of the arbitration agreement, an arbitral tribunal does not have jurisdiction.[60] Arbitration agreements often contain a choice of law clause. This shall be understood as instructions to the tribunal in respect of the law applicable to the substance of the dispute. These instructions may be considered as a delimitation of the tribunal's authority.[61] If an arbitral tribunal disregards these instructions, it exceeds its authority and renders an award that may be set aside or refused enforcement by the courts. However, under some circumstances, an arbitral tribunal does not exceed its power even if it does not follow the choice of law made by the parties (more on this in Section 3.1.3 below).

60 I am not considering in this context jurisdiction on investment disputes between states and foreign investors, in which the power of the arbitral tribunal may be based on public international law sources, on investment legislation of the host country etc.

61 See Redfern *et al.*, *Redfern and Hunter on International Arbitration*, para. 3.96f. See also the International Commercial Arbitration Committee, 'International Law Association Report Ascertaining the Contents of the Applicable Law in International Commercial Arbitration' (paper presented at the International Law Association Conference, Rio de Janeiro, 2008), formulating, under the heading Conclusions and Recommendations (page 19), the following general principle: '*First*, the principal task of arbitrators in a commercial case is to decide the dispute within the mandate defined by the arbitration clause. Arbitration is a creature of contract. The parties can agree to its scope. That agreement is binding on the arbitrators.'

3.1.2 Arbitration rules

In the case of institutional arbitration, arbitration rules issued by the institution chosen by the parties are applicable to the arbitral proceeding as a supplement to the arbitration agreement. By choosing arbitration in the framework of a certain institution, the parties have submitted to that institution's rules, and those rules become binding on the parties as well as on the tribunal. In the case of *ad hoc* arbitration, the parties may have chosen the UNCITRAL Arbitration Rules or they may have regulated the arbitral procedure in their agreement. In such cases, these rules will be applicable as a supplement to the arbitration agreement.

Both institutional arbitration rules[62] and the UNCITRAL Arbitration Rules[63] contain provisions relating to the law applicable to the merits of the dispute, and they all state that the arbitral tribunal shall apply the law chosen by the parties to the merits of the dispute.

3.1.3 Arbitration law and the New York Convention

As mentioned above, the territoriality principle applies in respect of the arbitral procedure. This does not mean that the law of the place of arbitration shall be applied to the merits of the dispute, but that law may contain rules on how the arbitral tribunal shall choose the law that is to apply to the merits of the dispute.

Arbitration laws usually provide that the arbitral tribunal shall apply the law chosen by the parties.[64] Furthermore, they usually also provide that an arbitral award may be set aside if the arbitral tribunal has exceeded its authority,[65] and the relevance of this provision will be discussed immediately below in respect of a similar provision contained in the New York Convention.

The New York Convention does not contain any rules directly regulating the choice of law applicable to the substance of the dispute. However, it contains a provision that indirectly affects this matter. According to article V(1)(c), one of the defences that may be brought

[62] See, for example, article 22(3) of the London Court of International Arbitration Rules, article 17 of the International Chamber of Commerce Rules, article 22 of the Stockholm Chamber of Commerce Rules and article 33 of the Swiss Rules.

[63] See article 35.

[64] See, for example, article 28 of the UNCITRAL Model Law, section 46 of the English Arbitration Act and article 187 of the Swiss Private International Law Act.

[65] See, for example, article 34(2)(a)(iii) of the UNCITRAL Model Law, article 34(2) of the Swedish Arbitration Act and section 68(2)(b) of the English Arbitration Act and article 190(2)(c) of the Swiss Private International Law Act.

against enforcement of an award is the eventuality that the tribunal has exceeded its power: 'The award deals with a difference not contemplated by or not falling within the terms of the submission to arbitration, or it contains decisions on matters beyond the scope of the submission to arbitration [. . .].'

The wording of the New York Convention's exception of excess of power expressly covers the object of the dispute. It does not contain an express rule for the eventuality that the award, despite deciding on an issue submitted by the parties to arbitration, applies a law different from the law chosen by the parties.

As a general rule, the enforcement of an arbitral award may not be used as a basis for the courts to review the arbitral tribunal's decision, including its application of the law. This is confirmed by the circumstance that article V of the New York Convention contains an exhaustive list of grounds for refusing enforcement[66] and that there is a strong consensus on the necessity to interpret this list restrictively.[67] Nothing in article V's wording suggests that the courts have the authority to review the merits of the arbitral decision, either in respect of the evaluation of the facts or in respect of the application of the law.[68] This applies both to errors in the application of the substantive law and to errors in the choice of which law to apply. Therefore, application by the arbitral tribunal of a law that should not have been applied is not, as a general rule, a ground for invalidity or unenforceability of the award.

Whether the tribunal had the authority to apply a certain law, however, is a matter that may be considered as relating to the power of the tribunal. The tribunal's power is conferred by the parties, and under article V(1)(c) of the New York Convention an award exceeding this power may be refused enforcement. An analysis of the reported cases concerning the New York Convention, or the corresponding provisions in the UNCITRAL Model Law on International Commercial Arbitration, shows that the defence of excess of power is seldom accepted for the purpose of sanctioning the arbitral tribunal's application of the law.[69] To the extent that the question has been given attention, it seems

66 See Redfern *et al.*, *Redfern and Hunter on International Arbitration*, para. 11.5.

67 See Born, *International Commercial Arbitration*, vol. 2, pp. 2714ff., and Redfern *et al.*, *Redfern and Hunter on International Arbitration*, para. 11.60.

68 See Born, *International Commercial Arbitration*, vol. 2, p. 2730, Redfern *et al.*, *Redfern and Hunter on International Arbitration*, para. 11.56.

69 See Nicola Christine Port and Scott Ethan Bowers, 'Article V(1)(c)', in Herbert Kronke and Patricia Nacimiento (eds.), *Recognition and Enforcement of Foreign Arbitral*

that it has mainly been answered negatively, both in practice and in theory.[70] However, even if it is not very practical, it cannot be excluded that an award may be refused enforcement on the ground that the arbitral tribunal has gone beyond its powers in connection with the application of the law. This, however, assumes that the arbitral tribunal directly and openly disregards or contradicts the parties' instructions.[71] The matters submitted to arbitration depend closely on the criteria that they have to be measured against. The dispute is to be solved on the basis of certain rules that have been agreed upon by the parties; if the tribunal applies a different law, and assuming that the two laws regulate the question in different ways, it could be considered as if the tribunal had applied a different contract: the assumptions for resolving the dispute would not be the same as those agreed upon by the parties. Therefore, the decision would be on matters different from those submitted by the parties and this would fall within the scope of article V(1)(c).[72] Thus, it is possible to assert that a court may refuse enforcement of an arbitral award under article V(1)(c) of the New York Convention if the arbitral tribunal manifestly and expressly disregards the parties' choice of law.

Indirectly, article V(1)(c) of the New York Convention may thus be deemed to confirm that the arbitral tribunal shall comply with the instructions that the parties have given in the arbitration agreement. If the parties' instructions are not followed, there is a risk that the resulting award will be unenforceable.

Awards: A Global Commentary on the New York Convention (Kluwer Law International, 2010), pp. 271f.

70 In theory see, for example, Emmanuel Gaillard and John Savage (eds.), *Fouchard, Gaillard and Goldman on International Commercial Arbitration* (KluwerArbitration, 2004), para. 1700. In practice, see US District Court, Southern District of California, 7.12.1998 Civ. No. 98–1165-B, 29 Federal Supplement, Second Series (S.D.Cal.1998) pp. 1168–1174, excluding that a decision rendered *ex bono et aequo* exceeded the arbitral tribunal's power. From the reasons of the decision, however, it appears that the court based its reasoning on the conclusion that the parties had actually empowered the tribunal to decide *ex bono et aequo* (therefore it is not surprising that the court did not see any excess of power). Also, a German decision decided similarly, even mentioning, in an *obiter dictum*, that the arbitral tribunal's choice of law may not be reviewed by the court. However, in this case the court also based its conclusion on the fact that the parties had empowered the tribunal to decide *ex bono et aequo* (Landesgericht Hamburg, 18.9.1997, available at *ICCA Yearbook Commercial Arbitration*, vol. XXV, 512).

71 Giuditta Cordero Moss, 'Can an Arbitral Tribunal Disregard the Choice of Law Made by the Parties?', *Stockholm International Arbitration Review*, 1(2005), 1, 6ff.

72 For a similar reasoning see Redfern *et al.*, *Redfern and Hunter on International Arbitration*, para. 3.91 as well as the International Commercial Arbitration Committee, 'International Law Association Report Ascertaining the Contents of the Applicable Law in International Commercial Arbitration', p. 19.

3.2 *Restrictions to the applicability of the law chosen by the parties*

The foregoing section showed that arbitration is mostly based on the will of the parties and that the applicable sources of law confirm the central role of the parties' will. The tribunal is bound to follow the parties' instructions, because it does not have any powers outside of the parties' agreement. Therefore, tribunals are generally, and correctly, very reluctant to deviate from the instructions of the parties.

However, the primacy of the parties' agreement needs to be coordinated with applicable rules on validity and enforceability of the arbitral award.[73] It is possible that the parties' instructions contradict certain requirements for the award's validity in the applicable arbitration law or certain requirements for the award's enforceability in the New York Convention. In this situation, if the arbitral tribunal follows the will of the parties, it may face the prospect of rendering an award that is invalid or cannot be enforced. To avoid these undesirable results, the arbitral tribunal may be tempted to disregard the parties' instructions, including their choice of law. This, however, may be done only under limited circumstances and according to restrictive criteria in order to avoid exposing the award to the risk of being annulled or refused enforcement based on the arbitral tribunal exceeding the scope of the power that the parties had conferred on it. The ground for invalidity of an award and the corresponding exception to enforceability that may indirectly restrict applicability of the parties' choice of law by the arbitral tribunal may be found in article 34(2)(b)(ii) of the UNCITRAL Model Law and article V(2)(b) of the New York Convention, and it is based on the already mentioned rule on public policy.

If application of the law chosen by the parties leads the arbitral tribunal to render an award that may conflict with the public policy of the country where the award was rendered or is sought to be enforced, the award runs the risk of being, respectively, invalid or unenforceable. Consequently, the arbitral tribunal might be inclined to restrict the

[73] See, for a more extensive reasoning, Giuditta Cordero-Moss, 'Arbitration and Private International Law', *International Arbitration Law Review*, 11(2008), 153. For a similar reasoning see Redfern *et al.*, *Redfern and Hunter on International Arbitration*, para. 3.102, adding also, as the only additional basis to restrict the parties' choice, that the parties' choice must have been made bona fide. See also the International Commercial Arbitration Committee, 'International Law Association Report Ascertaining the Contents of the Applicable Law in International Commercial Arbitration', p. 21, affirming that the only restriction to parties' choice is the public policy exception.

choice of law made by the parties, thus avoiding rendering an invalid or unenforceable award. Does the arbitral tribunal in this case run the risk of exceeding its power? In other words: is the arbitral tribunal forced to choose between two grounds for invalidity or unenforceability of the award, i.e. excess of power or conflict with public policy? In my opinion there is room to argue that an arbitral tribunal is not affected by the choice of the parties, to the extent necessary to comply with article V(2)(b) of the New York Convention and the corresponding provision in the applicable arbitration law.[74] Useful guidance in respect of how to supplement the choice made by the parties is to be found in private international law, as will be seen below.

3.3 *What is the relevance of private international law?*

That courts do not have the power to review the award in respect of the application of the law does not mean that arbitral tribunals should not seek to apply the law accurately. In respect of the choice of the applicable law, however, accuracy has to be measured against parameters that are different from those applicable by courts. This is because the sources applicable to arbitration all confirm that the arbitral tribunal shall apply the law chosen by the parties, as seen in Section 3.1 above. Other rules of choice of law are mentioned, if at all, only to a restricted extent in the sources applicable to arbitration.[75] Therefore, in respect of choice of the applicable law, accuracy of application of the law does not extend to a duty to apply private international law.[76] This does not mean, however, that private international law is totally irrelevant to arbitration.

[74] For a more extensive analysis see Cordero-Moss, 'Can an Arbitral Tribunal Disregard the Choice of Law Made by the Parties?'

[75] For the eventuality that the parties have not made a choice of the applicable law, arbitral tribunals are supposed to choose the law that is applicable according to the conflict rules that the tribunal considers applicable (see, for example, article 28(2) of the UNCITRAL Model Law and section 46(3) of the English Arbitration Act), or the law that has the closest connection with the disputed matter (see, for example, article 187 of the Swiss Private International Law Act) or the law that the tribunal deems applicable (see, for example, article 1496 of the French Civil Procedure Code).

[76] See the International Commercial Arbitration Committee, 'International Law Association Report Ascertaining the Contents of the Applicable Law in International Commercial Arbitration', pp. 4, 12. That arbitrators are not bound to apply the principles of private international law that are applicable to courts is considered to be an uncontested point by Gaillard, *Fouchard, Gaillard and Goldman on International Commercial Arbitration*, p. 849. At the same time, arbitrators are said to be under no

In private international law, party autonomy is usually the main choice of law rule for determining which law governs a contract.[77] Party autonomy, however, is not the main choice of law for areas beyond contract law.[78] For contracts that have implications for, by way of example, property, company or insolvency law, the choice made by the parties does not extend to these aspects of the relationship. The applicable law will be determined on the basis of other rules of private international law.

Moreover, private international law usually provides that the choice of law made by the parties may be overridden under some exceptional circumstances.[79] Overriding mandatory rules are rules that the judge (or, under certain circumstances, the arbitral tribunal) is entitled to apply irrespective of the choice of law made by the parties, also known as *lois de police*. It must be emphasised that not all mandatory rules are so important that they have the power to override other choice of law rules, as expressly clarified in Recital No. 37 of the Rome I Regulation.

Although these restrictions to party autonomy do not, as a general rule, have relevance to arbitration, they may give guidance to the arbitral tribunal when the arbitral tribunal has to restrict the parties' choice of law in order to avoid conflict with the applicable public policy. Within the framework provided by the applicable rules on validity and enforceability of awards, therefore, private international law may become relevant to arbitration and may be used as guidance by the arbitral tribunal in determining the extent to which the parties' choice of law may be restricted. Indeed, it is desirable in this context to apply private international law principles, because they enhance predictability in such a crucial area, namely the choice of the applicable law.[80]

In particular, private international law contains rules on the scope of party autonomy and on restrictions to party autonomy by overriding

public duty to enforce state laws: see International Commercial Arbitration Committee, 'International Law Association Report Ascertaining the Contents of the Applicable Law in International Commercial Arbitration', p. 20. See also Radicati Di Brozolo, 'Arbitration and Competition Law', pp. 16f.

77 This is the main rule, for example, in the EU Rome I Regulation No. 593/2008, article 3.

78 Thus the EU Rome I Regulation states in article 1(2) that areas such as company law, property law and insolvency fall outside of its scope of application. For a more extensive analysis of the choice of law rules in these areas, see Cordero-Moss, 'Arbitration and Private International Law'.

79 See, for example, article 9 of the EU Rome I Regulation.

80 For a more extensive analysis see Cordero-Moss, 'Arbitration and Private International Law' and Giuditta Cordero-Moss, 'Revision of the UNCITRAL Arbitration Rules: Further Steps', *International Arbitration Law Review*, 13(2010), 96.

mandatory rules. These criteria permit the determination as to what extent rules different from those chosen by the parties may be applied – provided, however, that they are relevant to the validity or enforceability of the award.

3.4 *Which private international law is applicable?*

In respect of courts of law, it is generally recognised that judges always apply the private international law of their own country to designate the applicable substantive law. In respect of international commercial arbitration there is no corresponding automatic and absolute reference to the private international law of the place where the arbitral tribunal has its venue. The international character of international arbitration has led various legislatures and arbitral institutions to loosen the link between the place of arbitration and the applicable private international law.

The ICC Rules of Arbitration, in particular, were described as a landmark when they, in 1998, deleted any reference to private international law,[81] and are followed now by other arbitration rules.[82] Under article 17 of the ICC Rules of Arbitration, if the parties have not made a choice, the arbitral tribunal may freely choose the applicable law directly and without applying any conflict rules (the so-called *voie directe*). If they choose to submit a dispute to arbitration under the ICC Rules, the parties thus agree that the arbitral tribunal is not bound to apply any private international law.

Arbitration laws present a variety of solutions, ranging from the application of the private international law of the place of arbitration,[83] to the application of the private international law that the arbitral tribunal deems most appropriate,[84] the application of conflict rules

[81] See Yves Derains and Eric Schwartz, *Guide to the ICC Rules of Arbitration* (Wolters Kluwer, 2005), p. 233.

[82] The rules of the London Court of International Arbitration, of the Arbitration Institute of the Stockholm Chamber of Commerce and the revised UNCITRAL Arbitration Rules give the arbitral tribunal the authority to directly apply the substantive law that it deems appropriate, without going through the mediation of a choice of law rule.

[83] This is the traditional approach that is still followed in some modern arbitration legislation; for example, article 31 of the Norwegian Arbitration Act.

[84] This approach is followed, among others, by the UNCITRAL Model Law (article 28(2)) and the English Arbitration Act (article 46(3)), and it can result in the application of the private international law of the country where the arbitral tribunal has its venue, of another law that seems to be more appropriate, or even, of no specific law (often arbitrators compare the choice of law rules of all laws that might be relevant and apply a minimum common denominator).

specifically designed for arbitration[85] and the *voie directe*.[86] The *voie directe* is deemed to reflect the most modern approach.[87] It is not advisable, however, to abandon in full the guidance that private international law gives. Therefore, it is not unusual that arbitral tribunals exercise their discretion so as to enhance predictability and look to widely applied principles of private international law or to the private international law of the place of arbitration, even though they are not bound to do so.

4. Conclusion

This chapter has shown that, while international arbitration undoubtedly is based on the will of the parties and international sources to a large extent provide a uniform legal framework, national laws still have a significant relevance. In particular, parties and arbitral tribunals may not disregard the peculiarities of the law of the places of arbitration and enforcement.

[85] For example, article 187 of the Swiss Arbitration Act contains a choice of law rule that designates as applicable the law of the country with which the subject matter of the dispute has the closest connection.

[86] Article 1496 of the French Civil Procedure Code.

[87] Redfern *et al.*, *Redfern and Hunter on International Arbitration*, paras. 3.217, 3.218, 3.224.

2

International arbitration and domestic law

LUCA RADICATI DI BROZOLO

It is useful to premise the analysis of the current state and trends of international commercial arbitration with a discussion of its relationship to domestic law. The purpose of such a discussion is to show that, contrary to a frequent perception, international arbitration remains subject to a significant level of influence from national legal systems, but that such influence is perfectly normal and is, in most cases, even to be welcomed. An understanding of this point is useful in order to illustrate the scope of party autonomy in this field and how best the parties to an international arbitration can take advantage of it to avoid certain risks.[1]

1 Domestic law as the basis of international commercial arbitration

Arbitration is undoubtedly one of the areas of law in which party autonomy plays the greatest role and where the influence of states has receded more significantly. During the past few decades, arbitration has not ceased to disenfranchise itself from domestic legal systems, whilst at the same time becoming a fundamental dispute-settlement mechanism

[1] The issues relating to extraordinary or pathological state interference in arbitration are addressed in L. G. Radicati di Brozolo and L. Malintoppi, 'Unlawful Interference with International Arbitration by National Courts of the Seat in the Aftermath of *Saipem* v. *Bangladesh*', in *Liber Amicorum B. Cremades* (La Ley, 2010), pp. 993ff. and in L. G. Radicati di Brozolo, 'The Impact of National Law and Courts on International Commercial Arbitration: Mythology, Physiology, Pathology, Remedies and Trends', *Paris Journal of International Arbitration* (2011), 663. For a discussion of some additional aspects of the issue see L. G. Radicati di Brozolo, 'The Control System of Arbitral Awards: A Pro-Arbitration Critique of Michael Reisman's "Normative Architecture of International Commercial Arbitration"', *ICCA Congress Series No. 16, Proceedings of the 50th Anniversary Conference*, in J. van den Berg (ed.), *Arbitration: The Next Fifty Years* (Kluwer, 2012), pp. 74–102.

that is a complete alternative to the jurisdiction of state courts. The reasons for the preference shown by international business for arbitration over national courts, especially in the transnational context, are well known. However, arbitration can satisfy the needs of its users – particularly in terms of flexibility and of the finality of the award – only insofar as states are willing to relinquish some measure of control over it.[2]

Initially, the favourable attitude of domestic legal systems towards arbitration and party autonomy consisted essentially of the recognition of the right of the parties to contract out of the jurisdiction of domestic courts and, in terms of obligation, to enforce 'foreign' arbitral awards. Both these obligations derived from the 1958 New York Convention on the Recognition and Enforcement of Foreign Arbitral Awards (the 'Convention'). Although crucial for the development of international arbitration, these obligations did not entail *per se* a liberalization of arbitration. Indeed, even after the entry into force of the Convention, in the early stages arbitration remained subject to quite restrictive legislation in almost all states. Over time, however, particularly as regards international arbitration – as opposed to purely domestic arbitration – an ever-growing number of states began to adopt an increasingly liberal attitude, which led to the recognition of the central role of party autonomy in all aspects of arbitration, and to a retrenchment of the powers of national courts to control both the process and its outcomes.

As a consequence of this evolution in the attitude of states, international commercial arbitration has become less and less influenced and limited by domestic legal systems and controls. This is visible in the ever-broadening scope of arbitrability, in the almost total disappearance of any control over the substantive and procedural rules applied in arbitration, in the elimination of any review of the merits of the award and in the restrictive interpretation of the grounds for setting aside and for refusal of enforcement. All this affords the parties a great degree of freedom to resort to arbitration and to forge it as best suits their needs, both as regards the procedure and in terms of the substantive rules.

This led some authors to consider the theory that international arbitration had become 'delocalized' and that one could therefore speak of a 'stateless' or 'floating' arbitration or of an '*arbitrage sans loi*'. Nowadays,

[2] For a more in-depth discussion of these issues see L. G. Radicati di Brozolo, 'Arbitrage commercial international et lois de police: Considerations sur les conflits de juridictions dans le commerce international', in *Collected Courses of The Hague Academy of International Law*, 315 (2006), pp. 282 ff.

these theories have largely been abandoned.[3] Arbitration admittedly rests on party autonomy, and the parties enjoy a very considerable freedom in laying down the rules that they choose and state interference has become very limited. Nonetheless, it is a truism that party autonomy can produce the desired effects only insofar as this is permitted by national legal systems. This applies to arbitration, just as it does to any type of contract or relationship.

Inevitably, therefore, the tolerance and collaboration of states remains key in respect of every aspect of arbitration. Arbitration can operate meaningfully only if state courts are prepared to enforce arbitration agreements – and thus to stay actions brought before them in violation of such agreements – and to lend their assistance in enforcing awards that are not complied with on a voluntary basis. State courts, and domestic laws, must also be prepared to lend their assistance where party autonomy proves insufficient (for instance, when the process of appointing the arbitrators breaks down or the parties have failed to consider a given situation that arises in connection with an arbitration).

On the other hand, states retain the power to interfere with the arbitral process in different ways through the actions of their courts and other organs.

The reality, therefore, is not that arbitration has become stateless or delocalized, but that a great number of domestic legal systems (although by no means all) have come to accept solutions that are, to a significant extent, both liberal and arbitration-friendly. Nevertheless, despite the great degree of freedom from state interference that arbitration has acquired, in practical terms, this freedom remains a concession by states, so that, ultimately, arbitration must always take into account the existence of national legal systems and the limits or interference that may derive from them. In international arbitration the difficulty is, of course, particularly conspicuous, because potentially there are always several states that may, in one way or another, wish to impose their rules on a given arbitration.

Given this situation, the issue for consideration is how and to what extent national legal systems and courts exercise their influence over the arbitral process and how, depending on the circumstances, parties can best take advantage of the freedom granted by legal systems, use the tools that states make available to them and avoid unwanted interference.

[3] See, however, E. Gaillard, *Legal Theory of International Arbitration* (Martinus Nijhoff, 2010).

2 The *lex arbitri*

The starting point of this analysis must be what is generally known as the *lex arbitri*; that is, the law of the seat of the arbitration. Even in an era of maximum liberalization of international arbitration, that law maintains a crucial, although overestimated and to a certain extent unwarranted, role. To appreciate the features of international arbitration, it is indispensable to have a very clear understanding of the matters that are usually considered subject to the law of the seat and over which the courts of the seat tend to exercise jurisdiction. It is also necessary to understand how, according to the conceptions which still prevail today, the choice of the seat is arguably the most important decision for the entire destiny of an arbitration.

2.1 The lex arbitri *in the prevailing conception of arbitration*

According to the paradigm that still prevails today, the *lex arbitri*, together with the will of the parties, provides the main foundation of the arbitration and of its binding force. The *lex arbitri* also provides the framework for the arbitration. It determines the extent of the parties' right to resort to arbitration and defines the boundaries of their autonomy, which means, essentially, their right to fashion their arbitration as they wish. It also defines the powers and the duties of the arbitrators and provides the mechanisms for the control over the individual arbitration.

More specifically, it is the law of the seat that determines whether arbitration can be resorted to in the first place[4] and, more particularly, whether, in light of the local rules on arbitrability, it can be resorted to in relation to the subject matter of the dispute at hand. The law of the seat also lays down the requirements of the form and validity of the arbitration agreement. Equally importantly, the law of the seat contains the rules for the creation of the arbitral tribunal; namely, the number of arbitrators and the mechanisms for their appointment, removal and

[4] Even where the state in question is a party to the New York Convention, it is debated as to whether article II is applicable (and requires courts to refer the dispute to arbitration) only where the seat of the arbitration is located in another country or also when it is in the forum state, provided in the latter case that the contract to which the arbitration agreement relates is not a purely domestic contract (see J.-F. Poudret and S. Besson, *Comparative Law of International Arbitration* (London, 2007), § 489 *et seq.*; G. Born, *International Commercial Arbitration* (Wolters Kluwer, 2009), vol. I, pp. 278 ff.

replacement, as well as the qualifications and other conditions that arbitrators must possess. The *lex arbitri* also contains the rules of procedure for the arbitration. Finally, and fundamentally, the law of the seat governs the validity of the award. Additionally, the fact that an award is considered valid according to a given legal system can have an impact on its international circulation.

The law of the seat is therefore the first source to which one must turn to resolve most issues pertaining to a given arbitration. Similarly, the courts of the seat are the primary venue for the determination of such issues. It is those courts that will, in the first instance, lend their support to the proper functioning of the arbitration (for instance, in relation to the constitution of the arbitral tribunal) and that will have jurisdiction over actions on the setting aside of the award.

As mentioned, during the years following the entry into force of the New York Convention, the role of party autonomy in matters relating to arbitration has never ceased to grow as states have come to recognize the importance of allowing parties to govern arbitration, to a large extent, as they wish. In parallel to this, states have broadened the scope of arbitrability, with the result that, nowadays, most matters can be referred to arbitration, including all matters that in some way involve mandatory rules (typically anti-trust, securities, corruption, regulatory matters etc.). Obviously, parties tend to make use of the freedom accorded to them by the law of the seat, either by themselves defining the rules of the game or, more often, by reference to the myriad of arbitration rules now available from a wide variety of institutional bodies that have assumed the task of supporting and promoting arbitration.

The generalized use of the freedom accorded by states to the parties, coupled with the emergence of what may be viewed as a 'community' of international arbitration (consisting of arbitrators, practitioners, arbitral institutions and scholars), has, in turn, led to the development of a body of principles applicable to a considerable number of aspects of international arbitration, which are, to a large extent, followed in international arbitrations and which eventually contribute further to marginalizing the law of the seat. The best-known components of this burgeoning body of rules, which might be seen as the arbitration-specific facet of the *lex mercatoria*, are the International Bar Association's Guidelines on Conflicts of Interest in International Arbitration as well as its Rules on the Taking of Evidence.

The result of all this is that generally speaking, even according to the conception which remains dominant, the role of the *lex arbitri* will often be relatively residual, since it is limited essentially to filling gaps where the parties have not dealt with a particular issue, directly or by reference to some arbitration rules and where reference cannot be made to generally accepted practices. Even where an intervention from outside is required (for instance, for the appointment or the challenge of arbitrators), for the most part this occurs at the hands of arbitral institutions rather than at those of the courts.

This situation can generate the impression that the law of the seat has become mostly irrelevant and that parties therefore need not overly concern themselves about its impact on their arbitration. At least from a pragmatic perspective this impression is misleading.

Firstly, all legal systems contain at least some rules from which the parties will, under no circumstances, be permitted to derogate (for instance, those which lay down the number of arbitrators or some fundamental principles of procedure, such as the equality of parties). Likewise, in most circumstances it will be impossible to oust the local courts completely and to avoid some form of control by them over the arbitral process – in particular, over the validity of the award. The reason is that a certain measure of state control through the intervention of their courts remains crucial, even if it is only to ensure that the arbitral process continues to be respectful of its fundamental principles, some of which are inherent in the process itself, such as, for instance, the requirement that arbitration can occur only if all parties have agreed to it and subject to the respect of certain basic procedural safeguards. States may also insist that arbitrations seated in their territory respect principles that are viewed as crucial by their legal system, such as those which commonly go under the heading of public policy, but which may actually be considerably broader and touch upon different areas of the local legal system. States usually insist on exercising this type of supervision over all arbitrations having their seat on their territory, even when the link with that territory is relatively weak.[5] The constraints thus posed by the *lex arbitri* must, therefore, clearly always be borne in mind by the parties and by arbitrators.

It must also be considered that differences between the arbitration laws of individual states remain, and in some instances are considerable,

5 A few legislations do, however, allow the parties expressly to waive the right to challenge the award where the connection to the state of the seat is particularly weak (see article 192(1) of the Swiss Law on Private International Law, article 1717(4) of the Belgian Code Judiciaire and article 51 of the Swedish Arbitration Law).

notwithstanding the incessant relaxation of the constraints imposed by national laws and the central role accorded by these to party autonomy. Arbitration is not harmonized at the international level. The international convention that constitutes the basis of the system of international arbitration, the New York Convention, governs only two, albeit absolutely crucial elements of arbitration: the enforcement of arbitration agreements and of arbitral awards (in the latter case when they circulate beyond the frontiers of the state of the seat). Even in relation to these two aspects, it is very far from imposing a harmonized regime. This means that all other matters, from the appointment of the arbitral tribunal and standards of arbitrator independence to the grounds for setting aside and the nature of the review of arbitral awards, not to mention more abstruse issues such as the binding effect of the arbitration agreement to non-signatories or its effects in relation to multiple contracts, are not harmonized at the international level.[6] Consequently, states retain total freedom as to how to govern all these matters. The only important legal instrument which goes some way towards bringing about some level of harmonization is the UNCITRAL Model Law on International Arbitration, which, however, is not binding and, moreover, is silent on many matters.

Thus, the boundaries of party autonomy are not the same in all legal systems and there are differences in the rules of the individual legal systems to which recourse must be had when the need arises in order to fill gaps in the rules laid down by the parties. Likewise, there are differences in the mechanisms provided for by each legal system for the support and the control of the arbitral process. Despite a convergence towards a standard of review that mirrors the grounds for refusal of the enforcement of article V of the New York Convention, in line with the prescription of the Model Law, there remain disparities between the grounds for annulment of awards in different countries and in terms of the extent to which parties can broaden or restrict these grounds. Likewise, there remain considerable differences in the procedural regimes. One example concerns the fact that, in some countries, there is only one level of review of awards (e.g. in Switzerland), whilst in others there may be two or more levels (for instance in England, where

[6] An exception is the European Convention on International Commercial Arbitration of April 21, 1961 and the 1998 Mercosur Agreement on International Commercial Arbitration.

proceedings for the setting aside of an award may go through three steps, from the High Court to the Supreme Court).

Over time, there has undoubtedly been a significant convergence in the solutions to many of the important problems of international arbitration across legal systems. This is the product of the development of a culture of international arbitration and of a 'competition' and imitation between the various legal systems that has, to a significant extent, been the product of the New York Convention. By obliging states to recognize arbitration agreements providing for arbitration abroad and to enforce, on their territory, the awards which are the outcome of such arbitrations, the Convention has, in practice, allowed parties to opt out of less arbitration-friendly regimes with few adverse effects. This has provided an incentive for many states to abandon excessively restrictive regimes, the principal impact of which is to discourage recourse to arbitration on their territory and to favour other countries as arbitration centres.

Discrepancies nevertheless remain, even amongst countries with the most arbitration-friendly regimes. The range of solutions is predictably much broader if one considers all the countries of the world that can potentially be the seat of an arbitration. Certain countries are unquestionably less sympathetic to arbitration than others – and this despite the now almost universal acceptance of the New York Convention. In particular, in certain countries that in recent years have reached a central stage in their economic relations such as China, Russia and India, the attitude towards international arbitration remains considerably less favourable than in the legal systems where the culture of arbitration first emerged such as France and Switzerland, followed by other states such as England. These disparities in approach should not cause surprise. After all, it is worth underlining that even in countries that are now unquestionably arbitration-friendly, the approach was considerably less open in the past. Progress in this direction has required a change in culture and, more often than not, the intervention of the legislator, an open attitude of the courts and, more generally, an understanding of the advantages that furthering arbitration can bring to the development of business relations, as well as, rather more selfishly, to the local legal services industry. It is encouraging that, given the right climate, progress can rapidly occur. A case in point is obviously Latin America, and foremost amongst Latin American countries, Brazil, which until not long ago was perceived to be hostile to arbitration but has readily adopted a completely different attitude.

2.2 *The proper role of the* lex arbitri

Despite the undeniable trend towards the liberalization of arbitration and its disenfranchisement from national law, in today's world the seat of the arbitration clearly remains far from irrelevant. It still determines what law governs the arbitration and what courts will exercise jurisdiction over many of the crucial matters liable to impact on the fate of the arbitration. In other words, the seat is crucial to the parties' ability to achieve what they seek in terms of the overall regime of their arbitration. What is more, for the most part states still tend to attribute great relevance to the decisions of the courts of the seat, particularly as to the validity of awards.

This said, there is nothing inevitable or inherent in the role of the law of the seat. Unlike judicial dispute settlement mechanisms, which are inextricably bound to the legal system of the state of which they are part, arbitration is not rooted in the legal system of any one state. Arbitrations and arbitral awards are akin to contracts which, once entered into, live a life of their own and are capable of being assessed by any legal system according to its own rules, regardless of the way in which they are considered by other legal systems. This includes the legal system of the state that is considered the seat of the arbitration.[7]

There is therefore no overarching legal or logical reason for the systematic attribution by states of particular weight to the *lex arbitri*, in particular when it comes to assessing the validity of awards that have been set aside at the seat. That view is the product of an uncritical adhesion to a traditional view of the nature of arbitration and of its links to domestic law. Whilst such a view may be justified with reference to domestic arbitration, from the local system's perspective, it is much less justified with regard to international arbitration that by definition falls to be assessed in a multijurisdictional perspective. A more modern and pro-arbitration perspective militates in favour of attributing a significantly greater role to the law of the enforcing state than to the *lex arbitri*, and of not referring almost automatically to the latter, particularly when it comes to the assessment of the validity of awards.

Given the prevalence of the more traditional and conservative vision, which influences the effects that states are prepared to attribute to the decisions of the jurisdiction of the seat, from an empirical perspective the

[7] For an exhaustive discussion of this position in support of a deflation of the role of the *lex arbitri* see Radicati di Brozolo, 'The Control System of Arbitral Awards'.

role of the law of the seat remains very significant. It is therefore only for this purely practical reason, and not on any more cogent legal or policy grounds, that parties cannot lightly disregard the law and the courts of the seat, even when they have no particular interest in the effects of the arbitration in that country.

3 The seat of the arbitration as a connecting factor

Notwithstanding the role that is attributed to it in arbitration law, the seat of the arbitration is a mere legal fiction. This is because the seat does not actually designate the physical and geographic 'place' of the arbitration; that is, where the arbitration will be held (e.g. the hearings, the deliberations, the issue of the award etc.). Actually, where these phases will take place, and whether they must take place on the territory of the seat of the arbitration or whether they can take place abroad, is precisely one of the issues that falls to be determined by the law of the seat.

The term 'seat' of the arbitration is, instead, used to designate the legal system that governs the arbitration. In other words, and to use classic conflict-of-law terminology, the seat of the arbitration is nothing other than a connecting factor between the arbitration and a given system of law which is its governing law.

Nowadays, most states use the seat of the arbitration as the jurisdictional and conflict-of-law criterion in matters of arbitration. More specifically, they refer to the seat to establish whether their courts will exercise support and supervisory jurisdiction over a given arbitration and apply their arbitration law to that arbitration. Thus, if the seat of the arbitration is, say, in England, Norway or Mexico,[8] the consequence is that the courts of that country will usually consider themselves to have jurisdiction over the principal matters relating to the functioning and outcome of the arbitration (typically the constitution of the tribunal, the support for the proceedings and the setting aside of the award)[9] and will apply their law to the solution of those matters. Even if no proceedings are brought before those courts, the parties and the arbitrators will normally refer to that law to settle the matters that arise. Conversely,

[8] In practical terms, the seat is usually designated as a city rather than as a country. As such, the designation of the seat will normally also serve to identify the competent courts and applicable rules within that jurisdiction.

[9] This jurisdiction will clearly be entirely independent of the jurisdiction over the merits of the dispute in the absence of the agreement to arbitrate, which could well not rest with the courts of the seat.

the courts of other countries will, in principle, consider themselves as lacking jurisdiction over those matters and will often apply the law of the seat to certain matters relating to the arbitration that may come before them.

The seat of the arbitration is normally selected by the parties. Most legal systems allow the parties complete freedom in the selection of the seat. From the perspective of each state, this has a dual implication. On the one hand, it entails that the state in question will agree to consider its law applicable to the arbitration and to exercise jurisdiction over it if the designated seat is on its territory. In this case, the arbitration will be considered to be 'domestic' in that country. On the other hand, that state will agree to refrain from exercising its jurisdiction or from applying its law to arbitrations with a designated seat in another country. The relevance of the choice of the seat, in terms of both its positive and negative implications for the jurisdiction of the state in question and for the applicability of its law, is usually recognized by states regardless of the existence or absence of a significant connection with the selected seat in terms of both the parties and the subject matter of the arbitration.

The consequence of the combination of, on the one hand, the fact that the seat determines the legal regime of the arbitration and, on the other hand, the parties' freedom to select the seat is obviously that, in practice, the parties have the ability to choose the legal system governing their arbitration or, in other words, the law governing their arbitration. The situation is therefore not dissimilar to the one that prevails in relation to the law governing contracts, for which the freedom of choice is generally recognized. The main difference is that, whilst for contracts the choice occurs in straightforward terms, for arbitration it usually takes the somewhat more convoluted route of the choice of the seat.

This is not to say that problems cannot arise in this connection. One problem arises in the absence of a choice of the seat by the parties. In such situations, most legal systems have criteria to establish whether the seat is on their territory. The difficulty is, of course, that more than one state could consider the seat to be located in its territory, with the inevitable risks of parallel proceedings and other conflicts. The opposite risk is that no state might be prepared to consider that the arbitration is seated on its territory, which would leave the arbitration deprived of the support mechanisms.

Another problem is that, even where the seat has been designated, a state might refuse to attribute to that choice the positive or negative effect usually associated with it. In other words, it might refuse to exercise its jurisdiction in relation to an arbitration although the designated seat is on its territory; for instance, because it considers that the links with its territory or legal systems are nonexistent or excessively tenuous. Conversely, the state in question may insist on asserting its jurisdiction over the arbitration with a designated seat in another state (for example, setting aside awards rendered in another state), perhaps on the grounds that, in its view, the arbitration involves important interests of that state or of its nationals.

The reasons for this are obvious. Just as there are no internationally binding or harmonized criteria for the allocation of adjudicative jurisdiction between states, there are also no internationally valid criteria on the exercise of jurisdiction over arbitrations. This means that – despite the broad tendency to recognize the seat of the arbitration as the paramount connecting factor to determine such jurisdiction and the applicability of national arbitration laws – there is, in principle, little to stop a given state from applying such a connecting factor as it sees fit (for instance, in deciding where the seat of the arbitration is) or in disregarding that criterion altogether.

The fundamental importance of the choice of the seat in today's legal environment is therefore self-evident. Parties to an arbitration cannot expect to escape the influence of national law altogether. More often than not, they would actually even be well advised not to seek to do so. National law may not necessarily unduly hinder their freedom to govern their arbitration as best suits them. On the other hand, national law and courts may provide a useful complement to party autonomy, filling gaps and providing mechanisms to support the arbitration where needed and to control the process to protect it against pathologies.

At the same time, the parties have ample freedom – by way of the choice of the seat – to select from amongst all the available legal systems the one that they view as most favourable to their goals. It is clearly up to them to use this freedom wisely. In selecting the seat of the arbitration, they should take into account the extent to which its arbitration law recognizes their ability to govern their arbitration as they wish, as well as the content of those rules which will apply mandatorily and of those which may be called upon to fill gaps. They must also pay regard to the case law and, more generally, the attitude and the efficiency of the local courts to ensure that the rules in question will be applied competently and fairly.

In other words, the parties cannot simply expect to have solved all their problems simply as a result of having chosen arbitration and of having opted out of adjudication of their disputes through national courts. The failure to choose a seat altogether – or a choice which is not well considered – can be fatal because it can lead to the involvement of courts which may operate at cross-purposes with the parties' expectations and to the application of unwanted rules. As a first rule of thumb, since the choice of the seat implies submission to the local courts and local arbitration law, one should, in particular, try to avoid seating the arbitration in a country whose courts one would not be happy to have exercising their jurisdiction over the dispute; for instance, because they are considered to lack the requisite degree of competence and independence. In particular, considering that neutrality is one of the objectives of arbitration, it is generally unwise to accept that the seat should be in the country of the other party to the potential dispute, at least unless that country has high standards in terms of its arbitration law and practice.

Unfortunately, instead, the decision as to the seat of the arbitration is too often not pondered by the parties with due attention to its consequences, on the assumption perhaps that it simply designates the venue of the hearings or that it can be easily bargained away against other elements of the contractual negotiation.

4 Other laws

The law of the seat is not the only domestic law that may be relevant in relation to an arbitration. When considering the impact on arbitration of legal systems other than the *lex arbitri*, a distinction has to be drawn between the perspective of the arbitrator and that of national legal systems.

Laws other than the *lex arbitri* routinely become relevant in the context of the arbitral proceedings themselves. It is generally recognized that most of the issues that fall to be decided on by the arbitrators in order to reach their decision on the settlement of the dispute submitted to them, and which do not relate to the conduct of the proceedings themselves, fall outside the scope of the *lex arbitri* and must therefore be decided on the basis of other rules. Since international arbitration, by definition, involves contacts with a multitude of legal systems, in order to identify the rules that will be used to form the basis of the decision on such issues, the arbitrators will find themselves faced with what are, in practice, conflict-of-law issues.

Such issues do not arise in every circumstance. Certain questions – both pertaining to the merits of the dispute and more arbitration-specific questions such as, for instance, those relating to the arbitration agreement – can be decided on the strength of principles which are not part of any single system of law and that are known under a variety of names, each of which carries with it a slightly different meaning (transnational commercial law, *lex mercatoria*, general principles, *règles matérielles du droit du commerce international* etc.). Whether such principles can be applied in a given case – to the exclusion of national law or alongside it – requires careful consideration.

Contrary, perhaps, to a fairly generalized assumption in past decades, it cannot be presumed that parties to international transactions will always want the merits of these to be governed by non-national rules.[10] While there are undoubtedly cases where the parties may want this, at least as often, if not more so, they will prefer to have their disputes resolved according to the rules of national law – albeit on occasion taking into account such principles – and not to rely exclusively on transnational principles and rules. The main reason will frequently be the impression that such rules are not sufficiently well defined. Admittedly, the rules in question have become more elaborate and sophisticated over the years, so that the initial hostility from its critics is much less justified.[11] However, national laws have also evolved

[10] The position of the early crusaders of the *lex mercatoria*, who in the sixties and seventies of the last century believed that it should replace national law almost altogether in international transactions, is understandable in a historical perspective. In the era of national-liberation movements, they were, in essence, themselves a liberation movement formed to release the shackles and constraints of national law, which, at the time, was indeed largely unfit to govern many international transactions for manifold reasons. At the time, national substantive law was extremely inflexible and parochial and, with a poor understanding of the needs of international transactions, the role of party autonomy was more limited and contractual techniques were undeveloped. The sixties and seventies were also the heydays of state contracts, which raised understandable concerns about avoiding the unfairness and the risks of the application of the laws of the host state at a time when investor protection, as we now know it, was non-existent. In such a context, transnational law or the *lex mercatoria* seemed to provide the optimal solution to insulate transnational transactions from the rigidities of national law and it also seemed to provide adequate responses to the problems raised by such transactions that could not be adequately addressed by national laws.

[11] For a comprehensive survey of the definition, nature and content of transnational commercial law see R. Goode, H. Kronke, E. McKendrick and J. Wool, *Transnational Commercial Law* (Oxford University Press, 2011), 2nd edn. See also L. G. Radicati di Brozolo, 'The UNIDROIT Principles and the Courts: Rethinking the Role of Non-national Rules for the Settlement of Transnational Disputes?', *Mélanges en l'honneur de Jean-Michel Jacquet* (forthcoming); L.G. Radicati di Brozolo, 'Non-national Rules and Conflicts of Laws', *Rivista di diritto internazionale e processuale* (2012) (forthcoming).

significantly from the days when they were considered as unsuitable for governing international transactions. On the one hand, they have become more receptive to the needs of party autonomy, which, for its part, benefits from the progress in contract-drafting techniques. On the other hand, they have become much better able to govern sophisticated transnational transactions, also as a result of the incorporation of rules coming from diverse international and supranational sources as well as of an increasing harmonization and, in any event, of their ability to take such rules into account. The situation has thus changed dramatically from the early days of the debate on the appeal of the *lex mercatoria* and, consequently, the need to escape entirely from national law is less prominent.[12]

Given the enormous variety of situations, the respective appeal of non-national rules and of national law on issues of merit differs significantly, particularly depending on the type of transaction and the business community in which it takes place[13] as well as in terms of the existence of rules specifically relevant to the relationship at issue.

In this context, the power of arbitrators to apply non-national rules to the exclusion of national law to the merits[14] cannot always be assumed in the absence of an appropriate rule in the *lex arbitri* or of an express indication by the parties, including one contained in any set of applicable arbitration rules.[15]

Where the arbitrators cannot apply non-national rules exclusively, in most cases they will have to resort to some type of conflict-of-law analysis in order to identify the national rules governing the individual issues. This does not mean that arbitrators will necessarily have to abide

[12] This is true even with regard to state contracts as a result of the emergence of a coherent body of substantive and procedural law on investment protection and due to the fact that the rule of law has become more widespread and that many countries that were formerly not part of the market economy have embraced legal concepts compatible with the smooth running of international commercial transactions.

[13] Typically, banking and financial transactions will be the ones in relation to which the recourse to non-national rules will be almost unheard of while those rules will be predominant, for instance, in commodities' transactions.

[14] The issue is slightly different for issues pertaining specifically to the arbitration such as, for instance, those relating to the validity and effects of the arbitration agreement.

[15] It is true that, since most advanced systems do not permit courts to review the application of the law by the arbitrators (which would include not only substantive and procedural rules, but also conflict-of-law principles), the arbitrators' decision to apply non-national rules may not be reviewable. Nevertheless, the application of such rules by the arbitrators against the will of the parties could, in some circumstances, be held to amount to a violation of the arbitrators' mandate, liable to entail the setting aside or refusal of enforcement of the award.

strictly by the conflict rules of the *lex arbitri* or, indeed, by those of any other legal system, since it is generally acknowledged that such rules are destined for national judges and there is a tendency to consider that traditional conflict-of-law analysis should, to a greater or lesser extent, be banished from arbitration. Arbitrators thus often rely on variations of those principles that are specific to arbitration.[16]

Such an analysis will generally lead the arbitrators to apply different legal systems or sets of rules depending on the matter to be decided. Amongst the ones that come into play most commonly, one may point to the laws governing the substance and the form of the arbitration agreement, the laws governing the capacity of the parties and the law governing the merits of the dispute (which may be different depending on the issues at hand; for instance, contractual and non-contractual liability, security rights, bankruptcy etc.). Moreover, particularly in light of their generally acknowledged duty to render an enforceable award, the arbitrators may have to take into account the mandatory laws of yet other legal systems, including the law of the seat and the law of the place of enforcement.

Turning to the perspective of domestic legal systems, the agreement to submit a dispute to arbitration does not rule out the intervention of national courts, not only from the seat of the arbitration, as shown above, but also from other countries.

The most predictable intervention is that of the courts of the country (or countries) where enforcement of the award will be sought. Even though in most cases the New York Convention will apply, the courts of those states will nonetheless have to assess the enforceability. In so doing, they will need to pay regard to their own law and possibly to that of other states. The *lex fori* of the enforcing court will be relevant, in particular, as regards procedural issues (article III of the Convention) and for the ascertainment of some of the grounds of non-enforceability laid down in article V – particularly public policy and arbitrability. Other laws will come into play in order to verify the capacity of the parties to enter into the arbitration agreement, the validity of that agreement, the proper composition of the arbitral tribunal and the binding character of the award.

Equally predictable is the intervention of the courts of countries where interim or protective measures in support of the arbitration may be

[16] See G. Cordero-Moss, 'Arbitration and Private International Law', (2008), *International Arbitration Law Review*, 11 (2008), 153 ff.

requested. These courts will resort to their own law to determine the procedural issues relating to the conditions for the issue of such measures, and may have to look at other laws as well, such as, for instance, the law governing the merits of the dispute in order to assess the prospects for the success of the claim (*fumus boni iuris*) where this is a condition for the issue of such measures.

Issues relating to an arbitration may also arise before national courts if the dispute allegedly subject to arbitration is brought for resolution before a court – be it of the seat of the arbitration or elsewhere – in apparent disregard of the arbitration agreement. In these cases, too, the New York Convention will be applicable. However, depending on their approach to this matter, such courts will have to rely on their own law or on that of some other state, or on transnational principles, to determine whether the arbitration agreement is 'null and void, inoperative or incapable of being performed' as permitted by article II(3) of the Convention.

Finally, it is possible that issues relating to an arbitration arise in yet other countries which may seek to intervene in relation to it on the strength of their own jurisdictional rules.[17]

5 Conclusion

Arbitration has evolved very significantly since the era when, even in the first decades after the adoption of the New York Convention, it was entirely the captive of national law. Today it has gained a very marked freedom from domestic legal systems, and unwanted interferences from local law are probably more the exception than the rule. Whilst one can expect that the situation will further evolve as an ever greater number of states adhere to a more arbitration-friendly culture, it is unrealistic to expect that the influence of national law can recede entirely. Complete autonomy from national law will continue to operate only for arbitrations under the auspices of ICSID.

This should not necessarily be a reason for apprehension, even if one believes that international commercial arbitration should be a means for the settlement of disputes completely alternative to national court systems and is a system that must remain as detached as possible from national law. Indeed, in the majority of cases there are effective tools to keep the influence of national law within reasonable and acceptable

[17] See Radicati di Brozolo, 'The Impact of National Law and Courts'.

limits. For the parties, the key to achieving this goal is a sensible designation of the seat of the arbitration that gives them the desired degree of autonomy and affords them an efficient and arbitration-friendly regime, which ideally grants them all the freedom they need, while at the same time being available to provide the necessary support and oversight when needed. If the arbitration only has contacts with countries that subscribe to a liberal vision of arbitration, few problems are to be expected.

In a broader and systematic perspective, it is to be hoped that states will adopt a more nuanced approach to the influence of domestic law on arbitration and on the role of the *lex arbitri*. In the interest of furthering arbitration, states should avoid blindly deferring to the decisions of foreign states, including the state of the seat, in matters of arbitration. Those decisions should be taken into consideration and possibly recognized only insofar as they comport with truly pro-arbitration and generally accepted standards. When this is not the case, states should exercise their own control over awards at the enforcement stage, without paying regard to the decisions of foreign courts.

PART II

Ad hoc arbitration

3

Ad hoc arbitration v. institutional arbitration

CARITA WALLGREN-LINDHOLM

1 Analysis of the topic

In comparing *ad hoc* to institutional arbitration, we first need to determine what differentiates these two categories from each other, and then consider the relevant angle for comparison from the perspective of the relevant participants in the procedure from time to time. Additionally, some main institutions need to be considered. Finally, some thought should be given to the extent to which differences are ultimately relevant, and the degree of significance that can be attributed to the institution chosen, as determined mainly as a function of the identity of the user of the service.

To deal with this broad topic conclusively would be a challenging task and would require thorough research. While some statistics will be given, the views expressed here are based on personal and, hence, random empirical findings. One of the conclusions will be that, while ready-made sets of rules are important for procedural efficiency and predictability, as is also often an institutional body managing aspects of a dispute that may not be core to its substantive resolution, many extrinsic factors affect the proceedings – and even their outcome – which may reduce the importance of the set of rules adopted and whether or not such rules are, indeed, adopted.

The prime relevant element for comparison of *ad hoc* with institutional arbitration is procedure. Procedure will be referred to herein in the

This chapter is based on the presentation 'Ad hoc arbitration v. institutional arbitration' given at the conference *Trends and Features in International Arbitration* in Oslo on 6 May 2010, organized by the University of Oslo Faculty of Law Department of Private Law's Research Project on 'Choice of Law Clauses and Their Limitations', headed by Professor Giuditta Cordero-Moss and the Norwegian Committee of the ICC. The chapter has been updated as regards facts until end November 2011. I wish to express my thanks to associate lawyer Mari Antila, who has assisted in producing this chapter.

largest sense as encompassing not only the procedural law or laws that govern or apply to the proceedings and their outcome, including the relevant international treaties, but also other rules and practices governing or affecting the conduct of an international arbitration; that is, everything but the merits.[1] This chapter will endeavour to address the manner in which proceedings are conducted and managed in practice and the 'drivers' for such conduct and management from the perspective of the laws and rules that may govern the proceedings from time to time.

2 Statutory rules, institutional rules and other rules: mandating an institution

The rules relevant for an international arbitration can consist of statutory national law (*lex arbitri*), international conventions such as the New York Convention,[2] contractually binding provisions and rules adopted before or during the proceedings that are made contractually binding or serve as guidance in the proceedings at the discretion of the arbitral tribunal. Contractually binding provisions may include institutional rules agreed by the parties such as the ICC, LCIA or SCC arbitration rules, just to name a few, and model rules intended to be applied in *ad hoc* proceedings such as the UNCITRAL Arbitration Rules. Parties may also have agreed that in any future (or ongoing) dispute between them, specific procedural rules – for example, the IBA Rules on the Taking of Evidence in International Arbitration[3] (the 'IBA Rules of Evidence') – will apply or serve as guidance. Further, arbitral tribunals may, at their discretion, adopt case-specific rules during proceedings. In adopting their own case-specific rules, tribunals may seek inspiration from instruments such as the above-mentioned IBA Rules of Evidence, ICC Techniques for Controlling Time and Costs in Arbitration,[4] the Debevoise Protocol[5] or the UNCITRAL Notes on Organizing Arbitral Proceedings, without full application of such instruments, but rather

1 Yet including the manner of merit assessment and also deliberations.
2 Convention on the Recognition and Enforcement of Foreign Arbitral Awards 1958.
3 On 29 May 2010, the International Bar Association Council adopted a revised version of the 1999 IBA Rules on the Taking of Evidence in International Arbitration.
4 Techniques for Controlling Time and Costs in Arbitration, Report from the ICC Commission on Arbitration, ICC Publication 843 (Paris: International Chamber of Commerce, 2007).
5 Debevoise & Plimpton LLP Protocol to Promote Efficiency in International Arbitration.

with a view to incorporating into each individual arbitration the best-suited practices and procedures offered by such instruments.

As we can see, the building blocks for putting into place the infrastructure of an arbitration can be manifold. They can vary from rules that impose themselves without the exercise of the will of the parties (e.g. mandatory *lex arbitri* rules), to best practices and models that are more principle- than rules-based and, the implementation of which, to a greater extent than strict rules, will depend on the participants' willingness to honour them.

While institutions may also play the role of appointing authority,[6] and rules of institutions are sometimes adopted by contracting parties with the exclusion of the administrative function of the relevant institutions, these instances will be deemed peculiarities for purposes of this presentation. Institutional arbitration, hence, will be dealt with herein as referring only to instances where the rules of a particular institution have been contracted fully[7] and the institution whose rules have been adopted has been mandated to administer the arbitration by performing certain tasks.

These administrative tasks performed by institutions normally include managing the early phases of the proceedings such as receiving the request for arbitration and the response, initial jurisdictional and other procedural assessments such as fixing the seat and language of arbitration and possible consolidation, appointing the arbitral tribunal and determining, initially, challenges towards arbitrators. Institutions also, as a rule, manage the financial aspects of the case. They request advance deposits for the costs of the arbitration from the parties, administer the funds during the arbitration and, finally, determine the costs of the arbitration and hence the fees of the arbitrators. Institutions are also

[6] Many institutions including, *inter alia*, the AAA, the FCCC, the ICC, the LCIA and the SCC, have adopted procedures allowing them to appoint arbitrators in *ad hoc* proceedings if the parties fail to agree on such appointment. See, for example, the Rules of the ICC as Appointing Authority in UNCITRAL or Other Ad Hoc Arbitration Proceedings, in force as of 1 January 2004. According to Article 6(1) of the UNCITRAL Arbitration Rules as revised in 2010, '[u]nless the parties have already agreed on the choice of an appointing authority, a party may at any time propose the name or names of one or more institutions or persons, including the Secretary-General of the Permanent Court of Arbitration at The Hague (hereinafter called the 'PCA'), one of whom would serve as appointing authority'. If the parties fail to agree on the choice of an appointing authority, any party may request the Secretary-General of the PCA to designate the appointing authority.

[7] Which obviously does not exclude that certain provisions may have been amended or expanded.

in charge of ongoing case management and certain other administrative matters, including managing the relevant procedural time limits (such as extending time limits for rendering the award, if needed), removing and replacing arbitrators, if necessary, and, as is the case with the ICC, exercising quality control over the awards. The basis for the mandate to the institutions to exercise such functions is contractual, stemming from the agreement to arbitrate under the rules of the particular institution, as discussed in more detail below.

Arbitral institutions are also important opinion leaders in the development of international arbitration and when institutions amend their rules similar trends, not unsurprisingly, can be discerned in the revision work of different institutions. One recent example would be the rules concerning emergency arbitrators adopted by the SCC in 2009.[8] Similar rules were adopted by the SIAC in 2010[9] and the ACICA in 2011[10] and the ICC has now followed suit by its introduction of an opt-out emergency arbitrator scheme.[11] It has been reported that other institutions are also currently considering whether to include an emergency arbitrator procedure in their rules. The same effect can be perceived relative to UNCITRAL and the IBA, organizations that in 2010 revised their arbitration rules and Rules of Evidence, respectively. After the revision of the UNCITRAL Model Law in 2006, the SCC, as an example, aligned its rules on interim measures with the revised Model Law. Recent institutional

[8] Appendix II to the SCC Arbitration Rules in force as of 1 January 2010. Under the SCC rules, an application may be made until the case has been referred to an arbitral tribunal. While similar rules have been adopted even before 2010, e.g. by the ICC (Rules for a Pre-Arbitral Referee Procedure, in force as of 1 January 1990), the ICDR (article 37 of the ICDR International Dispute Resolution Procedures) and the Netherlands Arbitration Institute (Articles 42a–42o of the NAI Arbitration Rules, which apply only if the seat of arbitration is situated within the Netherlands), they have, to date, not been used very often. Unlike the SCC rules, parties must specifically opt in; i.e. agree to apply the ICC pre-arbitral referee rules (instead of merely adopting the ICC Rules). Further, under the ICDR Rules, the emergency arbitrator may be applied for only after the arbitral proceedings have commenced.

[9] Rule 26 and Schedule 1 of the Arbitration Rules of the Singapore International Arbitration Centre. SIAC Rules 4th Edition, 1 July 2010.

[10] Article 28 and Schedule 2 of the ACICA Arbitration Rules incorporating the Emergency Arbitrator Provisions, in force as of 1 August 2011.

[11] Article 29 and appendix V, titled 'Emergency Arbitrator Rules', of the ICC Rules in force as of 1 January 2012. The emergency arbitrator provisions shall apply if the arbitration agreement under the ICC Rules was concluded before 1 January 2012, i.e. the date on which the Rules came into force, the parties have not opted out of the emergency arbitrator provisions and the parties have not agreed to another pre-arbitral procedure that provides for the granting of conservatory, interim or similar measures.

revision work, such as that of the ICC, can also be expected to influence other institutional rules. Similarly, the IBA Rules of Evidence are often used as reference when institutional or other procedural rules need to be supplemented for evidentiary matters.

When rules are adopted, which occurs when parties choose institutional or administered arbitration, they are binding upon the parties as a contract. Arbitral institutions, based on this contract, perform many of the functions that otherwise will be brought before local courts of varying quality but with a certain dilatory effect. As we will see below, many contractual parties attach importance to the identity, or rather renown of the relevant institution, mainly as a perceived security for orderly proceedings but also as a 'brand' in support of enforcement. While some arbitrators complain of the modest fees they receive under the cost tables of institutions, most acknowledge the value of a third-party administrator of the financial aspects of the arbitration, normally the only element of the arbitration where the arbitrators and the parties can be deemed to have opposing interests. As dealt with in more detail below, most parties and arbitral practitioners would hold, not unsurprisingly, that institutional administration has pros and cons.

However, the proceedings are also governed by tacit rules that exist in the minds of the persons impacting the conduct of the proceedings in practice. Such tacit rules are often not defined or articulated at the outset and their existence is not always even fully recognized by their carriers. When all participants come from the same legal environment and the arbitration is in all relevant respects national, arbitrators and counsel alike generally operate on and from the same legal platform, formally and in practice. It is in international arbitration, where national boundaries are transcended,[12] that the inner landscapes and roadmaps among arbitrators and counsel can differ quite significantly, regardless of the wide expertise that often characterizes the participants. This, in turn, can sometimes be seen to create misunderstandings and discord that in some

[12] The term 'international arbitration' does not have an established definition. Factors determinative to whether an arbitration is international may be, e.g. the international character of the dispute, the nationality of the parties or their place of business and the seat of the arbitration. Under article 1(3) of the UNCITRAL Model Law, an arbitration is defined as international also if any place where a substantial part of the obligations of the commercial relationship is to be performed or if the place with which the subject matter of the dispute is most closely connected is outside the state in which the parties have their places of business or the parties have expressly agreed that the subject matter of the arbitration agreement relates to more than one country.

cases could be avoided or at least managed by the recognition of completely legitimate, albeit different, approaches to procedural measures. These 'tacit rules' will be dealt with alongside the formal rules or models of institutions and organizations.

3 Choice by corporations of institutional or *ad hoc* arbitration

Before discussing the relative weight and interplay of formal and tacit rules for the conduct of an international arbitration, it is useful to look at some statistics for the importance that companies attribute to various aspects of available dispute resolution options. The statistics in this section are derived from three studies conducted by the School of International Arbitration, Queen Mary University of London, which will be referred to as the '2006 Study',[13] the '2008 Study'[14] and the '2010 Study',[15] respectively.

These statistics tell us that a great majority of awards, 86%, are rendered through arbitral institutions rather than *ad hoc* arbitrations.[16] The statistics also reveal some differences between the attitudes of corporations and states or state-owned enterprises towards *ad hoc* arbitration. According to the 2006 Study, 76% of corporations opt for institutional arbitration (as opposed to *ad hoc* arbitration, which is favoured mainly by large corporations).[17] The figure is somewhat lower when it comes to arbitrations involving states or state-owned enterprises. Of such latter arbitrations, 67% are institutional.[18]

Institutional involvement offers many advantages for parties in arbitration, which probably explains the success of institutional arbitration. The most cited reasons for choosing institutional arbitration are, according to the 2006 Study, reputation, familiarity with proceedings

[13] School of International Arbitration, Queen Mary University of London, *International Arbitration: Corporate Attitudes and Practices 2006*.

[14] School of International Arbitration, Queen Mary University of London, *International Arbitration: Corporate Attitudes and Practices 2008*.

[15] School of International Arbitration, Queen Mary University of London, *2010 International Arbitration Survey: Choices in International Arbitration*. After this chapter was finalised (end November 2011) a 2012 study appeared.

[16] Queen Mary University of London, *International Arbitration: Corporate Attitudes and Practices 2008*, p. 15. The results are consistent with the 2006 Study.

[17] Queen Mary University of London, *International Arbitration: Corporate Attitudes and Practices 2006*, p. 12.

[18] Queen Mary University of London, *International Arbitration: Corporate Attitudes and Practices 2008*, p. 4.

(experience),[19] understanding (predictability)[20] of costs and fees and, finally, the convenience of the process.[21]

The identity, or rather renown of the relevant institution is perceived by many parties both as a security for orderly proceedings and as a 'brand' in support of award enforcement. Instead of parties and arbitrators having to spend time on reinventing the wheel, institutional arbitration offers procedural rules that have been proven to work in practice and that exist conveniently at the outset of the proceedings. Further, it may well be true that a recognized institutional brand carried by an award can make it easier at times to enforce the award in local courts, the brand serving as a form of guarantee of the legitimacy of the proceedings. Institutional quality control of awards may further help to ensure effective award enforcement and in the 2010 Study, scrutiny of the award by an institution was mentioned by 33% of participants as one of the factors that favourably influenced their choice of institution.[22]

Further, institutions make decisions in support of arbitration based on their experience. They make initial decisions whether the institution (or any arbitral tribunal that would be appointed by it) has or manifestly lacks jurisdiction to proceed with the case. They appoint or replace arbitrators, in which task they are assisted by their knowledge of the pool of available arbitrators, and of the arbitrators' expertise and track record of previous case handling (under the auspices of that institution). As the specialization of arbitration increases, so does the need for assistance in finding the right arbitrator for the dispute. Institutions also perform a gap-filling function where the arbitration agreement is silent (e.g. fixing the language or the seat of the arbitration). They handle the financial aspects of the arbitration, fixing advances on costs and confirming fees and expenses payable to arbitrators – costs being determined according to established schedules and thus predictable to the parties. Institutions also manage time limits and other administrative aspects of the case and their staff are available for consultation on various questions that may arise during the proceedings.

With institutional support, it is often argued, comes additional cost, administration (bureaucracy) and delay. Institutional involvement also,

[19] Redefinition by the author. [20] Redefinition by the author.

[21] Queen Mary University of London, *International Arbitration: Corporate Attitudes and Practices 2006*, p. 12.

[22] Queen Mary University of London, *2010 International Arbitration Survey: Choices in International Arbitration*, p. 22.

it is said, adds one layer of bureaucracy to the proceedings, as many aspects of the arbitration must be run through the institution. Institutional involvement can also be held to mean that the parties are no longer the masters of all aspects of the arbitration. One example that is sometimes advanced is the instance where the institution refuses to appoint an arbitrator that both parties have agreed on. Without detailed knowledge of the particular cases, it cannot, however, be excluded that any such decision, albeit circumscribing party autonomy, would, ultimately, serve the parties' interest. In addition, institutional scrutiny of awards prior to their rendering may cause some delay.

While these time – and ultimately – cost effects cannot be ignored, they are relevant for comparison only with an alternative scenario; that is, what would the time and cost effect be without the gap-filling function of the institution? Administrative expenses themselves (disregarding any cost effect of additional time consumption), according to statistics, only constitute a fraction of the total costs of arbitration.[23] Where there is no clear address for solving the issues managed by the institution, the alternative cost and delay might, at the end of the day, exceed those adduced by the institutional involvement. Although it is clear that there are proceedings where the participants can be as, or more, efficient without institutional involvement, such involvement, in most cases, often provides a security to the parties and the arbitrators that may outweigh the extra cost and time that result.

It may also be asked of institutional arbitration whether a certain set of rules is itself prone to generate more (and possibly not useful) work for participants. This is a complex issue that it is not possible to deal with further here. Suffice it to say that in this author's view it is not obvious that one set of rules is more prone today to inflate and delay proceedings than others. The efficiency of the proceedings may have more to do with the culture and practices prevailing among those carrying out the administrative tasks and the standards they themselves set. Finally, any possibly perceived limitations in party autonomy by the decisions and acts of an institution can probably be outweighed by a reasonable transparency in its decision-making process coupled with it giving adequate reasons for the decisions that it has found necessary to make.

[23] According to statistics provided by the ICC, the institution's administrative expenses were approximately 2% of the total costs of arbitration in cases that went to a final award in 2003 and 2004. See Techniques for Controlling Time and Costs in Arbitration, Report from the ICC Commission on Arbitration 2007.

Turning to *ad hoc* arbitration, the advantages usually mentioned include, first, greater flexibility in designing the procedure to meet the parties' wishes and in accommodating the particularities of the dispute at hand. Parties may tailor case-specific procedural rules or they may apply established procedures such as the UNCITRAL Arbitration Rules that are commonly used in *ad hoc* arbitration. Selecting institutional arbitration rules to govern an *ad hoc* arbitration is not generally recommended, however, as they are unlikely to work properly or effectively without the involvement of the institution.[24]

In *ad hoc* arbitration, the parties avoid institutional expenses, which can be of some importance, especially where the value of the matter in dispute is high. The parties are also free to negotiate fees with the arbitrators directly instead of applying institutional cost schedules that primarily take the value of the dispute into account.[25] Through negotiation, arbitrators' remuneration can be set to depend more on the complexity of the case and the actual work performed. This way, arbitrators might also, in practice – as has sometimes been suggested – be perceived to be more directly accountable to the parties for the quality of their work. On the other hand, negotiating the fees with the person(s) who ultimately decides the dispute risks being an unbalanced negotiation not offering equality of arms. As mentioned, this is also the very aspect of the arbitration where arbitrators and the parties can be deemed to have opposing interests. In this regard, having a neutral case administrator removes the encounter or confrontation on monetary issues at the very outset of the proceedings, where establishing an atmosphere of confidence between the arbitral tribunal and the parties is key.

Avoidance of administrative costs, however, also means lack of immediately available institutional support. Arbitral institutions, as mentioned, perform many of the functions that, in cases where the parties fail to agree on the applicable procedure, are likely to be brought before local courts more or less qualified to deal with them. This, again, is often

[24] On occasion, parties have tried to mix and match arbitration rules and institutions. The 2007 SIAC case *Insigma*, in which the parties had agreed that their arbitration would be administered by the SIAC under the ICC Arbitration Rules, indicates that bringing institutional rules to an alien environment and to be administered by another body than that for which they were designed is not efficient dispute resolution. Indeed, the new ICC Rules expressly provide in their Article 1(2) that '[t]he Court is the only body authorized to administer arbitrations under the Rules, including the scrutiny and approval of awards rendered in accordance with the Rules'.

[25] Some institutions, such as the LCIA, apply hourly fees.

precisely what the parties wanted to avoid by choosing arbitration as their dispute resolution method. Effective cooperation between the parties and their counsel could thus be said to be the key component in, if not a *sine qua non* for, a successful *ad hoc* arbitration. In addition, reasonable experience and sophistication in international arbitration by all involved help ensure efficient *ad hoc* proceedings and a stable outcome. Parties should also see to it that they are seated in an arbitration-friendly legal environment that is adequate for responding to any need to turn to state courts, should the cooperation fail.

Flexibility in setting up the procedure is not necessarily the equivalent of procedural efficiency. *Ad hoc* arbitrations are said to proceed as smoothly as institutional arbitrations only from the moment when the tribunal is in existence and the procedural rules have been established. The principal weakness, or rather maybe risk, of *ad hoc* arbitration is precisely its dependence on cooperation between the parties and their lawyers.[26] After a dispute has arisen, parties, and the respondent in particular, may not be as cooperative in agreeing on the rules as they may have counted on when drafting the arbitration clause. Effective *ad hoc* proceedings essentially require that parties act responsibly and do not try to delay or otherwise obstruct the proceedings. However, there can be instances where counsel's legitimate responsibility to his or her client is to do just that.

When comparing institutional to *ad hoc* arbitration, it is worth remembering that even *ad hoc* arbitrations are not all free of institutional influence. In fact, the trend is towards greater institutional involvement in *ad hoc* arbitration, as reflected by the revised UNCITRAL Arbitration Rules. Institutions may appoint arbitrators and parties may seek a decision on the challenge of arbitrators from the institution acting as the appointing authority.[27] The revised UNCITRAL Rules provide that, in cases where an appointing authority has been agreed, arbitrators shall take the schedule or a method for determining arbitrator fees applied by such an appointing authority into account in their fee determination, to the extent that they consider it appropriate in the circumstances of the case.[28] This means that institutional schedules will also serve as an anchor in the negotiation, if any, on arbitrators' fees. Furthermore,

[26] Nigel Blackaby and Constantine Partasides with Alan Redfern and Martin Hunter, *Redfern and Hunter on International Arbitration*, 5th edn (Oxford University Press, 2009), at 1.157.

[27] Article 13(4) of the UNCITRAL Arbitration Rules.

[28] Article 41(2) of the UNCITRAL Arbitration Rules.

parties may refer the arbitrator's determination on fees for review to the appointing authority.[29]

To conclude, statistics suggest that institutional involvement is perceived by the parties more as a help than a hindrance and institutional arbitration is preferred by the majority. However, *ad hoc* arbitrations also have their own specific features that make the choice attractive to arbitrating parties, especially to those that are states or state-owned entities or large (sophisticated) corporations arbitrating high-value disputes. For parties wanting the 'best of both worlds', the UNCITRAL Rules, with certain support functions by institutions, may be the preferred choice.

4 How different are institutions?

In a general sense, four main aspects can be used to reflect differences between institutions: the profile of the institution, its arbitration rules, the manner in which the institution administers cases and the costs of arbitration.

The institutional profile and character have great weight in the choice of an institution. According to the 2010 Study, the top two influences in choosing arbitral institutions include 'neutrality/internationalism' and 'reputation/recognition'.[30] While it is questionable to what extent such distinctions are useful for the purpose of discovering true differences between institutions, an initial categorization between international, even non-national (see *infra*), and more regional institutions can be made.

It has been suggested that the ICC is the only truly non-national institution.[31] The ICC does indeed have a unique profile and a track record of successfully administering arbitrations globally for decades. Finding a precise definition for 'international institution', however, may prove as difficult as finding one for 'international arbitration'. The ICC can probably correctly be described as non-national and it would seem that the institution is not currently perceived as being particularly connected to France. As regards other institutions that could be characterized as international, they are necessarily perceived as, to some extent, being regional since their rules are often harmonized with the seat of the institution. As has

29 Article 41(4)(b) of the UNCITRAL Arbitration Rules.

30 Queen Mary University of London, *2010 International Arbitration Survey: Choices in International Arbitration*, p. 22.

31 Gerald Aksen, 'International Arbitration: Knowing the Practical Differences', in Gerald Aksen *et al.*, (eds.), *Liber Amicorum in honour of Robert Briner* (Paris: ICC Publishing S.A., 2005), p. 23.

been pointed out by Gerald Aksen, in an AAA, LCIA or SCC arbitration the odds are also good that one or more of the arbitrators will be from the country where the institution is based.[32] While an institution thus may have some regional features, it may qualify as international and enjoy recognition well beyond the borders of the country in which it is based and be able to administer (and also frequently administers) arbitrations in which parties come from a wide range of legal cultures. There are many such institutions, including the above-mentioned LCIA and SCC as well as the Swiss Chambers' Court of Arbitration and Mediation (the 'SCCAM').[33] When an institution is considered international in the sense described above, it is also probably more easily acceptable as a neutral institution to a party that otherwise would prefer the institution of its own country.

While internationalism is important, regional presence and knowledge are also valued as elements in themselves. Knowledge of features and requirements unique to different jurisdictions and legal cultures is part of the added value of institutional involvement. In addition, where the institution's staff master the language of the arbitration, even if this is not an absolute prerequisite, there is no need for (cost increasing) accommodation by the parties and the arbitrators. The 2010 Study shows that parties are increasingly 'considering "non-traditional" institutions in order to accommodate their counterparty in another region'. The use of regional institutions, however, requires that the institutions first have 'proven themselves' or have a 'track record' and presumably, as stated above, must be perceived as international/neutral enough.[34] The trend where an established 'brand' is combined with regional expertise, demonstrated by established institutions such as the LCIA moving to emerging markets,[35] may help in regional establishment and in getting acceptance from arbitration users.

[32] Ibid., p. 23.

[33] As of 1 January 2004, the Chambers of Commerce and Industry of Basel, Bern, Geneva, Ticino, Vaud and Zurich, joined by Neuchâtel in 2008, have applied the Swiss Rules of International Arbitration instead of their individual international arbitration rules. Since 2007, they have provided services collectively under the SCCAM.

[34] Queen Mary University of London, *2010 International Arbitration Survey: Choices in International Arbitration*, p. 22.

[35] On 28 July 2011, the LCIA-MIAC Arbitration Centre – the latest of the LCIA's foreign ventures to date – was established in Mauritius by an agreement between the LCIA, the government of the Republic of Mauritius and Mauritius International Arbitration Centre Limited (MIAC). Prior to this, in 2008, the LCIA had entered into a joint venture with the Dubai International Financial Centre to create the DIFC-LCIA Arbitration Centre, followed by the establishment of LCIA India, the first independent subsidiary of the LCIA, in 2009.

As between different institutions, at least in continental Europe, the difference as regards the basic procedure of the arbitration is limited. Institutions also seem to follow the same trends for rejuvenation and novelty, which is only natural, since issues to be addressed largely arise from arbitral practice. The UNCITRAL Arbitration Rules and other such established instruments have no doubt deeply influenced many institutional rules.[36] In view of the convergence that results from institutions following trends and practices set by international bodies and adopting other institutions' innovations, it may not be surprising that arbitration rules 'only' came in third in the 2010 Study for top influences when choosing arbitral institutions.[37]

Apart from some particularities that are sometimes singled out in discussions, such as the terms of reference and scrutiny of arbitral awards by the ICC Court and the SCC Rules' obligation, stemming from Swedish arbitration law, to terminate all arbitral proceedings by an award, most of the frequently quoted European rules (for example, the ICC, LCIA, SCC and Swiss Rules[38]) respect party autonomy and, where the parties have not agreed differently, allow the arbitral tribunal great room for manoeuvre in organizing the proceedings. This is not to say, however, that all rules are the same. Indeed, the 'default' rules do differ by institution to some extent[39] and, while the parties may in principle derogate from such rules, the reality of contract drafting often is that the default rule becomes the applicable rule. Furthermore, certain institutional rules function particularly well with the legal system of the country where the institution is based – a feature related to the 'regional' characteristics of institutions mentioned above. For example, the SCC Rules can be said to be aligned with Swedish arbitration law. The same is true of the LCIA and the English Arbitration Act 1996.

36 As an example, the website of the SCCAM expressly states that the Swiss Rules are based on the UNCITRAL Arbitration Rules, with modifications required to adapt the rules to institutional arbitration and changes and additions reflecting modern practice and comparative law in the field of international arbitration. See www.sccam.org/sa/en/rules.php.

37 Queen Mary University of London, *2010 International Arbitration Survey: Choices in International Arbitration*, p. 22.

38 Swiss Rules of International Arbitration 2006.

39 The present 1993 Rules of the Arbitration Institute of the Central Chamber of Commerce of Finland (FCCC) amended in 2005, as an example, provide that the default number of arbitrators is three (§6), as opposed to the more frequent default institutional rule that a sole arbitrator be appointed, unless the FCCC Institute considers it to be appropriate to appoint a sole arbitrator taking into account the nature of the dispute, the amount in dispute or other circumstances.

Further, the level of control institutions exercise over arbitral proceedings varies by institution. This control includes matters such as how vigorously time limits are imposed and enforced. The ICC could be viewed as one of the institutions exercising quite extensive control over proceedings, including its requirement of drafting terms of reference and timetables[40] at the beginning of the proceedings and its scrutiny of the award procedure, while other institutions take a fairly discreet role in the proceedings. While some prefer a high level of administration by the institution, others believe that the institution should adopt a lighter, rather more facilitative role. This facilitative role includes accessibility for consultation and advice on best practices that is especially important to those who do not have much experience in international arbitration. The degree of accessibility for consultation and its nature vary from one institution to another.

Finally, the cost and the manner of determining arbitrators' fees is one factor that differentiates institutions from one another. Most institutions calculate arbitrator fees and administrative expenses based upon the amount in dispute, with the exception of the LCIA, which applies hourly fees. Whether the calculation is mainly made on an *ad valorem* basis or by the hour does not, however, and quite logically, appear to be so important to arbitration users as long as the overall cost of service remains reasonable.[41] A recent study comparing arbitration costs indicates that there is substantial variance in arbitration costs between institutions.[42]

The costs will obviously depend on both the amount in dispute and whether a sole arbitrator or a three-member tribunal has been appointed. Fee and cost scales usually leave some judgmental room to the institution in its final determination of arbitrator fees and institutions generally make use of their margin of discretion by taking into account the complexity of the dispute and the amount of (necessary) work performed by the arbitrators. The ICC, with its close monitoring of matters, has been found to be among the most expensive institutions,[43] but the

[40] Timetables now required also by many other institutions, such as the SCC and the SCCAM.

[41] Queen Mary University of London, *2010 International Arbitration Survey: Choices in International Arbitration*, p. 22.

[42] Louis Flannery and Benjamin Garel, 'Arbitration Costs Compared', *Global Arbitration Review*, 5(5) (2010). A study comparing arbitration costs between the ICC, SCC, SIAC, DIAC, SCCAM, MKAS, CRCICA and HKIAC.

[43] Ibid.

point that should be taken into consideration – in addition to all other reasons for preferring a particular institution – is that the institutions that are expensive in cases with a comparatively low amount in dispute can, in fact, be among the most affordable when the amount is high and vice versa.[44]

From the arbitrators' point of view, institutions also differ with respect to the distribution of the fees among the chair, on the one hand, and the (normally two) 'wing' arbitrators, on the other, allocating a greater or lesser percentage of the total fees for the work of the chair.

In conclusion, under this heading, while institutions undoubtedly have their own particularities and different profiles, the conduct of an arbitration may not ultimately be greatly affected by the choice of one institution over another. The main institutional rules respect party autonomy and allow for broad room to manoeuvre in terms of arbitrators organizing the proceedings, as will be discussed below. It would, however, seem that the conduct of empirical studies into different aspects of arbitration is on the rise. While this chapter is not prepared to conclude on the cost aspect of a comparison between institutional and *ad hoc* arbitration, this is an area that will continue to attract much and decisive attention in the choice between the dispute resolution tools that are on offer.[45]

One final aspect that may be mentioned in this context is whether the choice of a particular regional institution can also be interpreted as a choice of arbitration culture; for example, to the effect that choosing the SCC signals a willingness to conduct a 'Nordic', somewhat minimalistic procedure. This is a complex issue that will not be elaborated here and which would benefit from further research.

5 How rational are choices? Imperfect communication between different legal traditions

An arbitration is always managed by someone's rules, articulated or just existing in the mind of the person managing it. Comparing institutional and *ad hoc* arbitration boils down to discussing procedure. In such a

[44] Ibid.

[45] For example, the Chartered Institute of Arbitrators conducted a Costs of International Arbitration Survey in 2010/2011. The findings of the survey were analyzed through a report and a conference, organized by CIArb, which took place on 27–28 September 2011 in London, England.

discussion participants are never wholly unbiased. The parties who are talking are often not fully communicating. Many layers of unarticulated preconceptions and matters taken for granted colour any such discussion (i.e. you talk out of your legal homeland irrespective of your international experience). One clear demarcation line is between the procedure that is applied in civil law countries versus that applied in common law jurisdictions. Having been raised in one or the other system is likely to colour a lawyer's approach to the rules – or modules – and their role in international arbitration.[46] These preconceptions and imperfect communication are also present in any comparison between different arbitral institutions and between institutional arbitration and *ad hoc* proceedings. Some of the true differences in how an arbitration actually turns out may lie elsewhere than in the adoption of a particular set of rules or in the continued presence of an administrative body therein.

6 The difference between institutional and *ad hoc* arbitration is one of degree rather than kind

There is some merit in the assertion that the difference between institutional and *ad hoc* arbitration is one of degree rather than kind.[47] As we have seen, the difference as regards the basic procedure is limited between different institutions, at least in continental Europe. Where the parties have not agreed otherwise, institutional rules allow the arbitral tribunal great room for manoeuvre in organizing the proceedings. Whether 'package' solutions are adopted as such (rules and institution) or whether structures are created for a particular arbitration by different modules as discussed above, including the UNCITRAL Arbitration Rules, and instruments such as the IBA Rules of Evidence, ICC Techniques for Controlling Time and Costs in Arbitration, the Debevoise Protocol or the UNCITRAL Notes on Organizing Arbitral Proceedings, may not ultimately matter, so long as the solutions that are adopted are based on experience, are thought through, respect basic access to justice rights and are identifiable and functional in the legal environments where they may be put to the test.

[46] An exception is made for the small number of arbitration practitioners who truly seem to rise above the distinction made between the systems.

[47] Fabien Gélinas, 'Re: The Institutionalisation of Ad Hoc Arbitration', on the OGEMID mailing list, 2 February 2010.

Proceedings can be regulated up front or in the course thereof in greater or lesser detail. Where parties, or more importantly counsel come from a similar legal background and have matching experience in international arbitration, certain procedures are taken for granted by both sides without much active monitoring from the arbitral tribunal. This is often also true when representatives of global arbitration firms appear on both sides.

However, where there is no conceptual symmetry between the sides, what happens when the adopted rules are silent? There are always gaps to be filled, interpretations to be made and approaches to be taken. Indeed, most rules of procedure actually do not regulate the issues that take up most procedural attention by counsel and that are invoked for purposes of equal and sufficient right to plead their case. These concern matters such as the form and contents of submissions and exhibits thereto, the timing and order of such submissions and evidence, the conduct of witness and expert hearings, production of documents and post-hearing measures (post-hearing briefs or oral closing). It is also not uncommon that parties have different views, by choice or by necessity, of the extent and level of support and infrastructure required for a hearing (number of counsel, premises, recording of the hearing, translation and interpretation etc.). Additionally, counsel's perceptions of the burden of proof and its impact on procedural decisions often vary greatly.

As regards most of the above-mentioned procedural issues, the rules and regulations contain some base provisions but the detailed procedure is ultimately established by the arbitral tribunal, which is granted such a right by most rules. In practice, this will often mean that the chair fills the gaps in procedural regulation, expressly or tacitly. It is therefore often the case that the chair's legal culture becomes decisive for the culture of the proceedings. This circumstance lessens the impact of the rules chosen by the parties, which mostly do not limit the tribunal's or the chair's possibility of conducting the proceedings in a manner that he or she feels is 'natural'. What feels natural, again, is often similar to the approach of counsel on one side of the dispute, whose procedural requests seem easily justifiable and legitimate, and indeed logical in the eyes of the chair. It is therefore possible, and not uncommon, that proceedings look the same with the same chair, irrespective of the rules that regulate them from time to time. While such similarity may be deemed desirable as such for the uniform development of international arbitration, it may still, in a particular arbitration, result in proceedings that are perceived as different from what one party thought it contracted for.

7 Concluding thoughts

In the discussion above, various pros and cons of institutional or administered arbitration and *ad hoc* arbitration have been addressed. The choice, where it is considered and informed regarding a particular dispute, could be made through the application of the following two tests:

(a) Efficiency of the proceedings;
(b) Stability of the outcome.

Efficiency obviously aims at achieving the most with as little input as possible and always needs to be balanced against the perception by both parties that they have been allowed to plead their case adequately. Efficiency also contains the notion of expediency and we know that there is a strong correlation between delay and increase in cost. We have also experienced that both arbitrators and parties are very preoccupied today with matters of procedure, also due to the increase in challenges of awards, mainly successful on procedural issues. It is therefore obvious that resorting to ready-made and tested procedural solutions frees up energy for the dispute itself. Procedure is a tool and should not *become* the arbitration.

The flyer for the conference[48] raised, *inter alia*, two questions, both of which are implicated by my heading:

(a) Institutional arbitration or *ad hoc*;
(b) If *ad hoc*, should the UNCITRAL Arbitration Rules be referred to?

The short answer from this author's perspective, trying to wear both the arbitrator's and counsel's hat, is that institutional arbitration is generally preferable to *ad hoc* and that if *ad hoc* is chosen, the UNCITRAL Rules should be referred to.

When it comes to the stability of the outcome – that is, the permanence and enforceability of the resulting arbitral award – due process, as reflected by established rules and the credibility of institutions, sometimes even referred to by courts in their rulings on challenges,[49] can be

[48] Conference: 'Trends and Features in International Arbitration' held in Oslo on 6 May 2010.

[49] Judgment by the Swedish Supreme Court in case no. T 2448–06, NJA 2007, p. 841. In the *Lind* case, the Swedish Supreme Court set aside an arbitral award on the basis of the existence of circumstances affecting an arbitrator's impartiality. In its ruling, the Supreme Court referred to both a statement given by the SCC Institute and the IBA Guidelines on Conflicts of Interest in International Arbitration.

held to point to the usefulness of referring to an institution or using established procedural modules.

It is my general view, which, I believe, is shared by most, that it is not possible to conduct an international arbitration today with the informality that was sometimes one of its inherent characteristics. The environment is much tougher, meaning, for example, that the products of international arbitration are increasingly tested before courts, with such lawsuits growing in inventiveness. Arbitrators, counsel and institutions are being sued for their acts and omissions in the context of arbitration and all participants in international arbitration have become more risk aware. However, not only fear or risk awareness is a driver: legitimate expectations of predictability of the procedure, the desire for interchangeability of counsel regardless of the seat and the overall economy of the system require sufficient standardization and best practices to prevail. Additionally, multiculturality and fundamental differences in legal systems need to be bridged in international arbitration to make all players reasonably comfortable in this environment and to preserve their trust in the system. Many arbitral institutions strike this balance to some degree. None of us can feel free to create or recreate the rules anew for every arbitration. There would be no economy in this. We need some generally accepted standard solutions. Finally, procedure should remain a support function in the arbitration. The less energy the arbitrators have to spend on matters of procedure dividing the parties, the more time will be freed up for the arbitrators to concentrate on the causes that drove the parties to arbitration: the merits of the dispute.

We have concluded here that standardized solutions are needed but that they are not enough to create a level playing field for different legal cultures. International best practices are often referred to in order to fill the gaps necessarily left by existing rules. However, is there a generally accepted uniform best practice and whose practice is that? In addition, can one say that best practice also depends on where you are seated; that is, that regionalism can be an element to determine what is best practice from time to time? Alternatively, is there a uniform best practice for international arbitration that is always prevalent? This author is not prepared to offer an answer but maybe a direction, as suggested further below.

While it is clear that knowledgeable and sophisticated parties can tailor-make their own rules from time to time, it would seem clear that choosing an institution is more likely to balance the rights of all parties and to offer a base system where none has been provided for. It is also possible that institutional rules are more on the pulse, normally being more quickly adaptable to new developments than national arbitration laws.

One argument against institutions and standardization that is repeatedly heard in the world of arbitration – and also in the corporate world – is that there is just too much regulation and that too much new regulation is added to the old one. This criticism is largely directed against institutions. The word 'micromanagement' is heard, as is the argument that the over-regulation of human behaviour can lead to absurd results, and many are afraid that increased regulation may not enhance best practices. In addition, there is, of course, a point in arguing that very casuistic handbook-type regulation has the nature to erode good principles and the instinctive good sense of the participants. I heard a colleague mentioning just recently – an international arbitrator of great renown – that he can see a movement away from institutions because those procedures are just too complicated. In his personal experience – which, hence, is anecdotal – arbitrations are increasingly agreed on to be *ad hoc* based upon the UNCITRAL Rules with the Permanent Court of Arbitration at The Hague acting as appointing authority and administrator.

There is no doubt that with one or three internationally experienced arbitrators and equally qualified counsel, who encounter one another frequently in a professional context, the procedure conducted *ad hoc* and without detailed rules under those circumstances will be of a nature to preserve the legitimate interests of all parties. The picture does, however, look different if – which is not infrequent – neither parties nor arbitrators, or only some among them, are particularly well versed in international arbitration. This is where a safety net will be needed.

Does this then mean, as we say in the corporate governance debate, that *one size does not fit all* and that we need *horses for courses*. Yes, maybe. Arbitral institutions are good sources for information and support for those who do not navigate naturally in this environment and these institutions are in the habit of ensuring equal treatment and the right for all parties to be heard. Arbitral institutions are also important opinion leaders for promoting and making known the best practices in the field. However, we all know that the choice on dispute resolution is often not educated – when it could be and even when made by major corporations. Clauses may be adopted out of habit – that of the company or of the house lawyer – and they may never have been tested or questioned. Not even law firms seem to successfully export best practices for various contracts from the dispute resolution to the corporate department.

So where does this leave us? Big law firms largely dominate the relevant market for arbitral clauses and this statement is completely neutral. It probably could not and should not be otherwise. There are certain large corporations and corporate counsel associations[50] that are active in the area but they, I believe, remain the exception, at least in Europe. Law firms in these circumstances have an important task of ensuring that the arbitral clauses that they include in their clients' contracts enhance predictability for the particular client and type of contract at hand. The biggest threat to arbitration today is cost and also time, which ultimately equal cost. Building up the dispute readiness through the use of considered ready modules is likely to reduce cost by allowing an arbitral tribunal to focus on the dispute itself. It is, of course, possible for sophisticated users to accomplish this by tailor-made solutions and shared practices, but if in doubt a tested and established system, such as an institution, is probably most prone to control cost. Additionally, dialogue and institutional transparency regarding the decisions taken is important to refine solutions in the myriad of new regulation. Solutions need time, discussion and a re-visiting of old issues, which may not always appear efficient.

The need for standardized solutions conflicts with the risk of regulating for the pathology and being in a state of fear as a result of today's belligerent climate. We have seen the effects of too much overly hasty technical regulation in the corporate world. The base values get lost or are forgotten in the focus on technical detail and compliance. One key element, however, cannot be stressed enough, and that is the need for chairs of arbitral tribunals to recognize and to be receptive to different expectations in the understanding that there may not be one set of best practices and that less familiar practices may also qualify.

[50] The Corporate Counsel International Arbitration Group (CCIAG), as an example.

4

The UNCITRAL Arbitration Rules and their use in *ad hoc* arbitration

CORINNE MONTINERI

1 Introduction

The United Nations Commission on International Trade Law (UNCITRAL or the 'Commission') was established by the United Nations General Assembly via resolution 2205 (XXI) of 17 December 1966. UNCITRAL plays an important role in developing a legal framework for the facilitation of international trade and investment in pursuance of its mandate to further the progressive harmonization and modernization of the law on international trade.[1] In an increasingly economically interdependent world, the importance of an improved legal framework for the facilitation of international trade and investment is widely acknowledged. Member states have also recognized that the activity of international trade could itself provide a basis for friendly relations if it were structured by a common set of rules, informed by the

The views expressed in this chapter are personal and do not necessarily reflect the views of the United Nations Commission on International Trade Law (UNCITRAL) Secretariat.

[1] UNCITRAL gives effect to its mandate by: '(a) Coordinating the work of organizations active in this field and encouraging cooperation among them; (b) Promoting wider participation in existing international conventions and wider acceptance of existing model and uniform laws; (c) Preparing or promoting the adoption of new international conventions, model laws and uniform laws and promoting the codification and wider acceptance of international trade terms, provisions, customs and practices, in collaboration, where appropriate, with the organizations operating in this field; (d) Promoting ways and means of ensuring a uniform interpretation and application of international conventions and uniform laws in the field of the law of international trade; (e) Collecting and disseminating information on national legislation and modern legal developments, including case law, in the field of the law of international trade; (f) Establishing and maintaining a close collaboration with the United Nations Conference on Trade and Development; (g) Maintaining liaison with other United Nations organs and specialized agencies concerned with international trade; and (h) Taking any other action it may deem useful to fulfill its functions' (see General Assembly Resolution 2205 (XXI), sect. II, para. 8).

principles of equality and mutual respect. Governments have recognized the relationship between trade facilitation and the broader goals of the United Nations, such as in the promotion of world peace and human development. Since UNCITRAL texts contribute to building an open trading and financial system that is rule-based, predictable and non-discriminatory, supporting good governance, development and poverty reduction, UNCITRAL texts are also instrumental in achieving the United Nations Millennium Development Goals and, in particular, Goal 8: fostering a global partnership for development. In the years since its establishment, UNCITRAL has been recognized as the core legal body of the United Nations system in the field of international trade law.[2]

UNCITRAL is well known for its works in the field of international commercial arbitration and mediation, but obviously the scope of its work is much wider. At its first session in 1968, after considering a number of suggestions by member states, the Commission adopted nine subject areas as the basis of its work programme: the international sale of goods, international commercial arbitration, transportation, insurance, international payments, intellectual property, the elimination of discrimination in laws affecting international trade, agency and the legalization of documents. Some of these subjects have not been taken up by the Commission; for example, intellectual property, insurance, the elimination of discrimination in laws affecting international trade, agency and the legalization of documents. Priority status was initially accorded to the international sale of goods, international commercial arbitration and international payments, with trade-financing contracts, transportation, electronic commerce, government contracts and insolvency subsequently being added.

On a number of occasions since its first session, the Commission has considered and revised its work programme on the basis of new developments in technology, changes in business practices, international trends and developments, economic and financial crises and other forces affecting and shaping international trade. In considering whether particular topics should be added to the programme, factors such as global significance, areas of special interest to developing countries and the evolution of commercial practice are taken into account.

[2] See *The UNCITRAL Guide, Basic Facts about the United Nations Commission on International Trade Law*, United Nations publication, Sales No. E.07.V.12.

The legislative and non-legislative instruments[3] prepared and promoted by UNCITRAL are negotiated through an international process involving a variety of participants, including member states of UNCITRAL, who represent different legal traditions and levels of economic development: non-member states, intergovernmental organizations and non-governmental organizations. Thus, these texts are widely acceptable as offering solutions appropriate to different legal traditions and to countries at different stages in their economic development. It may also be noted that UNCITRAL undertakes a range of technical-assistance activities to promote its work and to promote the use and adoption of the legislative and non-legislative texts it has developed to further the progressive harmonization and unification of international trade law.[4]

Instruments produced by UNCITRAL may only become binding law after a state has decided to adopt them – either by ratification or by domestic enactment – but no state is obliged to do so. Thus, the entire work in terms of harmonization that is carried out by UNCITRAL is of a voluntary nature and takes full account of state sovereignty. This characteristic explains the continuous and often difficult search for consensus in the work of UNCITRAL, which relies only on the acceptability of its texts to achieve wide adoption.

2 UNCITRAL texts in the field of dispute settlement

UNCITRAL has adopted a flexible and functional approach with respect to the techniques it uses to perform its mandate to modernize and harmonize the law of international trade. These techniques fall into three broad categories. To some extent, they also show the process of

[3] UNCITRAL instruments are conceived and drafted in the six official languages of the United Nations (Arabic, Chinese, English, French, Russian and Spanish).

[4] These activities include organizing briefing missions and seminars and participating in conferences to familiarize participants with UNCITRAL texts and their use; undertaking law reform assessments to assist governments, legislative organs and other authorities to review existing legislation and assess their need for law reform in the commercial field; assisting with the drafting of national legislation to implement UNCITRAL texts; assisting international development agencies, such as the World Bank, to use UNCITRAL texts in their law-reform activities and projects; and providing advice and assistance to international and other organizations, such as professional associations, organizations of attorneys, chambers of commerce and arbitration centres, on the use of UNCITRAL non-legislative texts.

modernization and harmonization occurring at different stages of business development.[5]

The approach adopted by UNCITRAL in the field of international commercial arbitration has been to provide instruments to encourage modernization and harmonization of either legislation or practices, depending on the nature of the instrument, always respecting the diversity in application of the instrument itself so as to take into account the particular features and needs of international commercial arbitration. In addition, since UNCITRAL is composed of government representatives, with observers from international organizations active in the field of arbitration, the perspective with respect to issues regarding international commercial arbitration is quite unique.

2.1 The Convention on the Recognition and Enforcement of Foreign Arbitral Awards (New York, 1958), (the 'New York Convention'), and the Recommendation regarding the interpretation of article II, paragraph (2), and article VII, paragraph (1), of the New York Convention

The New York Convention is one of the most important and successful United Nations treaties in the area of international trade law. Although the Convention, adopted by diplomatic conference on 10 June 1958, was prepared by the United Nations prior to the establishment of UNCITRAL, promotion of the Convention is an integral part of the work programme of UNCITRAL. The Convention is widely recognized as a foundation instrument of international arbitration and requires the courts of contracting states to give effect to an agreement to arbitrate when an action is in progress concerning a matter covered by an arbitration agreement, and also to recognize and enforce awards made in other states, subject to specific limited exceptions. The Convention entered into force on 7 June 1959, and there are, to date, 147 state parties to the Convention.

The General Assembly adopted Resolution 62/65 on 6 December 2007, in which it recognized the value of arbitration as a method of settling disputes in international commercial relations in a manner that contributes to harmonious commercial relations, stimulates international trade and development and promotes the rule of law at the international and national levels. The General Assembly expressed its

[5] Information on the works of UNCITRAL can be found on its website: www.uncitral.org

conviction that the New York Convention strengthens respect for binding commitments, inspires confidence in the rule of law and ensures fair treatment in the resolution of disputes arising over contractual rights and obligations. It emphasized the necessity for further national efforts to achieve universal adherence to the Convention, together with its uniform interpretation and effective implementation. The General Assembly expressed its hope that states that were not yet parties to the Convention would soon become parties to it, which would ensure that the legal certainty afforded by the Convention would be universally enjoyed, so decreasing the level of risk and transactional costs associated with doing business and, thus, promoting international trade.

In line with the recommendation of the General Assembly, the Commission decided, at its forty-first session in 2008, that a guide to enactment of the New York Convention should be developed, with a view to promoting a uniform interpretation and application of the Convention.[6] This project is in the process of being implemented by UNCITRAL, through its secretariat.

The Commission also adopted, at its thirty-ninth session in 2006, a 'Recommendation regarding the interpretation of article II, paragraph 2, and article VII, paragraph 1, of the Convention on the Recognition and Enforcement of Foreign Arbitral Awards, done in New York, 10 June 1958'.[7] The Recommendation was drafted in recognition of the widening use of electronic commerce and enactments of domestic legislation as well as case law, which are more favourable than the New York Convention in respect of the form requirement governing arbitration agreements, arbitration proceedings and the enforcement of arbitral awards. The Recommendation encourages states to apply article II (2) of the New York Convention, 'recognizing that the circumstances described therein are not exhaustive'. In addition, the Recommendation encourages states to adopt the revised article 7 of the UNCITRAL Model Law on International Commercial Arbitration (the 'Model Law on Arbitration'), which deals with the form of an arbitration agreement. The revised article 7 establishes a more favourable regime for the recognition and enforcement of arbitral awards than that provided under the New York Convention. By virtue of the 'more favourable law provision' contained in article VII(1) of the New York Convention, the

6 Official Records of the General Assembly, Sixty-third Session, Supplement No. 17 (A/63/17), para. 355.

7 Official Records of the General Assembly, Sixty-first Session, Supplement No. 17 (A/61/17), annex 2.

Recommendation clarifies that 'any interested party' should be allowed 'to avail itself of rights it may have, under the law or treaties of the country where an arbitration agreement is sought to be relied upon, to seek recognition of the validity of such an arbitration agreement'.

2.2 *The UNCITRAL Arbitration Rules: A text of a contractual nature*

In the drafting of contracts, there are issues that can be resolved by reference to a standard or uniform clause or set of clauses or rules. The process of standardization of these clauses or rules has a number of advantages. It can identify all of the issues that parties should address in such clauses or rules; ensure that the clause is effective and that it is not (as sometimes occurs in the case of agreements to arbitrate) pathological and therefore ineffective or invalid; and provide internationally recognized and up-to-date solutions to specific issues. One common example is in the field of dispute resolution, where a contract can include a standard dispute resolution clause referring to the use of internationally recognized rules for the conduct of dispute-resolution proceedings. The UNCITRAL Arbitration Rules (1976),[8] the UNCITRAL Arbitration Rules as revised in 2010,[9] and the UNCITRAL Conciliation Rules (1980)[10] are examples of such internationally recognized uniform rules. The UNCITRAL Arbitration Rules, which are introduced in more detail below, should be chosen by parties, in particular when they wish to solve their disputes through *ad hoc* arbitration, as the procedures are carefully crafted and have proven their efficiency in solving disputes since their adoption in 1976.

2.3 *The UNCITRAL Model Law on International Commercial Arbitration: A text of a legislative nature*

The Model Law on Arbitration was preceded by the New York Convention and the UNCITRAL Arbitration Rules. In the preparation of the Model Law, the drafters were careful not to include any deviations from the two previous documents.

[8] Official Records of the General Assembly, Thirty-first Session, Supplement No. 17 (A/31/17), para. 57.

[9] Official Records of the General Assembly, Sixty-fifth Session, Supplement No. 17 (A/65/17), para. 187 and annex 1.

[10] United Nations publication, Sales No. E.81.V.6.

The main purpose of the Model Law on Arbitration is to reduce the discrepancy between domestic procedural laws affecting international commercial arbitration. The Model Law on Arbitration deals with the essential elements of a favourable legal framework for the conduct of arbitration proceedings, such as the arbitration agreement, the composition of the arbitral tribunal (including the appointment, substitution and challenge of arbitrators), the jurisdiction of the arbitral tribunal (including its competence to rule on its own jurisdiction and its power to order interim measures), the conduct of arbitral proceedings (treatment of parties, determination of rules of procedure, hearings and written proceedings, party default, appointment of experts, court assistance in taking evidence), the making of an award and the termination of proceedings (settlement, form and contents of award – its correction and interpretation), the application for setting aside as an exclusive recourse against arbitral awards, the conditions for recognition and enforcement of arbitral awards and the grounds for refusing the recognition or enforcement.

When preparation of the Model Law on Arbitration first began, it was thought that it would be primarily useful for the developing world. Developed countries believed that their law of arbitration was adequate, if not much better than whatever UNCITRAL might produce. Interestingly, the past 25 years have shown that the Model Law on Arbitration has indeed been highly useful for developing countries, but also for many developed countries, which have also reformed their law by adopting the Model Law. There are currently around 90 jurisdictions that have adopted legislation based on the Model Law on Arbitration.

2.4 *A few words about conciliation/mediation*

There are critical differences among the dispute resolution processes of negotiation, conciliation and arbitration. Once a dispute arises, the parties typically seek to resolve their dispute by negotiating without involving anyone outside the dispute. If the negotiations fail to resolve the dispute, a range of dispute-settlement mechanisms is available, including arbitration and conciliation. UNCITRAL adopted the Model Law on International Commercial Conciliation[11] in 2002 in order to

[11] UNCITRAL Model Law on International Commercial Conciliation with Guide to Enactment (2002), General Assembly Resolution 57/18, annex (model law only); Official Records of the General Assembly, Fifty-seventh Session, Supplement No. 17 (A/57/17), annex I (model law only); United Nations publication, Sales No. E.05.V.4.

assist states in designing dispute resolution processes that are intended to reduce the costs of dispute settlement, foster the maintenance of a cooperative atmosphere between trading parties, prevent further disputes and inject certainty into international trade. In many countries, the legal rules affecting conciliation are set out in various pieces of legislation and take differing approaches on issues such as confidentiality and evidentiary privilege and exceptions thereto. Uniformity on such topics helps to provide greater integrity and certainty in the conciliation process. The benefits of uniformity are even more obvious in cases involving conciliation via the Internet, where the applicable law may not be self-evident. The UNCITRAL Rules on Conciliation,[12] adopted in 1980, provide a sound framework for guiding mediators and parties in any attempt to solve their dispute.

3 Arbitrating under the UNCITRAL Arbitration Rules, as revised in 2010

3.1 The origin of the UNCITRAL Arbitration Rules

At the sixth session of UNCITRAL in April 1973, the Secretariat of UNCITRAL was requested 'to prepare a draft set of arbitration rules for optional use in *ad hoc* arbitration relating to international trade'.[13] The initial version of the draft was prepared by the UNCITRAL Secretariat in consultation with Professor Pieter Sanders, who served as a consultant to the Secretariat on the subject. The preparation of these Rules took a period of three years. The UNCITRAL Arbitration Rules were adopted by UNCITRAL in 1976, after extensive consultations with arbitral institutions and arbitral experts. In the same year, the General Assembly of the United Nations, by its resolution 31/98, recommended the use of these Rules in the settlement of disputes arising in the context of international commercial relations. This recommendation was based on the conviction that the establishment of rules for *ad hoc* arbitration that are acceptable in countries with different legal, social and economic systems would significantly contribute to the development of harmonious international economic relations.

The UNCITRAL Arbitration Rules do not compete with institutional arbitration, since the UNCITRAL Arbitration Rules do not provide for the

[12] United Nations publication, Sales No. E.81.V.6; Official Records of the General Assembly, Thirty-fifth Session, Supplement No. 17 (A/35/17), chap. V, sect. A, para. 106.

[13] Official records of the General Assembly, Twenty-eighth session, Supplement No. 17 (A/9017), para. 85 (*UNCITRAL Yearbook*, vol. IV (1973), Part One II, A).

administration of arbitration. As underlined by Professor Pieter Sanders in 'A commentary on the UNCITRAL Arbitration Rules',[14] earlier versions of the 1976 version of the Rules mentioned that they were designed for use in *ad hoc* arbitrations. The limiting reference in the title of the Rules to '*ad hoc* arbitration' was deleted for substantive reasons. While arbitration under the Rules cannot be regarded as institutionally administered arbitration, the Rules provide for reliance, in certain cases, on an appointing authority, and in most cases, arbitral institutions are designated to act as the appointing authority. Arbitral institutions are therefore not excluded from playing a role in arbitrations under the UNCITRAL Arbitration Rules.

At the fourteenth session of UNCITRAL in 1981, the Commission 'decided that it would be desirable to issue guidelines, in the form of recommendations, to arbitral institutions and other relevant bodies to assist them in adopting procedures for acting as appointing authority or for providing administrative services in cases to be conducted under the UNCITRAL Arbitration Rules'.[15] Such guidelines were adopted by the Commission at its fifteenth session in 1982, in the form of 'Recommendations to assist arbitral institutions and other interested bodies with regard to arbitration under the UNCITRAL Arbitration Rules'.[16] It should be noted that similar recommendations have been adopted by UNCITRAL in 2012 regarding the use of the UNCITRAL Arbitration Rules, as revised in 2010.

The UNCITRAL Arbitration Rules are designed for worldwide use. They are intended to be acceptable in developed and developing countries and in all legal systems, whether they are common law or civil law jurisdictions. Since their adoption in 1976, the UNCITRAL Arbitration Rules have become well known and are widely used around the world in *ad hoc* arbitrations, and far beyond *ad hoc* arbitrations. Contracting parties increasingly refer to these Rules in their arbitration clauses or agreements and a substantial number of arbitral institutions have, in a number of ways, accepted or adopted these Rules.[17] They were revised for the first time in 2010.

[14] Professor Pieter Sanders, *Commentary on UNCITRAL Arbitration Rules*, Yearbook Commercial Arbitration, vol. II (1977).

[15] Official Records of the General Assembly, Thirty-sixth Session, Supplement No. 17 (A/36/17), para. 59.

[16] Official Records of the General Assembly, Thirty-seventh Session, Supplement No. 17 (A/37/17), annex II.

[17] As noted in the Recommendation, '[o]ne way in which the UNCITRAL Arbitration Rules have been accepted is that arbitral bodies have drawn on them in preparing their own institutional arbitration rules'. This has taken two different forms. One has been to use the UNCITRAL Arbitration Rules as a drafting model, either in full (e.g. the 1978 Rules of Procedure of the Inter-American Commercial Arbitration Commission) or in

3.2 The mandate to revise the UNCITRAL Arbitration Rules

In 2006, at its thirty-ninth session, the Commission agreed that the UNCITRAL Working Group on Arbitration should undertake work on a revision of the original version of the Rules (referred to below as the '1976 Rules'). At that session, the Commission noted that, 'as one of the early instruments developed by UNCITRAL in the field of arbitration, the 1976 Rules were recognized as a very successful text, adopted by many arbitration centres and used in many different instances. In recognition of the success and status of the 1976 Rules, the Commission was generally of the view that any revision of the UNCITRAL Arbitration Rules should not alter the structure of the text, its spirit or its drafting style, and should respect the flexibility of the text rather than make it more complex.'[18]

part (e.g. the 1980 Procedures for Arbitration and Additional Rules of the International Energy Agency Dispute Settlement Centre). The other form has been to adopt the UNCITRAL Arbitration Rules as such, maintaining their name, and to include in the statutes or administrative rules of an institution a provision that disputes referred to the institution shall be settled in accordance with the UNCITRAL Arbitration Rules, subject to any modifications set forth in those statutes or administrative rules. Prime examples of institutions adopting this approach are the two arbitration centres established under the auspices of the Asian–African Legal Consultative Committee (see Rule I of the Rules for Arbitration of the Kuala Lumpur Regional Arbitration Centre; articles 4 and 11 of the Statutes of the Cairo Centre for International Commercial Arbitration). In addition, a provision similar to the one described above was included in the 'Declaration of the Government of the Democratic and Popular Republic of Algeria concerning the settlement of claims by the Government of the United States of America and the Government of the Islamic Republic of Iran' of 19 January 1981. In addition to the above cases, which concern an arbitral body's own and only rules, a great number of institutions which have their own established arbitration rules have accepted, in a number of ways, the use of the UNCITRAL Arbitration Rules if parties so wished. Some institutions have, for example, embodied that option into their established institutional rules (e.g. the London Court of International Arbitration, 1981 International Arbitration Rules; Foreign Trade Arbitration of the Economic Chamber of Yugoslavia, 1981 Rules). Another form of acceptance has been to offer the administrative facilities of an arbitral institution in co-operation agreements between arbitration associations or chambers of commerce and in recommendations or model clauses providing for the use of the UNCITRAL Arbitration Rules. The prime example, which was also the first international agreement to include the UNCITRAL Arbitration Rules, is the 'Optional Arbitration Clause for use in contracts in USA–USSR Trade – 1977 (prepared by American Arbitration Association and USSR Chamber of Commerce and Industry)', with the Stockholm Chamber of Commerce acting as appointing authority. The American Arbitration Association (AAA) adopted a specific set of administrative 'Procedures for Cases under the UNCITRAL Arbitration Rules', setting forth in detail how the AAA would perform the functions of an appointing authority and provide administrative services in conformity with the UNCITRAL Arbitration Rules.

[18] Official Records of the General Assembly, Sixty-first Session, Supplement No. 17 (A/61/17), para. 184.

The Working Group commenced its work on a revision of the 1976 Rules at its forty-fifth session, in September 2006. The work was completed on 25 June 2010 through the adoption by UNCITRAL of the revised version of the Rules. The revision of the Rules took four years, and eight sessions of the Working Group on Arbitration were devoted to that revision.[19]

When starting its work on the revision of the Rules, the Working Group agreed that the UNCITRAL Arbitration Rules had been one of the most successful instruments of UNCITRAL and therefore cautioned against any unnecessary amendments or statements being included in the *travaux préparatoires* that would call into question the legitimacy of prior applications of the Rules in specific cases. It was considered that the focus of the revision should be on updating the Rules to meet changes that had taken place over the previous 30 years in arbitral practice.

It was pointed out that the UNCITRAL Arbitration Rules were originally intended to be used in a broad range of circumstances and therefore a generic approach had been taken in drafting the Rules. The Working Group recalled that, for that reason, the reference to the word '*ad hoc*' in the title of the UNCITRAL Arbitration Rules had been deleted at the time when the Rules were drafted. It was noted that, in practice, there were at least four types of arbitration where the UNCITRAL Arbitration Rules were used; namely, disputes between private commercial parties where no arbitral institution was involved, investor-state disputes, state-to-state disputes and commercial disputes administered by arbitral institutions. Broad support was expressed for a generic approach that sought to identify common denominators that applied to all types of arbitration irrespective of the subject matter of the dispute, in preference to dealing with specific situations. The Working Group took note that the Rules had been easily adapted to be used in a wide variety of circumstances covering a broad range of disputes and that this quality should be retained.[20]

Among the more noteworthy changes to the 1976 Rules are revisions intended to provide for procedural balance between the parties by requiring the respondent to submit a response to the notice of arbitration early in the proceedings (new article 4), express references to the use of

[19] The *travaux préparatoires* regarding the revision of the UNCITRAL Arbitration Rules are posted on the UNCITRAL website at: www.uncitral.org

[20] Report of the UNCITRAL Working Group on Arbitration on the work of its 45th session, A/CN.9/614.

modern technologies (for instance, under article 2 on notice and article 28(4), referring to the use of videoconferences as part of evidentiary hearings), with changes to the provisions on interim measures (article 26, which includes provisions inspired from the provisions contained in the Model Law on Arbitration, in its chapter IVA) and the addition of language and express provisions addressing the possibility of multi-party proceedings (see, for instance, article 10) and joinder (articles 4(2)(f) and 17(5)). A number of innovative features contained in the Rules aim to enhance procedural efficiency, including revised procedures for the replacement of an arbitrator (article 14), the requirement for reasonableness of costs and a review mechanism regarding the costs of arbitration (articles 40 to 43).

3.3 Some features of the UNCITRAL Arbitration Rules, as revised in 2010

The UNCITRAL Arbitration Rules have been drafted as a straightforward set of procedural rules that are adapted to the circumstances of various types of disputes. The basic principle is that the parties and the arbitral tribunal decide on the procedure, within the framework of the Rules.

The UNCITRAL Arbitration Rules, as revised in 2010 (referred to below as 'revised UNCITRAL Arbitration Rules' or 'revised Rules'), apply to arbitrations where the arbitration agreement was concluded after 15 August 2010. Unless the parties agree otherwise, the 1976 Rules will remain in force for arbitrations in which the agreement to arbitrate was concluded before that date (article 1(2)).

The revised Rules maintain the structure of the 1976 Rules and continue to be divided into four sections corresponding to the main stages of the arbitral proceedings: introductory rules, composition of the arbitral tribunal, arbitral proceedings and the award.

The sections below provide a brief overview of only some selected aspects of the revised UNCITRAL Arbitration Rules.

3.3.1 Form of the arbitration agreement

There is no specific form requirement for an arbitration agreement under the revised UNCITRAL Arbitration Rules. That matter is dealt with under article 1 of the Rules. An interesting evolution to note relates to the requirement that an arbitration agreement be in writing. Article 1(1) of the 1976 Rules requires that the reference to dispute settlement under the UNCITRAL Arbitration Rules be in writing. The *travaux préparatoires* of the 1976 Rules indicates that the purpose of the requirement that an arbitration agreement be in writing is to avoid uncertainty as to whether the UNCITRAL Arbitration Rules are applicable.

During the revision of the 1976 Rules, it was questioned whether to retain the requirements in article 1(1) that both the agreement of the parties to refer disputes to arbitration under the UNCITRAL Arbitration Rules and any modification thereto should be in writing. It was noted that the writing requirement could have two functions. First, to remind the parties that, depending on the applicable law, the agreement to arbitrate may only be valid if made in writing and second, from the point of view of convenience, to provide the basis upon which an appointing authority can appoint arbitrators. After considering that issue, the Working Group decided to delete the reference to the writing requirement for the reason, *inter alia*, that the question of form should be a matter dealt with under the applicable law.

Annex 1 of the revised Rules proposes a model arbitration clause for contracts in order to provide guidance to parties wishing to arbitrate under the Rules.[21] The model clause contains a note recommending parties to agree when concluding their arbitration agreement on an appointing authority, on the number of arbitrators, on the place of arbitration and on the language to be used in the arbitral proceedings. In the interest of efficiency, it is wise to agree on those matters before a dispute arises. In case the parties have not agreed on those matters, default provisions in the Rules will apply: the appointing authority will then be selected by the Secretary-General of the Permanent Court of Arbitration at The Hague ('the Secretary-General of the PCA'), the number of arbitrators will be three, and the place of arbitration and the language used will be decided by the arbitral tribunal.

[21] Model arbitration clause for contracts

Any dispute, controversy or claim arising out of or relating to this contract, or the breach, termination or invalidity thereof, shall be settled by arbitration in accordance with the UNCITRAL Arbitration Rules.

Note. Parties should consider adding:

(a) The appointing authority shall be . . . [name of institution or person];
(b) The number of arbitrators shall be . . . [one or three];
(c) The place of arbitration shall be . . . [town and country];
(d) The language to be used in the arbitral proceedings shall be . . .

3.3.2 Time frame for the proceeding

The 1976 Rules do not contain a time limitation for rendering an award. A question was raised during the revision of the Rules as to whether a time limit should be imposed for the rendering of an award. It was noted that the existence of time limits was well known in institutional rules and that, in practice, extensions of such time limits were systematically given. Some support was expressed for the inclusion of a time limit with the arbitral tribunal having a one-time option to extend that period. Reservations were expressed on that proposal, given that, in non-administered arbitrations, there would be no institution to deal with possible extensions of the time limit. Additionally, it was indicated that in states having time limits in their arbitration laws, practical problems also existed and therefore strong opposition was expressed to a time limit. It was suggested that rather than imposing an arbitrary time period, flexibility should be retained through the inclusion of a general principle that there should not be undue delay in rendering an award.[22] As a matter of fact, article 17(1) of the revised Rules (revising article 15(1) of the 1976 Rules) provides that '[t]he arbitral tribunal, in exercising its discretion, shall conduct the proceedings so as to avoid unnecessary delay and expense and to provide a fair and efficient process for resolving the parties' dispute.'

The arbitration proceedings under the UNCITRAL Arbitration Rules start with the communication by the claimant of the notice of arbitration to the respondent. Under the revised Rules, the respondent has 30 days to reply to the notice of arbitration and the provision on the response to the notice of arbitration is a new provision in the Rules. It should be noted that article 4(3) of the revised Rules provides that '[t]he constitution of the arbitral tribunal shall not be hindered by any controversy with respect to the respondent's failure to communicate a response to the notice of arbitration, or an incomplete or late response to the notice of arbitration, which shall be finally resolved by the arbitral tribunal.'

After the commencement of the arbitration and the establishment of the arbitral tribunal, an important provision regarding the time frame of the proceedings is article 17(2) of the revised Rules: it provides that '[a]s soon as practicable after its constitution and after inviting the parties to express their views, the arbitral tribunal shall establish the provisional timetable of the arbitration. The arbitral tribunal may, at any time, after

[22] Report of the Working Group on Arbitration on the work of its 45th session, A/CN.9/614, paras. 118 and 119.

inviting the parties to express their views, extend or abridge any period of time prescribed under these Rules or agreed by the parties.' A general provision on 'periods of time' is contained in article 25, which provides that '[t]he periods of time fixed by the arbitral tribunal for the communication of written statements (including the statement of claim and statement of defence) should not exceed 45 days. However, the arbitral tribunal may extend the time limits if it concludes that an extension is justified.'

Those provisions are an illustration of the balance that the revised Rules seek to achieve between the principle of party autonomy and the discretionary power of the arbitral tribunal to decide on how to best lead the procedure, taking account of the circumstances of the case.

3.3.3 Identity and role of the appointing authority

The existence of an appointing authority is a distinctive feature of the 1976 Rules.

An appointing authority may be called upon to provide certain services in support of arbitral proceedings: under the 1976 Rules, an appointing authority may be called upon to appoint members of an arbitral tribunal (articles 6 and 7) and to rule on challenges to arbitrators (article 12). Under articles 39 and 41 (respectively) of the 1976 Rules, the appointing authority may also assist the parties in fixing the arbitrators' fees and assist the arbitral tribunal in fixing the deposit for costs. The 1976 version of the Rules included a mechanism whereby, in cases where the parties could not agree on an appointing authority, the Secretary-General of the PCA could, if so requested by a party, designate an appointing authority.

That mechanism has been maintained in the revised Rules. Article 6 of the revised Rules, which is a new provision, consolidates the provisions relating to the appointing authority, which were divided in the 1976 Rules between former articles 6 and 7. Article 6 seeks to underline the importance of the appointing authority, particularly in the context of non-administered arbitration. The appointing authority can be a person or an arbitral institution. Under the revised Rules, where the parties have not already agreed on an appointing authority at an earlier stage, article 6(1) provides that the parties may propose an appointing authority at any time during the proceeding. The default rule in article 6(2) envisages the possibility that the Secretary-General of the PCA, if so requested by a party, can designate an appointing authority.

Other provisions in article 6 clarify the role of the designating and appointing authorities. For example, article 6(4) provides that where the designated appointing authority fails to appoint an arbitrator within 30 days, or refuses to act or fails to comply with any other time limits as set forth in the Rules, the Secretary-General of the PCA will appoint a substitute appointing authority upon the request of any party. Article 6 (5) clarifies that an appointing authority and the Secretary-General of the PCA may require that the parties and the arbitrators provide any information that the authority deems necessary in order to be able to exercise its function (such as for the appointment of arbitrators pursuant to articles 8, 9, 10 and 14) or to render a decision (for instance, on the challenge to an arbitrator pursuant to article 13).

The possibility of the parties receiving the assistance of an arbitral institution or a third party in the course of their *ad hoc* arbitration provides the parties with crucial assistance and a level of security aimed at ensuring that the arbitration process does not derail.

3.3.4 Procedure for the appointment of the tribunal

Section II of the Rules deals with the composition of the arbitral tribunal and has been subject to revisions, including changes to the role of the appointing authority in replacing arbitrators.

Article 7 (revising article 5 of the 1976 Rules) maintains the default rule that if the parties have not agreed on the number of arbitrators in their arbitration agreement or otherwise, three arbitrators shall be appointed. Notwithstanding this default rule, under article 7(2) of the revised Rules, the appointing authority may appoint, if it deems it appropriate, a sole arbitrator when the responding party fails to respond to a proposal for the appointment of a sole arbitrator and fails to appoint a second arbitrator.

The mechanisms for the appointment of a sole arbitrator under article 8 (revising article 6 of the 1976 Rules) and for the appointment of three arbitrators under article 9 (revising article 7 of the 1976 Rules) remain unchanged.

The appointment of a sole arbitrator is regulated under article 8 (revising article 6 of the 1976 rules). The notice of arbitration, sent by the claimant to the respondent, may already contain a proposal for the appointment of a sole arbitrator (article 3(4)(b)). If the notice of arbitration does not contain such a proposal, either party may make such a proposal, including the respondent in its response to the notice of arbitration (article 4(2)(c)). If the parties have agreed that a sole arbitrator is to be appointed and, if within 30 days after receipt of a proposal for the appointment of a sole arbitrator the parties have not reached agreement thereon, a sole arbitrator shall, at the request of a party, be appointed by the appointing authority.

The appointment of three arbitrators is regulated under article 9 (revising article 7 of the 1976 Rules). The article follows international practice in giving each party the right to appoint one arbitrator. The appointment of arbitrators may be made in the notice of arbitration by the claimant (article 3(4)(c)) and in the response thereto by the respondent (article 4(2)(d)). If, within 30 days after the receipt of a party's notification of the appointment of an arbitrator, the other party has not notified the first party of the arbitrator it has appointed, the first party may request the appointing authority to appoint the second arbitrator. The two arbitrators, thus appointed, shall choose the third arbitrator, who will act as the presiding arbitrator of the arbitral tribunal. If, within 30 days after the appointment of the second arbitrator, the two arbitrators have not agreed on the choice of the presiding arbitrator, the presiding arbitrator shall be appointed by the appointing authority.

Article 10 is a new provision dealing with situations where parties agree to appoint a number of arbitrators other than one or three, in which case the arbitrators will be appointed by the method agreed by the parties. Article 10(1) provides that, where there are three arbitrators, and there are multiple parties as claimant or respondent, those parties shall jointly appoint an arbitrator. However, the parties can agree to a different method of appointment. Article 10(3) sets out a general default rule in case the parties fail to constitute the arbitral tribunal. That article provides that, upon the request of any party, the appointing authority will constitute the tribunal and, in doing so, may also revoke appointments already made, appoint or reappoint each of the arbitrators and designate one as the presiding arbitrator.

Articles 12 to 14 (revising articles 10 to 13 of the 1976 Rules) set out the procedure for the challenge and the replacement of arbitrators. It is noteworthy that article 14(2) (revising article 13 of the 1976 Rules) grants the appointing authority the power, in exceptional circumstances, to deprive a party of its right to appoint a substitute arbitrator (after giving the remaining arbitrators and the parties the opportunity to express their views). The reason for that important modification to the Rules is to provide a solution to possible dilatory tactics of parties.

3.3.5 Cost determination

There is no schedule of fees under the UNCITRAL Arbitration Rules. As was underlined in the *travaux préparatoires* of the 1976 Rules: 'since the UNCITRAL Arbitration Rules are designed to facilitate arbitration in all parts of the world, and in respect of different kinds of cases, a fee schedule under the Rules would probably have to establish a wide margin between minimum and maximum rates so as to allow flexibility in determining the fees. Therefore, the mere fact of a maximum rate being indicated in the schedule would not effectively inform the parties in advance what the cost of arbitration will be and would not necessarily, in every case, preclude the assessment of improper charges by arbitrators'.[23] It was considered that the effectiveness of a schedule of fees would depend on the intervention of an independent body and that the only arbitration rules that include a schedule of fees are those administered by arbitral institutions.

The matter of cost determination was the subject of careful consideration by the Working Group when revising the Rules. As was noted in a report commissioned by the UNCITRAL Secretariat for the preparation of works on revision of the 1976 Rules: 'there have been disturbing instances of "negotiations" regarding fees between arbitrators and the parties, especially where one party finds it tactically appealing to accept anything the arbitrators say. Such experiences can cause loss of respect for the process. (And of course the purpose of having rules is not for the easy cases, where the participants have similar expectations.) There is no simple solution in the context of *ad hoc* rules, but the subject deserves serious attention in order to avoid the spectre of self-dealing arbitrators'.[24]

The provisions of the 1976 Rules relating to costs have been revised by providing a more transparent procedure for agreeing on the method of calculating the arbitral tribunal's fees from the outset and by granting a role to the appointing authority in respect of fees.

Article 40 of the revised Rules provides that the tribunal may fix the costs of the arbitration and sets out specific different categories of costs.

[23] Note by the secretariat: draft UNCITRAL Arbitration Rules; schedule of fees of arbitrators (A/CN.9/114), *Yearbook of the United Nations Commission on International Trade Law*, vol. VII, Part Two (1976), p. 190.

[24] Jan Paulsson and Georgios Petrochilos, *Revision of the UNCITRAL Arbitration Rules*, Commissioned by the UNCITRAL secretariat, (September 2006), available at www.uncitral.org

Article 40 has been amended to clarify that the tribunal has the authority to determine and set the costs in any decision it might render at any stage of the proceedings, and not just in a final award. Article 40 further defines the term 'costs' to include: the fees of the arbitral tribunal to be stated separately as to each arbitrator; the reasonable travel and other expenses incurred by the arbitrators; the reasonable costs of expert advice and of other assistance required by the arbitral tribunal, and of witnesses, to the extent that such expenses are approved by the arbitral tribunal; the legal and other costs incurred by the parties in relation to the arbitration to the extent that the arbitral tribunal determines that the amount of such costs is reasonable; and fees and expenses of the appointing authority and of the Secretary-General of the PCA.

Article 41 of the revised Rules allows the appointing authority, if so requested by a party, to review the methods for determining the arbitrators' fees. Article 41(3) provides that, promptly after its constitution, the tribunal must inform the parties of its proposal as to how to determine its fees. Within 15 days after receipt of such a proposal the parties can refer any complaints about the fee proposal to the appointing authority, which shall 'within 45 days of receipt of such referral . . . make any necessary adjustments thereto, which shall be binding upon the arbitral tribunal'. If the appointing authority refuses or fails to make a decision on the fees and expenses of the arbitrators, any party may request the Secretary-General of the PCA to make that decision.

3.3.6 The possibility of interim measures and their enforceability

Article 26 of the revised Rules (revising article 26 of the 1976 Rules) adopts a generic approach in the definition of what is meant by 'interim measures' and significantly widens the express grounds upon which a party may apply for interim relief. It provides guidance as to the purposes of, and conditions for the granting of interim measures. For example, under article 26(2), a tribunal's power to grant interim measures is not merely limited to measures to preserve the *status quo*, but now expressly includes the authority to grant injunctions and order the preservation of evidence or of assets out of which a subsequent award may be satisfied.

Article 26(8) also expressly provides that the party that obtains an interim measure 'may be liable for any costs and damages caused by the measure to any party if the arbitral tribunal later determines that, in the circumstances then prevailing, the measure should not have been granted'.

3.3.7 Multi-party arbitration (including joinder and consolidation)

Consolidation Under the 1976 Rules, consolidation of cases is only possible where the parties specifically so agree, and under the revised Rules, the same ruling applies. During the revision of the Rules, the Working Group considered whether additional provisions on that matter should be added to the Rules. Some support was expressed for the inclusion of such provisions based, for example, on the approach taken in article 4(6) of the ICC Rules, which allows consolidation when all proceedings relate to the same 'legal relationship' and are subject to the consent of the parties to submit to rules that permitted such consolidation. Delegations in the Working Group considered that such a provision could be useful in situations where several distinct disputes arose between the same parties under separate contracts (e.g. related contracts or a chain of contracts) containing separate arbitration clauses or to avoid a situation where a party initiated a separate arbitration in respect of a distinct claim under the same contract in order to gain a tactical advantage. Consolidation in such situations might provide an efficient resolution of the disputes between the parties and also might reduce the possibility of inconsistent awards in parallel arbitrations.

However, doubts were expressed as to the workability of such a provision, particularly when the Rules were applied in non-administered cases: either a provision on consolidation would be intended to deal with new claims under the same contract, and that situation would be better dealt with under provisions on the amendment of the statement of the claim, or the provision was intended to cover several distinct disputes arising between the same parties under separate contracts containing separate arbitration clauses. In that latter situation, the application of a provision on consolidation might subject parties to arbitration proceedings under terms which differed from those that were agreed upon in their arbitration agreement. The Working Group considered that that situation raised complex issues and might result in unfair solutions. For those reasons, the Working Group agreed that it might not be necessary to provide for consolidation under the Rules.[25]

[25] Report of the UNCITRAL Working Group on Arbitration on the work of its 46th session, A/CN.9/619, paras. 116–120.

Joinder The revised Rules contain provisions on joinder, and this constitutes an important addition to the Rules. During the discussion on the revision of the Rules, the Working Group considered a proposed provision on joinder, inspired by article 22.1(h) of the LCIA Arbitration Rules. Some support was expressed for the inclusion of such a principle in the Rules, as it was said to fulfil the useful purpose of allowing interested third parties to join an arbitration in circumstances where the other party objected to such joinder. However, concerns were expressed that such a provision would run counter to the fundamental principle of the consent of parties in arbitration, and that such a provision would be acceptable only if it either contained an opt-in or opt-out proviso or if it were modified so that joinder would only be possible if all parties to the arbitration agreed thereto. It was pointed out that securing agreement of all parties would avoid possible difficulties at the stage of recognition and enforcement of the arbitral award, as it would put the agreement of all parties to the arbitration beyond doubt.[26]

There are currently two provisions in the rules dealing with that question. The first provision can be found under article 4(2)(f), which provides for the possibility of the respondent formulating, as part of its response to the notice of arbitration, 'a claim against a party to the arbitration agreement other than the claimant'. That provision seeks to encourage joinder at the early stage of the proceedings, before the arbitral tribunal has been constituted. The other provision can be found under article 17(5), and it provides that '[t]he arbitral tribunal may, at the request of any party, allow one or more third persons to be joined in the arbitration as a party provided such person is a party to the arbitration agreement, unless the arbitral tribunal finds, after giving all parties, including the person or persons to be joined, the opportunity to be heard, that joinder should not be permitted because of prejudice to any of those parties. The arbitral tribunal may make a single award or several awards in respect of all parties so involved in the arbitration.'

3.3.8 Conduct of arbitration (terms of reference, number of briefs, disclosure, written or oral evidence, modality of hearings, applicable law)

Section III of the Rules deals with the conduct of the arbitral proceedings.

Article 17(1) revised Rules (revising article 15(1) of the 1976 Rules) retains the key principle of the 1976 Rules; that is, that the tribunal 'may conduct the arbitration in such manner as it considers appropriate,

[26] Ibid., paras. 121–126.

provided that the parties are treated with equality and that at an appropriate stage of the proceedings each party is given a reasonable opportunity of presenting its case'. As already mentioned above regarding time frame, a new provision has been added to article 17(1), underlining the tribunal's duty to enhance procedural efficiency by determining that '[t]he arbitral tribunal shall conduct the proceedings so as to avoid unnecessary delay and expense'. Article 17(2) requires that '[a]s soon as practicable after its constitution and after inviting the parties to express their views, the arbitral tribunal shall establish the provisional timetable of the arbitration'. By making this practice an express requirement, the intent is to enhance the efficiency of proceedings.

For the sake of efficiency, in particular for small claims, articles 20 and 21 of the revised Rules (revising articles 18 and 19 of the 1976 Rules) allow for the notice of arbitration to be treated as a statement of claim and for the response to the notice of arbitration to be treated as a statement of defence (under the condition that those submissions comply with the relevant requirements for such statements). The revised Rules also clarify that the statement of claim and the statement of defence should be accompanied by all documents or evidence relied upon by the submitting party.

Articles 27 and 28 of the revised Rules (revising articles 24 and 25 of the 1976 Rules) address the giving of evidence and the conduct of hearings. Article 27 provides, *inter alia*, that 'each party shall have the burden of proving the facts relied on to support its claim or defence' and that 'the arbitral tribunal shall determine the admissibility, relevance, materiality and weight of the evidence offered'. Regarding hearings, article 28(2) provides that witnesses may be heard 'under the conditions and examined in the manner set by the arbitral tribunal'. Article 28(3) provides that 'hearings shall be held *in camera*, unless otherwise agreed by the parties', thus maintaining the principle that was already provided for under the 1976 Rules.

As to applicable law, article 35(1) of the revised Rules reflects the principle of party autonomy by providing that '[t]he arbitral tribunal shall apply the rules of law designated by the parties as applicable to the substance of the dispute. Failing such designation by the parties, the arbitral tribunal shall apply the law which it determines to be appropriate'.

3.3.9 Confidentiality

The 1976 Rules did not include any provision on confidentiality. Article 28(3) (revising article 25(4)) and article 34(5) (revising article 32(5)) of the revised Rules deals with the confidentiality of hearings and awards, respectively, but they do not contain rules regarding the confidentiality of the proceedings as such or of the materials (including pleadings) before the arbitral tribunal.

As part of the process of revising the Rules, the Working Group considered whether an express provision on confidentiality should be included in a revised version of the UNCITRAL Arbitration Rules. The Working Group noted that that matter was quite complex, that there were diverse views expressed on the importance of confidentiality and that the practice and the law were still evolving. Delegations considered that regulating that issue in too much detail would constitute a major departure from the UNCITRAL Arbitration Rules. In addition, it was observed that the scope of confidentiality needed could depend on the subject matter of the dispute and the applicable regulatory regimes. The opinion that a general confidentiality provision should not be included was expressed by many delegations. It was also suggested that the matter should be left to be addressed on a case-by-case basis by the arbitrators and the parties.[27]

The result is that there is no general duty of confidentiality in the Rules. Article 34(5) of the revised Rules makes clear that, even without the consent of all parties, an award may be made public to the extent required by legal duty or for the protection of legal rights in relation to legal proceedings.

3.3.10 The possibility of excluding the courts' review of an award's validity

Articles 34(1) and (2) of the revised Rules (revising articles 32(1) and (2) of the 1976 Rules) provide that a tribunal may make separate awards on different issues at different times, that 'all awards' shall be 'final and binding on the parties' and that 'the parties shall carry out all awards without delay'.

In addition, the revised Rules include a 'possible waiver statement', which parties can add to their arbitration agreement. The 1976 Rules did not contain a provision on a waiver to recourses against an arbitral award, and there had been extensive discussions in the Working Group on whether a provision should be included, spelling out the recourses that were excluded from the scope of the waiver. It was felt that a provision on that matter might create ambiguity regarding the scope of the waiver, in particular with regard to whether the waiver encompassed the ability to resist enforcement of an award. The concern

[27] Ibid., paras. 127–133.

was expressed that a general waiver without any qualifications might be ineffective and would not provide sufficient guidance to the parties. Parties might not be aware that certain forms of recourse could not be waived in most legal systems. In the few systems where a waiver was possible, various requirements had to be met for the waiver to be valid, depending on the applicable law. In view of the difficulties in properly defining the limits of the waiver, and on the basis that that matter should be left to be addressed by the applicable law, a proposal was made in order to deal with that issue in an annex to the Rules, following the model arbitration clause for contracts, and to provide the parties with the option to expressly agree to waive any recourse against an arbitral award that may be available and admissible under the applicable law. That proposal was adopted by the Commission with the waiver statement reading as follows: 'The parties hereby waive their right to any form of recourse against an award to any court or other competent authority, insofar as such waiver can validly be made under the applicable law.' It is accompanied by a note providing some information to the parties. That note reads as follows: 'If the parties wish to exclude recourse against the arbitral award that may be available under the applicable law, they may consider adding a provision to that effect as suggested below, considering, however, that the effectiveness and conditions of such an exclusion depend on the applicable law.'[28]

4 Final comments

The UNCITRAL Arbitration Rules are a universal text: the revisions made to the Rules in 2010 aim at enhancing procedural efficiency. If parties wish to arbitrate under *ad hoc* rules, the use of the UNCITRAL Arbitration Rules is recommended. As highlighted by recent books on the UNCITRAL Arbitration Rules,[29] the UNCITRAL Arbitration Rules provide the leading set of arbitration rules for international *ad hoc* arbitration: 'they are intended to deal with disadvantages of national *ad hoc* arbitration by providing for the possibility of international

28 Official Records of the General Assembly, Sixty-fifth Session, Supplement No. 17 (A/65/17), paras. 141–151.

29 James Castello, 'UNCITRAL Rules', in Frank-Bernd Weigand (ed.), *Practitioner's Handbook on International Commercial Arbitration* (Oxford University Press, 2nd edn, 2009); Thomas H. Webster, *Handbook of UNCITRAL Arbitration* (London: Sweet & Maxwell, 2010).

appointing authorities and by providing a framework for an international arbitration procedure'.[30]

In the decision to adopt the revised Rules,[31] states have expressed the belief that the UNCITRAL Arbitration Rules, as revised to reflect current practices, will significantly enhance the efficiency of arbitration under the Rules, and the conviction that the revision of the UNCITRAL Arbitration Rules in a manner that is acceptable to countries with different legal, social and economic systems can significantly contribute to the development of harmonious international economic relations. The preparation of the UNCITRAL Arbitration Rules, as revised in 2010, have been the subject of due deliberation and extensive consultations with governments and interested circles and the revised text is expected to contribute significantly to the establishment of a harmonized legal framework for the fair and efficient settlement of international commercial disputes.

[30] Webster, *Handbook of UNCITRAL Arbitration*, p. 11.

[31] Official records of the General Assembly, Sixty-fifth session, Supplement No. 17 (A/65/17), para. 187.

PART III

Institutional arbitration: Features of selected arbitration institutions in Europe

5

Arbitration in Austria: Features of the International Arbitral Centre of the Austrian Federal Economic Chamber (VIAC)

WERNER MELIS

1 Introduction

The Austrian Arbitration Law (hereafter 'the Law') is a part of the Austrian Code for Civil Procedure. The last update was made in 2006 in order to bring the Law into line with the UNCITRAL Model Law on International Commercial Arbitration. This revision entered into force on 1 July 2006. Since then, Austria has been considered as a UNCITRAL Model Law country.

The International Arbitral Centre of the Austrian Federal Economic Chamber (VIAC), based in Vienna, is an entity of the Austrian Federal Economic Chamber (*Wirtschaftskammer Österreich*) according to article 139(2) of the Law on Economic Chambers (*Wirtschaftskammergesetz*). According to article 139(4) of this law, the organs of VIAC (the Board and the Secretary General) are independent and are not subject to any directives. Identical provisions are contained in article 3(6) and article 5(3) of the VIAC Rules.

VIAC commenced its work in 1975. As Austria is a neutral state, VIAC was often used for companies from Eastern and Western countries for the settlement of commercial disputes during the so-called Cold War period. It is now a leading regional arbitration centre for Central Europe. There have been several revisions of the VIAC Rules. The present Rules of Arbitration and Conciliation (the Vienna Rules) were adopted in 2012 with effect from 1 July 2013.

VIAC recommends the following arbitration clause:

> All disputes arising out of this contract or related to its violation, termination or nullity shall be finally settled under the Rules of Arbitration and

Conciliation of the International Arbitral Centre of the Austrian Federal Economic Chamber in Vienna (Vienna Rules) by one or more arbitrators appointed in accordance with these Rules.

Appropriate supplementary provisions:

(a) The number of arbitrators shall be .... (one or three);
(b) The substantive law of .... shall be applicable; *)
(c) The language to be used in the arbitral proceedings shall be ....
(*) In this context, consideration may be given to the possible application of the United Nations Convention on Contracts for the International Sale of Goods, 1980.

2 Time frame for the proceeding

Neither in the Law nor in the VIAC Rules are there provisions concerning time limits for the termination of arbitral proceedings or the rendering of an award. However, according to article 594(1) of the Law, 'the parties are free to determine the rules of procedure. The parties may thereby refer to other rules of procedure. Failing such agreement, the Arbitral Tribunal shall, subject to the provisions of this Law, conduct the arbitration in such manner as it considers appropriate.' This means that the parties are free to agree upon arbitration rules which contain such time limits or they can agree upon such time limits if they so wish. In such a case, according to article 594(4), 'An arbitrator who does not or does not timely fulfil his obligation resulting from the acceptance of his appointment, shall be liable to the parties for all damages caused by his culpable refusal or delay.' In addition, according to article 590(2) of the Law, 'Any party may request the court to decide on the termination of the mandate when an arbitrator either becomes unable to perform his functions or fails to act without undue delay ... Such decision shall be subject to no appeal.'

Also under article 28(1) of the VIAC Rules, the sole arbitrator or arbitral tribunal may 'In the context of the Vienna Rules and the agreements between the parties ... conduct the arbitration proceedings at his (its) absolute discretion.' The parties can, therefore, agree upon time limits in the conduct of the arbitral proceedings or for the making of an award if they so wish. Also under article 21(2) of the VIAC Rules: 'Any party may request the termination of the mandate of an arbitrator if the latter's incapacitation is not merely temporary, if he otherwise fails to perform his duties or unduly delays the proceedings.' The decision is taken by the Board after hearing the arbitrator in question. Also under article 16 of the VIAC Rules, the liability of the arbitrators shall only be excluded 'insofar as such liability may be admissible by law.' This means that only slight negligence is excluded.

In this connection it is noteworthy to say that the Secretariat, after the deposit for fees and expenses has been fully paid, asks the chairman of the arbitral tribunal or the sole arbitrator to start proceedings and to send copies of his orders to the Secretariat of VIAC for information purposes. Parallel to this, the parties are also requested to send copies of their submissions to the Secretariat of VIAC for information purposes. This gives the Secretary General who deals with the cases, the opportunity to see what is going on and to contact the chairman of the arbitral tribunal or the sole arbitrator if he has the impression that the reference has not been properly conducted.

3 Cost determination (including security)

Article 609 of the Law contains detailed provisions concerning the decisions on the costs of arbitration. As a basic principle, it is stated in article 608(1) that, where the arbitral proceedings are terminated either by 'the final award, an arbitral settlement or by an order of the arbitral tribunal', the arbitral tribunal shall decide upon the obligation to reimburse the costs of the proceedings provided that the parties have not agreed otherwise. The obligation to reimburse may include any and all reasonable costs appropriate for bringing the action or defence. If the parties have agreed on the termination of proceedings and have communicated this to the arbitral tribunal, the parties may, according to article 609(1), request a decision on costs, together with the notification of the agreement to terminate the proceedings.

Of practical interest is the provision in article 609(2), according to which an arbitral tribunal may also decide upon the application of the respondent to reimburse its costs for the proceedings if the tribunal has decided that it does not have jurisdiction on the grounds that there is no arbitration agreement. Through this provision, an arbitral tribunal not having jurisdiction over the case now has the same standing as a state court in Austria, which is also entitled to award the respondent its costs for the proceedings, even in cases where it decides that it does not have jurisdiction over the case.

According to article 609(3) of the Law, the arbitral tribunal shall also, as far as possible and as long as the costs are not set off against each other, determine the amounts of the costs to be reimbursed.

The VIAC Rules contain detailed provisions on the costs of arbitration. According to article 10 of the VIAC Rules, 'on filing the claim (counter-claim) the claimant (counter-claimant) shall pay into the account of the Centre, free of charges, a registration fee in the amount stated [presently 2,000 euros – if there are only two parties involved]. That fee is intended to cover the costs up to the submission of the files to the sole arbitrator (arbitral tribunal). This registration fee is not repayable. According to article 10(4), a claim or counter-claim will only be served on the other party after the registration fee has been fully paid.

According to article 44, the costs of arbitration are determined by the Secretary General of VIAC. These costs comprise the administrative charges of VIAC, the arbitrators' fees and the arbitrators' expenses. The administrative charges are a percentage of the amount in dispute, as set out in annex 1 of the VIAC Rules (the Schedule of Arbitration Costs).

The arbitrators' fees are also determined as a percentage of the amount in dispute. Annex 1 of the VIAC Rules also contains a schedule for the fees for sole arbitrators as a percentage of the amount in dispute. Unlike in other institutional arbitration rules where the arbitrators' fees are determined by the institution between a minimum and maximum amount, the VIAC Rules determine the fees for sole arbitrators as a fixed percentage of the amount in dispute. If there are three arbitrators, the amount quoted in the schedule of arbitrators' fees shall be raised to two and a half times the amounts quoted (article 44(9)). The reason is that the fees for the sole arbitrators are also intended to cover the additional administrative work which the sole arbitrator has to undertake. In an arbitral tribunal composed of three persons, only the chairman has to do this administrative work. However, the Secretary General may raise this amount to up to 30%, in the event of a particular difficulty with a case. Finally, the arbitration costs determined by the Secretary General at the end of the proceedings also contain the expenses of the arbitrators during the proceedings. These expenses are determined at cost.

According to article 42(1) of the VIAC Rules, the Secretary General fixes the amount of a deposit against the expected costs of arbitration and asks the parties to pay it in equal shares before the transmission of the files to the arbitrators. If the full amount is not paid, according to article 42(3) the Secretary General may declare the proceedings as terminated.

However, if there are more than two parties to proceedings, the rates for the administrative costs of VIAC and the arbitrators' fees, as contained in the schedules attached to the VIAC Rules, shall be increased by 10% for each additional party (article 44(6)). According to article 36(3), the Secretary General may also make separate calculations of the arbitration costs for claims which are submitted to offset against the claims or counter-claims and that are in fact and in law of no connection to the cause of action (principle claims) or in the case of proceedings conducted concerning a number of individual claims or counter-claims which are both in fact and in law of no connection (article 44(6)). The Secretary General may also deviate from the statements of the parties in fixing the amount in dispute if they have made only a partial claim or if a request by them, whose purpose was not the payment of sums of money, was obviously undervalued (article 44(8)).

According to article 43(1) of the VIAC Rules, additional costs such as for the appointment of experts, interpreters or translators, for making verbatim records of the proceedings, and for a visual inspection or a relocation of the proceedings ordered by the sole arbitrator or the arbitral tribunal are considered as costs that are not covered by the deposit which the Secretary General has determined and requested the parties to pay. It is the obligation of the arbitrator(s) to collect the necessary advances from the parties and to inform the Secretary General thereof. The sole arbitrator (arbitral tribunal) may only undertake the procedural steps mentioned in article 43(1) 'if adequate cover for the expected costs exists' (article 43(2)).

4 Procedure for the appointment of the tribunal

The provisions of the Law on the appointment of arbitrators follow closely the provisions of articles 11(2)–(5) of the UNCITRAL Model Law. Thus, the parties are free to agree on a procedure of appointing the arbitrator or arbitrators (article 587(1)). Failing such an agreement, a sole arbitrator or arbitrators to be appointed by a party are appointed upon request of a party by the competent court as specified in article 615 of the Law if the parties cannot agree upon the person of the sole arbitrator, or a party fails to appoint its arbitrator(s) within four weeks of receipt of a request to do so from the other party, or if the parties do not receive the notification of the third arbitrator to be appointed by the party-appointed arbitrators within four weeks of their appointment (article 587(2) numbers 1–4). A party is bound by its appointment of an arbitrator as soon as the other party has received the written notice of the appointment (article 587(2) number 1). A party may also request the court to appoint the arbitrator when the parties have agreed on an appointment procedure and the parties fail to act according to this procedure, or they or the arbitrators are unable to reach an agreement according to this procedure or a third party fails to perform any function entrusted to it under such procedure within three months of receipt of the respective written notification (article 587(3) numbers 1–3). The latter is, in practice, the case when an agreed appointing authority refuses to act or fails to act upon the request of a party. The decision reached when an arbitrator is appointed by a court shall not be subject to any appeal (article 587(9)).

According to article 17(1) of the VIAC Rules, the parties can agree that the dispute is to be decided upon either by a sole arbitrator or by three arbitrators. In the case where no such agreement has been made or the parties do not agree on the number of arbitrators, according to article 17(2), the VIAC Board shall determine whether the dispute is to be decided upon by a sole arbitrator or by three arbitrators. The VIAC Board 'shall take into consideration in particular the difficulty of the case, the magnitude of the amount in dispute and the interest of the parties in a rapid and cost effective decision.' It can be said that in practice, the VIAC Board has determined in the past that three arbitrators shall decide the reference when the amount in dispute is more than one million euros and, unless there are special reasons to have the dispute decided upon by three arbitrators, by a single arbitrator when it is less.

The parties are notified of the decision of the VIAC Board and in the event that proceedings before a sole arbitrator are decided upon, they are requested to agree on a person within 30 days after service of the request. If no agreement has been reached between the parties within that period, the sole arbitrator will be appointed by the VIAC Board (article 17(3)).

If the dispute shall be decided upon by three arbitrators, the party that has not yet nominated an arbitrator shall be requested to indicate the name and address of a person within 30 days after the service of the request. If the party fails to do so within that time limit, then the arbitrator shall be appointed by the VIAC Board (article 17(4)). It has to be noted that, according to article 7(3.5) of the VIAC Rules, the statement of claim must include the name of an arbitrator if a decision by three arbitrators is requested. If this is not done, the Secretary General shall request the claimant to remedy this defect and inform the claimant that until this defect has been remedied, the claim shall not be processed. The Board of VIAC will, therefore, not make a default appointment of an arbitrator for a claimant.

According to article 17(5) of the VIAC Rules, the arbitrators nominated by the parties or appointed by the VIAC Board will be requested to agree on a chairman within 30 days after service of the request. If no such indication is made within that period, the chairman shall be appointed by the VIAC Board.

According to article 17(6) of the VIAC Rules, the parties are bound by their nominations of arbitrators as soon as the nominated person has been confirmed by Secretary General or the Board.

It follows from the above that the VIAC Board makes only default appointments of arbitrators. If an arbitrator appointed by a party, or by the arbitrators nominated by the parties or by the VIAC Board should resign from his office, or is successfully challenged or is removed from his office by the VIAC Board, the new arbitrator has to be appointed according to the original rules for appointment.

For multi-party arbitrations see Section 10 below.

5 Identity and role of the appointing authority

The term 'appointing authority' is not used in the Law. However, the main functions of an appointing authority – namely the default appointment of arbitrators, the procedure for the challenge of arbitrators and the early termination of an arbitrator's mandate – are dealt with in articles 587, 589 and 590 of the Law. According to this, the parties are free to agree on a procedure for appointing the arbitrator or arbitrators, a procedure for challenging an arbitrator and a procedure for the termination of an arbitrator's mandate. If no such procedure has been agreed between the parties, or when the agreed procedure is not successful, the interested party may refer the matter to the court for decision. A decision taken by the court shall not be subject to any appeal.

The provisions in the VIAC Rules concerning the appointment of arbitrators have been dealt with in Section 4 above.

The wording of article 20(1) of the VIAC Rules has been copied from article 588(2) of the Law. According to this, 'An arbitrator may be challenged only if circumstances exist that give rise to justifiable doubts as to his impartiality or independence, or that are in conflict with the agreement of the parties. A party may challenge an arbitrator appointed by him, or in whose appointment he participated, only for reasons of which he becomes aware after the participation of the appointment or after the appointment has been made.' The challenging party must within 15 days inform the Secretary General thereof, stating the grounds for the challenge (article 20(2)). Should the challenged arbitrator not withdraw from his office, the Board shall decide upon the challenge and, before making its decision, the Secretary General must obtain the comments of the arbitrator challenged and of the other parties (article 20(3)). The Board can also request comments from other persons. According to article 20(4) of the VIAC Rules, an arbitrator who has been challenged may continue the proceedings notwithstanding the challenging motion. However, an award may not be rendered until the final and binding decision of the VIAC Board. The latter provision is more restrictive than the provision in article 589(3) of the Law, according to which the arbitral tribunal, including the challenged arbitrator, may continue the arbitral proceedings and make an award. The reason for the more restrictive provision in the VIAC Rules is to avoid problems that may arise in a situation where the arbitral tribunal has made an award and the VIAC Board has decided to accept the challenge after this award has been made.

Article 21 of the VIAC Rules concerning early termination of the mandate of arbitrators follows closely the provision of article 590 of the Law. According to article 21(2), 'any party may request the termination of a mandate of an arbitrator if the latter's incapacitation is not merely temporary, if he otherwise fails to perform his duties or unduly delays the proceedings.' Such a request must be submitted to the Secretariat and the VIAC Board shall decide upon the request after hearing the arbitrator in question. In addition, the VIAC Board may terminate the arbitrator's mandate even without a request from a party if it is clear that his incapacitation is not merely temporary. To date, there has only been one case where the VIAC Board has terminated an arbitrator's mandate due to unjustifiable failure to act.

6 Form of the arbitration agreement

The Law follows closely the language of article 7(1) of the UNCITRAL Model Law for the definition of an arbitration agreement. The parties may, therefore, agree 'to submit to arbitration all or certain disputes which have a reason or which may arise between them in respect of a defined legal relationship, whether contractual or not'. This agreement may be a separate agreement or a clause within a contract (article 581(1)). The provisions of this law also apply to arbitral tribunals that are, in a manner admitted by the law, not based on agreements of the parties; for example, in testamentary dispositions or as provided by articles of incorporation (article 581(2)).

The provisions concerning the form of an arbitration agreement are an update of article 7(2) of the UNCITRAL Model Law. An arbitration agreement must, therefore, be contained either in a document signed by the parties or in letters, telefaxes, e-mails or other forms of communication exchanged between the parties which provide the evidence of a contract (article 583(1)). It follows from this that there are types of arbitration agreements which do not need to be signed by the parties and where a safe electronic signature is not required for e-mails. The new provisions cover all kinds of arbitration agreements on which parties have so far based their claims in cases submitted to VIAC: the Law expressly provides that a reference to a document which contains an arbitration agreement constitutes an arbitration agreement if the reference is such that it deems the arbitration agreement to be part of the contract and if the form requirements for arbitration agreements are met (article 583(2)). In addition, there is a provision that defects of the form of the arbitration agreement are overcome if they have not been raised at the latest point in time together with the defence plea (*Einlassung in die Sache*) on the merits of the claimant's claim (article 583(3)).

According to article 1008 of the Austrian Civil Code (ABGB), a special power of attorney in writing is necessary for the conclusion of an arbitration agreement. On 1 January 2007 a new Entrepreneurial Code (UGB) succeeded the former Commercial Code. According to article 54 UGB, any authorisation given orally or in writing by an entrepreneur, which is subject to this code, also includes the right to conclude arbitration agreements. Article 1008 ABGB is, therefore, no longer applicable in commercial arbitration, whether domestic or international.

There are no provisions concerning the form of an arbitration agreement in the VIAC Rules. Therefore, the provisions of the Law fully apply. In practice, there are numerous types of arbitration clauses to which parties frequently agree in Austria. The minimum arbitration clause for an *ad hoc* arbitration would simply be a provision where disputes arising out of a contract between the parties or out of an existing dispute should be settled by arbitration in Austria in one of the forms admitted by the Law as mentioned above. In institutional arbitration, the institutions usually propose standard arbitration clauses that the parties copy in their contracts. Also, VIAC recommends a standard arbitration clause (see Section 1 above).

7 Interference/support by the courts (including tribunals' powers to involve them)

There is no provision in the Law to give a court the power to intervene in arbitral proceedings. However, according to article 602 of the Law concerning court assistance in taking evidence, 'The arbitral tribunal, arbitrators who have been accordingly authorised by the arbitral tribunal or a party with the approval of the arbitral tribunal, may request from the Court the conduct of judicial acts for which the arbitral tribunal has no authorisation.' This concerns the swearing in of a witness and the compulsory attendance before a judge of a person who has refused to appear as a witness before the arbitrator or the arbitral tribunal. 'The arbitral tribunal or an arbitrator mandated by the arbitral tribunal and the parties may participate in the taking of evidence by the Court and may put questions.' If the witness who shall be heard lives in a third country, 'The judicial assistance may also consist of the Court requesting a foreign court or authority to conduct such acts.'

8 Tribunals' powers *ex officio*

According to article 592(1) of the Law, the arbitral tribunal may rule on its own jurisdiction either together with the ruling on the case or by separate arbitral award. According to article 592(3), the arbitral tribunal may continue the arbitral proceedings and make an award even while a request for the setting aside of an arbitral award by which the arbitral tribunal accepted its jurisdiction is still pending.

Failing an agreement of the parties on the rules of procedure, 'the arbitral tribunal shall, subject to the provisions of this law, conduct the arbitration in such manner as it considers appropriate' (article 594(1)). According to article 594(2), 'The parties shall be treated fairly. Each party shall be given a full opportunity of presenting his case.' This gives the arbitral tribunal the opportunity to adapt the arbitral proceedings to the circumstances of the case. Failing an agreement of the parties, 'the place of arbitration shall be determined by the arbitral tribunal having regard to the circumstances of the case, including the convenience of the parties' (article 595(1)). Failing an agreement of the parties on the language or languages to be used in the arbitral proceedings, the language or languages to be used shall be determined by the arbitral tribunal (article 596). The same applies for the applicable law. According to article 603(2) of the Law, 'the arbitral tribunal shall apply the provisions of law considered by it as appropriate' failing any designation by the parties of the applicable provisions of law or rules of law.

According to the provisions of the Law, the arbitral proceedings are terminated by a final award, an arbitral settlement or by an order from the arbitral tribunal. If the parties have agreed upon a settlement according to article 605(2) of the Law, the arbitral tribunal may, upon request of a party, record the settlement in the form of an arbitral award on agreed terms provided that the contents of the settlement are not in conflict with the fundamentals of the Austrian legal system (*ordre public*). If arbitral proceedings are terminated by an arbitral award according to article 606(1) of the Law, 'The award shall be made in writing and shall be signed by the arbitrator or arbitrators. Unless otherwise agreed by the parties, in arbitral proceedings with more than one arbitrator the signatures of the majority of all members of the arbitral tribunal shall suffice, provided that the reason for any omitted signature is stated on the arbitral awards by the presiding or another arbitrator.' Unless agreed otherwise by the parties, 'the award shall state the reasons upon which it is based' (article 606(2)). According to article 608(2) of the Law, the arbitral tribunal shall terminate the arbitral proceedings by an order when the claimant fails to file his claim within the period of time agreed by the parties or determined by the arbitral tribunal, when the claimant withdraws his claim 'unless the respondent objects thereto and the arbitral tribunal recognizes a legitimate interest on his part in obtaining a final settlement of the dispute', when the parties agree on the termination of the proceedings and communicate this to the arbitral tribunal or when the arbitral tribunal finds that the continuation of the proceedings has become impossible.

The provisions concerning tribunals' powers in the VIAC Rules are in line with the provisions of the Law. There is only a slight difference in article 25: namely, that the place of arbitration shall be Vienna unless the parties have agreed otherwise.

9 The possibility of interim measures and their enforceability

According to the Law, arbitrators are not only entitled to render interim measures of protection between the parties to the arbitration agreement, but such interim measures rendered by arbitrators are also enforceable by the state courts in the same way as interim measures rendered by the courts are. As there is 'competition' between arbitral tribunals and state courts, the provision of article 9 of the UNCITRAL Model Law that it is not incompatible with an arbitration agreement for a party to request from a court – before or during arbitral proceedings – an interim measure of protection and for a court to grant such a measure, has also been copied into the Law (article 585).

Article 593(1) of the Law provides: 'Unless otherwise agreed by the parties, the arbitral tribunal may, at the request of a party and after hearing the other party, order such interim or protective measures it deems necessary in respect of the subject-matter in dispute' and it is further provided that the arbitral tribunal is entitled to request appropriate security from any party in connection with such a measure. It follows from that language that the parties can by agreement exclude the power of an arbitral tribunal to grant interim measures of protection. In addition, the arbitral tribunal *may* order or refuse to order an interim measure of protection requested by a party. In addition, there is a mandatory provision that an arbitral tribunal can only order an interim measure of protection *after hearing such party*. It follows that *ex parte* interim measures are excluded from the jurisdiction of arbitral tribunals.

As interim measures of protection are now enforceable in the same way as interim measures of protection rendered by courts are, it is necessary to make clear that the decision of an arbitral tribunal is not simply a procedural order (which is not enforceable), but an enforceable interim measure of protection. The Law contains, therefore, specific form requirements. Interim measures are to be ordered in writing and a signed copy is to be served on each party; in cases with more than one arbitrator, the signature of the presiding arbitrator or in case of him being prevented from doing so, the signature of another arbitrator shall suffice, provided that the presiding arbitrator or another arbitrator records on the order the reason preventing the signature. Unless agreed otherwise by the parties, the order shall state the reasons on which it is based, it shall be dated and shall state the place of arbitration. The arbitral tribunal shall discuss with the parties a possible safekeeping of the order and the documentation of its service and, upon request of a party, the presiding arbitrator, or in case of his disability, another arbitrator, shall confirm the *res iudicata* and enforceability of the order on a copy of the order (article 593(2)). Furthermore, as interim measures ordered by an arbitral tribunal are now enforceable, the Law contains detailed provisions concerning the proceedings before the competent district court (article 593(3)–(6)).

Article 33 of the VIAC Rules on interim measures of protection complies largely with the wording of the law. As VIAC only administers international arbitrations, many parties to the arbitration have their place of residence in countries where interim measures of protection are not enforceable by the courts. For this reason, in article 33(1), which complies with article 593(1) of the Law, the following sentence is added: 'The parties are obliged to comply with such orders, whether or not they are enforceable by State courts.' Article 33(5) complies with article 585 of the Austrian Code for Civil Procedure, giving parties to an arbitration agreement the right to apply to any competent state organ for interim measures of protection. However, if this is done, 'The Secretariat and the arbitral tribunal must be immediately informed of any such application as well as of all measures ordered by the State organ.'

10 Multi-party arbitration (including joinder and consolidation)

According to the Law, the courts have no jurisdiction for joinder or consolidation in arbitral proceedings. Joinder to an arbitration requires, therefore, the existence of an arbitral agreement which binds all parties and the agreement of the parties and the arbitrators: consolidation of arbitral proceedings can be made by an order of the arbitrators if the arbitrators and the parties are identical. The only provision in the Law which deals expressly with several parties is found in article 587(5): 'When several parties that are to jointly appoint one or more arbitrators have not agreed upon such appointment within four weeks of receipt of a respective written notification from these parties, the arbitrators or arbitrator shall be appointed by the Court upon application by one of these parties, unless the agreement on the appointment procedure provides other means for securing the appointment.' It follows that upon request of the claimant(s), the court will appoint an arbitrator for the respondents if they do not agree upon a person. Article 18 of the VIAC Rules deals, therefore, mainly with the situation where multiple parties fail to agree on an arbitrator.

According to article 18(1) of the VIAC Rules, multiple parties are free to determine whether they wish to have the case decided by one or three arbitrators. In addition they are free to determine the mode for the appointment of the arbitrators. If this is not done and the parties do not agree on the number of the arbitrators, the Board will decide whether the dispute will be decided by one or by three arbitrators (article 18(2)).

If the dispute is to be decided by a sole arbitrator and the parties have not agreed upon the person within 30 days after service of the request, the sole arbitrator will be appointed by the Board of VIAC (article 18(3)).

If the dispute has to be decided by three arbitrators each side has to appoint an arbitrator. If a party fails to appoint its arbitrator the Board of VIAC will appoint the arbitrator for the failing party (parties). The appointment of the arbitrator of the other party remains valid (article 18(6)). Only in exceptional cases the Board may after having heard the parties reappoint the arbitrators appointed by the parties, or all arbitrators. This is in line with article 10(3) of the UNCITRAL Arbitration Rules (as revised 2010).

According to article 18(8), if a claim cannot be served on all respondents, the arbitral tribunal shall, upon application of the claimant(s), be continued only against those respondents on whom the claim was served. The claims against those respondents on whom the claim could not be served shall be subject to separate proceedings.

Whether a third person may participate in a pending arbitration under the VIAC-Rules, and the way of its participation will be decided by the arbitral tribunal upon application of a party or the third person after having heard all parties and the third person in question (article 14(1)). The consolidation of arbitral proceedings is, upon request of a party, only possible upon application of a party if the parties agree, or if they have named the same arbitrator, if in the cases which shall be consolidated the same arbitrators have been appointed or the Board has appointed the same arbitrators under articles 17 and 18, and the seat of the arbitration is the same (article 15(1)). The decision is taken by the Board of VIAC after having heard the parties and the arbitrators (article 15(2)).

11 Conduct of arbitration (terms of reference, number of briefs, disclosure, written oral evidence, modality of hearings, applicable law)

Subject to the mandatory provisions of the Law – that is, to treat the parties with equality and give each party the full opportunity of presenting his case – the parties are free to determine the rules of procedure. They may refer to other rules of procedure such as arbitration rules of arbitral institutions, or the UNCITRAL Arbitration Rules for *ad hoc* arbitrations. Failing such agreement between the parties, the arbitral tribunal sitting in the case shall conduct the arbitration in such a manner as it considers appropriate, subject to the mandatory provisions of the Law (article 594(1)). The parties shall be treated fairly and shall be given full opportunity to present their case (article 594(2)) and they may be represented or counselled by persons of their choice (article 594(3)). Arbitrators who do not perform their obligations resulting from the acceptance of their appointment in a timely fashion shall be liable to the parties for all damages caused by their culpable refusal or delay (article 594(4)).

In the Law, a series of non-mandatory procedural provisions have been largely or even wholly copied from articles 19, 22, 23, 24, 25 and 26 of the UNCITRAL Model Law which, in turn, largely have their origin in the UNCITRAL Arbitration Rules. Although these provisions did not introduce new elements to past practice in terms of conducting arbitral proceedings, it was felt useful to introduce them into the actual arbitration law, in particular in order to demonstrate to potential foreign users of arbitration in Austria that they would not be faced with unpleasant surprises when conducting an arbitration in Austria. For the same reasons, these procedural provisions have largely been copied in the VIAC Rules.

As in article 22(1) of the UNCITRAL Model Law, the parties are free to agree on the language or languages to be used in the arbitral proceedings: failing such agreement, the arbitral tribunal shall determine the language or languages to be used in the proceedings (article 596).

The provisions on statements of claim and defence correspond with article 23 of the UNCITRAL Model Law. According to this, the claimant shall submit, within the period of time agreed by the parties or determined by the arbitral tribunal, the points at issue and the facts supporting its claim and the respondent shall respond hereto. The parties may attach to their statements all documents that they consider to be relevant or they may merely refer to the documents or other evidence that they intend to submit (article 597(1)). Unless otherwise agreed by the parties, the parties are entitled to amend or supplement their claim or pleadings during the arbitral proceedings, unless the arbitral tribunal considers it inappropriate due to delay (article 597(2)).

The provisions on hearings and proceedings conducted in writing are taken from article 24(1) of the UNCITRAL Model Law. Subject to any contrary agreement by the parties, the arbitral tribunal has the power to decide whether to hold oral hearings or whether the proceedings shall be conducted in writing. Where the parties have not expressly excluded an oral hearing, the arbitral tribunal shall, upon motion of a party, hold such a hearing at an appropriate stage of the proceedings (article 598). These provisions reflect the actual practice of arbitration in Austria: arbitrators who think that they are able to render an award on the basis of the submissions and documents which have been submitted will inform the parties accordingly and will give them a time limit for the submission of a request to the contrary.

As in article 19(2) of the UNCITRAL Model Law, the arbitral tribunal is authorised to decide upon the admissibility of taking of evidence and to conduct such taking of evidence and freely evaluate the result of such evidence (article 599(1)). As in articles 24(2) and (3) of the UNCITRAL Model Law, the parties are to be given notice in a timely fashion of every hearing and of every meeting of the arbitral tribunal for the purpose of taking evidence (article 599(2)) and all written documents or other communications are to be brought to the notice of both parties (article 599(3)).

There are no particular rules of evidence that arbitrators have to respect in arbitration proceedings in Austria. It is also up to the arbitrators how they want to hear the witnesses. While in local arbitrations they may, in practice, follow the practice of civil court proceedings where witnesses are basically questioned by the judge and where counsel for the parties will then also be given the right to ask questions, one can say that in international arbitrations in Austria, the Anglo-American practice of questioning witnesses is increasingly used. Cross- and counter-examinations of witnesses are, therefore, possible. According to Austrian law, witnesses may not be sworn in by the arbitrators. There exists, however, the possibility to have a witness sworn in by a state judge, if this should be considered necessary by the arbitrators or by the parties. Arbitrators may ask a court to hear a witness domiciled in Austria who refuses to appear before the arbitral tribunal. Judicial assistance may also be requested from a court to hear a witness who is domiciled outside of Austria before a court in his country (article 602). Such requests have, in the past, been successfully made.

The provisions on experts have been copied from article 26 of the UNCITRAL Model Law. They confirm current arbitration practice before the entry into force of the new Law. Unless the parties have agreed otherwise, an arbitral tribunal can, therefore, appoint an expert to report to it on specific issues to be determined by the arbitral tribunal and require the parties to give the expert any relevant information and to assist the expert (article 601(1)). An arbitral tribunal can, therefore, also appoint an expert if one of the parties objects. An oral hearing with the parties and the expert can be ordered if a party so requests or if the arbitral tribunal considers it necessary, unless the parties have agreed otherwise (article 601(2)). An expert nominated by an arbitral tribunal may be challenged on the same grounds on which arbitrators may be challenged according to articles 588 and 589(1) and (2) and article 601(3).

The VIAC Rules concerning the conduct of the proceedings before the arbitrators (article 28) comply with the provisions of the Law. A sole arbitrator (arbitral tribunal) may conduct the arbitration proceedings at his (its) absolute discretion; the principle of equal treatment of the parties shall apply. 'However, subject to advance notice, the sole arbitrator (arbitral tribunal) is entitled to declare that pleadings and the presentation of documentary evidence shall be admissible only up to a certain stage of the proceedings' (article 28(2)). Through this provision, unnecessary extensions of time can be avoided. As under the Law, the proceedings may be oral or in writing, but 'oral proceedings shall take part at the request of one party or if the sole arbitrator (arbitral tribunal) to whom (which) the case has been referred considers it necessary' (article 30(1)). Hearings shall be private and a record 'of at least the results of the hearings' shall be made (article 30(2)). If the arbitrator(s) consider(s) it necessary, 'he (they) may on his (their) own initiative collect evidence, in particular may question parties or witnesses, may request a party to submit documents and visual evidence and may call in experts' (article 29(1)). This provision gives the arbitrators a larger discretionary power to collect evidence than article 599 of the Law. 'If one party does not take part in the proceedings, the case can be heard with the other party alone' (article 29(2)). A judgment by default is therefore not possible. 'If a violation by the arbitrator(s) of a provision of these arbitration rules or other provisions applicable to the proceedings comes to the notice of a party, that party must immediately enter an objection otherwise the party will be barred from entering an objection against that defect' (article 31). This provision complies with article 579 of the Law. Finally, as soon as the arbitral tribunal is convinced that the parties have had an adequate opportunity for such purposes, the sole arbitrator (arbitral tribunal) must declare the proceedings closed and inform the Secretary General and the parties when it intends to render the award' (article 32). Through this provision, parties to an arbitration are protected from a closure of the arbitral proceedings by surprise.

According to article 45 of the VIAC Rules the parties can agree upon accelerated proceedings as set out in this article. This means in parctice that all time limits in the VIAC-Rules are shortened and the arbitrator(s) have to render their award within six months after receipt of the file.

12 Confidentiality

According to article 616(2) of the Law, 'Upon application of a party the public can be excluded if a respective justified interest in the excluding of the public is shown.' In practice, it is generally accepted that arbitral proceedings are private.

According to the provisions of the VIAC Rules, arbitrations are private and the organs of the institution and the arbitrators acting in a case have to respect privacy. According to article 2(4) of the VIAC Rules, 'the members of the Board must perform their duties to the best of their ability; They are independent and are not subject to any directives in that respect. They are bound to secrecy on all matters coming to their notice in the course of their duties.' According to article 4(3) of the VIAC Rules, 'the Secretary General and his Deputy must perform their duties to the best of their ability and they are not subject to any directives in that respect. They are bound to secrecy on all matters coming to their notice in the course of their duties.' Finally, article 30 of the VIAC Rules provides that hearings are private. This implies that the arbitrators are also bound to secrecy on all matters coming to their attention in the course of the proceedings.

13 The institution's role

According to VIAC Arbitration Rules, proceedings are divided into three steps. The first step starts with the receipt of the statement of claim with the Secretariat. After receipt of the statement of claim, the Secretary General will ask the claimant(s) to pay the registration fee and after receipt of this registration fee, requests the respondent(s) to submit a memorandum in reply. If the respondent raises a counter-claim together with his memorandum in reply, the Secretary General will request the counter-claimant(s) to pay the registration fee and, after receipt of this registration fee, will request the claimant to submit a reply. The Secretary General will also determine fees and costs of arbitration for the claim and, if a counter-claim has been introduced at this stage, also for the counter-claim.

The Secretary General will also arrange for the composition of the arbitral tribunal. If there is no agreement between the parties about the number of arbitrators, or in the case where there are three arbitrators or the respondent(s) fail(s) to appoint an arbitrator, default appointments will be made by the Board of VIAC. When the sole arbitrator has been appointed and an arbitral tribunal consisting of three persons has been appointed according to VIAC Rules, and the advances on fees and costs determined by the Secretary General have been fully paid, the Secretary General shall transmit the files to the sole arbitrator (arbitral tribunal) according to article 11 of the VIAC Rules. With this second step, the proceedings before the sole arbitrator (arbitral tribunal) commences.

When the arbitrator(s) have terminated the proceedings, they have to inform the Secretary General and to request his determinations of fees and costs. Through this third step, the proceedings commence. According to article 36(4), 'awards are confirmed on all copies by the signature of the Secretary General and the stamp of VIAC. By this it is confirmed that the award is an award of VIAC and that it was made and signed by (an) arbitrator(s) chosen or appointed in accordance with these rules of arbitration.' The award shall be served on the parties by the Secretary General (article 36(5)).

The Board of VIAC makes default appointments of arbitrator(s) (article 17(3–5)), it decides on challenges of arbitrators (article 20(3)) and the termination of the mandate of an arbitrator 'if the latter's incapacitation is not merely temporary, if he otherwise fails to perform his duties or unduly delays the proceedings'. If it is clear that the incapacitation is not merely temporary, the Board may terminate an arbitrator's mandate even without the request from a party (article 21 (2)). According to article 7(6) of the VIAC Rules, 'the Board can refuse to carry out proceedings if the parties have designated the International Arbitral Centre of the Austrian Federal Economic Chamber in the arbitration agreement, but have made agreements that deviate substantially from the Vienna Rules and are incompatible with them.'

14 The possibility of excluding the court's review of an award's validity

According to the Austrian Arbitration Law, it is impossible to exclude a court's review of an award's validity.

15 Grounds for invalidity of the award

The grounds for setting aside an award largely follow article 34 of the UNCITRAL Model Law and article V of the 1958 New York Convention on the Recognition and Enforcement of Foreign Arbitral Awards. They are exclusive and they apply also for awards by which an arbitral tribunal has ruled on its jurisdiction. Upon application of a party, an arbitral award shall be set aside if:

(a) there is no valid arbitration agreement, or an arbitral tribunal denies its jurisdiction despite the existence of a valid arbitration agreement, or a party was under some incapacity to conclude a valid arbitration agreement under the law applicable to it (article 611(2) no. 1);
(b) a party was not given proper notice of the appointment of an arbitrator or of the arbitral proceedings, or was for other reasons unable to present its case (article 611(2) no. 2);
(c) the award concerns a dispute not contemplated, or not falling within the terms of the submission to arbitration, or contains decisions on matters beyond the scope of the submission to arbitration or beyond the plea of the parties for legal protection, provided that, if the default concerns only a part that can be separated from the award, only that part of the award shall be set aside (article 611(2) no. 3);
(d) the formation or composition of the arbitral tribunal was not in accordance with the provisions of articles 586–587 of the Law or with an admissible agreement of the parties (article 611(2) no. 4);
(e) the arbitral procedure was not carried out in accordance with the fundamental principles of the Austrian legal system (*ordre public*) (article 611(2) no. 5); and/or
(f) the requirements have not been met to which a judgment of a court can be appealed by an action for revision under article 530(1) nos. 1–5 (article 611(2) no. 6).

An arbitral award shall be set aside upon application of a party or by the court *ex officio*:

(a) when the subject matter of the dispute is not arbitrable under Austrian Law (article 611(2) no. 7); and/or
(b) if the award is in conflict with the fundamentals of the Austrian legal system (*ordre public*) (article 611(2) no. 8).

In addition, there are specific provisions for consumers (article 617), which also apply to labour law cases (article 618) for arbitral proceedings in which a consumer is involved.

The setting aside of an arbitral award has no effect on the validity of the underlying arbitration agreement. It follows that after the setting aside of an award, new arbitration proceedings can be commenced within the framework of the arbitration agreement. However, when an arbitral award on the same subject matter has already been finally set aside twice and when a further arbitral award on the same subject matter is to be set aside upon application of a party, the court shall concurrently declare invalid the arbitration agreement with respect to that matter (article 611(5)).

According to article 612, an applicant who has a legal interest can apply to the competent court, as specified in article 615, for a declaration of the existence or non-existence of an arbitral award.

6

Arbitration in Denmark: Features

GEORG LETT

1 Foreword

In 2005, Denmark enacted the UNCITRAL Model Law on Arbitration (lov nr. 553 af 24. juni 2005 om voldgift (hereinafter the 'Act')). There are some minor deviations from the Model Law.[1]

Denmark has, furthermore, an institutional arbitration institute called the Danish Arbitration Institute. All relevant information on the Danish Arbitration Institute may be found on their homepage, www.voldgiftsinstituttet.dk or www.danisharbitration.com. The procedure for arbitration under Danish Arbitration is set out in the Rules of the Arbitration Procedure for Danish Arbitration – 2013 (hereinafter the 'Rules').

On this homepage, the Rules are available in Danish, English, German and French alongside all other relevant information concerning the Arbitration Institute (statistics, standard clauses of arbitration etc.).

2 Time frame for proceedings

There is no specific time frame for the proceedings in the Act or in the Rules. However, there are provisions to enhance expedient procedure in the Rules. Article 18 states that the case shall be finalised within a reasonable time. Article 19 states that the arbitral tribunal shall, when taking on the handling of the case, convene the parties for a preparatory meeting and set out the issues of special importance to be addressed at the meeting including, for instance:

(a) The organisation of and timetable for any additional preparatory work,
(b) The time and place for the oral hearing.

[1] For details, see Georg Lett, *Cahiers de l'arbitrage*, 1(2007), 25 and Ketilbjørn Hertz, *Danish Arbitration Act 2005* (DJØF Publishing, 2005).

Article 43(1) states that the arbitral tribunal shall ensure that the arbitration is finalised within a reasonable time and in a cost-effective manner.

The Danish Institution of Arbitration has made a set of 'Rules of Simplified Arbitration Procedure (2008)' (hereinafter 'Simplified Rules'), which may be applied in case of agreement between the parties to settle in accordance with the Simplified Rules. These Simplified Rules stipulate very short deadlines. Article 26 of the Simplified Rules states that the arbitrator shall make his award as soon as possible and not later than three months after submission to the arbitrator of the documents of the case and of a copy of any existing correspondence. If the award has not been made before the deadlines stipulated in the first section of the article, the arbitrator shall notify the parties and Danish Arbitration Institute of the date by which he expects to be able to make an award for the case.

In all instances, the Rules or the Simplified Rules apply. The secretariat will follow up on any delays.

Article 14(2) of the Rules states that the Danish Arbitration Institute may revoke the appointment of one or more arbitrators if the arbitration case does not progress effectively and efficiently (Simplified Rules, article 14).

3 Cost determination (including security)

Section 34 of the Act states that the tribunal fixes the fees of the panel, including remuneration and reimbursement of expenses. The amount is payable 30 days after the termination of the arbitration. The parties are jointly liable for the costs due to the arbitration panel.

Section 35 states that the arbitral tribunal decides on the distribution of the costs of the arbitral tribunal between the parties. Furthermore, the arbitral tribunal can impose on a party the payment of the whole or part of the costs of the other party.

Section 36 states that the arbitral tribunal may order the parties to provide security for the fees and expenses of the arbitral tribunal. The arbitral tribunal may terminate the arbitral proceedings if the security is not provided. If a party does not provide the security as ordered, the other party may provide the security in full.

The Rules also contain detailed provisions as to costs.

Article 5(1) states that a fee of 10,000 DK is payable to the Danish Arbitration Institute. This registration fee is not refundable.

In addition to this registration fee, the parties shall pay a cash deposit as security for the estimated costs of the arbitration (article 6(1)), including a fee to the Danish Arbitration Institute (hereafter 'the Institute'). The Institute decides on the size of the deposit and normally the two parties will be asked to pay identical amounts.

The Institute has elaborated a schedule for the size of its fee and for the arbitrators' fees. Article 25(1) and (2) of the Rules states that the award shall contain provisions regarding the size and the payment of costs of the arbitration case, including the reimbursement of payments to experts appointed by the arbitral tribunal, the fee to the arbitrators and the charge payable to the Institute.

Article 26(1) states that the fee payable to the members of the arbitral tribunal shall be decided by the Institute on the basis of a reasoned written proposal drafted by the chairperson of the arbitral tribunal, setting out the size of the total fees and their distribution among the arbitrators. The Institute shall make the final computation of the total costs of the arbitration case, including its own charge. The fees to the arbitrators and the charge payable to the Institute shall be decided in accordance with the rates fixed by the Institute.

Article 26(2) and (3) states that the award shall indicate whether or not the losing party shall effect reimbursement to the other party of the costs incurred by the latter in connection with the case. In its determination of the amount of costs to be paid, the tribunal shall rely on the outcome of the award and other relevant circumstances including a possible agreement between the parties.

The tribunal when deciding on the cost distribution may take into consideration, *inter alia*, whether a party has cooperated in an expedient and cost-efficient manner to finalise the arbitration.

4 Procedure for the appointment of the tribunal

Section 11(2) of the Act gives details on the appointment of arbitrators when the parties have not agreed on the procedure. In this case the arbitral tribunal shall consist of three arbitrators. Each party shall appoint one arbitrator within 30 days after having received a request to this effect from the other party. These arbitrators shall appoint the third arbitrator (the chairperson) within

30 days after their appointment. If the panel cannot be established in this way or according to the agreement, each party may request the court to appoint the missing arbitrators. Furthermore, the Act gives details of how to handle conflicts of interest (for details see Section 7 below).

Article 10 of the Rules states that failing an agreement to the opposite the tribunal shall consist of one arbitrator unless the Institute after having heard the parties decides that the tribunal shall consists of three arbitrators. The Institute will when making this decision take into consideration the amount involved, the complexity and other relevent circumstances.

Article 11(1) of the Rules states that all the arbitrators are approved by the Institute. When a case is decided by three arbitrators, the claimant may, in his request for arbitration, nominate one arbitrator and the respondent may, in his answer, nominate the second arbitrator. The third arbitrator who will act as chairperson of the panel may be proposed by the parties jointly, before the expiration of the deadline for the statement of defence. If the Institute cannot approve a nominated arbitrator the party/parties may nominate another within a time fixed by the Institute, unless the Institute decides otherwise due to the delay this may incur. If the parties fail to nominate an arbitrator or fail to agree on a single arbitrator or chairperson the Institute will make the appoinment. The chairperson of the arbitral tribunal must have a law degree. The same applies for a single arbitrator (article 10(2)).

If there are two or more claimants in an arbitration case, they must all act jointly in proposing an arbitrator. The same is to apply if there are two or more respondents in a case. Failing such a joint proposal, the arbitrators in question are to be appointed by the Institute (article 11(5)).

When not all the parties in a dispute are domiciled in the same country, the person appointed as chairperson must be domiciled in a country other than those in which the parties reside unless otherwise agreed by the parties (article 11(6)). As may be seen, the Institute deviates from the ICC, where the emphasis is on nationality rather than domicile.

If the case is to be decided by one arbitrator, the parties may jointly propose a candidate not later than by the deadline fixed by the Institute (article 11(2)).

If, after having been appointed, an arbitrator dies, wishes to resign or has his appointment revoked by the Institute, a substitute arbitrator is appointed according to the same procedure as the arbitrator he is replacing, unless the Institute decides otherwise to avoid delay (article 11(2)). This appointment follows the same Rules as the appointment of the arbitrator who is being replaced.

If the arbitration case does not progress effectively and efficiently or if the other duties vested in the arbitrators are not fulfilled, the Institute may revoke the appointment of one or more arbitrators (article 14(2)).

Before being appointed by the Institute, an arbitrator must sign a statement of independence and impartiality, in which they must state any circumstances which may, in the opinion of either party to the arbitration case, give rise to justifiable doubt as to the arbitrator's impartiality or independence. The arbitrator must also produce information on his professional and educational background etc., and that information must be submitted to the parties and a deadline must be set for any relevant comments (article 14). The Rules then lay down specific procedural requirements for the further procedure as to the processing of any objection to the appointment of an arbitrator.

5 Identity and role of the appointing authority

The Institute, which is a non-profit private foundation, was founded in 1981 by the Danish Bar and Law Society, the Danish Society of Engineers, the Association of Danish Judges, the Danish Federation of Small and Medium-Sized Enterprises and the Federation of Danish Engineers. The Danish Construction Association, the Danish IT Industry Association, the Confederation of Danish Industry, the Institute of State-Authorized Public Accountants in Denmark, the Danish Shipowners' Association and Danish Arbitration Association have subsequently joined the circle of organisations behind Danish Arbitration.

The Institute is governed by a Council. The highest authority of the Institute is the Board of Representatives. The day-to-day management of the activities rests with the Managing Director.

Committees are formed with expertise in specific fields of arbitration. Thus, expert committees have been formed for the following areas: maritime law, IT law, mediation and international dispute resolution.

The role of the Institute as an appointing authority is to identify and appoint arbitrators in any case where the arbitration clause in the parties' agreement does not stipulate otherwise and the parties do not appoint arbitrators according to the Rules described above in Section 4.

The Institute relies on a network of internationally recognised arbitrators from European countries.

In older arbitration clauses, reference to a court president is often found as the appointing authority, leading to the appointment of a judge.

6 Form of the arbitration agreement

There are no requirements as to the form of the arbitration agreement. Danish law does not even request that arbitration is agreed upon in writing. In this respect, Danish law anticipated the revision of the UNCITRAL Model Law, which in 2006 introduced, as an option for the legislature, arbitration agreements without form requirements. The reason is that what can be considered as a written agreement has been seen as a major obstacle. As the existence of an arbitration agreement is subject to proof, it goes without saying that non-written arbitration agreements do not play any role.

7 Interference/support by the courts (including a tribunal's powers to involve them)

Section 5 of the Act refers to sections of the Act empowering parties or the tribunal to involve national courts and concludes that the request must be given to the court that would have been competent had arbitration not been agreed upon.

Section 11(3) states that the parties may request the courts to assist in the appointment of the tribunal. If one of the parties fail to appoint his arbitrator or if the two arbitrators fail to appoint the chairperson a party may request the courts to appoint the missing arbitrator, unless the arbitration agreement prescribes another procedure. This provision is not applicable when the Institute is agreed.

Section 13(3) states that the court may decide on a challenge to an arbitrator. Provided that no agreement has been made, including reference to the Institute, a reasoned challenge shall be made in writing to the tribunal within 15 days from the time the party became aware of the appointment of the arbitrator and must include the circumstances on which the challenge is based. Unless the arbitrator resigns or the other party agrees to the challenge, the tribunal decides whether the challenge is to be allowed or not.

If the challenge is not allowed, the challenging party may, within 30 days, request the court to decide whether the challenge should be allowed. However, while this request is pending the arbitration proceedings may continue.

Section 14 states that the court may also decide on challenges of already appointed arbitrators. This provision applies if legal or factual reasons make it impossible for an arbitrator to perform his mandate or if he does not do so within a reasonable time. His mandate will cease if he retires or if the parties agree that his mandate is to come to an end. In other cases, the parties may request the courts to decide whether the mandate should be terminated. Additionally, this section is only applicable if another agreement including reference to the Institute is not made.

Section 16 of the Act states that the competence of the arbitral tribunal is decided by the tribunal itself. This affects the validity and the existence of the arbitration agreement. Once the tribunal has decided on the issue, each party may, within 30 days of the decision, request the court to decide on the issue. However, such a request will not prevent the arbitral proceedings continuing.

Section 27(1) states that the arbitral tribunal or party with the approval of the arbitral tribunal may request the court's assistance in taking evidence according to the Administration of Justice Act. This is, in particular, relevant when it comes to recalcitrant witnesses, who can be forced to give evidence before the court.

Furthermore, it may be applicable when it comes to requests for information or documents from a person or entity not party to the arbitration. The procedure may be lengthy and subject to appeal and must therefore be considered at a very early stage of the arbitration.

Section 27(2) has an interesting feature, according to which the arbitral tribunals in matters relating to European law may request a court to request a preliminary decision from the European Court of Justice. The conditions under which the arbitral tribunal may request the assistance of the European Court of Justice are parallel to the conditions under which the court may itself, under the Treaty, request assistance from the European Court of Justice had the case been pending before the national court.

Section 34(3) of the Act states that the decision on the costs of the arbitral tribunal may be challenged by each party before the competent court within a time limit of 30 days after the parties received notification of the costs. If the costs of the arbitral tribunal are reduced, this reduction will also be effective in respect of the party who did not challenge the costs.

The court's role in preliminary measures will be dealt with in Section 9 concerning interim measures.

The court's decision in the above matters is subject to appeal according to chapter 37 of the Administration of Justice Act, except for the decisions according to section 11(3) on the appointment of arbitrators. When the courts appoint an arbitrator then the appointment is final. This is also applicable in cases where the court is designated as the appointing authority in the arbitration agreement. Appeal is made to the court of second instance (*landsretten*). A further appeal to the Supreme Court requires special permission from the Board of Appeal (*Procesbevillingsnævnet*).

Since matters brought before the court do not prevent the arbitration continuing, these appeals will not jeopardise the arbitration procedure.

8 Tribunal's powers *ex officio*

According to the Act, the courts have no competence in matters referred to arbitration except for those matters that are stipulated in the Act. These exceptions are described in the next section and if a matter is arbitrable and if a lawsuit is initiated the court shall dismiss such a case from its files (section 8 of the Act).

In cases of arbitration where the Institute is agreed, their Rules become part of the arbitration agreement. To the extent that decisions in an arbitration are referred to the Institute, it may be seen as a limitation of the autonomy of the arbitration tribunal (e.g. the review of the costs of arbitration).

To the extent that a procedural issue is not addressed in the Rules in cases of national arbitration, it is common to agree on the application of the Administration of Justice Act – *mutatis mutandis*. In international arbitration, the tribunal is free to decide on procedural rules that should be used in addition to the Rules.

The most important features of the procedural rules according to the Administration of Justice Act can be condensed as follows:

(a) No written witness statements are accepted,
(b) No party appointed experts are accepted, and

(c) No expert opinion that is required unilaterally by one party for the purpose of the arbitration is admissible.

The national rules on requests for further particulars are very close to the IBA Rules on Taking Evidence and do not cause any problems in an international context.

9 The possibility of interim measures and their enforceability

It is up to the tribunal to decide on interim measures. As to their enforceability, the tribunal may request the court to implement decisions on interim measures, especially on injunctions and arrests. As to the details of the procedure on implementing preliminary measures, the court will follow the Administration of Justice Act. Furthermore, the parties may request the court to secure evidence in the form of witness statements or expert opinions, which may be relevant in urgent cases even before the arbitration is initiated.

10 Multi-party arbitration (including joinder and consolidation)

The Rules have no provisions on joinder or consolidation. However, the Rules presuppose the possibility of multi-party arbitration, since it envisages how to appoint arbitrators if there are more than two parties (see Section 4 above). The Act has no provisions on this issue.

The issue has been considered by the courts, on one occasion. In the decision U2005, page 2560S, an insurer made a request for arbitration against all the reinsurers under a reinsurance contract. The case was decided on under the previous Act on arbitration from 1972. The court decided that the Act gave no power to the courts to decide that parties in arbitration cases that were not based on the same contract should be confined to appointing one arbitrator or bound to accept that the cases be consolidated.

This result would also be the likely outcome of a case decided on the basis of the present Act. However, the only problem was that the court obviously misunderstood the nature of the insurance contract, but this does not touch upon the basic issue concerning consolidation. The same result would be expected in the case of a joinder.

Having said this, it must be expected that the court will accept consolidation if all the parties in the arbitration are parties in the same contract.

11 Conduct of arbitration

As to the conduct of arbitration, much is left to the tribunal's discretion. The Danish Society of Arbitration has adopted a set of rules on taking evidence, addressing the same issues as the IBA Rules on Taking Evidence. The rules are presently only available in Danish, but are in the process of being translated into English, French and German. It is up to the parties or, if they disagree, the tribunal to decide whether these rules should be adopted. The following refers to cases where no specific rules are adopted. If no agreement is made to the contrary, it is up to the tribunal to decide whether to elaborate terms of reference, which is, however, unusual in Danish arbitration. It is, furthermore, up to the tribunal to decide on the number of briefs. Post-hearing briefs are not common.

As to disclosure, Danish practice is close to the IBA Guidelines on Taking Evidence. In Danish arbitration, requests for further particulars are often left undecided by the tribunal, in which case the legal consequences are difficult to foresee. It is therefore recommended in the case where there is a Danish chairperson to request a decision from the tribunal on requests for further particulars relating to a specific procedural order.

There are no restrictions as to the form of evidence. However, as already mentioned, written witness statements in a Danish context are unusual and it should, therefore, be decided on as to what extent written witness statements are admissible and whether written witness statements foreclose questions outside the written witness statement from the party who presents the witness.

The Rules have detailed provisions concerning experts. Article 35 stipulates that a party may request an expert to be appointed. It is up to the arbitral tribunal after having heard the other party to decide whether to appoint one or more experts to report to it on specific issues to be determined by the arbitral tribunal. It may, furthermore, order a party to give the expert any and all relevant information and to grant him access to inspect documents and other evidence. Article 35(2) states that the Institute shall produce one or more candidates for appointment as expert(s) by the arbitral tribunal after having heard the parties thereon. The ordinary way to identify a suitable expert is to approach relevant institutions and ask them to suggest one or several experts within a specific field of expertise. The Institute charges a fee for the appointment of experts amounting to 500 euros per expert. It will provide an estimate of costs and secure a deposit from the requesting party, but it is up to the tribunal to decide on the fee payable to the expert.

The appointment by the tribunal of an expert does not prevent the parties from calling their own expert witnesses (article 35(7)). Although not said explicitly, this provision implies that the parties may also be entitled to produce unilaterally requested expert opinions.

According to the Act, it is up to the tribunal to decide whether an oral hearing is necessary or whether the case should be tried on the basis of the written submissions. However, if one party so wishes, the tribunal shall accept an oral pleading.

When it comes to the applicable law, the tribunal is under no constraint. If the parties have not agreed on the applicable law, it is up to the tribunal to decide.

When the arbitration is under the Institute, there are certain requirements as to the procedure.

The Institute expects to be copied in on the ongoing correspondence between the tribunal and the parties and will, if necessary, assist in order to assure 'that the case progresses effectively and efficiently' (article 15(1)).

At the start of the case, the tribunal is expected, as mentioned in Section 2, to convene the parties for a preparatory meeting. In the notice convening the meeting, the arbitral tribunal shall set out the issues of special importance to be addressed at the meeting, including the position taken by the parties in relation to the facts and legal points of the case as well as:

(a) The parties' position on the factual and legal circumstances of the case including clarification of which circumstances of the case are not challenged by the parties and which circumstances shall be subject to presentation of evidence.
(b) The procedure for the presentation of evidence.
(c) The time and place of the oral hearing.
(d) Calls to a party for the submission of factual information, including the presentation of documents or others evidence.
(e) Requests for the commissioning of expert opinions or statements by organisations or authorities.

(f) The phrasing of questions to be put to experts, organisations or authorities.
(g) Costs which may accrue from the case, including the need to make decisions involving particularly cost-consuming activities.
(h) The organisation of the oral hearing including the date, time and place for it.

Article 8 states that, in addition to statement of claim and statement of defence, the parties shall be given the opportunity of exchanging a reply and rejoinder.

According to article 24(1), the arbitral tribunal shall, before making its award, forward a draft version of the award and a statement of the costs of the arbitration case to the Institute. The draft shall be forwarded as soon as possible after the case has been set down and, if possible, no later than six months after the case has been submitted to the Institute. If the draft is not available within the indicative time limit, the arbitral tribunal shall inform the parties and the Institute of when the draft is expected to be available.

The Institute uses this to suggest modifications, especially in terms of form, but to a much lesser extent than, for example, the ICC Court of Arbitration. The primary goal (see article 28) is to ensure the validity of the award, its recognition and enforcement.

Article 31 states that the parties may, within 30 days from receipt of the arbitral award, request from the arbitral tribunal corrections, interpretations or the making of an additional award with regard to claims which, although they were presented to the arbitral tribunal and should have been decided on by it, were omitted from the arbitral award. Furthermore, the arbitral tribunal may itself make corrections to the award within the same time limit. A hearing of the parties in both instances is envisaged.

12 Confidentiality

There is no provision under Danish law that arbitration proceedings or awards are confidential. However, the arbitrators are supposed to be bound by a confidentiality obligation. In the Rules of Danish Arbitration, this is specifically stipulated in article 34. Confidentiality may be agreed in the agreement that forms the basis of the arbitration.

In cases where confidentiality is breached, it is a matter to be decided under contract law of what the effect of that breach shall be. Generally, it is considered to be difficult to recover compensation, since it is hard to prove a financial loss.

13 The institution's role

The Rules are very comprehensive. They can be seen as an effort to secure a high standard for arbitration under the Rules. The Institution's involvement in the arbitration process is, as appears from the previous sections, primarily to control costs and to secure an expedient procedure and a high level of quality in its awards.

14 Possibility of excluding the court's review of the validity of an award

Under Danish law, the courts have no competence to review the award as such. For the matters decided on by the award, the award is final. However, the Act foresees the possibility of setting aside the award on the grounds of invalidity. It is not possible to exclude the court's review of the validity of an award.

15 Grounds for invalidity of the award

According to section 37 of the Act, an award may only be set aside by the courts as invalid if it is shown that:

(a) a party to the arbitration agreement was, under the law of the country in which that party was domiciled at the time of conclusion of the contract, under some incapacity, or the said agreement is not valid under the law to which the parties have subjected it or, failing any indication thereon, under Danish law;
(b) the party making the application was not given proper notice of the appointment of an arbitrator or of the arbitral proceedings or was otherwise unable to present his or her case;
(c) the award deals with a dispute not contemplated by or not falling within the terms of the submission to arbitration, or contains decisions on matters beyond the scope of the submission to arbitration;
(d) the composition of the arbitral tribunal or the arbitral procedure was not in accordance with the agreement of the parties or with the Act;

(e) the subject-matter of the dispute is not capable of settlement by arbitration;
(f) the award is manifestly contrary to the public policy of Denmark.

An application to set aside an award on grounds of invalidity shall be initiated within three months from the time the party making the application received the award.

7

Arbitration in Germany: Features of the German Institution of Arbitration

JENS BREDOW

1 Time frame for the proceeding

1.1 German arbitration law

The German arbitration law, that is, the 10th book of the *Zivilprozessordnung* (the 'GCCP': German Code of Civil Procedure),[1] is to a large extent a verbatim adoption of the UNCITRAL Model Law on International Commercial Arbitration 1985[2] and, accordingly, does not provide for a time frame in which arbitral proceedings shall be conducted.

However, under German arbitration law, parties enjoy the highest level of autonomy in terms of timing and, accordingly, they are free to agree on a time frame that they deem feasible for the conduct of their arbitral proceedings.

1.2 DIS Arbitration Rules and DIS Supplementary Rules for Expedited Proceedings

Such an agreement may be negotiated individually or by reference to a pre-fabricated set of arbitration rules, such as the Supplementary Rules for Expedited Proceedings ('SREP') of the *Deutsche Institution für*

The author wishes to thank Peter Kraft, Rechtsanwalt and counsel at the German Institution of Arbitration (DIS) for his very valuable contribution to this chapter.

1 Act on the Reform of the Law relating to Arbitral Proceedings of 22 December 1997, published in the Federal Law Gazette (*Bundesgesetzblatt*), 1997, part I, p. 3224; the law is available for download in different languages at www.dis-arb.de, last visited on 20 December 2010.

2 The UNCITRAL Model Law on International Commercial Arbitration 1985 is available for download in the official UN languages at www.uncitral.org/uncitral/en/uncitral_texts/arbitration/1985Model_arbitration.html, last visited on 20 December 2010.

Schiedsgerichtsbarkeit e.V. (the 'DIS': the German Institution of Arbitration).[3]

While the standard DIS Arbitration Rules of 1998 do not provide for a specific time frame in which the arbitral proceedings shall be conducted, the increasing criticism by the users of arbitration regarding the average duration of arbitral proceedings[4] persuaded the DIS to offer a ready-made set of rules for arbitral proceedings 'on the fast track'. The *raison d'être* for such a set of rules being that – on the one hand – it is difficult at the time of drafting the arbitration clause to predict, with a reasonable degree of certainty, whether the fast-track procedures will be suitable for those disputes.[5] Conversely, it will often be difficult for the parties to negotiate fast-track arbitration rules individually after the dispute has arisen. The DIS-SREP entered into force on 1 April 2008.

Pursuant to s. 1 subs. 2 of the DIS-SREP, the duration of arbitral proceedings should be no longer than six months after filing the statement of claim where the decision is to be made by a sole arbitrator and no more than nine months in the case of a three-member tribunal. The different time frames – that is, six and nine months, respectively – are due to the fact that the periods that are foreseen commence with the initial filing of a claim. Accordingly, the process of constituting the arbitral tribunal falls within the period, which almost inevitably requires more time in the case of a three-member tribunal. The six-month deadline is the general rule, because in deviation from s. 3 of the standard DIS Arbitration Rules, s. 3 subs. 1 of the DIS-SREP provides that the dispute shall be decided on by a sole arbitrator, unless the parties have agreed prior to the filing of the statement of claim that the dispute shall be decided on by a three-member tribunal.

Contrary to fast-track concepts in other arbitral institutions, the DIS-SREP do not stipulate automatic application in cases where a certain amount in dispute is not exceeded.[6] Accordingly, the DIS-SREP apply

3 The DIS-SREP entered into force as of 1 April 2008 and are available for download at www.dis-arb.de, last visited on 20 December 2010.

4 See K. P. Berger, 'The Need for Speed in International Arbitration: Supplementary Rules for Expedited Proceedings of the German Institution of Arbitration (DIS)', *Journal of International Arbitration*, 25(2008), 595 *et seq.*; M. McIlwrath and R. Schroeder, 'The View from an International Arbitration Customer: In Dire Need of Early Resolution', *Arbitration*, 74(2008), 3, 4 and at 10; R. L. Kleine, 'Die Schiedsgerichtsbarkeit aus Sicht ihrer Nutzer', *SchiedsVZ*, 6(2008), 145 *et seq.*

5 Berger, 'The Need for Speed', 595 at 596.

6 J. Bredow, 'Without Delay: Arbitrating in Six Months: The German Approach for Expedited Proceedings', in K. Hobér, A. Magnusson and M. Öhrström (eds.), *Between*

only if the parties have expressly referred to them in their arbitration agreement or if they have agreed on their application at a later stage prior to filing a statement of claim (s. 1 subs. 1).[7] After the filing of the claim, for the sake of clarity regarding the different deadlines set out in the DIS-SREP, it is not possible to agree on the applicability of the rules as such.[8] However, the parties may agree to apply certain elements therein in order to expedite their proceeding.[9] DIS practice shows that the agreement on the application of the DIS-SREP is usually reached only after the dispute has arisen, as it is difficult to predict the kind of dispute arising out of a contractual relationship and its suitability for expedited proceedings.[10]

2 Cost determination (including security)

2.1 German arbitration law

2.1.1 Determination of the arbitrators' fees

The German arbitration law is silent on the arbitrators' fees and it is for the parties and the arbitrators to exercise their autonomy when negotiating the remuneration of the arbitrators. In the absence of an express agreement between the arbitrators and the parties, the usual remuneration is deemed to have been agreed upon if the duties that are performed are not usually rendered free of charge (s. 612 of the *Bürgerliches Gesetzbuch*: 'BGB' – the German Civil Code).[11] The parties are jointly

East and West: Essays in Honour of Ulf Franke (Huntington: JurisNet, 2010), p. 51 at p. 53.

[7] Accordingly, the German Institution of Arbitration (DIS) advises all parties wishing to make reference to the Supplementary Rules for Expedited Proceedings when concluding the arbitration agreement to use the following arbitration clause: 'All disputes arising in connection with the contract (. . . description of the contract . . .) or its validity shall be finally settled according to the Arbitration Rules and the Supplementary Rules for Expedited Proceedings of the German Institution of Arbitration e.V. (DIS) without recourse to the ordinary courts of law.' Further, it is recommended that the arbitration clause is supplemented by the following provisions: 'The place of arbitration is (. . .) / The substantive law of (. . .) is applicable to the dispute. / The language of the arbitral proceedings is (. . .)'.

[8] Bredow, 'Without Delay', pp. 53 *et seq.*; Berger, 'The Need for Speed', 599.

[9] Bredow, 'Without Delay', p. 54. [10] Ibid., p. 53.

[11] I. Hanefeld, 'Chapter 7: Germany', in F.-B. Weigand (ed.), *Practitioner's Handbook on International Commercial Arbitration* (Oxford University Press, 2009), p. 475 at p. 525, para. 7.208; W. Voit, '§ 1035: Bestellung der Schiedsrichter', in H.-J. Musielak (ed.), *Kommentar zur Zivilprozessordnung* (Munich: Verlag Franz Vahlen, 2007), p. 2446 at p. 2456, para. 26; S. Wilske, 'Ad hoc Arbitration in Germany', in Böckstiegel, Kröll and

and severally liable for the payment.[12] In *ad hoc* arbitration, parties and their arbitrators frequently revert to the DIS cost schedule[13] or the model agreement by the *Deutscher Anwaltverein* (the 'DAV': the German Lawyers' Association).[14]

2.1.2 Advance on costs and orders to provide security for costs

German arbitration does not explicitly address the issue of deposits or advances for costs and fees. However, under German customary law, arbitrators are entitled to claim advance payments. Arbitrators may suspend their activities until such payment has been effected.[15] Even though the arbitral tribunal is generally entitled to request the parties to pay advances on costs, it remains an open question as to whether or not an arbitral tribunal may compel the parties to actually make such payments.[16]

There exists no specific provision under German law regarding the security for costs and – in practice – granting applications for security for costs is the exception rather than the rule. Nevertheless, the arbitral tribunal is not prevented from granting such security upon the reasoned request of a party.[17]

Nacimiento (eds.), *Arbitration in Germany: The Model Law in Practice* (Aalphen aan den Rijn: Kluwer Law International, 2007), p. 809 at p. 829 at para. 46. Some courts have held that the DIS cost scheme can be considered as the usual remuneration: see LG Arnsberg, Decision of 7 August 2006 – 2 O 83/06, available at www.dis-arb.de, last visited on 20 December 2010; see also J.-P. Lachmann, *Handbuch für die Schiedsgerichtspraxis* (Cologne: Verlag Dr Otto Schmidt, 2008), p. 910 at para. 4225 *et seq.*

12 Hanefeld, 'Chapter 7: Germany', p. 525, para. 7.208; Lachmann, *Schiedsgerichtspraxis*, p. 915 at para. 4250 with further references.

13 A cost calculator is provided on the DIS website www.dis-arb.de, last visited on 20 December 2010; for a model clause see Lachmann, *Schiedsgerichtspraxis*, p. 911 at para. 4231 with further references.

14 The model agreement of 10 March 2006 is available on the website of Deutscher Anwaltverein (DAV), anwaltverein.de/downloads/praxis/mustervertrag/SchiedsrichterverguetungDAV-DRiB.pdf; last visited on 20 December 2010; see H. H. Bischof, 'RVG: Erste Gebührenprobleme für Schiedsverfahren und Mediation', *SchiedsVZ*, 5(2004), 252 *et seq.*

15 F. von Schlabrendorff and A. Sessler, '§ 1057: Decision on Costs', in Böckstiegel, Kröll and Nacimiento (eds.), *Arbitration in Germany*, p. 421, para. 15; Wilske, 'Ad hoc Arbitration in Germany', p. 833, para. 53; Hanefeld, 'Chapter 7: Germany', p. 523, para. 7.200.

16 OLG Oldenburg, Decision of 31 March 1971 – 8 U 103/70, (1971), *NJW*, 1461 at 1462; AG Düsseldorf, Decision of 17 June 2003 – 36 C 19 607/02, *SchiedsVZ*, 5(2003), 240; but see Schlabrendorff and Sessler, '§ 1057: Decision on Costs', pp. 421 *et seq.* para. 16 with further references.

17 K.-H. Böckstiegel, S. M. Kröll and P. Nacimiento, 'Germany as a Place for International and Domestic Arbitrations: General Overview', in Böckstiegel, Kröll and Nacimiento (eds.), *Arbitration in Germany*, p. 38, para. 92; K. Haase, 'Das Erfordernis der Prozesskostensicherheit i.S.d. § 110 ZPO im schiedsgerichtlichen Verfahrens', *BB*, (1995), 1252 *et seq.*

2.1.3 Retainable costs

Under German law, the retainable costs comprise the arbitrators' fees, the parties' costs for legal representation and the parties' other costs for the proceedings that are deemed as necessary for their pursuit of the claim or for their defence.

Retaining legal representation is a recognized necessary cost. The remuneration of attorneys in Germany is governed by the *Rechtsanwaltsvergütungsgesetz* (the 'RVG': the Lawyers' Fees Act).[18] However, these rules do not apply *per se* to the reimbursement of parties' costs in arbitral proceedings and, in particular, not if the parties involved have a non-German counsel.[19] In arbitral proceedings where both parties are represented by German lawyers, the reimbursement of attorneys' costs will often, but not necessarily, be based on the fee schedule of the RVG.[20] In proceedings where both parties are represented by non-German lawyers, the system of reimbursement of attorneys' fees according to the RVG obviously does not apply.[21] However, if, in the country of origin of the parties or attorneys, a fee schedule for attorneys' costs exists, such a schedule may be taken into consideration.[22]

In complex arbitrations, in-house counsel are often also involved in both preparing for and accompanying the proceedings. Such costs have so far not been recoverable in proceedings before German state courts.[23] However, as the assessment of which costs are 'necessary' for the pursuit of a claim is at the arbitral tribunal's discretion, it may award such costs where the need for them is alleged substantively by the parties.

2.1.4 Allocation of the costs

Pursuant to s. 1057 of the GCCP, the arbitral tribunal shall decide, in the arbitral award, which party has to bear the costs of the proceedings. Section 1057 of the GCCP applies if the parties have not made other arrangements.[24]

[18] See s. 36 subs. 1 RVG. Under the RVG, remuneration of the attorney is generally based on the amount in dispute. However, attorneys and parties are entitled to agree on a scheme of remuneration that is higher than the statutory fee schedule, e.g. a fee calculated on the basis of an hourly rate, see s. 4 RVG.

[19] J. Bredow and I. Mulder, 'Section 35: Decision on Costs', in Böckstiegel, Kröll and Nacimiento (eds.), *Arbitration in Germany*, p. 778, para. 12.

[20] Ibid., p. 778, para. 14. [21] Ibid., p. 778, para. 16. [22] Ibid., p. 778, para. 16.

[23] See also Schlabrendorff and Sessler, '§ 1057: Decision on Costs', p. 424, paras. 23 *et seq.*; Bredow and Mulder, 'Section 35: Decision on Costs', p. 778, para. 16.

[24] See also Schlabrendorff and Sessler, '§ 1057: Decision on Costs', p. 417, para. 3.

The German law vests arbitral tribunals with broad discretion regarding the allocation of costs, so that the tribunal can fully consider the specific circumstances of each case and find flexible solutions.[25] Unlike in German state-court proceedings, the rule of costs following the event is not a mandatory principle and the arbitral tribunal is free to deviate from this rule if it considers it appropriate.[26] In deciding on the allocation of costs, the outcome of the proceedings is an important, but by no means exclusive or overriding criterion for the arbitral tribunal to consider. If, for example, the conduct of the proceedings by a party, though ultimately victorious, has caused unnecessary delays or additional and unwarranted procedural measures and expenses, these circumstances may be taken into consideration in the cost decision of the arbitral tribunal.[27]

2.2 *DIS Arbitration Rules*

2.2.1 Determination of the arbitrators' fees and the DIS administrative fee

Pursuant to s. 40 subs. 2 of the DIS Arbitration Rules, the arbitrators' fees are determined by reference to the amount in dispute. The amount in dispute will usually be assessed by the arbitral tribunal by reference to the specific relief requested or in consultation with the parties. If the arbitral tribunal and the parties do not reach agreement on the assessment, the arbitral tribunal determines the amount at its own discretion. If the parties consider the assessment to be grossly unreasonable, they may, at least to the extent that German law applies to the proceedings, have the assessment reviewed pursuant to s. 319 of the BGB.[28]

In addition, the DIS administrative fee is fixed on the basis of the amount in dispute (s. 40 subs. 4 DIS Arbitration Rules). The minimum DIS administrative fee amounts to EUR 350 for amounts in dispute of up to EUR 17,500. The maximum fee of EUR 25,000 falls due when the amount in dispute reaches EUR 3,900,000. In multi-party proceedings, an increase of 20% of the administrative fee per additional party is charged up to a

[25] Bill on the Reform of the Law relating to Arbitral Proceedings, published in BT-Drs. 13/5274, p. 57 available in German at www.dis-arb.de, Materials section, last visited on 20 December 2010; also Schlabrendorff and Sessler, '§ 1057: Decision on Costs', p. 427, para. 36.

[26] Schlabrendorff and Sessler, '§ 1057: Decision on Costs', p. 427, para. 36.

[27] Ibid., p. 428, para. 37.

[28] J. Bredow and I. Mulder, 'Section 40: Costs of Arbitral Proceedings', in Böckstiegel, Kröll and Nacimiento (eds.), *Arbitration in Germany*, p. 792 at p. 793, para. 3.

maximum increase of 50%; that is, a maximum administrative fee of EUR 37,500 will be charged.[29] If a counter-claim is filed or a subsidiary set-off (*Hilfsaufrechnung*) is declared, the DIS administrative fee is calculated on the basis of the combined amount in dispute of the claim and counter-claim or set-off.[30] The maximum combined DIS administrative fee for a claim and counter-claim also amounts to EUR 37,500.

2.2.2 Advance on costs and orders to provide security for costs

The parties are jointly and severally liable for the payment of the advance costs for the arbitral tribunal.[31] Pursuant to s. 25 of the DIS Arbitration Rules the arbitral tribunal may make the continuation of the arbitral proceedings contingent on the payment of advances for the anticipated costs of the arbitral tribunal. It should request each party to pay half of the advance.

The DIS Arbitration Rules do not expressly provide for orders for security concerning costs; that is, an order by an arbitral tribunal requiring a claimant or, in the case of a counter-claim, the respondent to provide security for the costs of its counter-party in the event that its (counter-)claim is ultimately unsuccessful. Security for costs relates only to legal fees and expenses arising from the defence of the relevant claims in the proceedings. It is still an open question as to whether the arbitral tribunal may require a party to provide appropriate security for costs in connection with any interim measures of protection pursuant to s. 20 subs. 1 of the DIS Arbitration Rules. As s. 20 of the DIS Arbitration Rules empowers the arbitral tribunal only to order any interim measures of protection that it considers necessary in respect of the subject matter of the dispute, orders ordering the party to provide for security for costs are the exception rather than the rule.[32]

2.2.3 Retainable costs and allocation of costs

Regarding the issue of retainable costs and the allocation of costs, reference may be made to the statements made above in the context of the German arbitration law (s. 1057 GCCP) as the German arbitration law and the DIS Arbitration Rules contain largely identical provisions.

[29] This amount is reached when three additional parties are involved on the claimant or respondent side and the amount in dispute exceeds EUR 3,900,000.

[30] Bredow and Mulder, 'Section 40: Costs of Arbitral Proceedings', p. 797, para. 33.

[31] Hanefeld, 'Chapter 7: Germany', p. 525, para. 7.208; Lachmann, *Schiedsgerichtspraxis*, p. 915 at para. 4250 with further references.

[32] See K. Pörnbacher and S. Thiel, 'Kostensicherheit in Schiedsverfahren', *SchiedsVZ*, 8(2010), 14 *et seq.*

As for the retainable costs, it is generally accepted that the DIS administrative fee is a retainable cost. Such an administrative fee, for obvious reasons, does not fall due in *ad hoc* proceedings.

3 Procedure for the appointment of the tribunal

3.1 German arbitration law

Section 1035 subs. 1 of the GCCP vests the parties with the autonomy to agree on an appointment procedure for the arbitral tribunal. Where the parties have not exercised their freedom to agree on an appointment procedure, the arbitration law provides for a default mechanism.

Pursuant to s. 1034, the parties are free to determine the number of arbitrators and, failing such a determination, the number of arbitrators shall be three. In arbitrations with three arbitrators, each party has to nominate one arbitrator within one month after receiving the respective request by the other party (s. 1035 subs. 3, sentences 2 and 3, GCCP). The appointment of an arbitrator will become binding as soon as the other party has received notice of the appointment, unless the parties have stipulated otherwise (s. 1035 subs. 2 GCCP). Unless otherwise agreed by the parties, the chairperson will be appointed by the two arbitrators appointed by the parties (s. 1035 subs. 3, sentence 2, GCCP).

If the parties have agreed on a sole arbitrator, but cannot agree on an individual to act as sole arbitrator (s. 1035 subs. 3, sentence 1, GCCP),[33] or if a three-member arbitral tribunal is to decide on the dispute and the respondent, within one month of receiving the notice of arbitration, does not appoint its arbitrator or, in the case of a three-member arbitral tribunal where the two party-appointed arbitrators fail to agree on the third arbitrator within one month of their appointment (s. 1035 subs. 3, sentence 3, GCCP), the appointment of the sole arbitrator, the arbitrator to be appointed by the respondent or the chairperson's appointment shall be made, upon the request of a party, by the competent court, unless agreed otherwise by the parties.[34]

[33] While s. 1035 subs. 3, sentence 1 of the GCCP does not expressly provide for the nomination of a sole arbitrator, it is common knowledge that the period of one month, which applies to other situations governed by s. 1035 of the GCCP, should be taken as a guideline; see Hanefeld, 'Chapter 7: Germany', p. 491, para. 7.52.

[34] Pursuant to s. 1062 subs. 1, no. 1 of the GCCP, the competent court is the *Oberlandesgericht* designated in the arbitration agreement or, failing such designation, the higher regional court in whose district the place of arbitration is situated.

With respect to such appointments, the courts shall have due regard to any qualifications required of the arbitrator by the parties' agreement and to such considerations as are likely to secure the appointment of an independent and impartial arbitrator. In the case of a sole or third arbitrator, the court shall take into account the advisability of appointing an arbitrator of a nationality other than those of the parties (s. 1035 subs. 5 GCCP). In exercising their power to appoint an arbitrator, courts tend to consider suggestions made by the party for which they make the substitute appointment.[35]

The German arbitration law provides for a mechanism to cure an arbitration agreement granting preponderant rights to one party with regard to the composition of the arbitral tribunal. In such a case, the disadvantaged party may request the competent *Oberlandesgericht* (the 'OLG': the Higher Regional Court) to appoint the arbitrator(s) in deviation from the agreed nomination procedure (s. 1034 subs. 2 GCCP). The request must be submitted within two weeks of the party becoming aware of the constitution of the arbitral tribunal.

3.2 DIS Arbitration Rules

In the absence of an agreement by the parties to the contrary, the number of arbitrators will be three (s. 3 DIS Arbitration Rules). In the case of a three-member panel, each party nominates one arbitrator and these two arbitrators jointly nominate the chairperson of the arbitral tribunal (s. 12 DIS Arbitration Rules). If the parties have agreed that the tribunal shall consist of one arbitrator, the parties jointly nominate the sole arbitrator (s. 14 DIS Arbitration Rules).

If the nomination procedure fails, then the nomination of a substitute arbitrator by the appointing committee of the DIS[36] can be requested by a party.

Section 13 of the DIS Arbitration Rules makes special provision for the nomination of arbitrators in situations where there is more than one party on the respondent side (multi-party proceedings). If the respondents fail to agree on a joint nomination within the time limit provided, the DIS appointing committee, after having consulted the parties,

[35] S. M. Kröll and P. Kraft, 'Ten Years of UNCITRAL Model Law in Germany', *World Arbitration & Mediation Review*, 1(2007), 439 at 474 *et seq*.

[36] The composition and functions of the appointing committee of the DIS are stipulated in s. 14 of the DIS Statutes, available at www.dis-arb.de; see also *infra* Section 4.2.

nominates two arbitrators, unless the parties agree otherwise.[37] A nomination made by the claimant side is set aside by the DIS appointing committee's nomination.

Arbitrators, upon being nominated, are required to submit a declaration (s. 16 DIS Arbitration Rules) regarding their acceptance and their impartiality and independence (s. 15 DIS Arbitration Rules) as well as regarding their compliance with any agreed qualifications. An arbitrator may only be confirmed in office (s. 17 DIS Arbitration Rules) after having submitted such a declaration.

The arbitrators' declarations are circulated to the parties and they are given the opportunity to comment. If no party has raised an objection to the confirmation of the arbitrator, the DIS Secretary General confirms the arbitrator as being in office. In all other cases, the appointing committee decides on the confirmation. The arbitral tribunal is constituted when all three arbitrators are confirmed in office.

4 Identity and role of the appointing authority

4.1 German arbitration law

Arbitration clauses for *ad hoc* proceedings often provide that the president of a local chamber of commerce or the president of a state court shall appoint an arbitrator or a chairperson on behalf of the defaulting party. The appointment of an arbitrator is considered to be a *nobile officium* but there exists no legal obligation for the designated appointing authority to act.[38] Accordingly, it is recommendable to verify whether (a) such appointing authority exists; (b) it is willing to perform the task assigned to it[39]; and (c) it is suited to assess which person has the required or sufficient qualification, availability and logistical support to act as arbitrator.[40]

[37] The DIS Arbitration Rules in this regard differ from other institutional rules, e.g. art. 12 subs. 8 ICC Arbitration Rules, art. 8 subs. 1 LCIA Arbitration Rules and art. 13 subs. 4 SCC Arbitration Rules, as these rules provide that if multiple respondents cannot jointly nominate an arbitrator, the institution will nominate all three arbitrators.

[38] Lachmann, *Schiedsgerichtspraxis*, p. 214 at para. 809.

[39] *Cf.* BayObLG, Decision of 20 June 2000 – 4 Z SchH 12/99, (2000), *Recht und Praxis der Schiedsgerichtsbarkeit* (RPS), 21, in which the president of the Court refused to appoint an arbitrator, although this meant that in the end his colleagues in the competent senate of his court, i.e. the Bavarian highest regional court, had to appoint the arbitrator.

[40] Wilske, 'Ad hoc Arbitration in Germany', p. 815, para. 13.

However, the German arbitration law provides for a mechanism to save arbitration agreements that designate an appointing authority when they are not suitable or where they are not willing to appoint an arbitrator. Pursuant to s. 1035 subs. 4 of the GCCP, where, under an appointment procedure that has been agreed upon a third party fails to perform any function entrusted to it under the procedure, any party may request the court to take the necessary measures, unless the agreement on the appointment procedure provides other means for securing the appointment. The German Institution of Arbitration is willing to act as the appointing authority in *ad hoc* arbitration cases.

In case the parties to an *ad hoc* arbitration have not agreed on an appointing authority or where the agreed procedure of appointment fails, the arbitrator or the presiding arbitrator is appointed, upon the request of a party, by the competent OLG.[41] This ensures that the appointment is conducted in a swift and efficient manner.

4.2 DIS Arbitration Rules

Pursuant to s. 14 subs. 1 of the DIS Statutes, the appointing committee of the DIS consists of three members and three alternate members, appointed by the DIS board of directors for a period of two years.[42] Decisions are taken by the three regular members of the appointing committee. If one or more of the regular members is not available, one or more alternate members take their place. Decisions are taken by the majority of the three members.[43]

In DIS proceedings, the appointing committee nominates arbitrators – at the request of a party – if the respondent does not nominate an arbitrator (ss. 12 subs. 1 and 13 subs. 2 DIS Arbitration Rules), if a party does not participate in the nomination of a sole arbitrator (s. 14 DIS Arbitration Rules) or if the party nominated arbitrators fail to nominate the chairman of the tribunal (s. 12 subs. 2 DIS Arbitration Rules).[44]

The appointing committee nominates arbitrators upon proposal of the executive committee. Prior to making a proposal, the executive

41 See *supra* Section 3.1.

42 The DIS Statutes are available for download at www.dis-arb.de.

43 J. Bredow and I. Mulder, 'Introduction to DIS', in Böckstiegel, Kröll and Nacimiento (eds.), *Arbitration in Germany*, p. 660, para. 19.

44 Ibid., para. 20.

committee will request the person it intends to propose to declare if he will accept the office in the event of a nomination by the appointing committee and to declare if he is impartial and independent and fulfils any qualifications the parties have agreed on.[45] Only if the prospective arbitrator makes an unqualified declaration of acceptance and of impartiality and independence – that is, if he does not disclose circumstances which may give rise to doubts as to the proposed person's impartiality and independence or fulfilment of agreed qualifications – will the executive committee propose the person to the appointing committee.[46]

Decisions of the appointing committee are usually taken by written procedure and are therefore rendered very quickly, usually within the course of a few days.[47] Upon a proposal by the DIS executive committee, each member of the appointing committee returns his vote on the nomination of the proposed person to the DIS secretariat. If the appointing committee adopts the proposal of the executive committee by at least a majority of the votes, the parties get the chance to comment on the proposal within a short time limit. If no objections are raised then the person is confirmed as arbitrator pursuant to s. 17 of the DIS Arbitration Rules.

The DIS does not maintain a list of persons from which the proposals for the appointing committee are drawn. Rather, the persons are selected on the basis of the circumstances of each individual case, having regard to its legal and factual specifics and the requirements for the arbitrator resulting therefrom.[48] In order to be able to make the selection, the DIS maintains a strictly confidential database of information on the professional know-how as well as the prior experience as arbitrators or arbitration counsel of persons – not restricted to DIS members – who are interested in acting as arbitrators in DIS proceedings. The data are recorded (and updated) on the basis of information provided by such persons.

The appointing committee also decides on the confirmation of arbitrators in cases where the arbitrator has submitted a contested declaration of acceptance and of impartiality and independence (s. 17 subs. 2 DIS Arbitration Rules).[49]

Other functions have been assigned to the appointing committee. Under the revision of the DIS Schedule of Costs, nos. 12 and 13 have been included to provide that the appointing committee has to decide on

[45] Ibid., para. 21. [46] Ibid., para. 21. [47] Ibid., para. 21. [48] Ibid., para. 23.
[49] Ibid., para. 24.

a request by the arbitral tribunal to calculate the fees of the arbitrators on the basis of the separate amounts in dispute for the claim and counterclaim (no. 12 Schedule of Costs) or to increase the fees of the arbitrators in complex cases (no. 13 Schedule of Costs).[50]

5 Form of the arbitration agreement

In s. 1029 subs. 1 of the GCCP, an arbitration agreement is defined as 'an agreement by the parties to submit to arbitration all or certain legal disputes which have arisen or which may arise between them in respect of a defined legal relationship'.

As to the minimum content of an arbitration agreement, German law imposes very few requirements. One indispensable requirement is that the parties in the arbitration agreement clearly express their intention to submit their disputes to arbitration and that they opt out of state-court jurisdiction.[51] Other details such as the number of arbitrators, their appointment or the place of arbitration are provided for by the 10th Book of the GCCP or in the institutional rules that the parties have agreed on. Thus, courts have enforced minimalistic agreements such as 'Arbitration: Hamburg'.[52]

Arbitration agreements may – pursuant to s. 1029 subs. 2 of the GCCP – either take the form of a separate agreement or may be included in a main contract as an arbitration clause. Even where the arbitration agreement is incorporated into the main contract as a clause, it is considered to be a separate contract, independent from the main contract in which it is included (s. 1040 subs. 1, sentence 2, GCCP).[53]

Section 1031 subs. 1 of the GCCP provides that the arbitration agreement 'shall be contained either in a document signed by the parties or in an exchange of letters, telefaxes, telegrams or other means of telecommunication which provide a record of the agreement'.

[50] Ibid., para. 25.

[51] R. Trittmann and I. Hanefeld, '§ 1029: Definition', in Böckstiegel, Kröll and Nacimiento (eds.), *Arbitration in Germany*, p. 94 at p. 100, para. 17; Hanefeld, 'Chapter 7: Germany', p. 478, para. 7.11; but cf. BGH, Decision of 1 March 2007 – III ZB 7/06, *SchiedsVZ*, 6(2008), 160 *et seq.*, where the BGH held that the parties may agree on a conditional submission to arbitration, in which case the party not satisfied with the arbitral award could appeal to the state courts within a certain time limit.

[52] OLG Hamburg, Decision of 11 March 2003 – 11 Sch 06/01, (2003) 1, *SchiedsVZ*, 284; OLG Dresden, Decision of 26 October 2004 – 11 SchH 03/04, available at www.dis-arb.de.

[53] S. 1040 subs. 1, sentence 2, GCCP stipulates that 'an arbitration clause which forms part of a contract shall be treated as an agreement independent of the other terms of the contract'.

The wording is a literal adoption of article 7, subs. 2 sentence 2 of the UNCITRAL Model Law on International Commercial Arbitration. Irrespective thereof, the form requirements of the German arbitration law are, in fact, much more lenient than those of the Model Law. Pursuant to s. 1031 subs. 2 of the GCCP, the form requirement of subs. 1 is also deemed to have been complied with if the arbitration agreement is contained in a document transmitted from one party to the other party provided that, in accordance with common usage, that document is considered to become part of the contract if no objection is raised.[54] Consequently, arbitration agreements concluded orally and later confirmed by one party in a confirmation letter, not simply an invoice, will fulfil the form requirement.[55] Under s. 1031 subs. 3 of the GCCP, the form requirement is also fulfilled by a general reference to general conditions containing an arbitration clause in a contract complying with the form requirements of subss. 1 and 2, 'provided that the reference is such as to make that clause part of the contract' and if the other side has a reasonable chance to take note of the arbitration agreement.[56] This is, for example, assumed, if the other side is in the possession of the standard terms and conditions.[57]

Section 1031 subs. 4 of the GCCP contains a special provision relating to bills of lading, commonly encountered in maritime transport. It retains, in principle, the opportunity for carriers of maritime cargo to enter into arbitration agreements with third parties, to whom they have issued bills of lading, even if the arbitration agreement is only contained in the charter contract between the carrier and charterer.[58]

In cases of consumer involvement, s. 1031 subs. 5 of the GCCP requires particular attention. Subsection 5 requires that the arbitration agreement to which a consumer is a party must be contained in a separate document that has been personally signed by the parties and which does not contain any other agreement, unless it is notarized.[59] Electronic signatures are permissible.[60]

[54] Hanefeld, 'Chapter 7: Germany', p. 479, para. 7.12; Kröll and Kraft, 'Ten Years', 459.

[55] Kröll and Kraft, 'Ten Years', 459; see, e.g., OLG Hamburg, Decision of 4 December 2008 – 6 Sch 12/08, available at www.dis-arb.de; OLG Hamburg, Decision of 25 January 2008 – 6 Sch 07/07, *SchiedsVZ*, 7(2009), 71 *et seq.*

[56] Hanefeld, 'Chapter 7: Germany', p. 479, para. 7.14 with further references.

[57] R. Trittmann and I. Hanefeld, '§ 1031: Form of the Arbitration Agreement', in Böckstiegel, Kröll and Nacimiento (eds.), *Arbitration in Germany*, p. 133, para. 18; Hanefeld, 'Chapter 7: Germany', p. 480, para. 7.14 with further references.

[58] Trittmann and Hanefeld, '§ 1031: Form of the Arbitration Agreement', p. 134, para. 21

[59] For further details, ibid., p. 132, paras. 16 *et seq.*

[60] Ibid., p. 136, para. 27.

Non-compliance with the form requirement, in general, renders the arbitration agreement invalid. However, in view of the generally accepted principle of *non venire contra factum proprium*, s. 1031 subs. 6 of the GCCP provides that formal defects are cured where a party enters into the argument on the substance of the dispute in arbitral proceedings without challenging the formal validity of the agreement. A general challenge to the tribunal's jurisdiction is not sufficient to preserve the right of a party to rely on the formal invalidity of the arbitration agreement.[61]

6 Interference/support by the courts (including the tribunal's powers to involve them)

Irrespective of the fact that an arbitration agreement excludes the jurisdiction of the state courts for the action on the merits (s. 1032 GCCP), courts can play an important supportive and supervisory role in the arbitral proceedings. The functions assigned to the courts are enumerated in the arbitration law and s. 1026 of the GCCP restricts the courts' interference in the arbitral proceedings to those instances explicitly provided for in the 10th Book. A good overview on almost all provisions that allow for court interference is given in s. 1062 subs. 1, nos. 1–4 of the GCCP, determining which courts have jurisdiction for the various tasks entrusted to the courts by other provisions in the 10th Book.

Limited intervention is observed by the courts, at least as far as supervisory powers are concerned.[62] In general, courts refrain from intervening in the arbitral process without being explicitly empowered to do so. By contrast, as regards to their supportive functions, some courts have interpreted their powers broadly.[63]

The few supervisory powers granted to the courts are intended to safeguard the constitutional protection of the parties during the course of the arbitration process.[64] The supervision is thus restricted to the composition of the tribunal (challenge of an arbitrator, s. 1037 GCCP; equal influence on composition, s. 1034 subs. 2 GCCP; and termination

[61] Böckstiegel, Kröll and Nacimiento, 'Germany as a Place for International and Domestic Arbitrations', p. 27, para. 55; BGH, Decision of 29 June 2005 – III ZB 65/04, (2005) 3, *SchiedsVZ*, 259 *et seq.*

[62] Böckstiegel, Kröll and Nacimiento, 'Germany as a Place for International and Domestic Arbitrations', p. 50, para. 121.

[63] Ibid.

[64] Ibid., para. 123; H.-P. Schroeder, 'Introduction to §§ 1062–1065', in Böckstiegel, Kröll and Nacimiento (eds.), *Arbitration in Germany*, p. 577, para. 10.

of an arbitrator's appointment, s. 1038 GCCP), the judicial review of an arbitral tribunal's decision on its jurisdiction (s. 1040 subs. 3 GCCP) and the arbitral process (s. 1059 subs. 2, no. 1, lit. b–d GCCP). By contrast, the substantive outcome of the proceedings is, in principle, beyond the control of the court; that is, the review of the merits of an award is, in principle, excluded.[65]

The various supportive functions provided for in the German arbitration law are intended to remedy the two 'deficiencies' of arbitration: the lack of coercive powers and the non-existence of a readily available tribunal.[66]

One of the most important supportive functions of state courts in arbitral proceedings relates to the constitution of the arbitral tribunal. In the absence of an agreement by the parties or where the agreed procedure for appointment fails, the sole arbitrator or the presiding arbitrator is appointed upon request of a party by the competent OLG.[67]

As the arbitral tribunal lacks compulsory powers over the parties to the arbitration and over third parties, state courts may support arbitrations and act on behalf of the arbitral tribunal where the latter lacks the power to act.[68] This is the case when witnesses or experts are not willing to appear voluntarily before the arbitral tribunal or where an oath is to be taken (s. 1050 GCCP).[69] Further, state-court support is required for the enforcement of interim measures ordered by an arbitral tribunal if they are not complied with voluntarily (s. 1041 subs. 2 GCCP).[70] Furthermore, the courts themselves may grant at any time – that is, before or after an arbitral tribunal is constituted – interim relief where requested by a party (s. 1033 GCCP) (see *infra* Section 8).[71]

The court support provided for by s. 1050 of the GCCP (support in the taking of evidence) as well as the right to request interim measures of

[65] Schroeder, 'Introduction to §§ 1062–1065', p. 577, para. 11.

[66] Böckstiegel, Kröll and Nacimiento, 'Germany as a Place for International and Domestic Arbitrations: General Overview', p. 50, para. 124; Schroeder, 'Introduction to §§ 1062–1065', p. 576, para. 8.

[67] See *supra* Sections 3.1 and 4.1; in detail see Nacimiento and A. Abt, '§ 1035: Appointment of Arbitrators', in Böckstiegel, Kröll and Nacimiento (eds.), *Arbitration in Germany*, pp. 190 *et seq*.

[68] Böckstiegel, Kröll and Nacimiento, 'Germany as a Place for International and Domestic Arbitrations', p. 51, para. 126.

[69] Ibid.; Hanefeld, 'Chapter 7 – Germany', p. 505 para. 7112.

[70] Böckstiegel, Kröll and Nacimiento, 'Germany as a Place for International and Domestic Arbitrations – General Overview', p. 51 para. 126.

[71] Wilske, 'Ad hoc Arbitration in Germany', p. 809 at p. 820 para. 22.

protection from the courts (s. 1033 GCCP) is also available in arbitral proceedings in which the place of arbitration is situated outside Germany (s. 1025 subs. 2 GCCP).[72]

In addition, pursuant to s. 1032 subs. 2 of the GCCP, parties may seek the support of the court to determine, before the tribunal has been appointed, whether or not arbitral proceedings are admissible or inadmissible.[73]

Pursuant to s. 1062 of the GCCP, the jurisdiction for nearly all arbitration-related proceedings is concentrated at the OLG; some *Bundesländer* (federal states) have assigned the functions to a special senate at a particular higher regional court. This ensures that the various court proceedings in support and in supervision of the arbitral proceedings are conducted in a swift and efficient manner. Only assistance in the taking of evidence is assigned to the *Amtsgerichte* (the 'AG': the local courts).

Section 1063 of the GCCP provides that all decisions are taken in the form of an order, with the consequence that no oral hearing is required, except where a party applies for the setting aside of an arbitral award pursuant to s. 1059 of the GCCP.[74] In addition, to ensure a speedy conduct of the arbitral proceeding, court proceedings are usually restricted to one instance. At the pre-award stage, the *Rechtsbeschwerde* (complaints on points of law) to the *Bundesgerichtshof* (the 'BGH': the Federal Court of Justice) are only available with regard to actions on the admissibility or non-admissibility of arbitral proceedings or the determination of the tribunal's jurisdiction.[75] The availability of such recourse is further limited by ss. 1065, 574 subss. 1 and 2, pursuant to which the action is only admissible if it is either of primary importance or necessary to develop the law or if a decision from the Federal Court of Justice is required to ensure consistent jurisprudence.

7 Tribunal's powers *ex officio*

Most of the arbitral tribunal's powers *ex officio* are described in more detail in other sections of this chapter. In summary, under German arbitration law, the arbitral tribunal's powers include:

[72] Böckstiegel, Kröll and Nacimiento, 'Germany as a Place for International and Domestic Arbitrations', p. 51 para. 127; Hanefeld, 'Chapter 7 – Germany', p. 479 para. 7.150.

[73] For more details, see *infra* Section 15.

[74] H. Becker and R. Schartl, '§ 1063: General Provisions', in Böckstiegel, Kröll and Nacimiento (eds.), *Arbitration in Germany*, at p. 607, para. 11.

[75] Böckstiegel, Kröll and Nacimiento, 'Germany as a Place for International and Domestic Arbitrations', p. 51, para. 127.

(a) The power to rule on its own jurisdiction and, in this connection, on the existence or validity of the arbitration agreement (s. 1040 GCCP);
(b) Unless otherwise agreed by the parties, and at the request of a party, the power to order such interim measures of protection as it may consider necessary in respect of the subject matter of the dispute (s. 1041 GCCP, see *infra* Section 8);
(c) Failing an agreement by the parties, the power to conduct the arbitration in such a manner as it considers appropriate (s. 1042 GCCP, see *infra* Section 10);
(d) In the absence of an agreement by the parties, the power to determine the place of arbitration (s. 1043 GCCP);
(e) In the absence of an agreement by the parties, the power to determine the language or languages to be used in the proceedings (s. 1045 GCCP);
(f) Unless otherwise agreed by the parties, the power to appoint one or more experts to report to it on specific issues to be determined by the arbitral tribunal (s. 1049 GCCP);
(g) The power to request from a court, assistance in taking evidence or the performance of other judicial acts which the arbitral tribunal is not empowered to carry out (s. 1050 GCCP);
(h) The power to decide on the dispute in accordance with such rules of law as are chosen by the parties as applicable to the substance of the dispute (s. 1051 GCCP), or failing a designation by the parties, in accordance with the law of the state with which the subject matter of the proceedings is most closely connected;
(i) If, during arbitral proceedings, the parties settle the dispute, the power to terminate the proceedings and, if so requested by the parties, the power to record the settlement in the form of an arbitral award on agreed terms (s. 1054 GCCP); and
(j) The power to allocate, by means of an arbitral award, the costs of the arbitration as between the parties, including those incurred by the parties necessary for the proper pursuit of their claim or defence (s. 1057 GCCP).

The DIS Arbitration Rules also explicitly empower the arbitral tribunal to assess, at its due discretion, the amount in dispute, which is the basis for fixing the arbitrators' fees and the DIS's administrative fees.[76] The

[76] See s. 40 subs. 2 DIS Arbitration Rules.

arbitral tribunal will usually assess the amount by reference to the specific relief requested or in consultation with the parties. If the arbitral tribunal and the parties do not reach agreement on the assessment, the arbitral tribunal determines the amount at its own discretion. If the parties consider the assessment to be grossly unreasonable, they may, at least to the extent that German law applies to the proceedings, have the assessment reviewed pursuant to s. 319 of the BGB.[77]

8 The possibility of interim measures and their enforceability

German arbitration law provides along with the DIS Arbitration Rules for a dual system to seek interim measures of protection.[78] In order to ensure that in all cases an effective protection can be obtained, parties may seek interim relief from the arbitral tribunal or the state courts (s. 1033 GCCP). The same applies for arbitral proceedings under the DIS Arbitration Rules (s. 20 DIS Arbitration Rules). Possible conflicts between interim relief ordered by a state court and similar orders by a private arbitrational tribunal are resolved by s. 1041 subs. 2, s. 1062 subs. 1, no. 3 of the GCCP, which provide that the competent OLG can allow for the execution of interim orders issued by an arbitral tribunal, unless the same party has already applied for such relief to an AG or *Landgericht* (an 'LG': a regional court). The court may amend such an order, if it is deemed necessary for enforcement of the measure.[79]

In practice, the majority of applications are filed with the state courts.[80] In particular, when the tribunal has not yet been constituted or when it is likely that the measure will have to be enforced, state courts are, generally, the more appropriate forum.[81] However, state courts are limited to those types of interim measure of protection provided for in ss. 916 *et seq.* of the GCCP: attachment measures (*Arrest*) or interim injunctions (*einstweilige Verfügung*).[82]

[77] Bredow and Mulder, '§ 40: Costs of Arbitral Proceedings', p. 793, para. 3.
[78] Wilske, 'Ad hoc Arbitration in Germany', p. 820, para. 22.
[79] Böckstiegel, Kröll and Nacimiento, 'Germany as a Place for International and Domestic Arbitrations', p. 43, para. 102.
[80] Ibid.; see also Hanefeld, 'Chapter 7: Germany', p. 510, para. 7.137.
[81] Hanefeld, 'Chapter 7: Germany', p. 510, para. 7.137.
[82] Ibid., para. 7.136; for details see R. Kreindler and J. Schäfer, '§ 1033: Arbitration Agreement and Interim Measures by Court', in Böckstiegel, Kröll and Nacimiento (eds.), *Arbitration in Germany*, p. 162, paras. 13 *et seq.*

The arbitral tribunal, by contrast, may, according to s. 1041 of the GCCP or s. 20 of the DIS Arbitration Rules, order such interim or preventive measures as it considers necessary in respect of the subject matter of the dispute, unless that power is excluded by the parties.[83] This is understood to exclude 'anti-suit injunctions' as they serve to protect the arbitral process rather than the subject matter of the dispute.[84] Where the measures ordered are not known in German courts, they will not be enforced by the courts but will be transformed into such measures for the purpose of enforcement.

Under German arbitration law and the DIS Arbitration Rules, the arbitral tribunal may grant an interim measure only on the motion of a party and not *sua sponte*.[85] In addition, the arbitral tribunal must be satisfied that it has *prima facie* jurisdiction concerning the subject matter and the scope of the interim measure.[86]

The substantive requirements that have to be met are limited to the 'necessity' requirement stipulated in s. 1041 of the GCCP and s. 20 of the DIS Arbitration Rules.[87] In practice, this requirement is often understood to mean that there is a risk that the applicant's rights might be infringed.[88] Moreover, it is required that the interim measure relates to the subject matter of the dispute.[89] In addition, the interim measure may, in general, not pre-empt the dispute, unless the applicant would otherwise suffer irreparable harm.[90] The applicant has to show *prima facie* (*Glaubhaftmachung*) that his allegations are correct.[91]

[83] R. Kreindler and J. Schäfer, '§ 1041: Interim Measures of Protection', in Böckstiegel, Kröll and Nacimiento (eds.), *Arbitration in Germany*, p. 263, paras. 2 *et seq.*; Böckstiegel, Kröll and Nacimiento, 'Germany as a Place for International and Domestic Arbitrations', p. 44, para. 104; Hanefeld, 'Chapter 7: Germany', p. 510, para. 7.136.

[84] Kreindler and Schäfer, '§ 1041: Interim Measures of Protection', p. 266, para. 13.

[85] Ibid., p. 263, para. 15; Hanefeld, 'Chapter 7: Germany', p. 509, para. 7.132.

[86] Kreindler and Schäfer, '§ 1041: Interim Measures of Protection', p. 265, para. 8; Hanefeld, 'Chapter 7: Germany', p. 509, para. 7.132.

[87] Kreindler and Schäfer, '§ 1041: Interim Measures of Protection', p. 266, para. 12; Hanefeld, 'Chapter 7: Germany', p. 510, para. 7.133.

[88] Kreindler and Schäfer, '§ 1041: Interim Measures of Protection', p. 266, para. 12; Hanefeld, 'Chapter 7: Germany', p. 510, para. 7.133.

[89] Kreindler and Schäfer, '§ 1041: Interim Measures of Protection', p. 266, para. 13; Hanefeld, 'Chapter 7: Germany', p. 510, para. 7.133.

[90] Kreindler and Schäfer, '§ 1041: Interim Measures of Protection', p. 266, para. 14; Hanefeld, 'Chapter 7: Germany', p. 510, para. 7.133.

[91] Kreindler and Schäfer, '§ 1033: Arbitration Agreement and Interim Measures by Court', p. 167, paras. 30 *et seq.*; Hanefeld, 'Chapter 7: Germany', p. 510, para. 7.134.

According to the prevailing view, the arbitral tribunal is empowered to proceed *ex parte* without a prior hearing of the other party, as s. 1063 subs. 3 of the GCCP even allows the presiding judge of the civil court to enforce an interim measure issued by an arbitral tribunal without a prior hearing of the other side.[92] In any event, the arbitral tribunal must give the opposing party *ex post* an effective opportunity to present its case.[93]

Furthermore, the arbitral tribunal may require any party to provide appropriate security in connection with such a measure (s. 1041 subs. 1, sentence 2, GCCP or s. 20 subs. 1, sentence 2, DIS Arbitration Rules). If an interim measure of protection ordered by the arbitral tribunal proves to have been unjustified from the outset, the party, who obtained its enforcement, is obliged to compensate the other party for damages resulting from the enforcement or from his security payment in order to avoid enforcement (s. 1041 subs. 4, sentence 1, GCCP).

9 Multi-party arbitration (including joinder and consolidation)

In the context of multi-party arbitration, the following scenarios may be distinguished[94]: first, arbitration proceedings in which claims are raised by several claimants or against several respondents. Second, cases in which several claims in a chain are combined in one proceeding, as it may be desirable in disputes between the principal, the general contractor and its subcontractors.[95] To combine the proceedings of the principal against the general contractor and its subcontractors may especially be desirable for the general contractor in order to avoid conflicting decisions.[96]

Irrespective of the fact that German arbitration law does not contain an explicit provision on the conduct of multi-party arbitration, such arbitrations are a frequent occurrence in German arbitration practice.[97]

92 Kreindler and Schäfer, '§ 1041: Interim Measures of Protection', p. 268, para. 19; Hanefeld, 'Chapter 7: Germany', p. 509, para. 7.138.

93 Ibid.

94 A special kind of multi-party arbitration proceeding form corporate law disputes; i.e. cases in which a claim has to be raised by a shareholder against its company and in which all other shareholders will be bound by the arbitral award (see *infra* Section 9.2).

95 Nacimiento and Abt, '§ 1035: Appointment of Arbitrators', p. 202, paras. 34 *et seq.*

96 Ibid., para. 35.

97 Hanefeld, 'Chapter 7: Germany', p. 483, para. 7.22; Böckstiegel, Kröll and Nacimiento, 'Germany as a Place for International and Domestic Arbitrations', p. 60, para. 159.

The two crucial elements for the admissibility of multi-party arbitrations are (a) that all parties must have entered into an arbitration agreement, and (b) that the parties involved have equal influence on the composition of the arbitral tribunal.[98]

As regards the first element, it is generally accepted that in case of a multi-party contract providing for arbitration, the arbitration clause may usually be interpreted as contemplating multi-party arbitration.[99] Further, it is generally accepted that in chain contracts with separate arbitration agreements, a third party – following a third-party notice – may join arbitration proceedings if the parties to the arbitration consent to the third-party joinder.[100] This implies, on one hand, that a third party cannot (unless there is an existing multi-party arbitration agreement) be forced to join an arbitration proceeding.[101] Conversely, it implies that in the absence of any provisions for third-party intervention (*Nebenintervention*) or third-party notice on that party's own accord (*Streitverkündung*), a unilaterally declared joinder of a third party does not oblige the other parties or the arbitral tribunal to agree on this joinder.[102] However, the parties may – in exercising their autonomy – enter into an agreement on the joinder of a third party, either in the arbitration agreement itself or in the course of the proceedings.[103]

With respect to the consolidation of two or more pending arbitration proceedings, neither the German arbitration law nor the DIS Arbitration Rules contain any specific provision. Yet, it is the prevailing opinion that consolidation requires the consent of all parties and the arbitrators involved.[104]

As regards the second element – that is, the equal influence on the composition of the arbitral tribunal – the DIS Arbitration Rules and the German arbitration law offer different solutions.

[98] Hanefeld, 'Chapter 7: Germany', p. 483, para. 7.23 with further references; Lachmann, *Schiedsgerichtspraxis*, p. 664 at para. 2806 and at p. 667 para. 2818; H. Labes, 'Arbitration of Insurance Disputes in Germany', in Böckstiegel, Kröll and Nacimiento (eds.), *Arbitration in Germany*, p. 933 at p. 946, para. 50.

[99] Hanefeld, 'Chapter 7: Germany', p. 483, para. 7.23. [100] Ibid.

[101] Ibid.; K. Sachs and T. Lörcher, '§ 1042: General Rules of Procedure', in Böckstiegel, Kröll and Nacimiento (eds.), *Arbitration in Germany*, p. 277 at p. 293, para. 43; Labes, 'Arbitration of Insurance Disputes in Germany', p. 946, para. 50.

[102] Hanefeld, 'Chapter 7: Germany', p. 484, para. 7.25; S. H. Elsing, 'Streitverkündung und Schiedsverfahren', *SchiedsVZ*, 2(2004), 88 *et seq.*

[103] Hanefeld, 'Chapter 7: Germany', p. 484, para. 7.25; Elsing, 'Streitverkündung und Schiedsverfahren', 88 *et seq.*

[104] Hanefeld, 'Chapter 7: Germany', p. 484, para. 7.24 with further references.

9.1 German law

In *ad hoc* arbitration solutions for the specific problems occurring in the context of multi-party arbitration are – in the absence of an agreement by the parties – achieved by applying the general rules of the German arbitration law.[105] Here, any agreement that meets the requirements set out above – that is, that the parties involved have equal influence on the composition of the arbitral tribunal – is permissible.[106] In cases where the agreed appointment mechanism grants preponderant rights to one of the parties, s. 1034 subs. 2 of the GCCP cures the existing deficiency by giving the disadvantaged party the right to request the court to appoint the arbitrator or arbitrators in deviation from the nomination that has been made or from the agreed nomination procedure.

9.2 DIS Arbitration Rules

As the question of what constitutes an 'equal influence' appointment process is not yet finally determined in German case law, the DIS Arbitration Rules provide that all parties on one side must agree to the choice of the arbitrator; otherwise, the DIS Appointing Committee will choose the arbitrators for both sides (s. 13 subs. 1). The two arbitrators so appointed will then appoint the chairperson.

In addition, since 15 September 2009, the DIS has offered a specific set of supplementary rules (the 'Supplementary Rules for Corporate Law Disputes': SRCoLD) for a certain category of multi-party disputes; that is, corporate law disputes requiring a single decision binding all shareholders and the corporation in which a party intends to extend the effects of an arbitral award to all shareholders and the corporation.[107]

[105] Böckstiegel, Kröll and Nacimiento, 'Germany as a Place for International and Domestic Arbitrations', p. 60, para. 59.

[106] OLG Frankfurt, Decision of 24 November 2005 – 26 Sch 13/05, *SchiedsVZ*, 4(2006), 219 *et seq*.

[107] See for details on the new DIS-SRCoLD: J. Bredow, 'Arbitrating Shareholder Resolution Disputes in Germany: The New DIS-Supplementary Rules for Corporate Law Disputes ('DIS-SRCoLD')', in Sad Arbitrazowy przy Krajowej Izbie Gospodarczej (ed.), *Ksiega pamiatkowa: 60-lecia Sadu Arbitrazowego pzy Krajowej Izbie Gospodarczej w Warszawie* (Warsaw, LexisNexis Polska, 2010), pp. 469 *et seq*.; C. Borris, 'Die "Ergänzenden Regeln für gesellschaftsrechtliche Streitigkeiten" der DIS ("DIS-ERGeS")', *SchiedsVZ*, 7(2009), 299 *et seq*.; K. Schwedt, A.-J. Lilja and M. Schaper, 'Schiedsfähigkeit von Beschlussmängelstreitigkeiten: Die neuen Ergänzenden Regeln für gesellschaftsrechtliche Streitigkeiten der DIS', *NZG*, 12(2009), 1281 *et seq*.

The SRCoLD were adopted in reaction to a decision of the German Federal Court of Justice,[108] which clarified that shareholder-resolution disputes in limited-liability companies are arbitrable provided that certain procedural requirements are met. The requirements established by the court are that:

(a) The arbitration agreement must be contained in the articles of incorporation or in a separate agreement entered into by all shareholders and the corporation;
(b) The arbitration agreement must guarantee that all shareholders and the corporation receive notice of the commencement of the arbitral proceeding and that they are continuously informed of the progress of the proceeding so as to allow them to participate in the proceeding at any time;
(c) The arbitration agreement ensures that all shareholders that choose to participate in the arbitral proceeding have the opportunity to participate in the selection of the arbitrators; and
(d) The arbitration agreement ensures that all disputes with the same subject matter will be decided on in the same arbitral proceeding by the same arbitral tribunal.

The DIS-SRCoLD implements these requirements and provides, in particular, for the following:

(a) In the statement of claim, the claimant must identify not only the respondent, but also all shareholders for whom the arbitral award will have a binding effect (concerned others);
(b) The DIS secretariat submits the statement of claim to all parties and others concerned and gives the identified other persons concerned the opportunity to join the proceedings within 30 days on the side of the claimant or respondent;
(c) Thirty days after the statement of claim has been served on the respondent and on the identified concerned others, or 30 days after a concerned other has validly joined the proceedings, the claimant side or the respondent side may each nominate one co-arbitrator. If, on the claimant's or respondent's side there is more than one party involved, they have to jointly nominate an arbitrator.

[108] BGH, Decision of 6 April 2009 – II ZR 255/08 ('Arbitrability II'), *SchiedsVZ*, 7(2009), 233 *et seq.* and *NJW*, 62(2009), 1962 *et seq.* English abstract by P. Kraft, *Int. A.L.R.*, 13(2010), N-1 *et seq.*

If either the claimants or the respondents cannot agree on a joint arbitrator, the DIS appointing committee will nominate both co-arbitrators. The co-arbitrators will then nominate the chairperson. If the arbitral tribunal consists only of one arbitrator, this arbitrator has either to be nominated jointly by all parties involved or – if the parties cannot agree on an arbitrator – the arbitrator will be appointed by the DIS appointing committee.

(d) The arbitral tribunal informs other persons concerned, who can be identified and who have not joined the arbitral proceeding, on the progress of the arbitral proceeding by delivering copies of written pleadings of the parties or interveners, as well as on decisions and procedural orders by the arbitral tribunal, unless the others concerned have expressly waived in writing receiving this information.

(e) Others concerned may join the arbitral proceedings at any later stage, provided they do not challenge the constitution of the arbitral tribunal; and

(f) In the event that more than one arbitration is filed against the same shareholders' resolution, the first arbitral proceedings block any subsequent proceedings and the parties of the subsequent proceedings may join the prevailing proceedings.

10 Conduct of arbitration (terms of reference, number of briefs, disclosure, written or oral evidence, modality of hearings, applicable law)

10.1 German law

Section 1042 subs. 3 of the GCCP provides that – as a general rule – 'subject to the mandatory provisions of this book, the parties are free to determine the procedure themselves or by reference to a set of arbitration rules'. There exist only a few mandatory provisions under the German arbitration law.[109] They ensure that the basic requirements of due process are observed; that is, that the parties are treated equally and that each party has the opportunity of presenting its case.[110] The latter principle encompasses that counsel may not be excluded from representing the parties in the proceedings (see s. 1042 GCCP). The principle of

[109] Böckstiegel, Kröll and Nacimiento, 'Germany as a Place for International and Domestic Arbitrations', p. 37, para. 86; Hanefeld, 'Chapter 7: Germany', p. 494, para. 7.63 and p. 495 at paras. 7.65 *et seq.*

[110] Ibid.

equal treatment requires that the proceedings be conducted in an even-handed and impartial manner.[111] The right to be heard entails the right to be duly informed, the opportunity to comment on the relevant facts and points of law and the arbitral tribunal's obligation to take into account the parties' arguments.[112] The other mandatory rules of the German arbitration law include a mandatory court review of any unsuccessful challenges of arbitrators (s. 1037 subs. 3 GCCP) and the court's decision on the arbitral tribunal's jurisdiction (s.1032 subs. 2 and s. 1040 subs. 3 GCCP).[113]

The remaining provisions are mere default provisions, and the parties may freely determine all other procedural rules such as the commencement of the arbitral proceedings (s. 1044 GCCP), the language of the proceedings (s. 1045 GCCP), the time limits for the statements of claim and defence (s. 1046 GCCP), whether an oral hearing shall take place or the proceedings shall be on a document-only basis (s. 1047 GCCP), the effect of a default by one party (s. 1048 GCCP) and the appointment of experts (s. 1049 GCCP).[114] In practice, such choice is often made by the submission of the parties to institutional arbitration or by an agreement to apply rules that are internationally accepted such as the IBA Rules on the Taking of Evidence.[115] In these cases, the tribunal is bound to follow the procedure agreed upon and any deviation may constitute a reason to challenge the award or to resist its enforcement.

In the absence of a specific agreement by the parties, the default rules contained in ss. 1044 *et seq.* of the GCCP provide for a basic structure for the proceedings. Within this structure, however, the actual conduct of the proceedings is largely left to the discretion of the arbitral tribunal.[116] While for some issues such as, for example, the admissibility of amendments or supplements to claims or defences, the law expressly indicates which considerations should be taken into account, all other cases are to be decided on through the arbitral tribunal exercising its

[111] Sachs and Lörcher, '§ 1042: General Rules of Procedure', p. 280, para. 4.

[112] Hanefeld, 'Chapter 7: Germany', p. 495, para. 7.65; Sachs and Lörcher, '§ 1042: General Rules of Procedure', p. 281, paras. 8 *et seq.* with further references.

[113] Hanefeld, 'Chapter 7: Germany', p. 495, para. 7.66 with further references.

[114] Böckstiegel, Kröll and Nacimiento, 'Germany as a Place for International and Domestic Arbitrations', p. 37, para. 87; Hanefeld, 'Chapter 7: Germany', p. 495, para. 7.64.

[115] Böckstiegel, Kröll and Nacimiento, 'Germany as a Place for International and Domestic Arbitrations', p. 37, para. 87.

[116] The DIS Arbitration Rules follow the same basic structure but are a little more detailed and explicit on certain issues, see *infra* Section 10.2.

discretion. Again, the tribunal's wide discretion is only limited by the few mandatory provisions contained in ss. 1025–1066 of the GCCP.

In *ad hoc* proceedings – in particular, where parties from different legal backgrounds are involved – it is common practice that the tribunal consults the parties as to the procedural rules governing the proceedings. If an agreement cannot be reached, the arbitral tribunal will take procedural decisions of a certain importance together and, if necessary, by a majority vote.[117] This does not exclude the possibility of empowering the chairperson to make procedural decisions of more weight alone.[118]

Pursuant to s. 1043 subs. 1 of the GCCP, the arbitral tribunal may determine the place of arbitration and, thereby, potentially also the law governing the arbitral proceedings. Furthermore, in relation to the conduct of the proceedings, s. 1042 subs. 4 of the GCCP provides as a general rule that the 'arbitral tribunal shall conduct the arbitration in such a manner as it considers appropriate'. That includes *inter alia* – as is, in part, also specifically set out in other sections – the taking of evidence, the language of the proceedings, time limits for submissions, the necessity of an oral hearing and the appointment of experts.[119] The parties are free to agree on the law to be applied to the merits as well as to the arbitration agreement itself (s. 1051 GCCP).

In addition, the parties may determine the court that has jurisdiction for the various supportive and supervisory actions either by a specific forum selection clause or by determining the place of arbitration (s. 1062 subs. 1 GCCP).

10.1.1 Written or oral evidence

In German civil litigation, documentary evidence has always been and remains to be the most important source of evidence (ss. 415 *et seq.* GCCP).[120] Documentary evidence is submitted as part of the parties'

[117] Böckstiegel, Kröll and Nacimiento, 'Germany as a Place for International and Domestic Arbitrations', p. 37, para. 88; Hanefeld, 'Chapter 7: Germany', p. 496, para. 7.68; F. von Schlabrendorff and A. Sessler, '§ 1052: Decision Making by the Panel of Arbitrators', in Böckstiegel, Kröll and Nacimiento (eds.), *Arbitration in Germany*, p. 363 at p. 369, paras. 14 *et seq*.

[118] Böckstiegel, Kröll and Nacimiento, 'Germany as a Place for International and Domestic Arbitrations', p. 37, para. 88.

[119] Ibid.

[120] R. Trittmann, 'Basics and Differences of the Continental and Common Law System and State Court Proceedings', in Böckstiegel, K. P. Berger and J. Bredow (eds.), *The Taking of Evidence in International Commercial Arbitration* (Cologne: Carl Heymanns Verlag, 2010), p. 15 at p. 18.

pleadings in support of their factual allegations. However, the provisions on the taking of evidence in civil courts (ss. 355 *et seq.* GCCP) only apply if the arbitration agreement or procedural rules expressly provide for the inclusion of these rules.[121]

10.1.2 Number of briefs

Unless otherwise agreed by the parties, s. 1044 sentence 2 of the GCCP provides the minimum requirements that a request for arbitration must fulfil. It shall state the names of the parties, the subject matter of the dispute and contain a reference to the arbitration agreement. The German arbitration law does not stipulate any specific form requirements.[122] Even though the law does not establish specific form requirements as to the submission of the request for arbitration, the claimant is well advised to choose a means of delivery that ensures that a record of receipt is established.[123] Unless otherwise agreed by the parties, arbitral proceedings commence on the date on which a request for the particular dispute to be referred to arbitration is received by the respondent (s. 1044 sentence 1 GCCP). The commencement of arbitration proceedings has the legal effect of suspending the applicable limitation period if German law is applicable with regard to the substance of the dispute (see s. 204 subs. 1, no. 11, BGB).[124]

With respect to the subsequent statement of claim, s. 1046 subs. 1, sentence 1 of the GCCP provides that within the period of time agreed by the parties or determined by the arbitral tribunal, the claimant shall state his claim and the facts supporting the claim in his statement of claim.[125]

With respect to the statement of defence, s. 1046 subs. 1, sentence 1 of the GCCP provides that the respondent, within the period of time agreed by the parties or determined by the arbitral tribunal, shall state his defence in respect of the particularities contained in the statement of claim.[126]

The parties usually submit all documentary evidence that they consider to be relevant with their statements (s. 1046 subs. 1, sentence 2, GCCP).[127] There are no specific time limits foreseen for the parties'

[121] Ibid.

[122] K. Sachs and T. Lörcher, '§ 1044: Commencement of Arbitral Proceedings', in Böckstiegel, Kröll and Nacimiento (eds.), *Arbitration in Germany*, p. 302 at p. 303, para. 8 with further references.

[123] Hanefeld, 'Chapter 7: Germany', p. 498, para. 7.77.

[124] Sachs and Lörcher, '§ 1044: Commencement of Arbitral Proceedings', p. 304, para. 9.

[125] Hanefeld, 'Chapter 7: Germany', p. 498, para. 7.78.

[126] Ibid., para. 7.79.

[127] Trittmann, 'Basics and Differences of the Continental and Common Law System and State Court Proceedings', p. 23.

submissions and they will vary depending on the complexity of the dispute and other relevant circumstances.[128]

Section 1046 subs. 2 of the GCCP empowers the arbitral tribunal to reject any late amendments or supplements to the claim and defence during the course of the proceedings if they would delay the proceedings without sufficient justification.[129] If any party fails to appear at an oral hearing or to produce documentary evidence within a set time limit, the arbitral tribunal may continue the proceedings and make the award on the evidence before it (s. 1048 subs. 3 GCCP).[130]

Furthermore, all statements, documents or information supplied by one party to the arbitral tribunal as well as any expert report or evidentiary documents must be communicated to both parties (s. 1047 subs. 3 GCCP).

10.1.3 Disclosure

The arbitral tribunal has the discretion to decide what kind of documents and in which form documents are to be presented to it.[131] Pursuant to s. 1045 subs. 2 of the GCCP, the arbitral tribunal may request that any documentary evidence shall be accompanied by a translation into the language of the arbitral proceedings. In practice, it is for the parties to submit to the arbitral tribunal all documents on which they wish to rely.[132] The original document only needs to be produced if its authenticity is contested.[133]

Discovery procedures such as those used in the United States of America are not known in German civil procedure.[134] However, the parties are free to agree to a full US discovery procedure.[135] In the absence of an express agreement by the parties, the arbitral tribunal might risk that its award is successfully challenged, if it ordered a full discovery procedure *sua sponte*.[136]

[128] Hanefeld, 'Chapter 7: Germany', p. 498, para. 7.81. [129] Ibid., p. 500, para. 7.88.

[130] Ibid. [131] Ibid., p. 505, para. 7.114.

[132] Ibid.; see also Trittmann, 'Basics and Differences of the Continental and Common Law System and State Court Proceedings', pp. 16 and 23.

[133] Hanefeld, 'Chapter 7: Germany', p. 505, para. 7.114.

[134] Trittmann, 'Basics and Differences of the Continental and Common Law System and State Court Proceedings', p. 18; Hanefeld, 'Chapter 7: Germany', p. 506, para. 7.117.

[135] K. Sachs and T. Lörcher, '§ 1047: Oral Hearings and Written Proceedings', in Böckstiegel, Kröll and Nacimiento (eds.), *Arbitration in Germany*, p. 318 at p. 326, para. 23.

[136] Hanefeld, 'Chapter 7: Germany', p. 505, para. 7.118; W. Voit, '§ 1042: Allgemeine Verfahrensregeln', in Musielak (ed.), *Kommentar zur Zivilprozessordnung*, p. 2474 at

The arbitral tribunal is not vested with compulsory powers to force a party to produce documents. However, it may request a state court to compel a party to produce a document pursuant to s. 1050 of the GCCP. Alternatively, the arbitral tribunal may continue the proceedings and make the award on the evidence before it (s. 1048 subs. 3 GCCP). When making the award, the arbitral tribunal may treat the failure to produce documentary evidence without a valid excuse as an admission of the other party's allegation.[137]

10.1.4 Modality of hearings

Under German arbitration law, in the absence of an agreement by the parties, the arbitral tribunal is empowered to decide whether or not an oral hearing is to be held (s. 1047 subs. 1 GCCP). There exists no obligation to hold an oral hearing.[138] The parties may agree that the arbitral proceedings shall be conducted on a document-only basis (s. 1047 subs. 1 GCCP). However, at the request of a party, the arbitral tribunal is obliged to hold an oral hearing.[139] In arbitral practice, the conduct of an oral hearing is the rule rather than the exception.

If an oral hearing or any other meeting of the arbitral tribunal for the purpose of taking evidence is conducted, the parties must be given sufficient notice in advance (s. 1047 subs. 2 GCCP). If any party fails to appear at an oral hearing or to produce documentary evidence within a set time limit, the arbitral tribunal may continue the proceedings and make the award on the evidence before it (s. 1048 subs. 3 GCCP). The parties may agree otherwise on the consequences of default (s. 1048 subs. 4, sentence 2, GCCP).

Regarding the conduct of the hearing itself, a common law lawyer should not be surprised if a totally German arbitral tribunal takes a more active approach to the conduct of the hearings than he is used to. Regarding the

p. 2483, para. 26 with further references; R. A. Schütze, 'Two Issues of Taking Evidence in International Arbitration Under Civil and Common Law Systems: Production of Documents and Examination of Witnesses', in R. A. Schütze (ed.), *Ausgewählte Probleme des deutschen und internationalen Schiedsverfahrensrechts* (Cologne: Carl Heymanns Verlag, 2006), p. 71 at 77 *et seq.* for the hearing of witnesses in the common-law tradition.

[137] See also art. 9 subs. 5 of the 2010 IBA Rules on the Taking of Evidence that stipulates comparable consequences.

[138] Hanefeld, 'Chapter 7: Germany', p. 505, para. 7.67; Lachmann, *Schiedsgerichtspraxis*, p. 392 at para. 1586.

[139] Sachs and Lörcher, '§ 1047: Oral Hearings and Written Proceedings', p. 319, paras. 3 *et seq.*; see OLG Naumburg, Decision of 21 February 2002 – 10 Sch 8/01, *NJW-RR*, 18(2003), 71 *et seq.*

taking of witness evidence, the arbitral tribunal – in the absence of an agreement of the parties to the contrary – has discretion as to whether or not written witness statements shall be admitted. In arbitral practice, written witness statements have become accepted practice.[140] Preparation of witnesses is admissible, yet in German arbitration proceedings this is not the rule.[141] Witness preparation has its limits, where it amounts to witness manipulation or the fabrication of evidence.[142] US-style cross-examination is not known to German civil procedure. It is, however, within the parties' and the arbitrators' autonomy to allow for a cross-examination.[143] To ensure a fair proceeding and in order to give the parties equal opportunity to prepare for a cross-examination, the arbitral tribunal should give prior notice to the witness and the parties' counsel of its intention to allow for cross-examination.

Under German arbitration law, the arbitral tribunal is not empowered to take an oath from a witness. However, pursuant to s. 1050, the arbitral tribunal or a party with the approval of the arbitral tribunal may apply for assistance of the state courts in the taking of an oath or the affirmation in lieu of an oath.[144]

As for experts, s. 1049 of the GCCP stipulates that, under German arbitration law, experts are, in principle, appointed by the arbitral tribunal. The arbitral tribunal may appoint one or more experts to report to it on specific issues to be determined by the arbitral tribunal, unless the parties agreed otherwise (s. 1049 sub. 1, sentence 1, GCCP). The arbitral tribunal may also require a party to give the expert any relevant information or to produce, or to provide access to any relevant documents or property for his inspection (s. 1049 subs. 2, sentence 1, GCCP). The arbitral tribunal's power does not prevent the parties from appointing their own experts.[145] Unless

[140] Sachs and Lörcher, '§ 1047: Oral Hearings and Written Proceedings', p. 323, para. 13.

[141] Lachmann, *Schiedsgerichtspraxis*, p. 375 at para. 1513 with reference to art. 4.3 of the IBA Rules on the Taking of Evidence; P. Schlosser, 'Verfahrensrechtliche und berufsrechtliche Zulässigkeit der Zeugenvorbereitung', *SchiedsVZ*, 2(2004), 225 at 228 *et seq.*

[142] Hanefeld, 'Chapter 7: Germany', p. 504, para. 7.104, Lachmann, *Schiedsgerichtspraxis*, p. 375 at para. 1515 with further references.

[143] Hanefeld, 'Chapter 7: Germany', p. 505, para. 7.110; Voit, '§ 1042: Allgemeine Verfahrensregeln', p. 2482, para. 23 with further references; Schütze, 'Two Issues of Taking Evidence', 77 *et seq.* for the hearing of witnesses in the common-law tradition.

[144] Hanefeld, 'Chapter 7: Germany', p. 505, para. 7.112; Sachs and Lörcher, '§ 1042: General Rules of Procedure', p. 292, para. 39.

[145] Hanefeld, 'Chapter 7: Germany', p. 508, para. 7.125; K. Sachs and T. Lörcher, '§ 1049: Experts Appointed by the Arbitral Tribunal', in Böckstiegel, Kröll and Nacimiento (eds.), *Arbitration in Germany*, p. 335 at p. 336, para. 3.

otherwise agreed by the parties, if a party so requests, or if the arbitral tribunal considers it necessary an expert shall, after delivery of his written or oral report, participate in an oral hearing where the parties have the opportunity to put questions to him and to present expert witnesses in order to testify on the points at issue (s. 1049 subs. 2 GCCP).[146]

In the absence of an agreement by the parties, it lies within the discretion of the arbitral tribunal as to whether or not and how the arbitral tribunal wishes to establish a record of the arbitral proceedings.[147] In arbitral practice, most arbitral tribunals establish a record of the oral hearing. Whether the arbitral tribunal will resort to tape recording, verbatim court reporters, dictated minutes or a short-summary protocol will depend on the nature and complexity of the dispute and other particularities of the case.[148]

10.1.5 Applicable substantive law

Pursuant to s. 1051 subs. 1, sentence 1 of the GCCP, the arbitral tribunal shall decide the dispute according to the rules of law agreed upon by the parties. The parties' choice of law shall be construed, unless otherwise expressed, as a direct reference to the substantive law of a state and not to its conflict-of-law rules (s. 1051 subs. 1, sentence 2, GCCP). Section 1051 of the GCCP gives the parties the freedom to also choose rules of law such as the UNIDROIT Principles of International Commercial Contracts 2010 in their entirety or partially.[149] The tribunal shall always take into account the usages of the trade applicable to the transaction (s. 1051 subs. 4 GCCP).

Failing a designation by the parties of the applicable substantive law, the German arbitration law contains autonomous conflict-of-law provisions pursuant to which the tribunal shall apply the law of the state with which the subject matter of the proceedings has the closest connection (s. 1051 subs. 2 GCCP). The closest-connection test is an objective test.[150] This commonly accepted rule of private international law will

[146] Hanefeld, 'Chapter 7: Germany', p. 508, para. 7.126.

[147] Sachs and Lörcher, '§ 1047: Oral Hearings and Written Proceedings', p. 321, para. 8.

[148] Hanefeld, 'Chapter 7: Germany', p. 504, para. 7.111.

[149] Bill on the Reform of the Law Relating to Arbitral Proceedings, published in BT-Drs. 13/5274, p. 52 available in German at www.dis-arb.de, Materials section, last visited on 20 December 2010; B. Friedrich, '§ 1051: Rules Applicable to Substance of Dispute', in Böckstiegel, Kröll and Nacimiento (eds.), *Arbitration in Germany*, p. 346 at p. 352, paras. 19 *et seq*.

[150] Hanefeld, 'Chapter 7: Germany', p. 520, para. 7.84.

usually lead to the application of the law where the party rendering the characteristic performance of the contract has its seat or residence.[151]

The arbitral tribunal may not decide a dispute *ex aequo et bono* or as *amiable compositeur* unless expressly authorized by the parties to do so (s. 1051 subs. 3 GCCP). Such authorization may not be inferred from the parties' request to propose a settlement[152] but must be given explicitly, that is unambiguously and in a crystal-clear manner.[153] If the tribunal decides *ex aequo et bono* without the express authorization by the parties, the award may be challenged.[154]

10.2 DIS arbitration

As for the conduct of the arbitration under the DIS Arbitration Rules, reference may be made to what has been said regarding German arbitration law (see *supra* at 10.1). In essence, it may be said that the arbitration procedure under the DIS Arbitration Rules is very flexible and combines a high degree of party autonomy with full independence of the arbitral tribunal in the conduct of the proceedings. There exist two distinct features of the DIS Arbitration Rules that deserve mentioning.

It is one of the special characteristics of the DIS Arbitration Rules that every stage of the proceedings should seek to encourage amicable settlement of the dispute or of individual issues in dispute (s. 32 subs. 1 DIS Arbitration Rules). In fact, approximately 30% of all DIS arbitrations result in such a settlement.[155]

The wording of s. 32.1 of the DIS Arbitration Rules should not be understood to mean that it is the main task of the arbitral tribunal to urge the parties to settle the dispute amicably. The arbitrators are mainly

151 Friedrich, '§ 1051: Rules Applicable to Substance of Dispute', p. 358, paras. 40 *et seq.*

152 Hanefeld, 'Chapter 7: Germany', p. 519, para. 7.181; OLG München, Decision of 22 June 2005 – 34 Sch 10/05, *SchiedsVZ*, 3(2005), 308, 309 *et seq.*; Friedrich, '§ 1051: Rules Applicable to Substance of Dispute', p. 360, para. 54.

153 Hanefeld, 'Chapter 7: Germany', p. 519, para. 7.181; J. Münch, '§ 1051 Anwendbares Recht', in T. Rauscher, P. Wax and J. Wenzel (eds.), *Münchener Kommentar Zivilprozessordnung §§ 803–1066 EGZPO, GVG, EGGVG, IZPR* (Munich: Verlag C.H. Beck, 2001), p. 1305 at p. 1316, para. 20.

154 Lachmann, *Schiedsgerichtspraxis*, p. 414 at para. 1677.

155 Approximately 30% of all DIS proceedings are terminated by an award on agreed terms. See J. Bredow, 'Schiedsspruch mit vereinbartem Wortlaut: Form und Inhalt', *SchiedsVZ*, 8(2010), 295 at 295; see for *ad hoc* arbitration Böckstiegel, Kröll and Nacimiento, 'Germany as a Place for International and Domestic Arbitrations', p. 23, para. 45.

appointed in order to finally decide the dispute and, in the course of the arbitral proceedings, they should never give the impression to the parties that they are more interested in the parties entering into a settlement agreement than they are on deciding on the dispute through a final award.

Nevertheless, the arbitral tribunal should take into consideration that a settlement might be in the interests of both parties and it should address the issue once it has the impression that it is the right time to do so. However, before presenting a proposal for the settlement of the dispute, the arbitral tribunal should obtain the approval of the parties. Otherwise, the arbitral tribunal may run the risk that the manner of presentation of the settlement proposal or the settlement proposal itself will be regarded as a sign of partiality and lead to the challenge against an arbitrator or against the whole arbitral tribunal. By obliging the arbitrators to seek to encourage a settlement at every stage of the proceedings, s. 32.1 of the DIS Arbitration Rules protects the arbitrators against the accusation of partiality in the event that they propose a settlement.[156]

In addition, since 1 April 2008, the DIS has offered the DIS-SREP.[157] In order to achieve their goal – that the arbitral proceedings should not last longer than six months (in the case of a sole arbitrator) or nine months (in the case of a three-member tribunal) – after filing the statement of the claim, the DIS-SREP contain a number of guiding procedural maxims that are intended to ensure and safeguard the route of the arbitral proceedings conducted under those Rules. The most important of these being:[158]

(a) Section 5 subs. 1 of the DIS-SREP provides that the arbitral tribunal shall, at the outset of the proceedings and in agreement with the parties, establish a schedule to ensure that the arbitral proceedings can be concluded within the six- or nine-month time frame;
(b) The exchange of written submissions is limited to the statement of claim within the meaning of s. 6 of the DIS Arbitration Rules and the statement of defence within the meaning of s. 9 of the DIS Arbitration Rules, as well as one further written submission by each party;
(c) Section 5 subs. 2 of the DIS-SREP provides that only one oral hearing, including any taking of evidence, shall be held; no further

[156] R. Kreindler, J. Schäfer and R. Wolff, *Schiedsgerichtsbarkeit: Kompendium für die Praxis* (Frankfurt am Main: Verlag Recht und Wirtschaft, 2006), p. 90 at para. 296.

[157] See *supra* Section 1.2.

[158] For a detailed description see Berger, 'The Need for Speed', 595 *et seq.*; J. Bredow, 'Without Delay', pp. 51 *et seq.*

written submissions ('post-hearing briefs') shall be exchanged after the closing of the oral hearing;

(d) Section 4 subs. 4 of the DIS-SREP provides that counter-claims and set-offs shall only be admissible with the consent of all parties and the arbitral tribunal; and

(e) Section 5 subs. 3 of the DIS-SREP requires the tribunal to take a proactive approach and, at the earliest possible stage of the proceedings and, as a rule, after each round of written submissions, to identify to the parties the issues it may regard as relevant and material for the outcome of the case.

11 Confidentiality

11.1 German arbitration law

The German arbitration law, just like its model – the UNCITRAL Model Law in International Commercial Arbitration – is silent on confidentiality issues. Consequently, according to the prevailing opinion among legal commentators, the parties are – unless any stipulation has been made to the contrary – not restricted from disclosing to the public the existence of arbitral proceedings or particular details thereof.[159] Accordingly, when drafting an *ad hoc* arbitration clause, the issue of confidentiality should be considered. However, in Germany it is a generally recognized principle that arbitrators in *ad hoc* proceedings are bound to treat the proceedings confidentially.[160]

11.2 DIS Arbitration Rules

In contrast, the DIS Arbitration Rules contain a detailed provision on confidentiality. Pursuant to s. 43 subs. 1 of the DIS Arbitration Rules, the duty of confidentiality rests on all participants in the proceedings: the parties, their legal representatives, the arbitrators, the persons assisting the parties or the arbitral tribunal in the conduct of the proceedings (e.g. secretarial staff, translators etc.) and the persons at the DIS secretariat

[159] Lachmann, *Schiedsgerichtspraxis*, pp. 41 *et seq.* at paras. 143–51; Wilske, 'Ad hoc Arbitration in Germany', p. 824, para. 30.

[160] Wilske, 'Ad hoc Arbitration in Germany', p. 824, para. 30; Lachmann, *Schiedsgerichtspraxis*, p. 42 at para. 145; BGH, Decision of 5 May 1986 – III ZR 233/84, *BGHZ*, 98(1985), 32 at 35.

involved in administering the proceedings. Not included in this list, however, are witnesses and experts.[161]

Confidentiality includes the duty to refrain from passing information to anyone not involved in the proceedings. The duty of confidentiality does not prevent any participant from complying with statutory duties of information where such duties take precedence or where the parties have agreed to exclude confidentiality.[162]

If a request for information about an arbitration is addressed to the German Institution of Arbitration (the DIS) by someone not involved in the proceedings, the DIS will inform the parties accordingly and ask them if the requested information may be submitted to the third party. Unless the parties consent expressly, the DIS will not provide the information requested.[163]

However, since under German law the obligation on the DIS to maintain the confidentiality of the proceedings does not create a privilege to deny access to the information, the DIS will have to produce the requested information or documents if a third party – for example, a public prosecutor – requests information on the basis of a court order requiring the DIS to produce the information in question.

Pursuant to s. 43 subs. 2 of the DIS Arbitration Rules, the DIS retains the right to publish statistical information on the development of DIS arbitration to the extent that no specific data concerning individual cases can be discerned from it.

12 Institution's role

The German Institution of Arbitration (the DIS) is a registered association with its seat in Berlin,[164] whose roots go as far back as 1920. The main secretariat is situated in Cologne. The DIS, in its current form, is the result of a merger between the German Arbitration Committee and the German Arbitration Institute on 1 January 1992.

161 J. Bredow and I. Mulder, 'Section 43: Confidentiality', in Böckstiegel, Kröll and Nacimiento (eds.), *Arbitration in Germany*, p. 803 at p. 803, para. 2; Kreindler, Schäfer and Wolff, *Schiedsgerichtsbarkeit*, p. 90 at paras. 299 *et seq.*

162 J. Bredow, 'Part O: Schiedsgerichtsordnung der DIS', in H. Kronke, W. Melis and A. K. Schnyder (eds.), *Handbuch Internationales Wirtschaftsrecht* (Cologne: Verlag Dr Otto Schmidt, 2005), p. 1947 at p. 1969, para. 631.

163 Bredow and Mulder, 'Section 43 – Confidentiality', p. 803, para. 4.

164 The DIS Statutes may be downloaded from the DIS website at wwww.dis-arb.de, last visited on 20 December 2010.

With more than 1,100 members domestically and overseas, including numerous major trade organisations and chambers of commerce, leading German companies, judges, lawyers and academics, the German Institution of Arbitration is the leading German arbitration institution. In 2011, 178 new proceedings were commenced at the DIS. The aggregate amount in dispute of all cases filed directly with the DIS in 2011 amounted to approximately EUR 3.333 billion, and to EUR 3.925 billion, including extensions of claims and counter-claims in 2011, in arbitration proceedings commenced in previous years. The goal of the DIS is to promote arbitration and other methods of alternative dispute resolution ('ADR') and to serve the purpose of a central support for arbitration tasks in Germany.

The most important way in which the DIS promotes arbitration is through its arbitration rules and the rules supplementing its standard arbitration rules. In its role as the administrator of the proceedings, the DIS plays an important role in the phase of the commencement of the proceedings, as the statement of claim must be filed with the DIS secretariat[165] and the proceedings must commence when the statement of claim is received by the DIS (s. 6 DIS Arbitration Rules). After the claimant has paid the DIS administrative fee as well as a provisional advance on the costs of the arbitrators (s. 7.1 DIS Arbitration Rules) to the DIS, the statement of claim is delivered to the respondent by the DIS (s. 8 DIS Arbitration Rules). Compared to *ad hoc* proceedings under German law, this ensures that the claimant will be sure about the commencement of the proceedings.

The DIS safeguards that the constitution of the arbitral tribunal will proceed in a swift manner and if the nomination procedure agreed by the parties fails, that the nomination of a substitute arbitrator by the appointing committee of the DIS[166] can be requested by a party. Upon constitution, the arbitral tribunal takes charge of the proceedings, subject to any specific party agreement. While the DIS Arbitration Rules do not foresee an active involvement of the DIS in this phase of the proceedings, the parties and arbitrators may, at any time, seek advice from the secretariat. Once the arbitral tribunal has rendered its award,

[165] Apart from the main secretariat in Cologne, the DIS has secretariats in Berlin and Munich, where statements of claim may be filed. From there, the statements of claim are transmitted to the main secretariat in Cologne, where all proceedings under the DIS Arbitration Rules are administered.

[166] The composition and functions of the appointing committee of the DIS are stipulated in s. 14 of the DIS Statutes, see also *infra* Section 4.2.

the DIS delivers one original of the award to each party (s. 36 subs. 2 DIS Arbitration Rules).

Apart from its own arbitration rules, the DIS promotes arbitration by assuming a number of functions. The DIS acts as an appointing authority under the UNCITRAL Arbitration Rules where the parties have so agreed or at the request of the Permanent Court of Arbitration. In addition, the DIS also nominates arbitrators in *ad hoc* proceedings (domestic or international) if the parties have so agreed.

The DIS also provides technical support to arbitral tribunals and parties, mainly but not restricted to DIS arbitrations. At its main secretariat in Cologne, the DIS makes available hearing rooms for domestic and international arbitrations. The hearing-room facilities are available free of charge for DIS arbitrations. The DIS will also assist in obtaining the services of translators, court reporters and other clerical staff that are required for the proceedings.

The DIS and the Frankfurt Chamber of Industry and Commerce jointly founded the Frankfurt International Arbitration Centre (FIAC) in 2005. The FIAC provides hearing- and meeting-room facilities that are specially equipped for arbitrations as well as ancillary services in connection with the conduct of hearings at this venue.[167]

Further, the DIS promotes the development of arbitration-related scholarship and teaching. The DIS offers, amongst other things, conferences on current issues in the field of arbitration or ADR several times a year. Furthermore, it participates as a cooperation partner in numerous other events (e.g. the Petersberg Arbitration Days).

Since 2003, the DIS, in cooperation with Verlag C. H. Beck, has published the *German Arbitration Journal* (*Zeitschrift für Schiedsverfahren: SchiedsVZ*) six times per year. The journal contains German- and English-language contributions. DIS members receive the journal free of charge.

In addition, the DIS makes an award (*DIS-Förderpreis*) every two years for outstanding academic work in the area of arbitration or ADR. The DIS also holds the Arbitration Documentation and Information Centre e.V. (ADIC), which offers the most comprehensive access to arbitration-related literature in Germany.

[167] Further information on the services and costs of such services is available at www.frankfurt-main.ihk.de/english/legal_matters/disputeregulation/fiac/index.html, last visited on 20 December 2010.

13 The possibility of excluding the courts' review of an award's validity

The parties may not agree to exclude the right to apply for the setting aside of the award in advance; that is, before the arbitral proceedings have started.[168] The reason being that the constitutionally required minimum control must be maintained.[169]

However, this prohibition to exclude setting aside proceedings *per se* is to be distinguished from a waiver to rely on a particular ground for setting aside. The parties may not validly exclude reliance on the two grounds listed in s. 1059 subs. 2, no. 2 of the GCCP, as these grounds serve a public-interest function and they cannot validly be waived in advance. By contrast, reliance on the grounds in no. 1 may, in principle, be waived, with the effect that applications based on such grounds have to be rejected as unfounded.[170] That applies without restriction to the time after the award has been rendered but also to waivers, where the relevant defect is already known before the award has been rendered.[171] Waivers contained in some institutional arbitration rules such as, for example, article 28 subs. 6 of the ICC Arbitration Rules, pursuant to which the parties renounce 'any form of recourse', are not considered a waiver of the right to initiate setting aside proceedings. They are understood to exclude a review on the merits or the right to appeal on points of law existing in some legal systems[172] but not to exclude setting aside proceedings.[173]

14 Grounds for invalidity of the award

An action to set aside an arbitral award pursuant to s. 1059 of the GCCP is only admissible against domestic arbitral awards; that is, arbitral

[168] BGH, Decision of 26 September 1985 – III ZR 16/84, *BGHZ*, 96(1986), 40 at 42; Lachmann, *Schiedsgerichtspraxis*, p. 560 at para. 2346.

[169] Kröll and P. Kraft, '§ 1059: Application for Setting Aside', in Böckstiegel, Kröll and Nacimiento (eds.), *Arbitration in Germany*, p. 436 at p. 440, paras. 6 *et seq.*; Bill on the Reform of the Law Relating to Arbitral Proceedings, published in BT-Drs. 13/5274, p. 59 available in German at www.dis-arb.de, last visited on 20 December 2010.

[170] BGH, Decision of 26 September 1985 – III ZR 16/84, *BGHZ*, 96(1986), 40 at 42.

[171] Lachmann, *Schiedsgerichtspraxis*, p. 560 at para. 2346; Kröll and Kraft, '§ 1059: Application for Setting Aside', p. 440, paras. 7 *et seq.*

[172] Ibid.

[173] BayObLG, Decision of 15 December 1999 – 4 Z SchH 23/99 (2000), *Recht und Praxis der Schiedsgerichtsbarkeit* (RPS) 16 at 17 = CLOUT case No. 403; confirming BGH, Decision of 26 September 1985 – III ZR 16/84, *BGHZ*, 96(1986), 40 at 42.

awards rendered in arbitral proceedings that have their seat in Germany. Subsections 1–3 of s. 1059 are, to a large extent, a literal adoption of article 34 of the UNCITRAL Model Law on International Commercial Arbitration.

One distinct feature of s. 1059 of the GCCP is that pursuant to subs. 4 – in cases where the award is (partially or fully) set aside by the competent court – in cases of doubt, the arbitration clause again comes into effect and the case may, in appropriate cases, be referred to the arbitral tribunal.[174]

The grounds for setting aside an award are enumerated in s. 1059 subs. 2 of the GCCP and its wording ('may be set aside only') emphasizes the exhaustive character of the list.[175] The parties are not empowered to provide for additional grounds, in particular to allow for a review on the merits.[176] Despite its vague language ('may be set aside'), s. 1059 subs. 2 of the GCCP has to be read as meaning 'shall be set aside'. *Ergo*, whenever a ground for the setting aside of an arbitral award exists, courts have no discretionary power to refuse the setting aside of the award.[177]

Section 1059 subs. 2 of the GCCP distinguishes between two categories of grounds for the setting aside. Firstly, grounds which have to be pleaded by the applicant in the first category ('shows sufficient cause') and, secondly, those which are taken into account *ex officio* in the second category ('the court finds').

The following grounds fall into the first category, i.e. the party applying for the setting aside of the award has to show sufficient cause that:

(a) Lit. a: the arbitration agreement is invalid. This ground covers various instances where the arbitral tribunal lacked jurisdiction

[174] E.g., OLG Hamburg, Decision of 30 May 2008 – 11 Sch 09/07, available in German at www.dis-arb.de, last visited on 20 December 2010.

[175] Bill on the Reform of the Law Relating to Arbitral Proceedings, published in BT-Drs. 13/5274, p. 59 available in German at www.dis-arb.de, last visited on 20 December 2010; Lachmann, *Schiedsgerichtspraxis*, p. 522 at para. 2172.

[176] For the second alternative see OLG Naumburg; Decision of 20 May 2005 – 10 Sch 01/05, *SchiedsVZ*, 4(2006), 103 at 104 *et seq.* (the 'arbitration clause' did not provide the required finality to qualify as 'arbitration' in the sense of ss. 1025 GCCP *et seq.*); such a lack of finality has to be distinguished from cases in which the finality of an award is subject to a condition, e.g. the expiry of a time limit, see BGH, Decision of 1 March 2007 – III ZB 7/06, *SchiedsVZ*, 6(2008), 160 *et seq.*

[177] Kröll and Kraft, '§ 1059: Application for Setting Aside', p. 452, para. 40; J. Münch, '§ 1059 Aufhebungsantrag', in Rauscher, Wax and Wenzel (eds.), *Münchener Kommentar Zivilprozessordnung*, p. 1382, para. 2.

due to defects with regard to the arbitration agreement. While the defence of a lack of objective arbitrability is specially regulated (see *infra* s. 1059 subs. 2, no. 2, lit. a, GCCP), s. 1059 subs. 2, no. 1, lit. a of the GCCP covers cases of a lack of subjective arbitrability (incapacity of a party to conclude the arbitration agreement) and questions as to the conclusion of an arbitration agreement in a wider sense.[178]

(b) Lit. b: it was not given proper notice of the appointment of an arbitrator or of the arbitral proceedings or was otherwise unable to present his case. The various grounds listed in lit. b are special emanations of the right to be heard; that is, the right to be informed about the proceedings and the right to present one's case.

(c) Lit. c: the arbitral tribunal exceeded its authority. An award may be set aside if the arbitral tribunal has exceeded its authority, either because the dispute or parts of it were outside the scope of the arbitration agreement or because the arbitral tribunal has *ultra petita* awarded more or something different than the parties have requested.[179] By contrast, awards ruling *infra petita* cannot, in principle, be set aside pursuant to lit. c.[180]

(d) Lit. d: that there exist flaws in the composition of the arbitral tribunal or the arbitral procedure. An award is to be set aside if either the arbitral tribunal was not properly composed or the award was rendered on the basis of an incorrect procedure. The relevant standards for determining the incorrectness are the provisions of the 10th Book of the GCCP and the existing procedural agreements by the parties, as far as they are admissible. Section 1059 subs. 2, no. 1, lit. d GCCP – in deviation from art. 34 subs. 2 lit. c UNCITRAL Model Law on International Commercial Arbitration – furthermore requires that these defects presumably have affected the award. This additional requirement is intended to ensure that the award may not be set aside for minor formal defects which did not affect the outcome of the proceedings.[181]

[178] Kröll and Kraft, '§ 1059: Application for Setting Aside', p. 452, para. 40; Münch, '§ 1059: Aufhebungsantrag', p. 1382, paras. 5 *et seq.*

[179] Lachmann, *Schiedsgerichtspraxis*, p. 538 at para. 2243; Kröll and Kraft, '§ 1059: Application for Setting Aside', p. 462, para. 63; favouring the inclusion of a decision *ultra petita* in (d) W. Voit, '§ 1059: Aufhebungsantrag', in Musielak (ed.), *Kommentar zur Zivilprozessordnung*, p. 2522 at p. 2526, para. 14.

[180] Kröll and Kraft, '§ 1059: Application for Setting Aside', p. 463, para. 64.

[181] A presumed effect was denied e.g. in OLG Hamm, Decision of 18 October 1999 – 17 SchH 05/99, available at www.dis-arb.de, last visited on 20 December 2010.

It is the general understanding that the second category of grounds listed in s. 1059 subs. 2, no. 2 of the GCCP have to be considered by the competent court *ex officio* because they concern fundamental public interests (see also the UNCITRAL Model Law on International Commercial Arbitration: 'if the court finds').[182] However, the competent court will decide on the basis of the facts presented to it by the party to whom the ground for the setting aside will be of advantage.[183] The court has no obligation to start an independent investigation of the facts.[184]

The grounds of s. 1059 subs. 2, no. 2 of the GCCP comprise:

(a) Lit. a: the non-arbitrability of the dispute. The non-arbitrability of the dispute according to s. 1030 of the GCCP constitutes a ground for setting aside the award irrespective of the validity of the arbitration agreement in all other respects. By defining the arbitrability, the national legislator determines conclusively the extent to which disputes are open to arbitration and, at the same time, reserves certain disputes for state-court jurisdiction.[185]
(b) Lit. b: a conflict with public policy (*ordre public*). Awards are to be set aside if their enforcement would be contrary to German public policy. The German courts take a very narrow approach as to what constitutes a violation of public policy. Courts have constantly held that violation of public policy exists only if 'the award leads to a result that obviously violates basic principles of German law, especially if it is inconsistent with constitutional rights'. According to the commonly used definition, public policy is only affected if the award or the procedure upon which it is based disregards mandatory laws that form the basis for a functioning public and economic life[186] and/or violates the most basic notions and principles of German law.[187] The latter is only assumed if the award is likely to undermine confidence in the predictability of legal decisions generally and the

[182] Kröll and Kraft, '§ 1059: Application for Setting Aside', p. 466, para. 76.
[183] Ibid.; Münch, '§ 1059: Aufhebungsantrag', p. 1394, para. 25. [184] Ibid.
[185] Kröll and Kraft, '§ 1059: Application for Setting Aside', p. 467, para. 77 with further references.
[186] Ibid., p. 468, para. 80; OLG Dresden, Decision of 20 April 2005 – 11 Sch 01/05, *SchiedsVZ*, 3(2005), 210 at 211; Lachmann, *Schiedsgerichtspraxis*, p. 549 at para. 2300.
[187] Kröll and Kraft, '§ 1059: Application for Setting Aside', p. 468, para. 80; BayObLG, Decision of 20 November 2003 – 4Z Sch 17/03, *IHR*, 4(2004), 81 at 82 = *XXIX Yearbook* (2004), 771 (773 *et seq.*); see OLG Stuttgart, Decision of 3 June 2003 – 1 Sch 02/03, available at www.dis-arb.de, last visited on 20 December 2010.

reliability of arbitral procedures.[188] German law, therefore, has a much narrower concept of domestic or national public policy than many other legal systems in which all mandatory rules are considered to form part of the national public policy.

Unless otherwise agreed by the parties, an application to set aside an award may not be made after three months have elapsed since the date the party seeking to appeal the award received the award.

15 Other specific features in the arbitration rules or the arbitration law

Most of the distinct features of the German arbitration law and the DIS Arbitration Rules have been contemplated in the more specific sections above. They include *inter alia* the proactive arbitrator (see *supra* Section 10.2) and the possibility of submitting a dispute to an expedited arbitration procedure under the DIS-SREP (see *supra* Sections 1. 2 and 10. 2).

As mentioned above (see *supra* Section 6), there is one additional specific feature of arbitration proceedings which is of particular importance in the light of the revision of the Brussels I Convention. Pursuant to s. 1032 subs. 2 of the ZPO, prior to the constitution of the arbitral tribunal, an application may be made to the competent court to determine whether or not arbitration is admissible. This provision has no parallel in the UNCITRAL Model Law on International Commercial Arbitration. The German legislator decided to adopt this provision for reasons of procedural economy so as to provide the possibility of an early binding determination of the jurisdiction issue.[189] Pursuant to s. 1032 subs. 2 of the GCCP, the court can determine whether or not arbitration proceedings are admissible. Thus, s. 1032 subs. 2 of the GCCP covers both positive declarations (arbitration being admissible) and negative declarations (arbitration not being admissible). According to s. 1032 subs. 3 of the GCCP, where an action or application under s. 1032 subs. 1 of the ZPO or s. 1032 subs. 2 of the ZPO has been filed, arbitral proceedings may nevertheless be commenced or continued, and an arbitral award may be made, *while* the issue is pending before the

[188] Kröll and Kraft, '§ 1059: Application for Setting Aside', p. 467, para. 78; OLG Köln, Decision of 3 June 2003 – 9 Sch 23/02, available at www.dis-arb.de, last visited on 20 December 2010.

[189] Böckstiegel, Kröll and Nacimiento, 'Germany as a Place for International and Domestic Arbitrations', p. 21, para. 43.

court. The purpose of this provision is to prevent the parties from using the court procedures as a tactical tool to delay the arbitral proceedings.[190] The arbitral tribunal, at its discretion, may, however, stay its proceedings until the competent court has decided with binding force on the admissibility of the arbitral proceedings.

This procedure safeguards procedural efficiency, as the question of jurisdiction will be determined with binding force at an early stage of the proceedings.

[190] Bill on the Reform of the Law Relating to Arbitral Proceedings, published in BT-Drs. 13/5274, p. 38 available in German at www.dis-arb.de; W. Voit, '§ 1032: Schiedsvereinbarung und Klage vor Gericht', in Musielak (ed.), *Kommentar zur Zivilprozessordnung*, p. 2437 at p. 2442, para. 15.

8

Arbitration in Italy: Features of the Milan Chamber of Arbitration

STEFANO AZZALI

Established in 1985, the Chamber of Arbitration of Milan[1] (hereinafter 'CAM' or the 'Chamber') is a special branch of the local Chamber of Commerce and has been managing arbitration proceedings since 1986. The CAM has, since then, widened its range of activities and now also offers other alternative dispute resolution (hereinafter 'ADR') tools, including mediation, online mediation and domain name reassignment.

The Chamber features a research centre for ADR ('Centro Studi e Documentazione G. Schiavoni') with its own library and carries out international projects, also being a board member of the International Federation of Commercial Arbitration Institutions (IFCAI) and partner of the Italy–China Business Mediation Center (ICBMC).[2]

The opinions here expressed are those of the author alone and they do not reflect the official position of the Chamber of Arbitration of Milan nor are they binding upon it. The author wishes to thank Giada Caravello for her invaluable support and assistance.

1 See also the Chamber's official website: www.camera-arbitrale.it/

2 On the CAM see, *inter alia*: M. Cicogna, 'Milan Chamber of Arbitration', in P. Gola, C. Gotz Staehelin, K. Graf (eds.), *Institutional Arbitration: Tasks and Powers of Different Arbitration Institutions* (Geneva: Schulthess, 2009), pp. 169–190; B. Coppo, 'The New Arbitration Rules of the Chamber of Arbitration of Milan', in C. Finkelstein, J. B. Vita, N. Casado Filho (eds.), *Arbitragem Internacional: Unidroit, CISG e Direito Brasileiro* (São Paulo: Quartier Latin, 2010), pp. 23–42; B. Coppo, 'The 2010 Revision of the Arbitration Rules of the Chamber of Arbitration of Milan', *The Vindobona Journal of International Commercial Law and Arbitration*, 14(2010), 283; G. De Berti and N. Milone, 'New Rules for Milan Chamber of Arbitration', *International Law Office* (12 August 2010), available at: www.internationallawoffice.com/newsletters/Default.aspx (last visited on 11 November 2010); T. Giovannini and V. Renna, 'The Italian Experience of Arbitration and the Arbitration Rules of the Chamber of Arbitration of Milan: A Parallel View', *The Vindobona Journal of International Commercial Law and Arbitration*, 14(2010), 297; U. Draetta and R. Luzzatto (eds.), *The Chamber of Arbitration of Milan Rules: A Commentary* (New York: Juris, 2012).

In 2010, the CAM adopted new arbitration rules (hereinafter the 'Rules'), which entered into force on 1 January 2010: the previous set of rules dated back to 2004. The Rules apply both to domestic and international arbitration. The 2010 revision takes into consideration the changes brought by the 2006 reform of Italian arbitration law[3] as well as the CAM's growing practice: from 2004 to 2009 the caseload of the CAM has constantly increased, the total number of cases being 105 in 2004 and 153 in 2009. Significantly, during the same time frame, the number of international cases administered by the Chamber also increased from 11 in 2004 to 35 in 2009.

The aim of the 2010 revision was to provide the parties with an expeditious, transparent and effective administration for the proceedings. Before addressing the specific features of the Rules, some preliminary remarks as to the CAM's structure are necessary. The CAM's two main bodies are the arbitral council and the secretariat. The former is the Chamber's technical body and is in charge of a general competence over the administration of arbitral cases, while the latter is in charge of the actual case management and of all the functions set out in the Rules or delegated to it by the council. The secretariat performs its tasks through the Secretary General, the Deputy Secretary General and its delegated officers.

As to the 2010 revision, amendments concerned the functions of the CAM's bodies as well as the powers of arbitrators, confirming the institution's control over their independence and over the duration and the costs of the proceedings. The CAM's model arbitration clause was also amended in order to bring it into line with current international practice and with the reformed Italian arbitration law. The official text of the Rules is in Italian and it has been translated into and published in a number of other languages.

1 Time frame for the proceedings

Time is one of the key issues when commencing an arbitration. When parties opt for arbitration, they expect it to be faster and less expensive than going to court: from a business point of view, disputes are seen as both a cost and a risk, so that it is essential for the parties to monitor the time schedule of the arbitral proceedings.

[3] See Legislative Decree No. 40/2006, which entered into force on 2 March 2006.

According to article 32, paragraph 1 of the Rules, the final award must be rendered within six months from the constitution of the arbitral tribunal, unless otherwise agreed by the parties. In the event of a complex case, though, the CAM is aware that it may take longer than six months to reach the final award: for this reason, article 32, paragraph 2 provides that this term may be extended by the arbitration council, even on its own initiative or, when there is consent by the parties for an extension, by the secretariat itself. Therefore, the CAM maintains control over any extension of the said time limit, so that the parties are granted a time-efficient case. It is also relevant to note that article 4 of the CAM's Code of Ethics of Arbitrators requires that: 'When accepting his/her mandate, the arbitrator shall, to the best of his/her knowledge, be able to devote the necessary time and attention to the arbitration to perform and complete his/her task as expeditiously as possible.'

In 2009, the average length of CAM's arbitrations was 13.1 months and, in particular, the average length of arbitrations concluded by an award, rendered by an arbitral panel, was 18.8 months.

2 Cost determination (including security)

Along with time, predictability of costs is also critical for the parties involved. As for CAM's arbitrations, costs are calculated according to a predetermined schedule of fees attached to the Rules (hereinafter the 'Schedule'), which draws a connection between the value of the dispute and the fees for both the arbitrators and the CAM. In accordance with article 35, the value of the dispute is determined by the secretariat taking into account both the request for arbitration and the statement of defence, as well as any further indications by the parties and the tribunal. Specific criteria for determining the said value are listed in annexe A of the Rules. Once the value of the dispute has been calculated, the arbitral council determines the costs of the arbitration before the award is filed.

More specifically, article 36[4] states that costs of arbitration shall include the fees of the Chamber, the fees of the arbitral tribunal, the fees of the experts of the arbitral tribunal (if any) and the reimbursement of expenses of the CAM, of the arbitrators and of the experts. The Chamber's fee consists of a fixed cost connected to the different baskets listed by the Schedule: annexe B of the Rules lists which activities are

[4] See art. 36, paras. 4 and 5.

included and which are excluded in terms of its determination. No registration fee is due when filing the request for arbitration.

As for the arbitrators' fees, in accordance with article 36, paragraph 6, they are determined on the basis of the value of the dispute, according to the Schedule. In order to determine the precise amount of the said fees, the arbitral council takes into consideration the work done, the complexity of the dispute, the arbitration's length and any other relevant circumstances. The arbitral council can determine different fees for each member of the tribunal and, in exceptional cases, it may deviate from the amount set in the Schedule, going either below or above that figure.

The fees of the experts of the arbitral tribunal shall be determined by the arbitral council in equity, also considering the schedule of professional fees for the expert, national court schedules of fees and any other circumstances.[5]

Once the request for arbitration and the statement of defence are filed, the secretariat directs the parties to make an advance on the costs of arbitration and sets a time limit for the parties to make payment.[6] During the proceedings, further advances may be requested by the secretariat in connection with the activities performed by the arbitral tribunal or when any change as to the amount in dispute occurs.[7] Before the filing of the award, the secretariat shall direct the balance of the costs of the proceedings on the basis of the final determination of the arbitral council, setting a proper time limit. The parties are jointly and severally liable for the costs of arbitration; nevertheless, the secretariat may determine separate costs when the parties submit different claims. In this case, the Rules[8] make clear that both the Chamber's and the tribunal's fees cannot exceed the maximum set for where such a division did not occur.

When a party fails to pay the requested advance, the secretariat requests the other party to make a substitute payment when a counterclaim has been filed or it can divide the value of the dispute (if it has not already done so) and direct each party to deposit an amount based on the value of its claims within a set time limit.[9] If the requested amount remains unpaid, the proceedings may be suspended by the secretariat in regard to the claims whose costs remain unpaid. After a month of suspension and still with a lack of any payment, the secretariat may declare the closing of the case: the parties are constantly updated by the secretariat as to the economical situation of the case, so that both the

[5] See art. 36, para. 7. [6] See art. 37. [7] See art. 37, para. 2. [8] See art. 35, para. 4.
[9] See art. 38.

suspension and the possible dismissal of the proceedings are not unpredictable events to them.

It is to be noted that, according to article 30, the award itself shall indicate the decision on the costs of the proceedings, with reference to the decision on the costs of the arbitral council and on the legal costs of the parties.

3 Procedure for the appointment of the tribunal

The number of arbitrators and the manner of their appointment are determined by the parties in the arbitration agreement: failing any indication thereon, the CAM provides for supplementary rules. According to article 14, paragraph 2, unless otherwise agreed by the parties, the arbitral tribunal consists of a sole arbitrator appointed by the arbitral council. A panel of three arbitrators may be appointed when there is additional complexity or a higher economic value in the dispute.[10]

Where the parties have agreed to appoint the sole arbitrator jointly without indicating a time limit, this time limit shall be set by the secretariat. If the parties fail to reach an agreement, the sole arbitrator is appointed by the arbitral council.[11]

Under article 14, paragraph 4, unless otherwise agreed in the arbitration agreement, the arbitral panel shall be appointed as follows: (a) each party appoints an arbitrator: if one of the parties fails to do so, the arbitrator will be appointed by the arbitral council; and (b) the President of the arbitral tribunal shall be appointed by the arbitral council unless the parties agreed for him/her to be appointed by the two co-arbitrators[12] or by another appointing authority.

When the parties have different nationalities or when they have registered offices in different countries, the arbitral council shall appoint, as sole arbitrator or President of the arbitral tribunal, a person of a third nationality, unless otherwise agreed by the parties.

4 Identity and role of the appointing authority

As already anticipated, the CAM's appointing authority is the arbitral council. The arbitral council has general competence over all matters relating to the administration of arbitral proceedings and issues all orders relating thereto, in respect of the secretariat's functions under

[10] See art. 13, para. 2. [11] See art. 14, para. 3. [12] See art. 14, para. 4b.

the Rules. The council is composed of a minimum of seven and up to a maximum of eleven members, one of whom acts as President and one as Deputy: they are all appointed for three years by the Board of the Chamber of Arbitration and may be either Italian and/or foreign experts. According to the Preamble of the Rules (the 'Preamble'), the meetings of the arbitral council are valid where at least three members are present, while the 2004 Rules required the attendance of five members. This amendment, together with the possibility of attending the meetings by using any means of communication was made to allow for the prompt intervention of the council on the administration of cases.

The arbitral council reaches its decisions via the majority of the voting members: in the event of deadlock, the vote of the meeting's President will prevail. The President also has the power to make any decision – including those regarding the appointment of arbitrators – under urgent circumstances.

Additionally, the CAM itself can act as the appointing authority. According to the Preamble, upon the request of the parties, the Chamber can appoint arbitrators for proceedings which are not subject to the Rules (i.e. so-called *ad hoc* arbitrations). Through this service, the parties can refer the appointment of arbitrators to the arbitral council; the President of the CAM's arbitral council; or the President of the CAM. The application for the appointment shall be filed within the secretariat of the CAM and shall contain the following requirements: the name of the parties and of the parties' counsel, if any; the names of the arbitrators, if appointed by the parties; a short description of the dispute, of the parties' claims and their value; any indications as to the number of the arbitrators and the manner of their selection; and the arbitration agreement.

At the request of the parties, moreover, the CAM appoints arbitrators under the Arbitration Rules of the United Nations Commission for International Trade Law (UNCITRAL).

5 Form of the arbitration agreement

In order to start an arbitration under the Rules, the parties are prompted to make express reference to the Chamber of Arbitration of Milan in the arbitration agreement. More specifically, article 1 states that a reference in the clause to the CAM or to the Chamber of Commerce of Milan shall be deemed to permit the application of the Rules.

The CAM provides for the following model clause, attached to the Rules: 'Any dispute arising out of or related to the present contract shall be settled by arbitration under the Rules of the Chamber of Arbitration of Milan (the Rules), by a sole arbitrator/three arbitrators, appointed in accordance with the Rules'. The 2010 revision involved the model clause as well: the previous version of the clause only made reference to disputes 'arising out' of the contract, while the current one also refers to any dispute 'in connection with' the contract itself. The new version of the clause seems consistent with current international practice: similar wordings can be found in the models attached to the 1998 ICC Rules, the 2010 SCC Rules and the 1998 LCIA Rules.[13]

Further examples of model clauses can be found on the CAM's website and include a model clause for international arbitration, a clause for company arbitration, a multi-step clause (mediation and arbitration), a clause for arbitration with a seat in continental China, a submission agreement and a clause for *irrituale* arbitration.[14] In any case, parties can also agree on, and therefore indicate in the arbitration clause: the applicable law for the merits of the dispute; the seat of the arbitration; and the language of the arbitration. These requirements are of particular relevance, especially when the parties are of different nationalities or when a relevant part of the agreement must be performed in a foreign country.

Under article 1, paragraph 2, moreover, the Rules shall apply where: (a) a party files a personally signed request for arbitration proposing arbitration under the Rules; and (b) the other party accepts this proposal by a personally signed statement within the time limit set by the secretariat.

6 Interference/support by the courts (including the tribunal's powers to involve them)

While the 2004 Rules still contained reference to the Italian law (see article 9, 2004 Rules), the current version of the Rules does not make reference to any national law in order to strengthen the international spirit of the revision. As a result, the Rules do not contain any specific provision as to the relationship between the arbitral tribunal and the

[13] ICC stands for the International Chamber of Commerce; SCC stands for the Stockholm Chamber of Commerce; and LCIA stands for the London Court of International Arbitration.

[14] *Irrituale* arbitration is regulated by the Italian Civil Procedure Code (art. 808 bis) and, to put it in a nutshell, provides for the arbitral tribunal to render arbitral awards, the effects of which are contractual, as opposed to the judicial effects of a *rituale* arbitral award.

courts: issues such as the one of interference or of support by the courts as well as of the tribunal's powers to involve them will then be dealt with according to the law applicable to the arbitration.

As to the Italian arbitration law – should the seat of the arbitration be in Italy or the Italian law be applicable – article 816-ter ICPC[15] is of relevance. Article 816-ter, paragraph 3 ICPC, in fact, states that when a witness refuses to appear before the arbitral tribunal, the arbitrators can ask the President of the court, in the seat where arbitration takes place, to order their appearance. Moreover, under article 816-ter, paragraph 6, the arbitrators can request information, in writing, to any public-administration bodies in relation to their acts and documents that need to be considered in the arbitral proceedings.

7 The tribunal's powers *ex officio*

In order to allow the arbitrators to conduct each case in accordance with its peculiarities and to find a tailored solution thereto, the 2010 Rules extended the tribunal's powers in regard to several aspects. The said revision was due in light of the changes that occurred between 2004 – the year of the previous edition of the CAM's Rules – and 2009: during this time frame, the CAM significantly increased the number of its administered cases as well as the percentage of foreign parties involved, not to mention the increasing complexity of arbitrations that the CAM encountered.

As to the 2010 Rules, under article 3, paragraph 3, the tribunal has the power to apply to the merits of the dispute the rules that it deems appropriate, taking into account the nature of the contractual relationship, the quality of the parties and any other relevant circumstance of the case at hand. This provision is in line with international practice[16] and anchors the arbitrators' determination to objective criteria – the predictability of the tribunal's decision remaining crucial for the parties.

In the absence of any agreement between the parties, the tribunal also has the power to determine the language used in the arbitration.[17]

As to the conduct of the proceedings, article 22 is of the essence. First of all, according to article 22, paragraph 1, the arbitrators have the power to attempt a settlement of the case between the parties, and may delegate it to the mediation service of the CAM. Under article 22, paragraph 2,

[15] Italian Civil Procedure Code. [16] See, for example, art. 17, ICC Rules 1998.
[17] See art. 5.

then, the tribunal can adopt urgent and interim measures of protection, also of an anticipatory nature, which are not barred by mandatory provisions applicable to the case.

The arbitrators' power to consolidate or separate proceedings is stated by, respectively, article 22, paragraph 3 and article 22, paragraph 4, while article 22, paragraph 5 provides that the tribunal shall decide on third-party joinders.

Article 25 is also of relevance, as it gives the arbitrators the power to take all the relevant and admissible evidence adduced by the parties in a manner that they deem appropriate. This provision departs from any given national legislation and allows the tribunal to conduct this phase of the proceedings in accordance with the peculiarities of the case.

At the request of the parties or through their own initiative, the arbitrators can also appoint one or more experts or delegate such an appointment to the Chamber.[18]

In the event of new claims, it is within the power of the arbitrators to decide whether they are admissible or not:[19] the Rules omit any definition of when a claim shall be considered as 'new', so that any determination is left to the arbitrators themselves.

Finally, according to article 28, the tribunal shall close the evidence-taking phase and invite the parties to file their conclusions once it is ready to issue the award. In doing so, the tribunal has the power to set any subsequent time limit for filing final statements or rebuttal briefs, as well as scheduling a final hearing. From then on, parties are barred from filing new claims, pleading new facts or adducing new evidence, unless the tribunal decides otherwise.

8 The possibility of interim measures and their enforceability

As already underlined, the possibility of issuing interim measures is contained in article 22, paragraph 2. According to the said provision, such measures must not be barred by any mandatory provisions applicable to the proceedings. This rule acknowledges the limits of the Italian arbitration law (where applicable): according to article 818 ICPC, the arbitrators are, in fact, prevented from granting attachments or other interim measures of protection, except where the law provides otherwise. In fact, such a restriction acknowledges a gap in the (Italian) corporate law field.[20]

[18] See art. 26. [19] See art. 27. [20] See art. 35, para. 5, Legislative Decree No. 5/2003.

9 Multi-party arbitration (including joinder and consolidation)

In line with the increasing complexity of the cases and with the fact that both the 2006 Italian arbitration law reform and the 2003 Italian Corporate Law Act[21] ruled on these issues, multi-party arbitration as well as joinder and consolidation played a major role in the 2010 revision of the Rules.

As to the first issue, article 15 of the Rules contains a dedicated provision: in this regard, it should be noted that the CAM Rules have been in line with international practice since their 1996 edition. Article 15, paragraph 1 rules that in case of multiple parties acting as two sides, each one appoints an arbitrator (i.e. one arbitrator per side) and then the Chairperson is appointed in accordance with the parties' will. If this bilateral scheme does not take place, the tribunal is appointed by the arbitral council, regardless of any appointment eventually made by the parties:[22] such an explicit provision is consistent with the current revision of the UNCITRAL Arbitration Rules.[23]

On the other hand, when a third party requests to join a pending arbitration or if one of the parties calls for third-party intervention, any decision is left to the arbitral tribunal, which shall take into account both the parties' positions and the other relevant circumstances of the case (i.e. the applicable law).[24]

The tribunal may also order the consolidation of multiple proceedings pending before it when it deems them to be connected. Differently from the previous version of the Rules, the tribunal does not have to rely in its decision on an objective connection between the proceedings.

10 Conduct of arbitration (terms of reference, number of briefs, disclosure, written or oral evidence, modality of hearings, applicable law)

When a party seeks to commence an arbitration administered by the Chamber, the first step consists of filing a request for arbitration with the secretariat. The request shall be signed by the party or by its counsel with

[21] See art. 35, para. 2, Legislative Decree No. 5/2003. [22] See art. 15, para. 2.

[23] Reference is made to art. 10 of the UNCITRAL Rules, as revised in 2010: available at www.uncitral.org/uncitral/en/uncitral_texts/arbitration.html

[24] See art. 22, para. 5.

power of attorney and has to contain or be accompanied by the requirements stated in article 9. Within five working days, the secretariat will then send the request for arbitration to the respondent, and any time limit set by the Rules will run from this sending date. The respondent can file its statement of defence, with counter-claims, if any, within thirty days from the receipt of the request from the secretariat. This time limit may be extended by the secretariat for justified reasons.

Under article 10, paragraph 2, the statement of defence has to be signed by the party or by its counsel with power of attorney, and contains the indicated requirements. The statement of defence will then be sent by the secretariat to the claimant within five working days. The Rules make clear that if the respondent does not file a statement of defence, the arbitration shall proceed without it.

After the request for arbitration and the statement of defence are filed, the secretariat directs the parties to make an advance on the costs of arbitration within a set time limit: after the payment, the said pleadings (together with all annexed documents) are sent to the arbitrators. Within 30 days from the receipt of such briefs and documents, the arbitrator(s) shall constitute the arbitral tribunal: the secretariat may extend the said time limit for justified reasons. The arbitrators may formally 'constitute' the tribunal by way of an act contained in an order or by scheduling a hearing: in both cases, the arbitrators set the procedural steps of the case and a proper calendar, granting the parties the opportunity to file further pleadings and documents. The six-month time limit set for the arbitrators to render the final award runs from the constitution of the tribunal.

As to the terms of reference (hereinafter 'TOR'), the Rules do not contain any express provision about them.[25]

According to article 24, the dates of the hearings shall be determined by the arbitral tribunal after consultation with the secretariat and shall be communicated to the parties, which may appear either in person or through duly empowered representatives, and may be assisted by counsel.

After the constitution, the tribunal leads the case by taking all the relevant and admissible evidence, adduced in a manner that it deems

[25] When revising the Rules, the CAM discussed whether to introduce them for both the parties and arbitrators to sign: finally, it was decided not to necessarily bind the CAM proceedings to the TOR practice, leaving it up to the tribunal and the parties to agree on signing the TOR where they deem it appropriate (and when they are familiar with its practice).

appropriate.[26] On the basis of article 25, paragraph 2, the arbitrators can freely evaluate all evidence, with the exception of that which constitutes legal proof under mandatory provisions applicable either to the proceedings or to the merits of the dispute. In respect of the said limit, therefore, the tribunal may evaluate both oral and written evidence, as well as appoint one or more experts.

During this phase of the proceedings, the secretariat may request the parties to make a further advance on the costs of arbitration.

When the arbitral tribunal is ready to issue the final award, it closes the phase for taking evidence and invites the parties to file their conclusions. The tribunal may set a time limit for filing final statements and for rebuttal statements and it may also schedule a final hearing.

As to article 24, paragraph 3, minutes shall be taken of the hearings of the arbitral tribunal: when the hearings are held at the CAM's premises, this can also be done by one of the CAM's officers (as happens for almost 100% of the hearings are hosted by the Chamber).

As to the law applicable to the proceedings, the Rules do not make any reference to any national law. Article 2 provides that the case is governed by the Rules and by the rules chosen by the parties before the constitution of the tribunal, as long as they are consistent with the Rules themselves, or, in default, by the rules set by the arbitral tribunal. In any case, mandatory provisions applicable to the proceedings cannot be excluded and the principles of due process and equal treatment of the parties shall apply.

As to the merits of the dispute, the applicable rules are chosen by the parties: in the absence of such an agreement, the arbitral tribunal applies the rules that it determines to be appropriate, taking into account the nature of the relationship, the qualities of the parties and any other relevant circumstances.[27] In any case, the arbitral tribunal shall take trade usage into account.

11 Confidentiality

One of the advantages of arbitration is that the parties are able to handle their dispute in private. Confidentiality is, in fact, one of the main features of international arbitration and the 2010 Rules show a new attitude towards this issue. The duty of confidentiality is stated in article 8: departing from the previous version of the Rules, this provision now

[26] See art. 25. [27] See art. 3.

extends the said duty not only to the CAM, the arbitral tribunal and the experts but also to the parties. Both the proceedings and the arbitral award have to be kept confidential, 'except in the case where it has to be used to protect one's rights'. When revising the Rules, such a general and open exception was preferred to a detailed list of exceptions, since under national rules cases present so many differences. It goes without saying that a breach of the confidentiality duty is permissible if a party has a legal duty to breach it, as this would, in any case, prevail over the parties' agreement.

Article 8, paragraph 2 provides that, for purposes of research, the CAM may publish the arbitral award in anonymous format, unless any of the parties expressly objects to the publication during the proceedings. Additionally, this article has been amended by the 2010 revision: while the 2004 Rules provided for an 'opt-in' attitude towards the publication of sanitized awards (i.e. only with the prior written consent of the parties), the current Rules provide for an 'opt-out' solution.

12 Institution's role

When opting for administered arbitration, the parties look for an efficient, transparent and expeditious way to resolve their dispute. The Chamber's role in the management and administration of the cases is intended to provide the parties with such a result.

First of all, the Chamber provides assistance to the parties through all the proceedings, from the filing of the request of arbitration to the issuing of the award. The CAM actually helps the parties and the arbitrators through each step of the arbitration, providing practical assistance as well as clarifying the meaning and interpretation of the Rules, or helping with the drafting of the arbitration agreement itself. Every case filed with the Chamber is referred to one of the CAM's officers who will be in charge of the case's management as a member of the secretariat. The secretariat[28] informs the arbitral council on the status of arbitral proceedings and forwards the council's orders, as well as its own orders, to the parties and the arbitral tribunal, thus serving as a channel of communication between the players in the case. The CAM's officers also receive all written submissions and documents from both the parties and the arbitral tribunal and maintain the files for the proceedings.

[28] As to the role and functions of the secretariat, see the Preamble of the Rules.

As to the conduct of the proceedings, the CAM pays close attention to the independence of the arbitrators. Such a requirement is of crucial importance, since there is a deep connection between the arbitrator's behaviour and respect for the due process principle: any lack of independence by the arbitrators might affect the proceedings and the enforceability of the award as well. As a result, the Chamber and its Rules provide for strict control over the existence of the said requirement. Firstly, the arbitrators are required to be independent and impartial, and to stay so during the proceedings: this is stated in the CAM's Code of Ethics of Arbitrators, which is annexed to the Rules. Moreover, when accepting his/her appointment, each arbitrator is requested to sign a statement of independence, disclosing his/her connections with the case (if any).[29] The secretariat then forwards the said statement to the parties, who can file written comments within ten days. After the said time limit, the arbitrator is confirmed by the secretariat if he/she has filed an unqualified statement of independence and none of the parties has objected to it. In any other case, the confirmation is up to the arbitral council.

When the arbitral council has to make a decision on the independence of an arbitrator, it also takes into consideration – though it does not strictly apply them – the *IBA Guidelines on Conflict of Interests in International Arbitration*:[30] this is in line with the already mentioned 'international spirit' of the Rules and grants the parties a further grade of predictability as to the decision of the council.

As far as predictability is concerned, article 16 is also of relevance. According to this rule, neither the members of the arbitral council nor professionals working in the same law firm can be appointed as arbitrators. This rule is intended to provide the parties with the highest grade of transparency: nevertheless, under article 16.c, the parties can agree on derogating from it, while the CAM is bound to it when acting as appointing authority.

The Institution also plays an important role in terms of the conclusion of the proceedings. Once the final award is issued by the tribunal, in order to be sure that it is valid and it can be enforced, the Chamber provides for a formal check of the draft. Upon request of the arbitral tribunal, any non-compliance with the requirements set out in article 30

[29] See art. 18.

[30] See www.ibanet.org; these guidelines were approved by the International Bar Association in 2004.

shall be indicated by the secretariat to the arbitrators before they sign the award.

13 The possibility of excluding the courts' review of the award's validity

As already pointed out, the Rules do not make reference to any national law. Therefore, as to the validity of the award, the law applicable to the proceedings must be considered. In any case, article 30 states that the award shall be in writing and enlists the requirements it has to contain. This provision also states that the award shall be rendered with the participation of all the members of the tribunal and may be via a majority decision: in contrast to the previous edition, the 2010 Rules do not require any specific manner in which the arbitrators need to deliberate (i.e. there is no reference to a meeting in person).

As to the specific issue of the validity of the award, the Rules do not contain any provision granting the parties the possibility of excluding the courts' review of the award's validity, leaving the subject to the law applicable to the arbitration.

Under Italian arbitration law such a possibility is excluded by both article 825 ICPC and article 829 ICPC. While the first provision requires that the courts make a formal check of the award in order to enforce it, the latter expressly states that parties can always file a request of nullity (of the award), even when they previously renounced doing so.

14 Grounds for the invalidity of the award

The Rules do not contain any provision dealing with the issue of invalidity of the award. The only relevant rule is article 30, which – as already pointed out – deals with the form and content of the award, as well as with its deliberation. In order to define the grounds for the invalidity of the award, again, reference is to be made to the national law applicable to the proceedings.

Under Italian arbitration law such grounds are listed in article 829 ICPC. For example, the award may be set aside when rendered by a person who lacked the legal capacity to be appointed as arbitrator.[31] Moreover, the award may be challenged when it does not contain the reasons for the decision, or the decision (*dictum*) or the arbitrators'

[31] See art. 829, para. 1.3.

signatures.[32] The first two requirements are the same as those stated in article 30, paragraph 2.e and paragraph 2.f of the Rules. Another hypothesis of invalidity of the award includes the one in which the award is not valid when it does not contain any decision as to the merits of the dispute and the merits themselves had to be decided by the arbitrators.[33] Additionally, the award will be invalid when it fails to decide on any of the issues submitted to arbitration.[34]

In any case, according to article 2, paragraph 3 of the Rules, the award will be invalid each time the due process principle is not respected. Such a provision can also be found in article 829, paragraph 1.9 of the Italian arbitration law.

15 Other specific features in the arbitration rules or the arbitration law

As a concluding remark, reference will be made to the relationship between the Rules and the Italian arbitration law. Here, article 832 ICPC is of the essence. This provision was introduced in 2006 and deals with the issue of administered arbitration: prior to 2006, no such provision existed in Italian law.

According to the said article, the arbitration agreement may refer to pre-existing arbitration rules. In case of conflict between the provisions of the arbitration agreement and the arbitration rules chosen by the parties, the agreement of the parties will prevail. Article 832, paragraph 5 is of particular relevance, as it states that if the arbitral institution refuses to manage an arbitration, the arbitration clause maintains its validity and the Italian arbitration law should rule the (at that point, *ad hoc*) proceedings. As a matter of fact, all the cases filed with the CAM in 2009 had their seat of arbitration in Italy, as was the case in 2008. In this regard, article 4 of the Rules provides that, except where the parties have agreed otherwise, the seat of arbitration will be Milan.

[32] See art. 829, para. 1.5. [33] See art. 829, para. 1.10. [34] See art. 829, para. 1.12.

9

Rules of Arbitration of the International Chamber of Commerce

SIMON GREENBERG AND ANDERS RYSSDAL

1 Introduction

International commerce is greatly facilitated by allowing business firms to settle their differences and adjust their obligations through the mechanism of final, enforceable international arbitration. The benefits of freedom of contract are well known in economic theory, but the benefits of sorting out conflicts and differences through a relatively peaceful, private, mutually trustful mechanism such as international arbitration are still sometimes underestimated. This may be because the ground rules for international arbitration have been in place for a long time and are taken for granted. The New York Convention on the Recognition and Enforcement of Foreign Arbitral Awards of 10 June 1958 is invaluable because it basically states that an award made in accordance with the requirements of the Convention will be enforced directly in any Convention country where a losing party holds assets, without having to go through judicial proceedings anew.

International Chamber of Commerce ('ICC') arbitration has been around for much longer than the New York Convention. Multinational companies have been using the ICC Rules of Arbitration since the establishment of the ICC International Court of Arbitration ('Court') in 1923. The Court's headquarters are in Paris, but most ICC arbitrations do not take place there. On the contrary, the Court operates on a truly international field, supervising arbitrations all over the world. The Court

A significant portion of this chapter, although with various modifications, was extracted (with permission from the editors) from S. Greenberg, 'ICC Arbitration and Australia', in L. Nottage and R. Garnett (eds.), *International Arbitration in Australia* (Federation Press, 2010), chapter 6. Any views expressed in this chapter are the authors' only, and not necessarily those of the ICC.

has its Secretariat in Paris, but also has a branch of the Secretariat in Hong Kong to service the Court's considerable Asian caseload.

The Court remains one of the world's best-known and most respected international arbitration institutions and, as the figures below attest, ICC arbitration is a frequently sought after mechanism for business firms seeking to settle their differences. In fact, a recent empirical survey of leading global corporations found that 'the ICC is the most preferred and widely used arbitration institution', with 50% of survey participants indicating that the ICC was their preferred arbitral institution. The second most preferred institution scored 14% of participants' preferences.[1]

What, then, characterizes the Court's services in comparison with the alternatives? Generally, the Court has developed a system for quality control of the arbitration procedure and awards which, when considered as a package, remains somewhat unique. First, the Secretariat of the Court monitors the entire arbitration from beginning to end, starting with a review of the request for arbitration to ensure that it fulfils minimum requirements. The Court in some cases may then conduct a *prima facie* control of jurisdiction. This is to set the proceedings on the right track from the beginning. Then, after providing any necessary assistance in the constitution of the arbitral tribunal, once that tribunal has been fully constituted, the ICC 'terms of reference' serve to define the dispute and the mandate of the arbitrators, and to focus the further proceedings. Since the terms of reference are drafted and either approved or communicated to the Court at an early stage, the parties are encouraged to specify their claims and grounds from the outset of the arbitration. Using terms of reference reduces the chances of the arbitration drifting off track where proceedings linger until the parties are finally required to nail down their grounds and claims prior to a final hearing. Managing time and costs is an important feature of the ICC Rules of Arbitration, and several improvements were made in that respect in the 2012 version of those Rules ('2012 Rules'). For example, around the time of drafting the terms of reference, the arbitral tribunal must hold a case-management conference to design an effective and efficient procedure. The 2012 Rules also specifically oblige both the parties and the arbitral tribunal to make every effort to conduct the arbitration in an expeditious and cost-effective manner, and empower the arbitral tribunal to adopt appropriate procedural measures in that respect. At the end of a case, the

[1] School of International Arbitration, Queen Mary University of London, *2010 International Arbitration Survey: Choices in International Arbitration*, pp. 2 and 23.

Court's scrutiny of all awards is a vital safeguard to increase the award's enforceability and compatibility with the New York Convention's requirements. The Court has, over the years, developed vast experience with regard to how arbitral decisions should be fashioned in order to maximise the chances of the award being resistant to attack. Even experienced arbitrators benefit from this service when formulating the reasoning and dispositive parts of their awards. Finally, the Rules of Arbitration also provide for the granting of interim measures of protection both during the arbitration and, new to the 2012 Rules, by way of a special emergency arbitrator process at the outset of an arbitration.

2 Statistics

By the end of 2011, the Court had received some 18,500 arbitration cases since 1923.[2] In 2011, that caseload included 795 new requests for arbitration involving 2,293 parties from 139 different countries. Also in 2011, the arbitrations were seated in 63 different countries throughout the world and the Court appointed or confirmed 1,341 arbitrators and scrutinised and approved 508 arbitral awards. At the end of 2011, the Court was administering over 1,500 pending arbitrations, of which about 10% involved at least one state or state entity as a party, and with a growing number of investment disputes, some arising from bilateral investment treaties. In terms of the economic values of cases, at the beginning of 2011 the total value of all claims in the pending ICC arbitrations was US$ 86.8 billion. Several arbitrations involved total claims of over US$ 1 billion, with the average value for all cases being US$ 64 million as of 1 January 2012.

The ICC has national committees in over 90 different countries. The national committee in each country plays various roles. With most relevance to arbitration, the national committee is the body that proposes its nationals as members of the Court and as arbitrators for appointment by the Court. Thus, where the Court appoints an arbitrator, it ordinarily does so upon the proposal of the ICC's national committee from the same country (although under the 2012 Rules the

[2] ICC arbitration statistics can be found in the annual statistical report on ICC dispute resolution services. See for example '2010 Statistical Report', *ICC International Court of Arbitration Bulletin*, 21(1) (2011), 5. Many of the statistics referred to in this chapter have been published in such statistical reports, or will appear in future editions. The reports are also available online in the ICC Dispute Resolution Library at www.iccdrl.com.

Court is no longer *required* to seek an arbitrator proposal from a national committee).

3 Function and structure of the Court

Despite its name, the Court is not a judicial body. It does not make substantive decisions with respect to the arbitrations it administers, such as who wins or loses on any particular claim. Nor does it take decisions regarding the conduct of arbitrations, such as how many witnesses will be called, when and where the hearings will be held, how many written submissions there will be and so on.

The Court is rather an administrative body, supervising arbitrations conducted under the Rules of Arbitration. Broadly, the Court watches over the entire case from the moment a request for arbitration is filed to the moment a final award is delivered to the parties (unless the case is withdrawn earlier, for example due to a settlement, which occurs in about 47% of ICC arbitrations). The Court's decisions in exercising its administrative functions include examining whether there is a *prima facie* agreement to arbitrate, confirming or appointing arbitrators, fixing the seat or place of arbitration in the absence of party agreement, deciding challenges against arbitrators, removing arbitrators who are not performing their functions,[3] scrutinising all draft arbitral awards, fixing a cost deposit (called the 'advance on costs') for the arbitration and determining the fees of the arbitrators and of the ICC at the end of the case. In certain cases the Court will also administer the pre-arbitration step of an emergency arbitration process, a new mechanism under the 2012 Rules.

The Court is composed of about 120 Court members, experts in international arbitration and other relevant fields from more than 90 countries. Until recently the Court sat once per week in three-person committee sessions and once at the end of each month in a full plenary session. The Court has recently begun to hold a second weekly committee session by teleconference to cope with its growing case load. Those sessions are often held in either Spanish or German, rather than one of the Court's official working languages (English and French), so as to deal with cases in those

[3] A detailed discussion of the process of appointing, challenging and removing ICC arbitrators, including numerous recent examples, can be found in J. Fry and S. Greenberg, 'The Arbitral Tribunal: Applications of Articles 7–12 of the ICC Rules in Recent Cases', *ICC International Court of Arbitration Bulletin*, 20(2) (2009), 12.

languages. Court sessions involve a lively debate with notable variation in the views and opinions that are exchanged. Nonetheless, the Court's decisions are ultimately almost always unanimous.

The Court is assisted by an active Secretariat, a full-time permanent staff of about 80 people, including about 45 lawyers. Secretariat staff collectively speak approximately 26 different languages and hold about 28 different nationalities. The lawyers that manage the arbitration cases are divided into eight teams. Each team specialises in a different region, for example, North America, Latin America, Eastern Europe and Russia, France, Africa and the Middle East, and so on. Seven of the teams are based in Paris. In late 2008, the Secretariat set up the eighth team based in Hong Kong, which deals with its Asian caseload.

4 Revision of the ICC Rules of Arbitration

The ICC Rules of Arbitration had just been revised at the time of writing. A new version came into effect on 1 January 2012 (previously defined as the '2012 Rules'), applying to all arbitrations commenced on or after that date, unless the parties agree otherwise.[4]

The previous Rules of Arbitration came into force on 1 January 1998 ('1998 Rules'). In the 14 years that the 1998 Rules were applicable, the Court received over 8,600 new requests for arbitration. This is an enormous volume of cases to have been administered under a single set of arbitral rules. Moreover, it accounts for almost half of the Court's total case load since it was established in 1923.

The 1998 Rules stood the test of time well. They proved flexible, adaptable and able to accommodate the evolving demands of users. However, after ten years of use the ICC felt that it might be time to consider freshening up the Rules to take account of new developments and practices, particularly in relation to multi-party arbitration and finding ways further to reduce time and expense.[5]

[4] Both the 2012 and 1998 versions of the Rules of Arbitration can be downloaded in numerous different languages from the Court's website: www.iccarbitration.org. The 2012 Rules are also discussed in detail in *The Secretariat's Guide to ICC Arbitration: A Practical Commentary on the 2012 ICC Rules of Arbitration from the Secretariat of the ICC International Court of Arbitration* (ICC Publishing, 2012) (co-authored by J. Fry, S. Greenberg and F. Mazza).

[5] In 2007 the ICC Commission's Task Force on Saving Time and Costs in International Arbitration published a 'Report on Techniques for Controlling Time and Costs in Arbitration', available at www.iccwbo.org/policy/arbitration/id2882/index.html.

The process for revising the Rules began with broad consultation of the users of ICC arbitration in January 2008. In September 2008, the ICC decided to form the Task Force on the Revision of the ICC Rules of Arbitration ('Task Force'). The Task Force was a sub-committee of the ICC Commission on Arbitration ('Commission'), the Court's legislative and policy organ. The Commission is composed of more than 500 members worldwide and, at any one time, deals with a wide range of important projects through numerous task forces. Task Force members are designated by the ICC national committee of the country of which they are a national. The national committees designated in excess of 175 members for the Rules Task Force! The Chairman and Co-Chairs of the Task Force therefore decided to set up a core Drafting Sub-Committee ('DSC'). The DSC comprised approximately 20 members including the Chairman and Co-Chairs of the Task Force; the Chairman and Secretary General of the Court; two representatives of major global corporations who bring the users' perspective; six international arbitration experts representing both counsel and arbitrators; a representative of the Court; and the Vice-Chairs of the Commission as *ex officio* members. At the end of the process, the Task Force's recommendations were submitted to the ICC's national committees and then to the Commission as a whole for approval. The text was finally approved and enacted by the ICC's governing bodies at the ICC World Council meeting in Mexico in June 2011.

Two overriding principles guided the substance of the revision process. The first recognised the fact that the Rules were unlikely to be revised again for at least another 10 years. This meant that the changes should be viable for the next ten years and even beyond. The second overriding principle was that only useful or necessary changes should be made.

One of the key mandates for the DSC was to address concerns regarding the time and cost efficiency of arbitrations. This was implemented with some modifications to existing provisions (for example by streamlining the *prima facie* assessment of arbitral jurisdiction) and some additions designed specifically to combat time and costs (for example, the new requirement for a mandatory case-management conference at the outset of the process aimed at designing an appropriately efficient procedure,[6] as mentioned above).

[6] Such measures were recommended by the Commission's Task Force on Saving Time and Costs in International Arbitration: above note 5.

A second significant change was to introduce certain mechanisms for arbitrations involving more than two parties. Until the last amendments to the Rules, which took place in 1998, multi-party arbitration was relatively unusual and thus there appeared to be no particular need at the time to include special multi-party provisions (with some exceptions, such as article 10 of the 1998 Rules). Over the course of the last ten years, the Court was able to adopt and develop special practices to accommodate the rise in such arbitrations.[7] However, by 2008 it was felt that it was time to incorporate specifically tailored provisions to address certain multi-party issues. The 2012 Rules (in new articles 7–10) include simple, transparent provisions on joinder and multi-contract arbitration and a revised provision on consolidation.

As mentioned previously, the 2012 Rules also include a completely new process for the appointment of an emergency arbitrator who can issue an urgent interim measure of protection. The 2012 Rules provide for the emergency arbitrator's appointment within two days of the filing of the request for interim measures and for that emergency arbitrator to make his or her order within a maximum of 15 days.

There is also a range of smaller but sometimes symbolically significant changes. For example, changes were made to make the Rules gender neutral and to modernise certain provisions (for example to replace the reference to telex with email).

5 Distinguishing features of the ICC Rules of Arbitration

The Rules are designed to be flexible and can be used for virtually any kind of commercial dispute, whether involving individuals, companies or governments, and whether arising from contracts, non-contractual commercial relationships or international treaties. The 2012 Rules contain a number of provisions designed specifically to facilitate treaty-based arbitrations and arbitrations involving state entities as parties. The only requirement is an arbitration agreement providing for arbitration under the Rules. Some distinguishing features of the Rules are described below.

7 A detailed recent discussion of the Court's practices relating to multi-party and multi-contract arbitrations can be found in S. Greenberg, J. Feris and C. Albanesi, 'Consolidation, Joinder, Cross-Claims, Multiparty and Multicontract Arbitrations: Recent ICC Experience', in B. Hanotiau and E. A. Schwartz (eds.), *Multiparty Arbitration*, Dossier VII, ICC Institute of World Business Law, ICC Publication No. 701 (Paris, September 2010).

5.1 *Prima facie jurisdictional decisions, multi-party and multi-contract arbitrations*

Article 6.2 of the 1998 Rules empowered the Court to examine the *prima facie* existence of an arbitration agreement before an arbitral tribunal is even constituted. Under that provision, the Court did not analyse *sua sponte* whether an arbitration agreement under the Rules exists. Article 6.2 was rather triggered only when the respondent did not file an answer to the request for arbitration and/or objected to the arbitration clause. If there was no ICC arbitration agreement, the case was dismissed. Conversely, if the Court found *prima facie* that an ICC arbitration agreement existed, the arbitral tribunal would rule on its own jurisdiction after hearing full argument on the issue.

The main advantage of a provision such as article 6.2 is that it saves significant time and cost where there appears to be no way that an arbitral tribunal could accept jurisdiction over the case. A party aggrieved by a negative article 6.2 decision maintains the right to ask any court having jurisdiction whether or not there is a binding arbitration agreement.

The 2012 Rules maintain this basic notion of filtering out at an early stage any case where there is clearly no basis for ICC arbitral jurisdiction. However, there is a fairly important change to the manner in which this is achieved. Former article 6.2 has been split into new articles 6.3 and 6.4. Article 6.3, an entirely new provision, provides that the default will be for all jurisdictional issues to be decided by the arbitral tribunal, once constituted, unless the Secretary General of the Court decides to refer the issue to the Court for decision under article 6.4. Article 6.4 is the equivalent of former article 6.3, although with some changes which set out more transparently how the Court makes its decision as to whether there is *prima facie* ICC arbitral jurisdiction. In particular, the provision now refers to what happens when there is more than one party to the arbitration and what happens when claims are made on the basis of more than one contract.

New article 6.3 thus means that the Secretary General of the Court will act as a kind of gate-keeper, determining which cases are worthy of transmission to the Court for the Court to decide whether there is a *prima facie* jurisdictional basis for them to proceed. The advantage of this gate-keeping mechanism is to improve efficiency. Practice under the 1998 Rules showed that the vast majority of cases decided by the Court under article 6.2 resulted in a positive decision. In many of those cases the article 6.2 process itself caused unnecessary delay. New article 6.3 will ensure that only those cases where there is a chance of the Court deciding that the case cannot proceed will be transmitted to the Court.

In taking decisions under former article 6.2 of the 1998 Rules and new article 6.4 of the 2012 Rules, especially where complex multi-contract or multi-party issues are involved, the Court uses the expertise of its members and is guided by the experience of the Secretariat. In doing so, the Court is able to be pro-active in identifying and taking steps to eliminate procedural irregularities that could, at worst, frustrate the enforceability of arbitrations or, at least, cause inefficiency, delays and wasted costs. That said, the Court exercises extreme caution. It is cautious primarily by virtue of the limitations on its role: it is an administrative body that does not settle disputes. It is not the Court's role to decide disputed issues that can be submitted to fully briefed arbitral tribunals.

5.2 Terms of reference

As briefly mentioned above, a key feature of ICC arbitration is the terms of reference, drafted by the arbitral tribunal in consultation with the parties. The 2012 Rules maintained the requirement for terms of reference, which has been a hallmark feature of ICC arbitration since the Court was established. The terms of reference describe the case, define the issues and indicate the place and applicable rules for the arbitration. The terms of reference are submitted to the parties for comment (the arbitral tribunal may or may not amend the document according to the parties' input), then submitted to the parties for signature and ultimately to the Court. If any of the parties refuses to sign the terms of reference, the Court will decide whether or not to approve them. If all parties sign, the Court will only take note of the terms of reference.

Whether or not the terms of reference are a necessary part of arbitral proceedings has been the subject of a long-standing debate within the international arbitration community. It has been said that the usefulness of terms of reference is not sufficient to justify the time and cost spent on their preparation. In this regard, article 23.2 of the 2012 Rules provides a two-month deadline for the arbitral tribunal to prepare the terms of reference. In practice, it is not uncommon for this deadline to be extended by the Court, meaning that in some cases the terms of reference process takes three to four months, occasionally even longer. Whatever time it takes could be considered as additional to the overall time of resolving the parties' dispute. There is, similarly, an additional cost associated with preparing terms of reference because lawyers and arbitrators will need to spend time working on them.

Despite the perceived drawbacks of delay and cost, there has developed an emerging international consensus that some form of preliminary procedure – such as the terms of reference – is useful.[8] The ICC considers that terms of reference are an essential part of the procedure and contribute significantly to refining the issues in dispute, thereby increasing the effectiveness of subsequent hearings and, in a significant number of instances, showing the parties that their legal positions are not so different, thus creating the conditions for a possible settlement negotiation. While it is very difficult to measure scientifically, ICC experience suggests that these advantages can actually help to reduce time and costs, thus defraying any additional time and costs caused by establishing the terms of reference in the first place. As one case illustrates, terms of reference may even create a limited arbitration agreement for ruling on costs where an arbitral tribunal has decided that it has no jurisdiction.[9] Moreover, terms of reference can be prepared very quickly and cheaply if it is the desire of the parties to do so and/or if the arbitral tribunal is diligent and experienced. In a large number of cases, terms of reference are completed within a month. For these reasons, the task force that revised the Rules of Arbitration (discussed above) did not give serious consideration to changing the requirement of the terms of reference in ICC arbitration.

[8] See, for example, G. Born, *International Commercial Arbitration* (Kluwer Law International, 3rd edn, 2009), p. 1819: 'The criticism of the [ICC] Terms of Reference and procedural timetable requirements is misconceived: the ICC Rules perform a useful function by ensuring that arbitral tribunals attend at the beginning of a case to routine house-keeping (e.g. the parties' precise identities, representatives and contact details) and to less routine case management and timetabling. An experienced tribunal will usually attend to all of the issues required by the ICC Rules, even without an institutional requirement to do so. Nonetheless, no harm, and potentially much benefit, comes from requiring less experienced tribunals to complete these same tasks in a systematic manner.'

[9] *Commonwealth Development Corp (UK)* v. *Montague* (unreported, Supreme Court of Queensland Court of Appeal, Thomas JA, Ambrose and Fryberg JJ, 27 June 2000). See the discussion of the case in S. Greenberg and M. Secomb, 'Terms of Reference and Negative Jurisdictional Decisions: A lesson from Australia', *Arbitration International*, 18(2) (2002), 125.

5.3 *Awards and award scrutiny*

A large number (a little less than half[10]) of ICC arbitrations are settled or otherwise withdrawn at some stage before a final award is issued. If a case is not withdrawn, obtaining a well-reasoned enforceable award is the ultimate outcome of an arbitration. In 2011 alone, the Court received, scrutinised and approved 508 draft awards, comprising 347 final awards, 120 partial awards and 41 awards by consent.

The scrutiny of draft awards is a cornerstone feature of ICC arbitration. A great deal of work goes into the scrutiny process, both on the part of the Court and of the Secretariat. Article 33 of the 2012 Rules (which is identical to Article 27 of the 1998 Rules) provides:

> Before signing any Award, the Arbitral Tribunal shall submit it in draft form to the Court. The Court may lay down modifications as to the form of the Award and, without affecting the Arbitral Tribunal's liberty of decision, may also draw its attention to points of substance. No Award shall be rendered by the Arbitral Tribunal until it has been approved by the Court as to its form.[11]

The language of this provision makes clear that the Court's scrutiny process cannot require the arbitral tribunal to change the substance of its award, nor does it involve a review of the facts or a re-examination of questions of law. The tribunal's 'liberty of decision' remains untouched and – while the arbitrators' attention can be drawn to matters of substance – it is not the Court's role to interfere with the tribunal's discretion to decide the case as it sees fit.

5.3.1 Scrutiny process

An ICC arbitral tribunal decides the case alone and without any input or interference from the Court. Once the tribunal's deliberations are complete

[10] Over 2003–2008, an average of 47% of ICC arbitrations were withdrawn by the parties after the request for arbitration had been filed but before the arbitral tribunal issued its final award. Almost half of those withdrawals (an average of 43%) occurred after the request for arbitration was filed but prior to the arbitral tribunal being fully constituted. A further average of 22% of the withdrawals occurred between the time the arbitral tribunal was fully constituted and the time the terms of reference were finalised.

[11] Under article 6 of appendix II to the 2012 Rules (identical in the 1998 Rules), the Court may consider the impact of any mandatory laws at the place of arbitration in the following terms: 'When the Court scrutinises draft Awards in accordance with Article 33 of the Rules, it considers, to the extent practicable, the requirements of mandatory law at the place of arbitration.'

and the decisions are taken, they are drafted into the form of an award. The draft is submitted to the Court's Secretariat and reviewed by the Counsel in charge of the case. He or she occasionally spots an obvious discrepancy, which can be brought to the tribunal's attention even before the award goes to Court. The award is then reviewed by the Deputy Secretary General and possibly the Secretary General and/or General Counsel.

The award is then submitted to the Court itself and reviewed by several Court members. If the award goes to a plenary session, and also occasionally at committee sessions, a Court member is assigned the task of reporting to the rest of the Court on the award.

5.3.2 Outcomes of scrutiny

The Court can either not approve an award, approve it subject to the arbitral tribunal considering certain comments or approve it without any comments. On 37 occasions in 2011, the Court decided not to approve an award and requested the arbitral tribunal to resubmit it after dealing with the Court's comments. Of the 508 awards that the Court did approve in 2011, the Court laid down modifications as to the form of the award and/or drew the arbitral tribunal's attention to points of substance when approving 496 of those awards, leaving 12 awards approved without comments by the Court.

The problems found in awards can be broadly divided into three categories: formalistic, quasi-substantial and substantial. Comments of form include, for example, whether the award recites the arbitration agreement, the seat of arbitration, the parties' and counsel's details, the procedural history of the case, extensions of time for rendering the final award as well as typographical errors.

Examples of quasi-substantive points include whether all of the issues have been decided (*infra petita*), whether the tribunal has decided on issues not raised by the parties (*ultra petita*), whether reasons are given for the tribunal's decisions, whether the dispositive section of the award is clear, whether costs and interest are addressed (sometimes forgotten or given scant attention) as well as mathematical calculation errors. The Court may further draw the arbitral tribunal's attention to compulsory statutes of limitation in a given country that may affect the enforcement of the award.

More substantive points include drawing the arbitral tribunal's attention to apparent contradictions or inadequacies in the reasoning, potential flaws in the analysis and inconsistencies between the dispositive section and the body of the award.

However frustrating it may be for Court members to limit their comments when confronted with draft awards they simply do not agree with, the Court is careful to respect its role. As noted above, the Rules do not allow the Court to interfere with the arbitral tribunal's liberty of decision. While the scrutiny process occasionally leads an arbitral tribunal to modify an aspect of its decision, this is because the Court will have identified, for example, missing elements in the decision, inconsistencies in different parts of the award, a failure to deal with certain claims or a decision that is *ultra petita*.

Finding the delicate boundary between form and substance in scrutinising draft arbitral awards can also be a difficult task for Court members. While the quality of awards is by and large very good, there are still a number of inexperienced or overcommitted arbitrators who produce work of a lower quality. The Court's (and Secretariat's) review of draft awards plays a key role in increasing the chances of an award being enforceable.[12]

6 Conclusion

The ICC has to exercise considerable caution before changing any practices or Rules of the Court. This is because of the influence that any such change will have on international arbitral practice generally. The Court is probably the world's busiest and best-known international arbitral institution. It also has the broadest geographical reach across the broadest range of industry sectors. The changes to the Court's Rules will surely impact upon the practice of international arbitration globally.

ICC arbitration has and will continue to play an important role worldwide. The twenty-first century will bring new challenges. Whatever the future may hold, the Court and Secretariat are well equipped to cope thanks to the institution's long and diverse experience and the quality and experience of the Court members, both present and future, and staff of the Secretariat. The Court has been able to generate practices and to find practical solutions to the many challenges that face parties engaged in international arbitration. It should continue to do so.

[12] Both the Court and arbitral tribunal are obliged to do all that they can to ensure the enforceability of awards. Article 41 of the 2012 Rules (identical to article 35 of the 1998 Rules) provides: 'In all matters not expressly provided for in these Rules, the Court and the Arbitral Tribunal shall act in the spirit of these Rules and shall make every effort to make sure that the Award is enforceable at law.'

10

Arbitration in London: Features of the London Court of International Arbitration

JOHANNES KOEPP, DORINE FARAH AND PETER WEBSTER

1 Time frame for the proceeding

It used to be said that one of the main reasons for choosing to settle a dispute by arbitration instead of by resort to the courts was speed. Indeed, when the London Chamber of Arbitration (the precursor of the London Court of International Arbitration (the 'LCIA')) was founded, Edward Manson wrote in the *Law Quarterly Review*: 'it is to be expeditious where the law is slow'.[1] No longer. Now, delay is the most frequently voiced complaint about arbitration.[2] There is particular concern about the length of time it can take to constitute an arbitral tribunal and the length of time that a tribunal can take to render its award.

The LCIA Rules (hereafter, the 'Rules') attempt to address the concerns of delay. They contain a distinctive provision for the expedited formation of the tribunal in cases of urgency[3] and impose a general duty on the tribunal to adopt suitable procedures for the conduct of the arbitration to avoid unnecessary delay and expense.[4]

The Rules also attempt to avoid unnecessary delays through other mechanisms. For example, while the Rules do not impose any maximum duration on the arbitral proceedings as a whole or a time limit after the end of proceedings within which the award must be rendered,[5] they lay

1 E. Manson 'The City of London Chamber of Arbitration', *LQR*, 9(1893), 86 at p. 86.

2 N. Blackaby and C. Partasides with A. Redfern and M. Hunter, *Redfern and Hunter on International Arbitration*, 5th edn (Oxford University Press, 2009), para. 1.103.

3 Article 9, considered at pp. 231–2 below.

4 Article 14.1, considered at p. 258 below.

5 The explanation offered is that the number of situations in which an extension would be required defeats the purpose of setting a limit in the first place: J. L. Greenblatt and P. R. Griffin 'Towards the Harmonization of International Arbitration Rules:

down a series of deadlines which must be met once proceedings are commenced, although the tribunal may, in its discretion, extend or abridge these time limits.[6]

To commence arbitration proceedings under the LCIA Rules, the claimant must send a request for arbitration to the Registrar of the LCIA Court (the 'Registrar'), and simultaneously serve copies upon all other parties to the arbitration by one or more of the means of service specified in article 4.1.[7] The arbitration is deemed to have commenced on the date on which the Registrar receives the request for arbitration.[8] The respondent has 30 days from the date on which it receives service of the request for arbitration in which to send a response to the request.[9] The LCIA Court then takes steps to constitute the tribunal. It is required to appoint the tribunal as soon as practicable after receipt by the Registrar of the respondent's response or, if no response is received, after the expiry of 30 days following service of the request upon the respondent.[10]

Although the parties are encouraged to agree on the conduct of the proceedings,[11] it is rare for them to do so, especially after a dispute has arisen. In the absence of party agreement, the arbitrators routinely establish at the outset of the arbitration a timetable for the proceedings, including the time limits for lodging written pleadings.[12] Obviously, where an arbitration requires extensive factual investigations, the disclosure of evidence and the examination of several witnesses and experts, the time frame for rendering a final award may be longer than in a case with simpler factual issues.[13] Scheduling a hearing will depend upon the availability of the arbitrators, parties' counsel, witnesses and experts, among other factors, whilst the duration of the hearing will depend

Comparative Analysis of the Rules of the ICC, AAA, LCIA and CIET', *Arb Intl*, 17(2001), 101 at p. 107. Sometimes the parties may wish to impose on the arbitrators a mandatory time limit for rendering the final award (or the arbitrators may themselves provide for one in the timetable that they establish for the case). The merits of imposing such a limit are debateable: Blackaby and Partasides, *Redfern and Hunter on International Arbitration*, paras. 9.131–2.

[6] Articles 4.7 and 22.1(b).

[7] Article 1.1. Article 1.1 details what the request for arbitration should contain.

[8] Article 1.2.

[9] Article 2.1. The LCIA Court may fix a shorter period. Article 2 details what the response should contain.

[10] Article 5.4. [11] Article 14.

[12] Regulation of the conduct of the arbitration is discussed in more detail in Section 10 below.

[13] Article 15.

upon the complexity of the issues involved and the number of witnesses and experts to be examined.

2 Costs determination (including security)

Costs are determined in accordance with article 28, which distinguishes between the costs of the arbitration itself (articles 28.1 and 28.2) and the legal or other costs incurred by the parties (article 28.3).

The costs of the arbitration itself consist of the fees and expenses of the arbitrators as well as the administrative charges of the LCIA. The costs of the parties include the fees and expenses of the lawyers engaged to represent the parties in the arbitral proceedings in addition to other professional fees and expenses, such as those of expert witnesses. Expenses will include the hotel and travelling expenses of the lawyers, witnesses and others involved in the preparation and presentation of the case and other expenses such as photocopying, telephone calls, research, interpreters, court reporters, the hearing venue etc.

2.1 Determination of arbitration costs

The arbitration costs are determined by the LCIA Court (rather than the arbitral tribunal) in accordance with the Schedule of Costs set out in the preamble to the Rules.[14] A distinguishing feature of the Rules is that the arbitrators' fees and the administrative charges levied by the LCIA are based on the time spent by the arbitrators, the LCIA Court and the Secretariat of the LCIA Court (the 'Secretariat'), rather than being a flat fee based on the amount in dispute.[15] Thus, while parties cannot predict at the outset of the proceedings what the costs of an LCIA arbitration will be, the fact that costs are calculated on the basis of time spent on the dispute is perceived to be a fair solution for all parties. The fact that a claim is for a substantial sum of money does not necessarily mean that it is complex and that its handling requires particular expertise.[16]

[14] Article 28.1. For a discussion on the role, function and composition of the LCIA Court, see Section 12 below.

[15] Under the ICC Rules, for example, costs are determined in accordance with an *ad valorem* scale: Appendix III Rules of Arbitration of the International Chamber of Commerce (in force as from 1 January 2012; hereafter referred to as 'the ICC Rules').

[16] J. M. Hunter and J. Paulson 'Rules of the London Court of International Arbitration: A Commentary on the 1985 Rules of the London Court of International Arbitration', *Ybk Comm Arb*, 10(1985), 167 at p. 171.

The current Schedule of Costs, effective as of 1 July 2012, provides for the following:[17]

(a) A registration fee of £1,750 is payable in advance with the request for arbitration. It is non-refundable.[18]
(b) A fee of £225 per hour is charged for time spent by the Registrar, his deputy and his counsel in the administration of the arbitration.
(c) A fee of £100 or £150 per hour is charged for the time spent by other Secretariat personnel in the administration of the arbitration. The rate charged depends on the type of activity.
(d) Time spent by members of the LCIA Court in carrying out their functions in deciding any challenge is charged at hourly rates advised by members of the LCIA Court.
(e) The fees and expenses of the tribunal itself are calculated by reference to time spent in connection with the arbitration and according to the circumstances of the case. Rates are agreed prior to the tribunal's appointment. They should not exceed an hourly rate of £450 other than in exceptional cases.
(f) A sum equivalent to 5% of the tribunal's fees is payable to the LCIA in respect of its general overhead.

In determining the costs of the arbitration, the LCIA Court relies on a financial record prepared by the Secretariat. The LCIA Court reviews the dossier and notifies the Secretariat of the amount it has determined for the arbitration costs.[19] The tribunal must specify in its award the total amount of the costs as determined by the LCIA Court. Unless the parties agree otherwise, the tribunal must determine the proportions in which these costs are to be borne by the parties.[20] The parties are jointly and severally liable to the arbitral tribunal and the LCIA for the arbitration costs.[21] The basis upon which arbitration costs are apportioned is the same as for the apportionment of legal costs, which is discussed below.[22]

[17] Available at: www.lcia.org/Dispute_Resolution_Services/LCIA_Arbitration_Costs.aspx (accessed 12 November 2012).

[18] If the LCIA is requested to act as an appointing authority only, a non-refundable appointment fee of £1,000 is payable with the request.

[19] P. Turner and R. Mohtashami, *A Guide to the LCIA Arbitration Rules* (Oxford University Press, 2009), paras. 8.14–15.

[20] Article 28.2. [21] Article 28.1 [22] See p. 222 below.

2.2 *Deposits*

Unlike some arbitral institutions, the LCIA takes a 'pay as you arbitrate' approach. Article 24.1 permits the LCIA Court to direct the parties, in such proportions as it thinks appropriate, to make one of several interim or final payments on account of the costs of the arbitration. The deposits are held by the LCIA and, as the arbitration progresses, they may from time to time be released by the LCIA Court to the arbitrator(s), any expert(s) appointed by the tribunal and the LCIA itself. The aim of these payments is to ensure that the arbitrators and the LCIA encounter no difficulties in being paid. The funds are held on trust in interest-bearing accounts.[23] Although the Rules provide for the LCIA Court to exercise the power to issue directions regarding payments that the parties must make on account of the costs of the arbitration, this authority has been delegated to the Registrar and, in practice, is exercised by the Secretariat.[24] The LCIA will typically call for payment of deposits shortly after the tribunal's constitution and in anticipation of a hearing.[25] The LCIA Court may limit such payments to a sum sufficient to cover fees, expenses and costs for the next stage of the arbitration.[26] In practice, the LCIA Court decides that sum following consultation with the arbitrators.[27] Interim costs are paid from the sums held on deposit upon the Registrar submitting an invoice. If insufficient funds are held on deposit, an invoice can be submitted directly to the parties.[28]

The tribunal should not proceed with the arbitration without ascertaining that the LCIA has the required funds.[29] There is a close dialogue between tribunals and the Registrar regarding the financial position of each arbitration. If a shortage of funds is discovered, the arbitration may

[23] Interest is credited to the party depositing the sum (LCIA Schedule of Arbitration Costs, para. 6). This also distinguishes the LCIA from other institutions, which require the payment of costs in advance of the arbitration.

[24] Turner and Mohtashami, *Guide to the LCIA Rules*, para. 8.37. The delegation is by means of the directive 'Procedure for the Registrar in the Application of Articles 24.1 and 24.3 of the LCIA Rules' (19 October 2000), reproduced as Appendix 6 to Turner and Mohtashami, *Guide to the LCIA Rules*. There are monetary limits on the amount of each individual direction that the Registrar can issue (up to $240,000 or £120,000). The Registrar must advise the Court when the cumulative total of directions issued in one case exceeds $500,000 or £250,000 and of all directions for deposits thereafter. See also the LCIA Schedule of Arbitration Costs, para. 8.

[25] Turner and Mohtashami, *Guide to the LCIA Rules*, para. 8.38.

[26] Schedule of Arbitration Costs, para. 5(a).

[27] Turner and Mohtashami, *Guide to the LCIA Rules*, para. 8.38.

[28] LCIA Schedule of Arbitration Costs, para. 7. [29] Article 28.2.

be brought to a halt. The LCIA Court will only transmit the award to the parties if the costs of the arbitration have been paid.[30]

Article 24.3 provides that if one party fails or refuses to pay any deposit as directed, the Registrar may direct the other party or parties to effect a substitute payment to allow the arbitration to proceed, subject to any award on costs.[31] The party making the substitute payment is entitled to recover that amount as a debt immediately due from the defaulting party.[32] On several occasions, tribunals have issued partial awards ordering defaulting parties to pay their outstanding shares of the directed deposits, facilitating recovery of that sum by the party who has had to make a substitute payment.[33] Moreover, the LCIA Court and the tribunal may treat failure by a claimant or a counter-claiming party to provide the required deposit promptly and in full as a withdrawal of the claim or counter-claim.[34]

2.3 *Liability for legal costs*

The tribunal has the power to order that all or part of the legal and other costs of one party be paid by the other party, unless the parties have agreed otherwise.[35] As the tribunal's power is discretionary, a party must apply for its legal costs if it wishes to ensure that the issue is determined by the tribunal in the award.[36] In exercising this discretion, the tribunal is guided by the principle in article 28.4 that 'costs should reflect the parties' relative success and failure in the award or arbitration'.[37] The tribunal, however, may depart from this general principle 'where it appears to the Arbitral Tribunal that in the particular circumstances this general approach is inappropriate'.[38] The typical circumstances that will be relevant, other than the parties' relative success and failure on the merits, include the respective conduct of the parties throughout the arbitration proceedings and the relative success of the parties at different stages of the proceedings (for example, on preliminary issues or

30 LCIA Schedule of Arbitration Costs, para. 9(b).

31 The Rules refer to the LCIA Court issuing this direction, but this power has also been delegated to the Registrar.

32 Article 24.3.

33 Turner and Mohtashami, *Guide to the LCIA Rules*, para. 8.50.

34 Article 24.4.

35 Article 28.3.

36 This is in contrast with the determination of the arbitration costs under article 28.2, where the tribunal is mandated to address the costs of the arbitration.

37 Article 28.4. Article 28.4 applies to the apportionment of both the arbitration costs and legal costs.

38 Article 28.4.

challenge of an arbitrator). The tribunal will also be guided by the approach of the law of the seat to the apportionment of costs.[39]

In 93 cases in which a decision on liability for costs was made between 2007 and 2011, legal costs were awarded in their entirety to one party in 31 (a third) of those cases.[40] In 55 cases, the tribunal awarded part of a party's legal costs, and in seven, no decision was made on the apportionment of legal costs. Liability for arbitration costs was distributed differently. They were awarded in full to one party in more than two-thirds of the sample cases (68). In the other 25 cases, they were apportioned between the parties.

3 Procedure for the appointment of the tribunal

The Rules contain default provisions and also certain mandatory rules for the appointment of the arbitral tribunal. A unique feature of the Rules is that the LCIA Court alone is empowered to appoint the tribunal. Parties nevertheless often provide the procedure for the appointment of the arbitral tribunal in their arbitration agreement, which the LCIA Court will take into account. Thus, they may decide on the number of arbitrators, any required qualifications and the method of appointment.

The LCIA Court is the only arbitral institution that provides reasoned decisions in respect of challenges to arbitrators. It recently published anonymous versions of these decisions.[41] Although previous decisions are not binding in subsequent challenges, they do give some indication of how challenges are being decided by the LCIA Court.

3.1 Selection of arbitrators

The Rules do not limit the parties' freedom to choose their arbitrators to a roster of arbitrators selected by the institution.[42] Rather, parties

[39] Blackaby and Partasides, *Redfern and Hunter on International Arbitration*, paras. 9.99–100. In England, s. 61 Arbitration Act 1996 gives the tribunal a wide discretion in relation to how the parties' costs may be allocated.

[40] Information provided by the LCIA to the authors.

[41] They are summarised in T. W. Walsh and R. Teitelbaum, 'The LCIA Court Decisions on Challenges to Arbitrators: An Introduction', *Arb Intl*, 27(2011), 283. The abstracts of the decisions begin at p. 315.

[42] The LCIA Court does, however, maintain a database of arbitrators, which it will consult both when assessing the suitability of party nominees and in cases where the parties have

and their counsel are free to select any individual whose judgment and, in the case of a three-member tribunal, force of persuasion they trust. Article 5.2 categorically prohibits any arbitrator, whether before or after the appointment, from advising any party on the merits or outcome of the dispute.

The selection of the arbitrator(s) is subject to the scrutiny of the LCIA Court. Article 5.5 provides that it is the LCIA Court alone that is empowered to appoint arbitrators and that it is to have 'due regard' for any particular method or criteria of selection agreed in writing by the parties. It is to consider the nature of the transaction, the nature and circumstances of the dispute, the nationality, location and languages of the parties and the number of the parties. Prior to appointment, each arbitrator must make certain disclosures to the LCIA Court, which the LCIA Court will consider.[43] In practice, the LCIA Court will almost always appoint the party nominee where such nomination has been made.[44]

The LCIA Court may proceed with the formation of the tribunal notwithstanding that the request for arbitration is incomplete or the response is missing, late or incomplete.[45] This prevents a party from deliberately delaying the proceedings by attempting to obstruct the formation of the tribunal.

3.2 Number of arbitrators

Arbitral tribunals can be composed of one or more arbitrators, taking into account any prohibitions laid down in the law of the seat of the arbitration.[46] Article 5.4 contains the default rule. It provides for the appointment of a sole arbitrator, unless the parties have agreed otherwise or unless the LCIA Court determines that a three-member tribunal is

not nominated an arbitrator: S. Nesbitt, 'LCIA Arbitration Rules', in L. A. Mistelis (ed.), *Concise International Arbitration* (The Hague: Kluwer Law International, 2010), p. 414.

43 Article 5.3. See p. 231 below.

44 For a discussion of the three instances in which the LCIA Court refused to affirm the party nominee, see Turner and Mohtashami, *Guide to the LCIA Rules*, para. 4.73.

45 Article 5.4.

46 E.g., some jurisdictions prohibit arbitration with an even number of arbitrators. English law does not, although there is an interpretative presumption that, unless agreed otherwise, an agreement for an even number of arbitrators is to be understood as requiring the appointment of a further arbitrator as chairman of the tribunal: s. 15(2) Arbitration Act 1996. See, generally, G. Born, *International Commercial Arbitration*, 3rd edn (Alphen aan den Rijn: Kluwer Law International, 2009), pp. 1351–3.

more appropriate 'in view of all the circumstances of the case'.[47] There are no strict criteria for determining how this discretion is exercised.[48] When determining whether the 'circumstances of the case' require a three-member tribunal, the LCIA Court will take into account a variety of factors, including the complexity of the case, the amount at stake, the need for particular linguistic or other skills and whether one of the parties is a state.[49] This is consistent with the practice of other leading international arbitration institutions.[50]

3.3 *The nationality requirement*

Where the parties are of different nationalities, the LCIA Court will not appoint a sole arbitrator or chairperson of the nationality of one of the parties, unless the parties who are not of the same nationality as the proposed appointee all agree in writing.[51] Determining the nationality of a party requires the application of a 'substantive test as opposed to a merely formal one'.[52] A natural person can have a de facto nationality as well as a de jure nationality. A person will be deemed to be a de facto national of a country 'where his connections to it were so concentrated that his technical nationality did not ensure neutrality'.[53] For example, a person who is not a Swedish citizen but who had served as the Swedish consul to a South American port city for 30 years would be unsuitable as a sole arbitrator in a case involving a Swedish party.[54] Moreover, a person who had spent a considerable amount of time in England would not be deemed to be a de facto British citizen in circumstances where he

[47] Similar rules can be found in article 12 of the ICC Rules and article 6 of the Arbitration Rules of the Swiss Chamber of Commerce. There are obvious advantages associated with the appointment of a sole arbitrator. It normally costs less, the person is easier to select and is likely to be able to resolve a dispute more quickly than three- or five-member tribunals. The selection process in cases of a multi-member tribunal may cause significant delays in the composition of the tribunal. On the other hand, a three-member tribunal often allows parties to have a greater say in the selection of the decision-makers. Arbitration tribunals composed of more than three arbitrators are rare in commercial cases.

[48] S. Konrad and R. Hunter, 'LCIA-Schiedsregeln', in R. A. Schütze (ed.), *Institutionelle Schiedsgerichtsbarkeit: Kommentar*, 2nd edn (Cologne: Carl Heymanns Verlag, 2011), article 5, para. 15.

[49] S. Nesbitt, 'LCIA Arbitration Rules', p. 412.

[50] Born, *International Commercial Arbitration*, p. 1363. [51] Article 6.1.

[52] LCIA Reference No. 8086 (30 Sept 1998), *Arb Intl*, 27(2011), 328, para. 3.2.

[53] Ibid. [54] Ibid.

had worked for foreign companies and held legal qualifications from the United States.[55] A person who is a citizen of two or more states is treated as a national of each. European Union citizens are treated as nationals of the relevant Member State and are not treated as all having the same nationality.[56]

The nationality of legal persons will usually be the place of incorporation, but it is not necessarily limited to that nationality. Article 6.2 provides that the nationality of the parties 'shall be understood to include that of controlling shareholders or interests'. This will be fairly straightforward in companies with a clear controlling shareholder. In a company with a large and diverse shareholding, however, nationality will be taken to be only that of the place of incorporation.[57] For more complex shareholdings, the situation is unclear. None of the LCIA Court's published challenge decisions grapple with the various complexities of determining corporate nationality and, in particular, establishing what amounts to a 'controlling' shareholder or interest.[58]

3.4 Requirements as regards the qualifications/background of the arbitrator

The Rules do not restrict the parties' freedom to stipulate specific qualifications that the nominated arbitrators must meet, such as knowledge of a particular legal system, specific languages or industry practices. In 2010, the English Court of Appeal's decision in *Jivraj* v. *Hashwani*[59] sparked widespread concern that requirements in arbitration clauses using criteria such as religion or nationality might be void under English law, at least in relation to arbitrations seated in England. In *Jivraj*, an arbitration clause in a joint venture agreement provided that

[55] Ibid. [56] Article 6.3.

[57] Turner and Mohtashami, *Guide to the LCIA Rules*, paras. 4.63–4.64. Given the burdens that investigating shareholdings or interests in companies would impose on the LCIA Court, it does not undertake to research these points. It may be clear from the face of the Request for Arbitration or the Response that one (or more) of the parties has controlling shareholders or interests. If this is not clear from the face of those documents, the parties themselves must make representations about nationality if they wish the LCIA Court to consider this point.

[58] The issue arises prominently in international investment arbitration: see R. Dolzer and C. Schreuer, *Principles of International Investment Law* (Oxford University Press, 2008), pp. 49–52.

[59] [2010] EWCA Civ 712; [2010] ICR 1435; [2011] 1 All ER 50.

arbitrators appointed under it had to be respected members of the Ismaili community. The Court of Appeal found that the appointment of an arbitrator was 'employment' for the purposes of the Employment (Religion or Belief) Regulations 2003, which prohibited discrimination on grounds of religion or belief in determining access to employment.[60] As the clause was directly discriminatory, it was held to be void. This decision was of particular concern to the LCIA, given that the Rules specifically refer to nationality in the conduct of the selection of the arbitrators.[61] In July 2011, the UK Supreme Court unanimously allowed an appeal against that decision. It held that arbitrators are not 'employees' within the meaning of UK and EU discrimination legislation.[62] Parties are therefore free to agree the qualifying criteria that they deem necessary to ensure that the most suitable individuals are selected to resolve their dispute.

3.5 *Independence and impartiality of arbitrators*

Arbitrators must be impartial and independent of the parties at all times.[63] An arbitrator must not act in the arbitration as an advocate for any party.[64] Although the Rules do not provide any guidance as to the meaning of 'impartiality' and 'independence', the published abstracts of LCIA Court decisions give some indication as to how those concepts are being applied. All of the challenges that have been considered by the LCIA Court to date have arisen from arbitrations seated in England.[65] The Departmental Advisory Committee on Arbitration Law (which was instrumental in drafting what became the Arbitration Act) viewed 'independence' and 'impartiality' as distinct concepts and considered that mere dependence was not problematic.[66] The text of the Arbitration Act 1996 therefore requires arbitrators to be impartial but not necessarily independent.[67] By contrast, the LCIA Court has reasoned that the need to interpret the Arbitration Act 1996 compatibly with article 6(1) of the

[60] SI 2003/1660, regulation 6. The regulations implemented Council Framework Directive 2000/78/EC (OJ 2000 No. L303, p. 16) in the UK. They have now been replaced by the Equality Act 2010, which is in materially identical terms on this point.

[61] Article 6.3. [62] [2011] UKSC 40; [2011] 1 WLR 1872. [63] Article 5.2.

[64] Article 5.2. [65] This statement is accurate as at February 2012.

[66] Departmental Advisory Committee on Arbitration Law, *Report on the Arbitration Bill* (1996), para. 101. (The report is reproduced as Appendix 8 to R. Merkin and L. Flannery, *Arbitration Act 1996*, 4th edn (London: Informa, 2008).)

[67] ss. 24(1)(a) and 33 Arbitration Act 1996.

European Convention of Human Rights[68] means that it should be read as requiring arbitrators to be both impartial and independent.[69]

The LCIA Court has drawn upon English law in giving content to the concepts of 'independence' and 'impartiality' in the Rules. The LCIA Court's decisions treat independence as an objective concept. The test for dependence looks for the existence of circumstances that create the appearance of potential bias on the part of the arbitrator. Impartiality, on the other hand, is treated as a subjective concept. The test for impartiality looks for the actual presence of bias, as demonstrated by the actions of the arbitrator.[70] When applying tests regarding independence and impartiality, the relevant standpoint under the Rules is that of the 'fair-minded and informed observer'. The question is whether such a person, having considered the facts, would conclude that there is a 'real possibility' that an arbitrator is either dependent upon or partial to a party.[71]

When interpreting the concepts of 'independence' and 'impartiality', the LCIA Court has referred to the International Bar Association Guidelines on Conflicts of Interest in International Arbitration (2004) (the 'IBA Guidelines'), as they 'reflect actual practice in significant parts of the international arbitration community'.[72] In common with other arbitral institutions, however, it does not consider itself bound by these guidelines.[73] The LCIA Court has also, in some decisions, referred to the English law concept of 'automatic disqualification', which applies where a judge has 'objective connections with the interests at stake' in the dispute.[74] This has been treated as part of the analysis of whether the arbitrator is independent. If the LCIA Court were to apply the English law test, an arbitrator would be automatically disqualified if he has a

[68] Article 6(1) provides that everyone is entitled to a 'fair and public hearing . . . by an independent and impartial tribunal established by law'.

[69] LCIA Reference No. 81160 (28 August 2009), *Arb Intl* 442, 27(2011), paras. 3.3–3.5; LCIA Reference No. 81224 (15 March 2010), *Arb Intl* 461, 27(2011), para. 3.4.

[70] Walsh and Teitelbaum, 'LCIA Court Decisions: An Introduction', pp. 287–288; e.g. LCIA Reference No. 81160 (28 August 2009), *Arb Intl*, 27(2011), 442, paras. 3.8–3.9; LCIA Reference No. 81224 (15 March 2010) *Arb Intl*, 27(2011), 461, paras. 3.7–3.8.

[71] The 'real possibility' test for apparent bias in English law was established in *Porter* v. *Magill* [2001] UKHL 67, [2002] 2 AC 357 at paras. 100–3 and applied by the House of Lords in *Helow* v. *Secretary of State for the Home Department* [2008] 1 WLR 2416 (HL). It is a development of the previous test of 'real danger' of bias, referred to in cases such as *R* v. *Gough* [1993] AC 646 (HL).

[72] LCIA Reference No. 81160 (28 August 2009), *Arb Intl*, 27(2011), 442 para. 3.7; LCIA Reference No. 81224 (15 March 2010), *Arb Intl*, 461, 27(2011), para. 3.6.

[73] Walsh and Teitelbaum, 'LCIA Court Decisions: An Introduction', p. 288.

[74] LCIA Reference No. 81160 (28 August 2009), *Arb Intl*, 442, 27(2011), para. 3.10.

pecuniary interest in the outcome of the case and also if his decision would lead to the promotion of a cause in which he was involved together with one of the parties.[75]

One issue that has led to various challenges is the impact of professional and personal relationships between the arbitrator and either one of the parties or their counsel. In particular, members of the solicitors' and barristers' professions are treated differently because of the different business structures of those professions. The LCIA Court has held that 'a partner in a law firm had to be identified with his partners, at least insofar as their professional activities were concerned'.[76] Unsurprisingly, a partner in a law firm could not sit as an arbitrator in an arbitration in which that law firm was representing a party. Moreover, where partners of a prospective arbitrator had advised one of the parties on contracts related to the dispute that was the subject of arbitration, the LCIA Court declined to appoint the proposed arbitrator.[77] In contrast, the LCIA Court, in common with other national courts,[78] has held that a barrister may sit as an arbitrator in an arbitration in which a barrister from the same chambers is representing a party.[79] Chambers are groupings of barristers who share administrative resources, clerks and office space. The members do not share income and profits, are individually instructed in matters and frequently appear against other barristers from the same chambers. Some suggest that it is not safe to assume that the rule in respect of barristers is absolute and that this practice may be changing.[80] A possible reason for this shift in approach is that

[75] Famously applied in *R* v. *Bow Street Metropolitan Stipendiary Magistrate, Ex p Pinochet Ugarte (No. 2)* [2000] 1 AC 119 (HL).

[76] LCIA Reference No. UN96/X15 (29 May 1996), *Arb Intl*, 27(2011), 317, para. 4.1.

[77] LCIA Reference No. 9147 (27 January 2000), *Arb Intl*, 334, 27(2011), para. 3.1.

[78] England: *Laker Airways Inc* v. *FLS Aerospace Ltd* [2000] 1 WLR 113; France: *Kuwait Foreign Trading Contracting and Investment Co* v. *Ikori Estero* (Cour d'appel de Paris), *Rev Arb* (1992), 568, 570–1.

[79] LCIA Reference No. UN97/X11 (5 June 1997), *Arb Intl*, 320, 27(2011), para. 4.3. Apparently the ICC Court upheld a challenge in these circumstances (although, in line with ICC practice, the decision would not have been reasoned or published): K. Karadelis, 'Bar Council to Address Barristers' Conflicts', *Global Arbitration Review*, 12 March 2012.

[80] Walsh and Teitelbaum, 'LCIA Court Decisions: An Introduction', p. 295, referring to *Hrvatska Elektroprivreda, d.d.* v. *Slovenia* (ICSID Case No. ARB/05/24 6 May 2008, para. 34). In this ICSID decision, it was held that a respondent could not, at a late stage, change its legal team so as to include a barrister from the same chambers as the tribunal chairperson. See, also, W. W. Park 'Rectitude in International Arbitration', *Arb Intl*, 27(2011), 475 at pp. 516–18. He notes that the 'orange list' in the IBA Guidelines

barristers' chambers increasingly market themselves in a way similar to solicitor firms.[81] A group of barristers is currently working with the Bar Council to prepare guidelines to address potential conflicts, although it is thought unlikely that they will recommend an absolute bar on the practice of counsel from the same chambers appearing as arbitrator and counsel.[82]

Past relationships between counsel and arbitrators do not, by themselves, imperil impartiality.[83] The LCIA Court has considered the relevance of repeat appointments and their impact upon dependence. It reasoned that the 'mere fact that an arbitrator is regularly nominated (by different arbitral parties) on the recommendation of the same counsel or the same firm of solicitors ought not of itself to give rise to justifiable doubts as to his independence and impartiality'.[84] The arbitrator's relationship with those lawyers can, however, be such that it gives rise to a real possibility of bias. Unlike the IBA Guidelines, which include repeat appointments on their 'orange list' and consider only the number of appointments, the LCIA Court has considered the actual economic significance of appointments.[85] In the only challenge concerning this matter, the LCIA Court considered the position of an arbitrator who was a barrister and had received 11% of his instructions over the previous five years from the respondent's counsel. He had received a further two sets of instructions from the respondent's counsel during the period between his nomination as arbitrator and his disclosure, one of which was from the respondents themselves. The LCIA Court held that there was a real possibility of bias because the arbitrator had current instructions to act in a case from one of the parties to the dispute referred to arbitration.[86] This was compounded by the 'obvious professional importance' to the arbitrator of his relationship with the respondent's counsel. The LCIA Court did, however, stress that the mere fact that an arbitrator was regularly nominated (by different arbitral parties) on the recommendation of the same counsel or firm of solicitors was not, alone, enough to give rise to justifiable doubts over independence or impartiality.[87]

includes the fact that the arbitrator and another arbitrator or the counsel for one of the parties are members of the same barristers' chambers.

[81] Karadelis, 'Bar Council to Address Barristers' Conflicts'. [82] Ibid.

[83] Walsh and Teitelbaum, 'LCIA Court Decisions: An Introduction', pp. 295–7.

[84] LCIA Reference No. 81160 (28 August 2009) (2011), 27 *Arb Intl* 442, para. 4.6.

[85] An approach also adopted in recent ICSID challenges: Walsh and Teitelbaum, 'LCIA Court Decisions: An Introduction', pp. 300–1.

[86] LCIA Reference No. 81160 (28 August 2009), *Arb Intl* 442, 27(2011), paras. 4.1–4.6.

[87] Ibid., para. 4.6.

3.6 *Duty of disclosure*

Article 5.3 of the Rules provides for a duty of disclosure. A prospective arbitrator must furnish the Registrar with a declaration that there are no circumstances known to him likely to give rise to any justified doubts as to his impartiality or independence,[88] other than any circumstances disclosed by him in the declaration.[89] The duty of disclosure is not limited to the duration of the appointment procedure. An arbitrator is under a continuing duty to disclose any such circumstances to the LCIA Court, to any other members of the arbitral tribunal and to all the parties if they arise after the date of his declaration and before the arbitration is concluded.[90] Before appointment, each arbitrator must also submit to the Registrar a written résumé of past and present professional positions and must agree in writing upon fee rates conforming to the Schedule of Costs.[91]

3.7 *Expedited formation*

In cases of exceptional urgency, on or after commencement of the arbitration, any party may apply to the LCIA Court for the expedited formation of the arbitral tribunal, including the appointment of any replacement arbitrator under articles 10 and 11 of the Rules.[92] If successfully invoked, one of the main advantages of this procedure is that it allows for an application for interim or conservatory measures to be promptly considered by the same tribunal that will, in time, hear the substance of the dispute. This is a unique feature of the Rules and allows for continuity between

88 In *A v. B* [2011] EWHC 2345 (Comm) Flaux J interpreted Article 5.3 to mean that arbitrators are under a duty to disclose circumstances that amount to a breach of the impartiality or independence standard, and not some wider category of circumstances: para. 88.

89 There are two declarations. Declaration A: 'I am impartial, and independent of each of the parties, and I intend to remain so, and there are no circumstances known to me likely to give rise to any justified doubts as to my impartiality or independence.' Declaration B: 'I am impartial, and independent of each of the parties, and I intend to remain so, but I wish to disclose certain circumstances for the consideration of the LCIA Court prior to my appointment, whether or not any such circumstance is likely to give rise to any justified doubts as to my impartiality or independence. Other than such circumstances here disclosed by me, there are no circumstances known to me likely to give rise to any justified doubts as to my impartiality or independence.'

90 Article 5.3. 91 Article 5.3. 92 Article 9.1.

the expedited tribunal and the tribunal that will ultimately decide the merits of the case.[93]

An application for the expedited formation of the tribunal should be made in writing to the LCIA Court and copied to all other parties to the arbitration.[94] It must set out the specific grounds on which the applicant claims exceptional urgency in the formation of the tribunal. When considering the application, the LCIA Court may, in its complete discretion, abridge or curtail any time limit under the Rules for the formation of the tribunal, including the service of the response and of any matters or documents adjudged to be missing from the request.[95]

Article 9 allows the LCIA Court to form a tribunal in a matter of days (or sometimes even within hours) if necessary.[96] In the past five years, there have been 866 arbitrations conducted under the LCIA Rules.[97] Applications for expedited formation were made in 55 cases, 22 were granted, 13 were rejected and 20 were not decided.[98] In the applications that were granted, the average time from the date of the application to the appointment of the tribunal was 18 days. In one of the cases, the tribunal was appointed within 48 hours of the application.[99]

3.8 Revocation of appointment and procedure for challenge of arbitrators

Article 10 of the Rules concerns the revocation of appointment and the procedure for challenge of an arbitrator's appointment. Under article

[93] The rules of the Singapore International Arbitration Centre provide both for expedited formation (article 5) and the appointment of an emergency arbitrator (article 26.2 and schedule 1). Expedited formation takes place as part of the expedited procedure generally available under those rules and will therefore only be suitable for those cases to which the expedited procedure is otherwise suited. Under that procedure, for example, the tribunal will give reasons in summary form and the award should be rendered within six months, other than in exceptional circumstances, and this will not be appropriate for all types of dispute.

[94] Article 9.2. [95] Article 9.3.

[96] V. V. Veeder, 'London Court of International Arbitration: The New 1998 LCIA Rules', *Ybk Comm Arb*, 23(1998), 366 at p. 368.

[97] This does not include cases in which the LCIA was the designated appointing authority and/or was administering the arbitration.

[98] Some cases were not decided either because the parties agreed to expedite formation, the application was withdrawn or because the application was made close to or after the time when the response was due or after the file had already been passed to the LCIA Court for the appointment of the tribunal.

[99] Information provided by LCIA to the authors.

10.1, the LCIA Court, either upon challenge by a party or at the request of the remaining arbitrators, may revoke an appointment if the arbitrator (a) gives a written notice of his desire to resign as arbitrator or (b) dies, falls seriously ill, or refuses or becomes unable or unfit to act.[100] Article 10.2 provides that an arbitrator may be considered to be unfit if he acts in deliberate violation of the arbitration agreement (including the Rules); does not act fairly and impartially as between the parties; or does not conduct or participate in the arbitration proceedings with reasonable diligence, avoiding unnecessary delay or expense. Under article 10.3, a party may also challenge an arbitrator if circumstances exist that give rise to justifiable doubts over his impartiality or independence (although a party may only challenge an arbitrator it has nominated, or in whose appointment it has participated, for reasons of which it became aware after the appointment was made).

A challenge must be submitted within 15 days from the formation of the arbitration tribunal or (if later) from when the party became aware of the grounds of challenge.[101] The party must send a written statement of the reasons for its challenge to the LCIA Court, the tribunal and all other parties. Unless the challenged arbitrator withdraws or all other parties agree to the challenge within 15 days, the LCIA Court shall decide on the challenge.[102]

Challenges are considered by the President or a Vice President of the LCIA Court, or by a division of three or five of its members.[103] The Rules do not identify the procedure to be followed. Typically, written submissions, including supporting documentation, will be accepted from the challenging party, the challenged arbitrator and the other party or parties. Often, multiple rounds of written submissions are allowed. Challenges are usually decided based solely on written submissions without the need for an oral hearing.[104] Finally, the LCIA Court's decisions are administrative decisions, not arbitration awards or orders. Although not obliged to do so, the LCIA Court gives reasons for its decisions. Indeed, it is one of the few major arbitration institutions

[100] The LCIA Court may not, therefore, act on its own initiative to remove an arbitrator. Contrast this to the ICC Court's power under article 15.2 ICC Rules.

[101] Article 10.4. [102] Article 10.4. [103] Article 3.1.

[104] To date, oral hearings have been held for only two challenges: Walsh and Teitelbaum, 'LCIA Court Decisions: An Introduction', p. 286. The two challenges are LCIA Reference No. UN 7949 (3 December 2007), *Arb Int*, 27 (2011), 413 and LCIA Reference No. 3488 (11 July 2007), *Arb Int*, 27(2011), 413.

to do so.[105] In some circumstances, the decision in respect of a challenge may be reconsidered.[106]

3.9 *Replacement of arbitrators*

If the LCIA Court determines that a nominee is not suitable, independent or impartial, or if an arbitrator is to be replaced for any reason, the LCIA Court has wide discretion as to what procedure to apply for selecting a replacement.[107] It decides on a case-by-case basis whether to follow the original nominating process. In every case in the last two years in which the LCIA Court has replaced an arbitrator, it has followed the original nominating process.[108] Where the LCIA Court does follow the original nominating process, any opportunity given to a party to make a re-nomination will be waived if not exercised within 15 days (or a lesser time fixed by the LCIA Court), after which the LCIA Court will appoint the replacement arbitrator.[109] Unlike the rules of other institutions, the Rules do not make any provision regarding the status of proceedings of the tribunal pre-dating the replacement of an arbitrator.[110] The procedure adopted must comply with the tribunal's overriding duty to act fairly and impartially as between all of the parties, giving each a reasonable opportunity of putting its case.[111] Some commentators have suggested that if witnesses have been heard by the original tribunal, they should normally be heard again by the reconstituted tribunal.[112]

4 Identity and role of the appointing authority

As discussed previously, only the LCIA Court is empowered to appoint arbitrators.[113] In doing so, it must have 'due regard for any

[105] See, generally, Born, *International Commercial Arbitration*, p. 1559; Walsh and Teitelbaum, 'LCIA Court Decisions: An Introduction', p. 283. The ICC, ICDR and SCC do not provide reasoned decisions in respect of challenges. In practice, reasons are provided for decisions in respect of challenges in ICSID arbitrations, although the ICSID rules do not require this.

[106] LCIA Reference No. UN3490 (Decision 21 October 2005 and Reconsideration 27 December 2005), *Arb Intl*, 27(2011), 377, para. 5.3.

[107] Article 11.1. [108] Information provided by the LCIA to the authors.

[109] Article 11.2. [110] Compare, e.g., article 15.4 ICC Rules.

[111] Article 14.1 (discussed in more detail at p. 258 below).

[112] Turner and Mohtashami, *Guide to the LCIA Rules*, para. 4.134. Contrast, D. Girsberger and N. Voser, *International Arbitration in Switzerland* (Zurich: Schulthess, 2008), p. 165.

[113] Article 5.5. See p. 235 below.

particular method of criteria of selection agreed in writing by the parties', but the LCIA Court retains a power of ultimate veto. The Rules provide a non-exhaustive list of factors that the LCIA Court will consider when selecting arbitrators: the nature and circumstances of the dispute; the nationality, location and languages of the parties and (if there are more than two of them) the number of the parties.[114] The LCIA Court will also appoint the chairperson of the tribunal.[115] This does not prevent the parties from agreeing that they will jointly nominate a chairperson or from agreeing that the two party-nominated arbitrators will nominate the chairperson. In each case, the appointment is subject to the ultimate control of the LCIA Court. It is an absolute rule that the chairperson will not be one of the party-nominated arbitrators.[116]

5 Form of the arbitration agreement

Under the Rules, the request for arbitration must be accompanied by a copy of the 'written arbitration clause or separate written arbitration agreement' that the claimant invokes.[117] This provision is interpreted broadly by the LCIA Court. Thus, for purposes of registration only, an unsigned arbitration agreement that is evidenced in writing – for example, by being referred to in correspondence between the parties – would normally suffice, as would an agreement reached by exchange of e-mail.[118]

The LCIA's approach is in line with the liberal approach of English law. Part I of the Arbitration Act 1996 applies only where the agreement to arbitrate is in writing. That is satisfied if (a) the agreement itself is made in writing (whether or not it is signed by the parties); (b) it is made by an exchange of communications in writing; or (c) it is 'evidenced in writing', which means that although the agreement itself is not in writing, it has been documented by one of the parties or by a third party with the parties' authority.[119]

The rationale behind the form requirement is that the right to have recourse to the courts is too important to be lost by oral agreement.[120]

114 Article 5.5. 115 Article 5.6. 116 Ibid. 117 Article 1.1(b).
118 Information provided by the LCIA to the authors. 119 s. 5 Arbitration Act 1996.
120 Blackaby and Partasides, *Redfern and Hunter on International Arbitration*, para. 1.45. In respect of English law, see Merkin and Flannery, *Arbitration Act*, p. 28.

Requiring writing ensures that the parties have actually agreed to refer their dispute to arbitration and also provides a record of the content of their agreement. Parties will likely also be concerned to ensure that the arbitration agreement meets the requirements of article II of the New York Convention 1958 so that the resulting award can be enforced in the signatory states of that convention. Article II refers to an 'agreement in writing', which includes 'an arbitral clause in a contract or an arbitration agreement, signed by the parties or contained in an exchange of letters or telegrams'. National courts have demonstrated various levels of flexibility in their interpretation of article II(2). It is by no means guaranteed that something the LCIA Court would recognise as a 'written arbitration clause' for the purposes of article 1.1(b) of the Rules would necessarily be accepted by a national court as satisfying the requirements of article II of the New York Convention for the purposes of enforcement of the subsequent award. For example, a Norwegian Court of Appeal refused recognition of an arbitral award rendered in London on the ground that an exchange of e-mails did not constitute a 'written agreement' for the purposes of the New York Convention.[121]

6 Interference/support by the courts (including tribunal's powers to involve them)

The extent to which a national court may interfere in or support an arbitration proceeding will depend on the seat of the arbitration. It is increasingly accepted that commercial arbitration should be independent from national courts. Court intervention in most stages of proceedings has, in general, diminished.[122] All legal systems and the UNCITRAL Model Law recognise, however, that courts retain a residual role, whether to ensure that the arbitration can commence, to support the conduct of the arbitration or to subsequently enforce the award that results from it. As a high proportion of LCIA arbitrations are seated in England, this section focuses on the powers of the English courts to interfere in arbitration proceedings.[123]

[121] Decision of the Hålogaland Court of Appeal, 16 August 1999, *Ybk Comm Arb*, 27(2002), 519.

[122] Blackaby and Partasides, *Redfern and Hunter on International Arbitration*, para. 7.04.

[123] Article 16.1 allows the parties to choose any jurisdiction as the seat of arbitration.

6.1 *Court power to extend the time for beginning arbitral proceedings*

An arbitration agreement often requires the parties to take particular steps once a dispute has arisen, before they can commence arbitration proceedings. English courts are empowered to extend any time limit stipulated in the arbitration agreement for beginning arbitral proceedings if either (a) the circumstances were outside the reasonable contemplation of the parties when they agreed to the provision in question and it would be just to extend the time; or (b) the conduct of one party makes it unjust to hold the other party to the strict terms of the provision in question.[124] Any available arbitral process for obtaining an extension of time, however, must first be exhausted.[125]

Article 4.7 of the Rules allows the tribunal to extend any period of time (either under the Rules or the arbitration agreement) for the conduct of the arbitration. The LCIA Court has taken the view that it – as opposed to an arbitral tribunal – does not have the power to extend a contractually agreed period.[126] In practice, the LCIA Court will decide on a case-by-case basis how to proceed and may appoint a tribunal to determine whether the time limit should be extended.[127]

6.2 *Stay of court proceedings in breach of an arbitration agreement*

English courts will order the stay of court proceedings brought in breach of an arbitration agreement.[128] The matter before the court must be one that is arbitrable under the arbitration agreement. A broad approach is adopted when interpreting arbitration clauses. Issues sometimes arise about exactly which disputes between parties to a commercial relationship are covered by an arbitration clause. The House of Lords (the precursor of the Supreme Court) has held that the construction of an arbitration clause should start from the assumption that the parties, as rational businessmen, are likely to have intended any dispute arising out of the relationship into which they had entered or purported to enter to

[124] s. 12(3) Arbitration Act 1996. See Merkin and Flannery, *Arbitration Act*, pp. 44–8.
[125] s. 12(2) Arbitration Act 1996.
[126] Information provided by the LCIA Court to the authors.
[127] Information provided by the LCIA Court to the authors.
[128] s. 9 Arbitration Act 1996. This is a mandatory provision of the Arbitration Act and therefore cannot be disapplied by the parties.

be decided by the same tribunal unless the language makes it clear that certain questions were intended to be excluded from the arbitration clause.[129]

If the subject matter of court proceedings is covered by an arbitration clause, the court must grant an application for a stay unless satisfied that the arbitration agreement is null and void, inoperative or incapable of being performed.[130] There is an obvious tension between these exceptions and the fundamental principle that the tribunal has jurisdiction to decide upon its own jurisdiction and that the arbitration agreement is separate from the contract in which it is contained.[131] The difficulty is how a court, deciding an application for a stay, is to determine whether the arbitration agreement is 'null and void, inoperative, or incapable of being performed' for the purposes of section 9(4) of the Arbitration Act 1996.

In *Fiona Trust*, the House of Lords held that an arbitral tribunal had jurisdiction to decide whether contracts containing the arbitration clause were void for bribery. It therefore ordered a stay of court proceedings on that issue. Following that case, it has been said that the 'presumption may now be that the arbitral tribunal will usually be the first port of call in any jurisdictional determination'.[132]

In *Albon* v. *Naza Motor Trading Sdn Bhd*,[133] the High Court held that it has no jurisdiction under section 9 of the Arbitration Act 1996 to order a stay of court proceedings where there is an issue as to whether a valid arbitration agreement has been concluded. It does, however, retain an inherent jurisdiction to order a stay of legal proceedings in exceptional circumstances if, for example, it is 'virtually certain' that there was a valid arbitration agreement. In *Albon*, a party who had commenced arbitration sought a stay of parallel court proceedings. The claimant in those proceedings maintained that the arbitration agreement was a forgery. The court refused to order a stay. The distinction between these two lines of authority is unclear.[134] It is clear, however, that a stay will be granted if the alleged defect (such as fraud) would render the arbitration agreement

[129] *Fiona Trust & Holding Corp* v. *Privalov* [2007] UKHL 40; [2008] 1 Lloyd's Rep 254; [2007] 4 All ER 951 at para. 13 (Lord Hoffmann).

[130] s. 9(4) Arbitration Act 1996. [131] See p. 244.

[132] Merkin and Flannery, *Arbitration Act*, p. 41.

[133] [2007] EWHC 665 (Ch); [2007] 2 Lloyd's Rep 1; [2007] 2 All ER 1075.

[134] Merkin and Flannery, *Arbitration Act*, p. 41 remark that it is not easy to see any real difference between the arguments in *Fiona Trust* (i.e. that the contracts containing the arbitration clause had been induced by bribery) and *Albon* (i.e. that the contract containing the arbitration clause was a complete forgery).

voidable only, as opposed to a defect (such as forgery) that would render the arbitration agreement void *ab initio*.[135]

6.3 *Anti-suit injunctions*

An English court may grant an anti-suit injunction to restrain foreign court proceedings in breach of an arbitration agreement.[136] An anti-suit injunction enjoins a person from commencing or continuing with proceedings in a court abroad. Generally, anti-suit injunctions are granted when the applicant seeking the injunction can show that he has a right not to be sued in the foreign jurisdiction.[137] An arbitration agreement providing for LCIA arbitration in London would normally suffice to give either party to the arbitration agreement the right not to be sued abroad.[138] An arbitration clause that provides exclusively for arbitration in England, contains within it a negative covenant that a party will not sue abroad.[139] It does not matter if arbitration proceedings have not been initiated when the court proceedings began, although an injunction will only be granted if the foreign proceedings are not too advanced.[140] Since the decision of the European Court of Justice in *West Tankers*,[141] however, English courts will not issue anti-suit injunctions to restrain proceedings in other EU member states that are said to be in breach of an arbitration agreement.[142]

135 Ibid.

136 An interim injunction may be made under either s. 37 Senior Courts Act 1981 or s. 44 Arbitration Act 1996, but a final injunction may be made only under s. 37. See, e.g., *Aggeliki Charis Compania Maritima SA* v. *Pagnan SpA* (*The Angelic Grace*) [1995] 1 Lloyd's Rep 87 (CA) at 96 (Millett LJ) and, generally, S. Gee, *Commercial Injunctions*, 5th edn (London: Sweet and Maxwell, 2004), chapter 14.

137 See *Turner* v. *Grovit* [2002] 1 WLR 107 (HL) and *American International Specialty Lines Insurance Co* v. *Abbott Laboratories* [2002] EWHC 2714 (Comm); [2003] 1 Lloyd's Rep 267.

138 *Turner* v. *Grovit* [2002] 1 WLR 107 (HL) at para. 25.

139 The same principles apply whether the anti-suit injunction is sought to enforce an arbitration clause or an exclusive jurisdiction clause: *American International Specialty Lines Insurance Co* v. *Abbott Laboratories* [2002] EWHC 2714 (Comm); [2003] 1 Lloyd's Rep 267 at 275.

140 *Steamship Mutual Underwriting Association (Bermuda) Ltd* v. *Sulpico* [2008] EWHC 914 (Comm); [2008] Lloyd's Rep 269.

141 Case C-185/07 *West Tankers Inc* v. *Allianz SpA* [2009] ECR I-663; [2009] 1 AC 1138.

142 The European Court of Justice there held that granting an anti-suit injunction in such circumstances would be inconsistent with the Brussels Regulation on Jurisdiction and the Recognition and Enforcement of Judgments in Civil and Commercial Matters. The European Court agreed with the Opinion of the Advocate General in which she

6.4 *Determination by a court of the tribunal's jurisdiction*

The Rules provide that parties to an LCIA arbitration are treated as having agreed not to apply to any state court or other judicial authority for any relief regarding the arbitral tribunal's jurisdiction or authority, except in three circumstances: (a) with the agreement of all the parties; (b) with the prior authorisation of the tribunal; or (c) following the tribunal's award ruling on the objection to its jurisdiction or authority.[143] Parties may therefore apply to a state court for a determination of the tribunal's jurisdiction after the tribunal has determined the matter for itself. In England, such an application would be made under section 32 of the Arbitration Act 1996.

6.5 *Court application for removal of an arbitrator*

Parties may apply to an English court under section 24 of the Arbitration Act 1996 to seek to have an arbitrator removed. This is a mandatory provision, which applies regardless of agreement to the contrary. The court may not exercise its power to remove an arbitrator unless it is satisfied that the applicant has first exhausted any available recourse to the arbitral institution. An application must therefore first be made to the LCIA Court, as described above.[144]

Section 24 specifies the grounds on which an applicant may challenge an arbitrator's appointment, many of which overlap with those which may be considered by the LCIA Court. These grounds are: (a) there are justifiable doubts as to the arbitrator's impartiality; (b) the arbitrator lacks the qualifications required by the arbitration agreement; (c) the arbitrator is physically or mentally incapable of conducting the proceedings or there are justifiable doubts as to his capacity to do so; and (d) that the arbitrator has refused or failed to properly conduct the proceedings

expressed concern that the effect of an anti-suit injunction would prevent the court of the member state in which litigation was commenced from considering the validity of the arbitration agreement. She was also concerned about the possible repercussions if member states were to issue anti-suit injunctions in such circumstances. She acknowledged the deficiency of the present state of the Brussels Regulation in that there is no mechanism to co-ordinate its jurisdiction with the jurisdiction of the national courts in relation to arbitration, since arbitration is not within the scope of the Regulation. The European Court agreed at para. 33 that a unilateral anti-suit injunction was not a suitable measure to rectify the situation. See also *West Tankers Inc* v. *Allianz SpA* [2012] EWCA Civ 27 at para. 10.

143 Article 23.4. 144 See pp. 232–3.

or to use all reasonable dispatch in conducting the proceedings or making an award, which has caused or will cause substantial injustice.

6.6 *Court orders in support of arbitration*

The Rules give the arbitral tribunal significant powers in its conduct of the arbitration proceedings.[145] In particular, article 22.1 lists various types of orders that the tribunal may make. These include orders requiring a party to make available for inspection property under its control relating to the subject matter of the arbitration and orders requiring either or both parties to produce documents and orders allowing third parties to be joined to the arbitration.[146] Article 22.2 provides that, by agreeing to arbitration under the Rules, the parties shall be treated as having agreed not to apply to any state court or judicial authority for any order available from the tribunal under article 22.1, except with the agreement in writing of all of the parties.

As tribunals have no power to compel compliance with their orders, parties are entitled to resort to a national court to obtain enforcement of tribunal orders. Section 42 of the Arbitration Act 1996, for example, enables a court to make an order requiring a party to comply with a tribunal's 'peremptory order'. A 'peremptory order' is one made by the tribunal after a party has failed to comply with a previous order or directions, and which prescribes a time for compliance.[147] This is a default provision that applies unless otherwise agreed by the parties. There is no provision in the Rules that prevents such an application. Section 42 of the Arbitration Act provides that the application may only be made (a) by the tribunal (upon giving notice to the parties); (b) by a party to the arbitration with the permission of the tribunal; or (c) where the parties have agreed that the powers of the court under this section are available.[148]

The law of the seat might also allow for parties to arbitrations to apply directly to court for orders to support the arbitration, such as orders to compel the attendance of witnesses or for the production of documents and the like. For example, section 43 of the Arbitration Act 1996 allows parties to arbitral proceedings to apply directly to the courts to secure the attendance of witnesses or to produce documents or other material evidence.[149] This may be used in respect of persons who are not party to

[145] See p. 258. [146] Articles 22.2(d), (e) and (h).
[147] ss. 41(5) and 82(1) Arbitration Act 1996. [148] s. 42(2) Arbitration Act 1996.
[149] Section 43 of the Arbitration Act 1996 cannot be used to support 'fishing expeditions' in search of documents. An application requiring a witness to attend to produce

the arbitration. Recourse to section 43 of the Arbitration Act 1996 may only be had with permission of the tribunal or agreement of the other parties, which acts as a safeguard against applications to court for irrelevant evidence. Moreover, section 43 is a mandatory provision that cannot be excluded by agreement of the parties. It therefore overrides the limitations set forth in article 22.2 of the Rules. Nevertheless, section 43 only applies if the witness is in the UK and the arbitral proceedings are being conducted in England and Wales or Northern Ireland.

A broad range of court powers is also available under section 44 of the Arbitration Act. These powers relate, for example, to the taking of evidence of witnesses, the preservation of evidence and the granting of an interim injunction. In large part, these issues are addressed by the Rules and, therefore, recourse to the English courts is excluded. Nevertheless, recourse to the courts can be made under section 44 if the arbitral tribunal has no power or is unable for the time being to act effectively.[150]

Section 45 of the Arbitration Act allows a party to arbitral proceedings, subject to contrary agreement, to apply to court for a determination of a question of law arising during the proceedings.[151] This is not a mandatory provision and can be excluded by the parties. There is some doubt over whether it is excluded by article 26.9 of the Rules, which provides, in part, that the parties 'waive irrevocably their right to any form of appeal, review or recourse to any state court or other judicial authority, insofar as such waiver may be validly made'.[152] The point has not been decided (either in relation to the LCIA Rules or those of the ICC, which has similarly worded exclusions). One view is that the reference to 'recourse' in article 26.9 would cover an application under section 45.[153] Another view is that article 26.9 is concerned solely with recourse to court *in connection with an award* and therefore does not cover an application under section 45, which allows applications to be made at any time during the proceedings.[154] In practice, the debate has

documents should refer to specific identified documents. A compendious description of several documents suffices provided that the exact document in each case is clearly indicated: *Tajik Aluminium Plant* v. *Hydro Aluminium AS* [2005] EWCA Civ 1218; [2006] 1 Lloyd's Rep 155.

150 s. 44(5) Arbitration Act 1996. E.g., an application may be necessary if the tribunal has yet to be appointed and urgent interlocutory relief is required. See Merkin and Flannery, *Arbitration Act*, p. 112.

151 s. 45 Arbitration Act. 152 Discussed in more detail at p. 267 below.

153 Konrad and Hunter, 'LCIA-Schiedsregeln', Article 23, para. 23.

154 B. Harris, R. Planterose and J. Tecks, *The Arbitration Act 1996: A Commentary*, 4th edn (Oxford: Blackwell Publishing, 2007), p. 225.

little significance. Section 45 is rarely used.[155] Even when it is invoked, the application is rarely successful, given the strict conditions that must be satisfied. The court must find that the question of law raised substantially affects the rights of one or more of the parties.[156] Moreover, the court may only consider the application if it is made (a) with the agreement of all parties to the proceedings; or (b) with the permission of the tribunal, and the court is satisfied that the determination is likely to produce substantial cost savings and that the application was made without delay.[157]

6.7 *Challenge to an award*

The scope for challenging an arbitral award in national courts is considered in Section 13 below.

6.8 *Recognition and enforcement*

Recognition and enforcement of an award in England will be governed by sections 66 or 101 of the Arbitration Act 1996 (or in some rare cases of foreign awards which are not New York Convention awards, by Part II of the Arbitration Act 1950).[158]

7 Tribunal's powers *ex officio*

The Rules provide the arbitral tribunal with broad powers in order to ensure sufficient flexibility when conducting the arbitration proceedings. The parties can agree on additional powers that should be vested in the arbitrators.

7.1 *Power of the tribunal to decide its own jurisdiction*

Article 23.1 provides that the tribunal has the power to rule on its own jurisdiction, including the power to decide on any objection to the

155 Merkin and Flannery, *Arbitration Act*, p. 113.

156 s. 45(1) Arbitration Act 1996.

157 s. 45(2) Arbitration Act 1996.

158 For arbitrations seated in the UK, enforcement will be governed by s. 66 Arbitration Act 1996. If the arbitration was seated outside the UK in a party to the New York Convention, an application for enforcement in England will be governed by s. 101 Arbitration Act 1996.

existence, validity or effectiveness of the arbitration agreement.[159] It therefore upholds the principle of *Kompetenz-Kompetenz*, which is embodied in most international conventions and national arbitration regimes.[160] The conceptual difficulty of a tribunal finding that a contract that contains an arbitration clause is invalid when the tribunal's very ability to do so depends upon the validity of a clause in that contract is dealt with by invoking the doctrine of 'severability'. Article 23.1 provides that 'an arbitration clause which forms or was intended to form part of another agreement shall be treated as an arbitration agreement independent of that other agreement. A decision by the Arbitral Tribunal that such other agreement is non-existent, invalid or ineffective shall not entail *ipso jure* the non-existence, invalidity or ineffectiveness of the arbitration clause.'

Parties to arbitration under the Rules are taken to have agreed not to apply to any state court or other judicial authority for any relief regarding the tribunal's jurisdiction or authority, except (a) with the agreement in writing of all parties to the arbitration; (b) with the prior authorisation of the tribunal; or (c) following the tribunal's award ruling on the objection to its jurisdiction or authority.[161]

In order for the Rules to be effective and confer jurisdiction upon the tribunal to determine jurisdictional issues, the law of the seat of arbitration must also accept the principles of *Kompetenz-Kompetenz* and severability. Section 30 of the Arbitration Act 1996 recognises the authority of an arbitral tribunal to rule on its own jurisdiction and section 7 recognises the principle of severability. The latter principle was considered recently by the House of Lords in *Fiona Trust*.[162] Lord Hoffmann stated that 'the arbitration agreement can be invalidated only

[159] A party raising a jurisdictional plea must do so within the time limits set down by article 23.2. Unless the respondent raises a jurisdictional plea no later than the statement of defence, it is treated as having been irrevocably waived. A jurisdictional plea by a claimant in response to a counter-claim is similarly treated unless raised no later than the statement of defence to counter-claim.

[160] s. 30(1) Arbitration Act 1996 (England); s. 16(1) UNCITRAL Model Arbitration Law 2006; Article 6(3) ICC Rules. See generally, J. D. M. Lew, L. A. Mistelis and S. M. Kröll, *Comparative International Commercial Arbitration* (The Hague: Kluwer Law International, 2003), paras. 14–13 *et seq*.

[161] Article 23.4. A tribunal applying the Rules may determine a plea as to its jurisdiction either in an award as to jurisdiction or later in an award on the merits, as it considers appropriate in the circumstances: article 23.3.

[162] *Fiona Trust and Holding Corpn* v. *Privalov* [2007] UKHL 40; [2008] 1 Lloyd's Rep 254; [2007] 4 All ER 951.

on a ground which relates to the arbitration agreement and is not merely a consequence of the invalidity of the main agreement'.[163] The question remains whether the law of the seat of arbitration will recognise that the tribunal should be the body that first determines whether it has jurisdiction (where the challenge is to the validity of the arbitration agreement itself, as opposed to that of the underlying contract). English law provides that a person alleged to be a party to arbitral proceedings may, at any time, question in court proceedings whether there is a valid arbitration agreement, subject to the conditions set forth in section 32(2).[164] A party, however, may lose this right if it participated in the proceedings without contesting the validity of the arbitration agreement.[165] Similarly, (as discussed above), a stay of court proceedings to allow for arbitration will not be granted if the arbitration agreement is null and void.[166]

7.2 Powers of the tribunal for determining the dispute

Articles 22 and 25 of the Rules provide significant powers to the arbitral tribunal. Article 22 is a collection of various powers under the heading 'additional powers of the arbitral tribunal'. It has no counterpart in the ICC Rules, which provide for tribunals to have many of the same powers, but do not collect them all under one article. Article 25 of the Rules gives the tribunal powers in respect of 'interim and conservatory measures'.[167] Both articles 22 and 25 are subject to the contrary written agreement of the parties. They are also subject to the tribunal's general duties at all times to act fairly and impartially as between all parties and to adopt procedures that are suitable to the circumstances of the case, avoiding unnecessary delay or expense, and providing a fair and efficient means of resolving the parties' dispute.[168]

Article 22.1 of the Rules lists various powers. The tribunal may exercise them either on application of any party or of its own motion, but in either case must first give the parties a reasonable opportunity to state their views. Below is a brief overview of these powers:

(a) To allow the amendment of written submissions. This provision allows only amendment of existing claims and not the addition of

[163] Ibid., para. 20. [164] s. 32(1) Arbitration Act 1996.
[165] s. 73(1) Arbitration Act 1996. [166] s. 9(4) Arbitration Act 1996. See p. 238 above.
[167] See Section 8 below. [168] Article 14.1, discussed at p. 258 below.

a new claim.[169] The significance of amendments to written pleadings is less in arbitration than in domestic court proceedings. It is common for a party's case to develop significantly as the arbitration progresses, but for this not necessarily to be reflected in a formal amendment to earlier submissions;[170]

(b) To alter time limits;

(c) To conduct enquiries itself. This provision gives the tribunal the power to adopt an inquisitorial approach, more in keeping with the civil law tradition, instead of adopting the position of the common law umpire in an adversarial procedure;[171]

(d) To order the inspection of property. The tribunal may order any party to make any property, site or thing under its control and relating to the subject matter of the arbitration available for inspection by the tribunal, any other party, its expert or any expert to the tribunal;

(e) To order production of documents. Lawyers from different legal traditions approach the production of documents with different expectations: common law lawyers are accustomed to an obligation in domestic courts to disclose relevant documents, an obligation which is alien to lawyers from a civil law tradition. Article 22.1(e) reinforces that there is no automatic right to disclosure in arbitral proceedings. Written statements must be accompanied by copies or, if they are especially voluminous, lists of all essential documents on which a party relies and which have not previously been submitted by any party.[172] To have disclosure of further documents, there must be a request. The Rules are not prescriptive about how the tribunal should deal with any request. The type and scope of any disclosure will largely depend on the *lex arbitri*, the parties, the arbitrators and the specific facts of the case. In that sense, the Rules do not differ from most other institutional rules on the issue of disclosure. Although not incorporated in the Rules, it is common that a tribunal will have regard to the 1999 International Bar Association 'Rules for the Taking of Evidence in International Commercial Arbitration', described by Redfern and Hunter as 'almost universally recognized

[169] Cf. article 23.4 ICC Rules, which imposes a general prohibition on the introduction of 'new claims', subject to the tribunal's permission.

[170] Turner and Mohtashami, *Guide to the LCIA Rules*, para. 6.14.

[171] Blackaby and Partasides, *Redfern and Hunter on International Arbitration*, paras. 6.84–8.

[172] Article 15.6.

as the international standard for an effective, pragmatic and relatively economical document production regime'.[173]

(f) To decide on the applicable rules of evidence. This provision re-enforces that the tribunal is not bound to apply the rules of evidence of the seat of the arbitration;[174]

(g) To order the correction of any contract between the parties or the arbitration agreement itself, but only to the extent required to rectify any mistake common to the parties and only if and to the extent that the applicable law permits such correction;[175] and

(h) To allow the joinder of third parties to arbitration. This is considered in more detail in Part 9 below.

8 Interim measures

Interim measures are awards or orders issued to safeguard the parties from injury caused by delay in the arbitral process. Unless the tribunal is able to grant interim measures, its ability to provide effective, final relief may be compromised during the pendency of the dispute resolution process.[176]

The arbitration tribunal will often be the best forum to determine whether specific interim measures are appropriate. If the tribunal has already been established and the proceedings have begun, the arbitrators will likely be more familiar with the details of the case than a judge who is not going to determine the substance of the dispute between the parties. The tribunal will also likely be better placed to evaluate the chances of success in the substantive dispute and the impact that the interim measures may have on the case. That impact may be very significant (sometimes virtually determinative). The tribunal will also probably be in a better position than a court to identify those applications for interim

173 Ibid., para. 6.107.

174 E.g., a tribunal could disregard the general rule of English law that pre-contractual negotiations are not admissible when interpreting a contract: S. Nesbitt, 'LCIA Arbitration Rules', p. 442.

175 There is some debate about whether this provision restricts a power, otherwise available in the applicable law to correct a contract, to circumstances in which there is a mistake common to the parties. The alternative view is that article 22.1(g) is superfluous. See Turner and Mohtashami, *Guide to the LCIA Rules*, para. 6.41; Konrad and Hunter, 'LCIA-Schiedsregeln', Article 22, para. 9.

176 Born, *International Commercial Arbitration*, p. 1943. See generally G. Marchac, 'Interim Measures in International Commercial Arbitration under the ICC, AAA, LCIA and UNCITRAL rules', *Am Rev Intl Arb*, 10(1999), 123.

measures that have been brought for dilatory, tactical or offensive purposes instead of in pursuit of a legitimate interest. All of the reasons for which the parties opted to have their dispute resolved by arbitration, as opposed to by a national court (such as independence of the panel), apply to the determination of whether interim measures should be granted.[177]

Article 25 grants the arbitral tribunal broad powers to order interim relief. Before considering its scope, it is important to consider the impact of the law of the seat of arbitration. The majority of national laws either expressly grant arbitration tribunals the power to order interim relief or at least allow the parties to confer such powers on the tribunal. Historically, this was not the case. Some jurisdictions continue to refuse to allow arbitrators to order interim measures. When choosing the seat of arbitration, therefore, parties should give thought to whether article 25 can receive effect. English law (like the law of all of the other major arbitral jurisdictions) allows it to do so.

Section 38(1) of the Arbitration Act 1996 provides that 'the parties are free to agree on the powers exercisable by the arbitral tribunal for the purposes of and in relation to the proceedings'. Section 39(1) provides that 'the parties are free to agree that the tribunal shall have power to order on a provisional basis any relief which it would have power to grant in a final award'. These two provisions give parties the ability to define the interlocutory powers of their arbitrators.

Article 25.1 is more descriptive than similar provisions found in the ICC Rules[178] and the Rules of the Stockholm Chamber of Commerce,[179] which merely provide that the tribunal may grant such provisional and conservatory measures as 'it deems appropriate'.

Article 25.1(a) enables a tribunal to order the respondent to a claim or counter-claim to provide security for all or part of the amount in dispute. The order can be made upon such terms as the tribunal considers appropriate. This type of relief will be useful in situations where there is a risk that the respondent (or the claimant who is a respondent to a counter-claim) will not be able to pay the amount in dispute by the time of the final award.

Article 25.1(b) allows the tribunal to order the preservation, storage, sale or other disposal of any property or thing under the control of a

[177] Born, *International Commercial Arbitration*, p. 1950. [178] ICC Rules article 28.1.
[179] SCC Rules article 32.1.

party to the arbitration that relates to the subject matter of the arbitration. It can be used to preserve monies in bank accounts and physical assets. It is also sometimes used, in conjunction with article 25.1(c), in asset-freezing cases to prevent a respondent from putting assets beyond the claimant's reach.[180]

Article 25.1(c) empowers the tribunal to order on a provisional basis any relief that it could order in a final award; for example, to continue shipping products pending resolution of the dispute. The most frequent types of orders made by tribunals under this article are freezing injunctions (i.e. orders restraining a party from dealing with assets), orders for the status quo to be maintained, prohibitory orders and anti-suit injunctions.[181] It could also be used to order the payment of sums that are unquestionably due. On one occasion it was used as the basis for an order that the respondent cause its subsidiary to seek a stay of court proceedings which it had started against the claimant in the arbitration, pending the outcome of the arbitration.[182] When considering providing such relief, arbitrators should be careful not to be seen as prejudging the merits of the dispute.[183]

A tribunal awarding the provision of security for the amount in dispute under article 25.1(a) may make its order contingent upon the applicant providing a cross-indemnity to the respondent for any costs or losses that the respondent incurs in providing the security. Article 25.2, which allows a tribunal to order that a party provide security for costs, contains a similar provision. Articles 25.1(b) and (c), however, do not do so, even though the grant of, for example, a freezing order can cause significant losses. Some commentators have suggested that it is unlikely that the drafters intended that the tribunal would be unable to order that applicants for interim relief under article 25.1(b) and (c) provide such a cross-indemnity.[184]

Despite the fairly broad scope of article 25.1, there are important limitations on tribunals' powers to order interim relief. In particular:

[180] Turner and Mohtashami, *Guide to the LCIA Rules*, para. 6.141. For general discussion of this type of order, see Lew, Mistelis and Kröll, *Comparative International Commercial Arbitration*, para. 23.42 and Born, *International Commercial Arbitration*, pp. 1998 *et seq.*

[181] Information provided by the LCIA Court to the authors.

[182] Turner and Mohtashami, *Guide to the LCIA Rules*, para. 6.144.

[183] See the discussion at p. 254 below.

[184] Turner and Mohtashami, *Guide to the LCIA Rules*, para. 6.139.

(a) The tribunal lacks power to order provisional measures against third parties. The tribunal's powers are limited to the parties to the arbitration and arbitration agreement.[185]

(b) The tribunal lacks power to directly enforce provisional measures. It can indirectly procure compliance through the express or implied threat of drawing an adverse inference against a non-compliant party, but for direct enforcement parties must resort to national courts.[186] By the time an order is enforced by a national court, however, the very danger against which protection is sought may have materialised.

(c) The tribunal lacks power to order provisional measures until it is constituted.[187] The most critical time for seeking provisional measures is often at the outset of the parties' dispute, when one party may seek to dispose of disputed property or evidence, or to alter the contractual or commercial status quo by terminating an agreement or commercial relationship. The Rules go some way to address this concern by providing for the expedited formation of the tribunal. For more immediate protection, however, the parties will have to resort to the national courts.

(d) Courts often grant interim measures *ex parte*. Whether a tribunal can make an order *ex parte* is controversial, given that a tribunal must respect a party's right to be heard.[188] The LCIA Rules are silent on this question. For arbitrations seated in England, the Arbitration Act 1996 does not give a specific power to hear *ex parte* applications.[189] The 2006 revisions to the UNCITRAL Model Law allow for *ex parte* applications to be made for preliminary orders. These revisions, however, have been controversial and no Model Law

[185] This limitation is laid down in most national arbitration regimes: e.g., s. 39(1) Arbitration Act 1996; article 17 UNCITRAL Model Law 2006. See Born, *International Commercial Arbitration*, p. 1965.

[186] E. Gaillard and J. Savage, *Fouchard Gaillard Goldman on International Commercial Arbitration*, 2nd edn (The Hague: Kluwer Law International, 1999), para. 1323. If the seat is England, courts have the power to enforce 'peremptory' orders of tribunals: see p. 241 above.

[187] Born, *International Commercial Arbitration*, pp. 1970–71; Lew, Mistelis and Kröll, *Comparative International Commercial Arbitration*, para. 23–32.

[188] See, generally, Born, *International Commercial Arbitration*, pp. 2015–18.

[189] Nor, as Turner and Mohtashami note, does it expressly forbid it. In the July 1995 draft of the Arbitration Bill, there was a clause enabling *ex parte* applications: Turner and Mohtashami, *Guide to the LCIA Rules*, para. 6.148.

jurisdiction has adopted them.[190] The prevailing view is that tribunals cannot grant *ex parte* applications.[191]

In order to obtain effective interim relief, therefore, a party may have no choice but to resort to the national courts. Most national laws allow for this. Article 25.3 of the Rules limits the circumstances in which a party may apply to the national court. It provides, '[t]he power of the Arbitral Tribunal under Article 25.1 shall not prejudice howsoever any party's right to apply to any state court or other judicial authority for interim or conservatory measures before the formation of the Arbitral Tribunal and, in exceptional cases, thereafter'. This broadly reflects the circumstances under which an English court would make an order under section 44 of the Arbitration Act 1996.[192] The court has jurisdiction to grant various orders in support of the arbitral process[193] if the arbitrators themselves either have no power to act effectively (by virtue of the arbitration agreement)[194] or are unable to act effectively (for example, because the panel has yet to be appointed or because remedies with effect against third parties, which a tribunal has no jurisdiction to grant, are required).[195] If the case is one of urgency, the court may make orders for the purpose of preserving evidence or assets on the application of a party or proposed party to arbitral proceedings.[196] In cases that are not urgent,

190 Born, *International Commercial Arbitration*, p. 2016.

191 Ibid., pp. 2016–19; Lew, Mistelis and Kröll, *Comparative International Commercial Arbitration*, para. 23–72. It has been suggested by one commentator that such power is incompatible with the consensual nature of arbitration and the respect for due process. See H. van Houtte, 'Ten Reasons against a Proposal for Ex Parte Interim Measures of Protection in Arbitration', *Arb Intl*, 20(2004), 85 at p. 89.

192 s. 44(5) Arbitration Act 1996: the court shall act only if or to the extent that the arbitral tribunal, and any arbitral or other institution or person vested by the parties with power in that regard, has no power or is unable for the time being to act effectively.

193 The matters in respect of which an order can be made are listed in s. 44(2) Arbitration Act 1996: (a) the taking of the evidence of witnesses; (b) the preservation of evidence; (c) making orders relating to property which is the subject of the proceedings or as to which any question arises in the proceedings – (i) for the inspection, photographing, preservation, custody or detention of the property or (ii) ordering that samples be taken from, or any observation be made of or experiment conducted upon, the property; and for that purpose authorising any person to enter any premises in the possession or control of a party to the arbitration; (d) the sale of any goods that are the subject of the proceedings; (e) the granting of an interim injunction or the appointment of a receiver.

194 *Starlight Shipping Co.* v. *Tai Ping Insurance Co.* [2007] EWHC 1893 (Comm); [2008] 1 Lloyd's Rep 230.

195 *Pacific Maritime (Asia) Ltd* v. *Holystone Overseas Ltd* [2007] EWHC 2319 (Comm); [2008] 1 Lloyd's Rep 371.

196 s. 44(3) Arbitration Act 1996.

however, the court will only act upon an application by a party to proceedings made with the tribunal's permission or the agreement in writing of the other parties.[197]

8.1 Security for costs

Unlike many other institutional rules, article 25.2 expressly grants the tribunal the power to order security for costs.[198] Upon the application of a party, the tribunal may order any claiming or counter-claiming party to provide security for either the legal or the other costs of any other party. This may be by deposit or bank guarantee or in any other manner ordered by the tribunal. The order to provide security may be upon such terms as the tribunal considers appropriate, which may include that the applicant is to provide a cross-indemnity for any costs and losses incurred by the party providing security. If the party ordered to provide security does not comply with the order, the tribunal may stay or dismiss that party's claims or counter-claims.

An order for security for costs therefore requires one or both parties to post security to cover the likely amounts that would be awarded to the counter-party in the event that the counter-party prevailed in the arbitration and was entitled to recover its legal costs.

Although there is no guidance specific to the LCIA Rules as to when security for costs may be ordered, the following factors will likely feature in a tribunal's consideration:

(a) The financial state of the party from whom security is sought;
(b) The extent to which that party's participation in the arbitration is being funded by third parties, who would be insulated from a final costs award; and
(c) The likely difficulties in enforcing a final costs award.[199]

197 s. 44(4) Arbitration Act 1996.

198 Contrast, the ICC Rules. In ICC arbitrations, security for costs can, however, be awarded under the general provision regarding interim or conservatory measures: Lew, Mistelis and Kröll, *Comparative International Commercial Arbitration*, para. 23–53.

199 Born, *International Commercial Arbitration*, p. 2004. See, by analogy, arbitral award of 4 July 2008 – ICC Arbitration, *ASA Bulletin*, 28(2010), pp. 37–45, where security for costs was granted against the claimant company that was insolvent. See also ICC arbitration tribunal decision on 29 May 2009, *ASA Bulletin*, 28(2010), pp. 71–7, where an application for security for costs was refused even though the party's financial

For example, where a party appears to lack assets to satisfy a final costs award, but is pursuing claims in an arbitration with the funding of a third party, a strong prima facie case for security for costs exists.[200] Where English law applies, the power to order security for costs may not be exercised on the ground that the claimant or counter-claimant is a non-UK individual or company.[201] Under the Rules, parties are not allowed to apply to the courts for an order for security for costs.[202]

The award of security for costs is more frequent in England (and some other Commonwealth jurisdictions) than it is elsewhere, where tribunals are often reluctant to order payment of security for costs.[203] In a recent analysis of fifty applications for security for costs in LCIA arbitrations, thirty-one applications were granted and nineteen dismissed.[204]

8.2 *Applicable standards for determining whether to order interim measures*

The Rules do not specify the standards that the tribunal should apply when determining whether to order interim measures under article 25. The law providing these standards need not be the law of the arbitral seat (which determines the tribunal's power to order interim measures in the first place). When considering which standards should be applied, an LCIA arbitral tribunal typically chooses between: (a) the law of the arbitral seat; (b) the law governing the underlying contract or

situation was not stable. The tribunal reasoned that a party who enters into a contract with another party that is not financially stable should only be awarded security for costs when the latter's situation deteriorated unexpectedly after the conclusion of the contract that is the subject of the arbitration claim.

200 See, by analogy, *Coppee-Lavalin SA/NV* v. *Ken-Ren Chem and Fertilizers Ltd* [1995] 1 AC 38, where the House of Lords ordered a party to an ICC arbitration to provide security for costs.

201 s. 38(3) Arbitration Act 1996.

202 This part of article 25.3 of the Rules is intended to prevent an application being made in respect of an LCIA arbitration as was made in *Coppee-Lavalin SA/NV* v. *Ken-Ren Chem and Fertilizers Ltd* [1995] 1 AC 38, where the House of Lords ordered a party to an ICC arbitration to provide security for costs. The decision was controversial. It was feared that courts ordering security of costs would discourage arbitration in England. English law was, in any event, changed by s. 38(3) Arbitration Act 1996 to provide that parties may not apply to court for an order for security of costs in respect of an arbitration (although it may do so in respect of the costs associated with some applications to court arising out of the arbitration: s. 70(6) Arbitration Act).

203 Born, *International Commercial Arbitration*, p. 2004; Lew, Mistelis and Kröll, *Comparative International Commercial Arbitration*, para. 23–54.

204 Information provided by the LCIA Court to the authors.

relationship; and (c) international standards.[205] There is considerable support for the view that 'international sources provide the appropriate standards for granting provisional measures in international arbitration'.[206] The terms of article 17A of the UNCITRAL Model Law, which sets down conditions for granting interim measures, are likely to prove significant as indicating international standards. Nevertheless, most international tribunals require a showing of:[207]

(a) 'Serious' or 'irreparable' harm to the claimant if the measures are not granted. This is usually accompanied by a 'balance of harms' analysis, which asks whether this harm substantially outweighs the harm that the other party would suffer if the interim measures were granted;[208] and
(b) Urgency.

Some tribunals also require the applicant to establish a prima facie case on the merits. The UNCITRAL Model Law requires that the applicant make out a 'reasonable possibility' that he will succeed on the merits of the claim.[209] The reason for this is commercial common sense. There is little sense in protecting one party by, for example, requiring the other party to continue providing goods or services if there appears to be little prospect that the first party will prevail in the final award.

When considering applications for interim measures, the tribunal will not prejudge the merits of the dispute. This can only be done in the final award after hearing the entirety of both parties' submissions. Prejudgment of the merits can be a ground for challenge of an arbitrator's impartiality. Indeed, the LCIA Court has recently published two decisions in which such a challenge was made, although both challenges were unsuccessful.[210] The LCIA Court's approach was to apply the test

[205] Born, *International Commercial Arbitration*, pp. 1975–6.

[206] Ibid., p. 1977. See, also, Turner and Mohtashami, *Guide to the LCIA Rules*, para. 6.115.

[207] Born, *International Commercial Arbitration*, p. 1980.

[208] Article 17A.1(a) UNCITRAL Model Law; Born, *International Commercial Arbitration*, pp. 1980–3. See the award in Summary Arbitral Proceedings Case No. 2212 (28 July 1999), *Ybk Comm Arb*, 26(2001), 198.

[209] Born, *International Commercial Arbitration*, pp. 1988–91 favours such a requirement. Lew, Mistelis and Kröll, however, suggest that the merits of a case rarely play any direct role in determining whether interim relief is granted: *Comparative International Commercial Arbitration*, para. 23–62.

[210] LCIA Reference No. 3488 (11 July 2007), *Arb Intl*, 27(2011), 413 and LCIA Reference No. 81007/81008/81024/81025 (16 June 2008), *Arb Intl*, 27(2011), 425. Both are

for apparent bias outlined above: would a fair-minded and informed observer conclude that there was a real possibility that the tribunal was biased? Conclusions in respect of applications for interim measures will be expressed as prima facie or provisional, so as to avoid the appearance of prejudgment on the merits. Where an application for interim relief concerns a measure that is also being sought as final relief in the substantive arbitration, the issue of prejudgment is brought into particularly sharp focus. A division of the LCIA Court has rejected the view – advanced by Professor Lew – that a tribunal will generally refuse to grant an interim measure where it essentially covers what the tribunal is asked to resolve in the substantive arbitration because to do so would prejudge the merits.[211] The division held that article 25.1(c) expressly anticipates the granting on a provisional basis of remedies that the tribunal could grant in a final award. By its very nature, this requires a preliminary judgment about the correctness of a party's position on at least some part of the merits of the case.[212] The fact that the claimant-nominated arbitrator dissented and favoured the granting of the claimant's application for interim measures did not mean that he was apparently biased.

8.3 *Form of interim measures*

The LCIA Rules do not specify whether interim measures are to be granted in the form of an order or a partial award. This will usually be left to the discretion of the tribunal. There are advantages and disadvantages to issuing interim measures in either form. An order can typically be issued more promptly than an award. It requires fewer formalities. Thus, the text of an order is typically shorter than an award and no statement of reasons is required. An award, however, may enjoy greater enforceability in national courts. Some jurisdictions do not recognise orders as final and binding for the purposes of enforcement under the New York Convention.[213] Moreover, although orders cannot be enforced by the tribunal, parties are reluctant to flout an order of the tribunal for fear that the tribunal would draw adverse inferences when

summarised in Walsh and Teitelbaum, 'LCIA Court Decisions: An Introduction', at pp. 304–5.

211 LCIA Reference No. 81007/81008/81024/81025 (16 June 2008), *Arb Intl*, 27(2011), 425, referring to J. D. M. Lew 'Commentary on Interim Measures and Conservatory Measures in ICC Arbitration Cases', *ICC Int Ct Arb Bull*, 11 (2011), at para. 30.

212 *Arb Intl*, 27(2011), 425 at para. 4.12.

213 Lew, 'Commentary on Interim and Conservatory Measures', 23 at para. 34.

making the final award. In some jurisdictions (including England, under section 42 of the Arbitration Act 1996), a party may apply to the court to enforce an interim order of the tribunal.

9 Multi-party arbitration

Multi-party arbitrations are arbitration proceedings that involve more than one party on one or both sides of the dispute. This might be due to there being multiple claimants or respondents from the outset of the arbitration, the joinder of a third party after the commencement of proceedings or the consolidation of two or more ongoing proceedings. Multi-party arbitrations are increasingly frequent. In 2008, multi-party proceedings represented about 25% of all arbitrations filed with the LCIA.[214] They raise many practical issues, such as how arbitrators should be appointed and how costs should be divided.

9.1 Appointment of arbitrators in multi-party proceedings

Article 8 of the Rules governs the appointment of the arbitral tribunal in the event that there are more than two parties. The LCIA Court will appoint the tribunal without regard to any party's nomination where (a) the arbitration agreement entitles each party to nominate an arbitrator; (b) there are more than two parties to the dispute; and (c) those parties have not all agreed in writing that the disputant parties represent two separate sides for the formation of the arbitral tribunal as claimant and respondent, respectively. This provision is designed to respect the parties' rights to be treated equally in respect of the appointment of arbitrators. In a dispute arising out of a contract with various parties, for example, each might wish individually to exercise the right to nominate an arbitrator. In theory, the issue could arise with either multiple claimants or respondents; in practice, it inevitably arises where there are multiple respondents who do not consider that they have the same interests.[215] In cases where there are likely to be more than two parties to a dispute, the parties would be advised to specify in the arbitration agreement which parties form the claimant side and which form the respondent side, in order to safeguard their right to nominate an arbitrator.

[214] J. Bellhouse *et al.*, 'LCIA', in J. W. Rowley (ed.), *Arbitration World*, 3rd edn (European Lawyer Reference, 2010), para. 14.2.

[215] Turner and Mohtashami, *Guide to the LCIA Rules*, para. 4.77.

9.2 *Costs and deposits*

Article 24.1 provides the Registrar with considerable discretion in the apportionment of the directed payments between the parties. Where there are two sides in an arbitration, the LCIA is likely to divide the costs equally between the two sides, leaving it to the parties on each side to apportion costs between themselves. In cases with three or more sides to the arbitration, the LCIA Court will determine the apportionment on the basis of the circumstances.[216]

9.3 *Joinder*

Article 22.1(h) of the Rules gives the tribunal the power to join one or more third parties as a party to the proceedings upon the request of a party. Joinder of a third party can therefore be done without the consent of the other original party or parties to the arbitration, provided that the third party agrees. This could be said to be a departure from normal arbitration practice, which is based on the consent of the parties.[217] Arguably, the non-consenting party can be taken to have consented to the joinder of a third party by having agreed to arbitration under the Rules. This would satisfy the requirement of the New York Convention that there be a written arbitration agreement.[218]

Two different circumstances in which joinder might arise should be distinguished. The first is the case of a multi-party contract where arbitration has started amongst some, but not all, of the parties to the contract, and the third party is also party to that contract. The second is where the third party is not a party to the same contract (for example, a sub-contractor of one of the parties). Article 22.1(h) of the Rules allows for joinder in both circumstances, even though the third party is only a party to the arbitration agreement in the first case.[219]

216 Ibid., para. 8.42.

217 This provision is consistent with other institutional rules. E.g., article 7(1) of the new ICC Rules 2012 does not require the consent of the other original party or parties to the arbitration on the joinder. The additional party, however, should be joined before the confirmation or appointment of any arbitrator. Otherwise, the consent of all parties, including the party to be joined, is required. For a detailed account, see Born, *International Commercial Arbitration*, pp. 2094–5.

218 See Turner and Mohtashami, *Guide to the LCIA Rules*, para. 6.49.

219 Article 7(1) of the new ICC Rules 2012 adopts a similar language to that provided in article 22(1)(h) of the Rules. Thus, parties not signatory to the same contract can be joined by an original party to the arbitration.

9.4 Consolidation

There is no provision in the Rules that deals with the consolidation of two or more arbitral proceedings.[220] The question is therefore governed by the law of the seat. In England, the parties are free to agree to consolidate the arbitral proceeding with other proceedings or to agree to keep the arbitrations separate, but to hold concurrent hearings.[221] However, unless the parties agree to confer such power on the tribunal (which they might do in the arbitration agreement itself or once a dispute has arisen), the tribunal has no power to order consolidation of proceedings or to conduct concurrent hearings. If the parties to the parallel proceedings are different from the parties to the main proceedings, consent of all the parties would be required to consolidate the proceedings.

10 Conduct of proceedings

Articles 14 to 21 of the Rules govern the conduct of the arbitral proceedings. Article 14.1 endorses the broad principle of party autonomy and empowers the parties to determine for themselves how the arbitration will be conducted. This freedom is subject to the tribunal's general duties (a) to act fairly and impartially as between the parties, giving each a reasonable opportunity of putting its case and dealing with that of its opponent; and (b) to adopt procedures suitable to the circumstances of the arbitration, avoiding unnecessary delay or expense, so as to provide a fair and efficient means for resolution of the parties' dispute.[222]

In practice, it is rare for the parties to agree on a comprehensive set of rules for the conduct of a particular proceeding (they are, after all, by that stage in dispute). It therefore often falls to the tribunal to determine the procedural framework. The starting point for a tribunal will almost always be the Rules. They are significantly more detailed than most other institutional rules, including those of the ICC, in their coverage of the procedural framework for the conduct of the proceedings, although they do not provide for 'terms of reference' or 'case

[220] This position can be contrasted with the ICC Rules (article 10) and the SCC Rules (article 11), which allow for the arbitral institution to consolidate claims.

[221] s. 35 Arbitration Act 1996.

[222] Article 14.1.

management conferences' as do the ICC Rules.[223] They are not, however, exhaustive and the tribunal will likely issue at least one procedural direction in the course of proceedings.[224] In practice, tribunals sitting under the Rules often schedule a case management meeting at the outset of the arbitration to determine all relevant procedural issues.[225] In the case of a three-member tribunal the chairperson may, with the other arbitrators' prior consent, make procedural rulings alone,[226] avoiding the need to assemble the entire tribunal to deal with what may be minor procedural points.[227]

10.1 Written pleadings

Article 15 sets out in detail the procedure for the submission of written pleadings. This provision is not mandatory and can be modified by the parties and tribunal to suit the particular needs of their case. Article 15, therefore, amounts to a default procedure in the event that the parties and the tribunal have not agreed or ordered specific procedural directions.

Within 30 days of receipt of written confirmation from the LCIA Registrar of the formation of the arbitral tribunal, the claimant must submit its statement of case. Alternatively, the claimant may choose to treat its request for arbitration as its statement of case, in which case, it must notify the Registrar in writing of its election.[228]

Within 30 days of receipt of the statement of case (or written notice from the claimant that it elects to treat the request as its statement of case), the respondent must submit its statement of defence. Any counter-claims must be submitted with the statement of defence.[229]

Within 30 days of receipt of the statement of defence, the claimant must submit its statement of reply and, if a counter-claim was made, its defence to the counter-claim.[230]

Article 15 does not permit the respondent to submit a statement of rejoinder. However, if the statement of reply contains a defence to a

223 Articles 23 and 24 ICC Rules. See Sir Michael Kerr, 'London Court of International Arbitration', in A. J. van der Berg (ed.), *Planning Efficient Arbitration Proceedings: The Law Applicable in International Arbitration*, ICCA Congress Series, vol. 7 (The Hague: Kluwer Law International, 1996), p. 213.

224 Turner and Mohtashami, *Guide to the LCIA Rules*, paras. 5.19–21.

225 M. Blessing, 'Die LCIA Rules – aus der Sicht des Praktikers', *Schieds VZ* (2003), 198 at pp. 199–200.

226 Article 14.3. 227 Nesbitt, 'LCIA Arbitration Rules', p. 428. 228 Article 15.2.

229 Article 15.3. 230 Article 15.4.

counter-claim, within 30 days of receipt, the respondent must submit its statement of reply to the counter-claim, which responds to the claimant's statement of defence to the counter-claim.[231]

Unlike other institutional rules, the Rules require the parties to set out in their initial pleadings sufficient detail of the facts and any contentions of law on which they rely.[232] Any subsequent changes may be considered as a formal amendment falling within the ambit of article 22.1(a).

All pleadings are to be accompanied by copies (or, if especially voluminous, lists) of all essential documents relied upon that have not already been submitted by either party.[233] Article 15, however, does not require that the submission of witness statements and expert reports be made simultaneously with the written pleadings. This will typically be the subject of a separate procedural order by the tribunal.[234] It might set an alternative date for the service of witness statements and expert reports or require these to be submitted with the written pleadings.[235]

A party's failure to submit any pleadings or a failure otherwise to avail itself of the opportunity to present its case does not prevent the tribunal from moving forward with the proceedings and rendering an award.[236]

10.2 Hearings and oral evidence

Most international arbitration proceedings will involve the conduct of oral hearings. Although parties usually submit very detailed written submissions, including written witness statements and expert reports, it is rare for arbitration proceedings to be based solely on written submissions and documents.[237] Under article 19.1, any party can unilaterally insist on having an oral hearing on the merits, unless the parties have agreed on a documents-only arbitration. This is not subject to the discretion of the tribunal or the consent of the other party. The provision is in accordance with arbitration practice. Oral hearings are usually

231 Article 15.5. 232 Articles 15.2 and 15.3. 233 Article 15.6.

234 Turner and Mohtashami, *Guide to the LCIA Rules*, para. 5.52.

235 The first approach is increasingly not favoured in contemporary international practice: Born, *International Commercial Arbitration*, pp. 1825 and 1830.

236 Article 15.8. To comply with the requirement of due process and prevent any risk of challenge against the award, the tribunal must inform the defaulting party or parties of each stage of the proceedings so that they have the opportunity to participate. See, in particular, Gaillard and Savage, *Fouchard Gaillard Goldman on International Commercial Arbitration*, para. 1224.

237 Blackaby and Partasides, *Redfern and Hunter on International Commercial Arbitration*, para. 6.183; Born, *International Commercial Arbitration*, p. 1832.

desirable to give the parties an opportunity to have their 'day in court'. They are also a valuable opportunity for members of the tribunal to meet the parties and their counsel and ask questions about the case in order to enhance their understanding of intricate issues and avoid any misunderstanding that may have arisen from the written submissions.

The conduct of the hearing, including fixing the date, time and duration, is at the discretion of the tribunal, which is usually exercised after consultation with the parties. Article 20 of the Rules governs witness testimony, both factual and expert, which is considered to be 'the most comprehensive set of rules on witnesses among institutional rules'.[238] Among other things, article 20 affirms the right to cross-examine a witness presented by the other side, clarifies that the preparation of a witness by counsel is permissible under the Rules, subject to the mandatory provisions of any applicable law and confirms that party representatives or employees can serve as witnesses in LCIA arbitrations. Finally, article 21 affirms the tribunal's power to appoint experts unless the parties have agreed otherwise.[239]

10.3 The seat of arbitration and applicable law

Article 16.1 provides that the parties may agree on the seat of arbitration, provided that such agreement is expressed in writing. If the parties have not agreed on a seat of arbitration, the default position is that London will be the seat unless and until the LCIA Court determines, after having given the parties an opportunity to make written comment, that another seat is more appropriate. The inclusion of a default seat of arbitration is unique to the Rules and it means that England is frequently the seat of arbitration. It is also appropriate considering the close relationship between the Rules and England. Out of all the cases filed with the LCIA in the last three years, 85% were seated in England.[240] No cases were seated elsewhere in the United Kingdom. Moreover, on the rare occasion the LCIA Court was called upon to determine the seat, it has never determined that London was not the appropriate seat of arbitration. For example, in 2011, the LCIA Court was

[238] Turner and Mohtashami, *Guide to the LCIA Rules*, para. 5.99.

[239] The tribunal may not exercise its power to appoint an expert if the parties agree otherwise in writing. This 'veto' is exceptional in arbitral rules. It may be useful if the parties wish to limit the costs of the arbitration and are confident that their own expert witnesses can provide sufficient assistance for the tribunal. Nesbitt, 'LCIA Arbitration Rules', p. 439.

[240] Information provided by the LCIA to the authors.

called upon twice to determine the seat. In both cases, it considered that London was more appropriate, having considered the circumstances and the parties' written comments.[241]

Article 16.2 allows the parties to hold hearings, meetings and deliberations in locations other than the seat of arbitration. This may be convenient from a logistical point of view, taking into account the respective locations of the arbitrators, counsel and witnesses. Nevertheless, the arbitration proceeding is still deemed to be conducted at the seat of arbitration and any award rendered would still be deemed to be made at the seat of arbitration.

Article 16.3 provides that the law applicable to the arbitration – that is, the law that governs the procedure of the arbitration – will be the law of the seat of the arbitration, unless the parties have expressly agreed otherwise in writing and that agreement is not prohibited by the law of the arbitral seat.[242] It is not clear why the parties would wish to complicate their arbitration by applying a law other than the arbitration law of the seat, especially given that the parties would not be able to exclude the mandatory provisions of the law of the seat even by express agreement. Nevertheless, article 16.3 of the Rules upholds the principle of party autonomy in arbitration, giving the parties the express freedom to determine the framework for the settlement of their dispute.

10.4 Language

The initial language of the arbitration will be the language of the arbitration agreement, unless the parties have agreed otherwise in writing.[243] If that agreement is in more than one language, the LCIA Court may decide which will be the initial language, unless the agreement provides that proceedings should be conducted in more than one language.[244] Unless the parties have agreed the language(s) to be used in the arbitration, the tribunal, upon its formation, will decide that matter after giving the parties an opportunity to make written comment, taking into account the initial language of the arbitration and any other matter it may consider appropriate in all the circumstances of the case.[245] The tribunal or LCIA Court can require a party to submit translations of documents in other languages.[246]

[241] Information provided by the LCIA to the authors.

[242] English law does permit such an agreement: s. 4(5) Arbitration Act 1996.

[243] Article 17.1. [244] Article 17.2. [245] Article 17.3. [246] Article 17.4.

11 Confidentiality

One of the main advantages of LCIA arbitration is that the LCIA Rules preserve the confidentiality of the proceedings and submissions. This is important to protect sensitive commercial information. The concept of confidentiality is often distinguished from the privacy of hearings, and extends to all documents created for or submitted in the proceedings (including pleadings, witness statements and the like), the award and, indeed, to the very existence of the arbitration.[247]

The confidentiality of arbitration proceedings is not always presumed. Most institutional rules, including the ICC Rules, do not contain a provision expressly providing for confidentiality.[248] Similarly, many jurisdictions, such as states in the United States, Sweden and Australia, take the position that there is no implied duty of confidentiality in arbitration.[249] In contrast, one of the distinguishing features of the LCIA Rules is that they expressly impose an obligation of confidentiality on the parties in article 30, which will apply to proceedings commenced under these rules, even if the seat of the arbitration is in a jurisdiction that does not adopt an implied duty of confidentiality.[250]

Article 30 reflects the English law position. Under English law, there is an obligation of confidentiality in arbitration that has been developed by the common law.[251] The scope of this obligation and its implications, however, have yet to be clearly defined. This area of the law remains uncertain.[252]

247 The privacy of hearings is provided for in article 19.4. See Born, *International Commercial Arbitration*, p. 2251.

248 The new ICC Rules allow the parties to apply to the tribunal for orders concerning the confidentiality of the proceedings (article 22.3), but do not provide a default rule that proceedings are confidential.

249 Born, *International Commercial Arbitration*, pp. 2261–4.

250 See generally Veeder, 'The New 1998 LCIA Rules', pp. 368–9. Veeder queries, however, how effective article 30 will be once the tribunal is *functus officio* and recourse has to be made exclusively to national courts to enforce the duty of confidentiality.

251 The English Arbitration Act 1996 contains no express provision for the duty of confidentiality.

252 *Ali Shipping* v. *Shipyard Trogir* [1999] 1 WLR 314 (CA) 314 at 326 (Potter LJ) held that a duty of confidentiality was implied at law into an arbitration agreement as a necessary incident of that type of contract. See also *Scally* v. *Southern Health Board* [1992] 1 AC 294 (HL) at 307. See, however, *Electric & Gas Insurance Services Ltd. (Aegis)* v. *European Insurance Co. of Zurich* [2003] UKPC 11; [2003] 1 WLR 1041, at para. 20 (Lord Hobhouse): 'Commercial arbitrations are essentially private proceedings and unlike litigation in public courts do not place anything in the public domain. This may mean that the implied restrictions on the use of material obtained in arbitration

Article 30 is divided into three sub-paragraphs. Article 30.1 provides the general duty of confidentiality. It extends to 'all awards ... together with all materials in the proceedings created for the purpose of the arbitration and all other documents produced by another party in the proceedings not otherwise in the public domain'. This would include all submissions, witness statements, expert reports and all other documents produced that are not otherwise in the public domain.

Importantly, the duty of confidentiality under article 30 is not mandatory and the parties may choose to opt out of it expressly in writing. Moreover, it is not absolute. Disclosure of otherwise confidential material is permissible 'to the extent that disclosure may be required of a party by legal duty, to protect or pursue a legal right or to enforce or challenge an award in bona fide legal proceedings before a state court or other judicial authority'.[253] For arbitrations seated in England, it is relevant that the Judicial Committee of the Privy Council held that it was permissible in one set of proceedings to disclose an arbitral award rendered in previous proceedings between the same parties. The disclosure was necessary to enable the parties to enforce their rights in the subsequent proceedings.[254]

Article 30.2 codifies the universally accepted principle that a tribunal's deliberations are confidential. There is an exception to this rule allowing arbitrators to make public an arbitrator's refusal to take part in the deliberations if required under article 10 (revocation of arbitrator's appointment), article 12 (truncated tribunals) and article 26 (awards).

Article 30.3 provides that the LCIA Court 'does not publish any award or any part of an award without the prior written consent of all the parties and the Arbitral Tribunal'. Thus, LCIA awards, even in redacted form, are not published. This is in contrast to the practice of some other institutions such as the ICC, which publishes some of its awards in anonymous form.

proceedings may have greater impact than those applying to litigation. But when it comes to the award, the same logic cannot be applied. An award may have to be referred to for accounting purposes or for the purpose of legal proceedings ... or for the purposes of enforcing the rights which the award confers ... Generalisations and the formulation of detailed implied terms are not appropriate.' See, also, N. Rawding and K. Seeger, '*Aegis* v. *European Re* and the Confidentiality of Arbitration Awards', *Arb Intl*, 19(2003), 483 and *Emmott* v. *Michael Wilson & Partners Ltd.* [2008] EWCA Civ 184 at para. 84.

253 Article 30.1.

254 *Electric & Gas Insurance Services Ltd (Aegis)* v. *European Insurance Co. of Zurich* [2003] UKPC 11; [2003] 1 WLR 1041.

The duty of confidentiality has also applied to challenges to arbitrators. In June 2006, however, the LCIA Court announced that it would publish, on an anonymous basis, its reasoned decisions on such challenges; being the first arbitral institution to do so. The initiative has been welcomed by the international arbitration community as a step towards the development of a consistent body of jurisprudence on the application of principles such as impartiality and independence.[255]

12 The role of the LCIA organs

The LCIA is governed by two main organs: the LCIA Court and the Registrar.

12.1 The LCIA Court

The LCIA Court is not a typical 'court'. Its role is administrative as opposed to judicial in nature. It performs a variety of administrative functions such as appointing the arbitral tribunal and determining any challenge submitted by a party to the appointment of an arbitrator. The LCIA Court does not, however, review and scrutinise the award before it is transmitted to the parties.[256] It also does not undertake a prima facie review of the existence of an arbitration agreement. This is consistent with the practice of most arbitral institutions, but differs from that of the ICC Court.[257] Other responsibilities of the LCIA Court include the removal and replacement of arbitrators under articles 10 and 11, the determination of costs under article 28[258] and bringing arbitration

255 N. Gray and D. Crosbie, 'Winds of Change? The Pending Publication of LCIA Reasoned Decisions on Arbitral Independence', *Practical Law Company*, 1 February 2009.

256 M. Blessing 'London Court of International Arbitration: Praxisbezogene Anmerkungen', *SchiedsVZ* (2008), 126 at p. 127.

257 ICC Rules article 33. In an ICC arbitration, no award may be issued by a tribunal until it has been approved by the LCIA Court as to its form. See also ICC Rules article 6.3 and 6.4: the Secretary General may refer a question of the existence of an arbitration agreement to the ICC Court. In that case, the arbitration may only proceed if the ICC Court is prima facie satisfied that an arbitration agreement may exist. Under the previous rules, the Court itself considered this question in more cases.

258 Under the 1985 LCIA Rules costs were determined by the arbitrators subject to confirmation by the Court. Under the current rules, all disputes regarding administrative charges, fees and expenses of the tribunal are determined by the Court.

proceedings to an end pursuant to article 24.4.[259] In its six-monthly meetings, the LCIA Court reviews the progress and conduct of pending arbitrations.[260]

The LCIA Court is made up of 35 members, typically chosen from among prominent members of the international arbitration community. It comprises one President, six Vice Presidents and 28 members. The LCIA Court's functions are carried out on a delegated basis, either by the President, a Vice President or by a sub-division of three or five members appointed by the President or a Vice President. They are not carried out on a plenary basis. The LCIA Court's constitution provides that arbitral appointments shall be made by the President or, if unavailable, by one of the Vice Presidents.[261] Challenges to arbitrators are usually resolved by a three-member subdivision.[262] The current and previous four Presidents have all been from outside the UK and the LCIA Court's overall membership is diverse.[263]

Given that the LCIA Court is composed of prominent arbitration practitioners, in many instances the short-list for arbitral appointments will contain one or more members of the LCIA Court. To ensure the integrity of the process for forming the arbitral tribunal, the LCIA Court's constitution provides that the President shall only be eligible for appointment if the parties agree to nominate him as sole arbitrator or chairperson, and that Vice Presidents shall only be eligible to serve as arbitrators if nominated by a party or the parties.[264] The President or Vice Presidents so nominated shall not take any part in the appointment of the tribunal or in any other function of the LCIA Court relating to the arbitration.[265]

12.2 The LCIA Registrar

The Registrar is responsible for all administrative functions of the LCIA Court. He operates under the supervision of the LCIA Court

[259] These powers would be relevant in the event that a claimant failed to participate in proceedings shortly after submitting the request for arbitration and prior to the constitution of the tribunal. See LCIA article 24.4: failure by a claimant or counter-claiming party to provide promptly and in full the required deposit may be treated by the LCIA Court and the Arbitral Tribunal as a withdrawal of the claim or counter-claim respectively.

[260] Veeder, 'The New 1998 LCIA Rules', pp. 367–8.

[261] Article D.2 of the Constitution of the LCIA Arbitration Court.

[262] Walsh and Teitelbaum, 'LCIA Court Decisions: An Introduction', p. 286.

[263] Details of the Court's membership can be found at http://www.lcia.org/LCIA/Members_bios.aspx (accessed 17 January 2012).

[264] Article F of the Constitution of the LCIA Court.

[265] Article F.2 of the Constitution of the LCIA Court.

and is the head of the LCIA Secretariat, which is responsible for transmitting any communications among the LCIA Court, the tribunal and the parties.[266] All communications from any party or arbitrator to the LCIA Court must be addressed to the Registrar.[267] He is also invariably requested to make informal reviews of awards on behalf of tribunals to ensure that dates, party names and procedural history have been accurately transcribed in the award.[268] Under the supervision of the Registrar, the London headquarters of the Secretariat is responsible for the day-to-day administration of all arbitrations referred to the LCIA.

12.3 *Reviewing decisions of the LCIA Court*

Article 29 provides that decisions of the LCIA Court with respect to all matters relating to the arbitration shall be conclusive and binding upon both the parties and the tribunal. The LCIA Court need not give reasons (although it does do so in respect of challenges to arbitrators): the decisions are treated as administrative in nature. Parties are taken, to the extent permitted by the law of the seat of arbitration, to have waived any right of appeal or review in respect of such decisions of the LCIA Court.[269]

13 Possibility of excluding the courts' review of an award's validity

Article 26.9 of the Rules provides that an award by a tribunal is final and binding on the parties. The parties undertake to carry out any award immediately and without any delay (subject only to article 27, which provides for the correction of awards). They also waive irrevocably their right to any form of appeal, review or recourse to any state court or other judicial authority, insofar as such waiver may be validly made. Jurisdictions vary as to the extent to which they give effect to such a waiver and to which they allow arbitral awards to be challenged in judicial proceedings.[270]

[266] Article 13. [267] Article 3.3.

[268] Turner and Mohtashami, *Guide to the LCIA Rules*, para. 7.21. [269] Article 29.2.

[270] Blackaby and Partasides, *Redfern and Hunter on International Arbitration*, para. 10.24.

If a party wishes to challenge an award's validity, it must bring a challenge before the national courts of the seat of the arbitration.[271] The Rules do not allow a party to make an application to the LCIA itself to challenge an award. Nor is there a provision by which parties can apply to the tribunal for an 'interpretation' of the award, so as to clarify any uncertainty.[272] In common with those of other arbitral institutions, the Rules do allow for the correction of errors in computation, clerical or typographical errors or any errors of a similar nature.[273] They also allow for additional awards to be made in relation to claims or counter-claims omitted from the award.[274]

The grounds for challenge of an award rendered by the Rules will be governed by the law of the seat of the arbitration. In most LCIA arbitrations, this will be the English Arbitration Act 1996, since most LCIA arbitrations are seated in England. The Arbitration Act 1996 recognises three grounds on which an award can be challenged: lack of substantive jurisdiction (section 67), serious irregularity (section 68) and error of law (section 69). The first two are mandatory provisions of English law[275] and article 26.9 is not effective to remove a party's right to challenge an award on those grounds. It is, however, effective to prevent a party appealing to court under section 69 on a question of law arising out of the award.[276]

14 Other specific features

Two additional specific features of the Rules are the provisions dealing with truncated tribunals and those regarding awards.

[271] Except for those rare cases in which parties have agreed to apply a different law to the arbitration from the law of the seat (see n 242 above).

[272] Contrast article 35.2 ICC Rules. The omission was deliberate: it was thought that allowing applications for interpretation would lead to delay in enforcement. See, Turner and Mohtashami, *Guide to the LCIA Rules*, para. 7.43.

[273] Articles 27.1 and 27.2. It is likely that this does not extend to correcting an error of reasoning: see *CNH Global NV* v. *PGN Logistics Ltd & Ors* [2009] EWHC 977 (Comm); [2009] 1 CLC 807 in which it was held that an erroneous failure to award interest did not fall within the analogous provision of the ICC Rules. (The ICC Court had taken a different view, as it had approved an addendum to amend the award.)

[274] Article 27.3. [275] ss. 4(1), 67 and 68 and Sch. 1 Arbitration Act 1996.

[276] In *Lesotho Development* v. *Impregilo SpA* [2006] 1 AC 221 it was held that a similarly worded provision in the ICC Rules (now found in article 34.6) was an agreement to exclude a right of appeal under s. 69, para. 3.

14.1 *Truncated tribunals: Majority power to continue proceedings*

Article 12 of the Rules addresses the difficulty of truncated tribunals and provides a mechanism to ensure that the proceedings are not disrupted in the event of an uncooperative tribunal member.[277] If any arbitrator on a three-member tribunal refuses or persistently fails to participate in its deliberations, the two other arbitrators may continue the arbitration, including the making of any decision, ruling or award, notwithstanding the absence of the third arbitrator.[278] In order to do so, they must give written notice of the third arbitrator's refusal or failure to the LCIA Court, the parties and the third arbitrator himself. In making a decision whether to continue, the arbitrators must take into account the stage of the arbitration, any explanation given by the third arbitrator and such other matters as they consider appropriate. If they determine that they will not continue without the third arbitrator's participation, they must notify the parties and the LCIA Court. In such circumstances, either they or any party may refer the matter to the LCIA Court for the revocation of the third arbitrator's appointment and his replacement.[279] These provisions in the Rules are broader than those that apply to some other arbitral institutions.[280]

14.2 *The award and the power to award interest*

Article 26 of the Rules makes various provisions in respect of the award. Much of this provision is not unique and reflects the approach of other arbitral institutions. The award is to be in writing and, unless all parties agree otherwise, is to state the reasons on which it is based.[281] The decision can be by majority.[282] Separate awards may be made on separate issues at different times.[283] If the parties settle their dispute before the award is rendered, the tribunal may, upon the parties' written request,

[277] On which, see generally Born, *International Commercial Arbitration*, chapter 11, part G. Relying on article 12 and proceeding with a truncated tribunal may be quicker than relying on articles 10 and 11 to have the arbitrator replaced. This may be particularly useful if the arbitration is at an advanced stage when the difficulty arises. Nesbitt, 'LCIA Arbitration', pp. 424–5.

[278] Articles 12.1 and 12.2. [279] Article 12.3.

[280] Cf., e.g., article 15.5 ICC Rules, which provides for a remedy at the hands of the ICC Court (and not the arbitrators themselves) and then only after the proceedings have closed.

[281] Article 26.1. [282] Article 26.1. [283] Article 26.7.

render a 'Consent Award' which records the terms of the settlement. Such an award need not contain reasons.[284] The provisions in respect of currency of awards and interest are, however, distinctive.[285] An LCIA award may be expressed in any currency.[286] The tribunal has a broad discretion in respect of interest. It may order that simple or compound interest be paid by any party on any sum awarded at such rates as the tribunal determines to be appropriate, without being bound by legal rates of interest that would bind a state court. Interest can be imposed in respect of any period that the tribunal determines to be appropriate, ending not later than the date upon which the award is satisfied.[287]

[284] Article 26.8.

[285] The ICC and SCC Rules do not make provision in respect of these two matters. Indeed, institutional arbitral rules do not usually make provision in respect of interest: Born, *International Commercial Arbitration*, p. 2504.

[286] Article 26.6.

[287] Article 26.6. Awards of interest will not be enforced in all countries: Lew, Mistelis and Kröll, *Comparative International Commercial Arbitration*, paras. 24–89.

11

Arbitration in Norway: Features of the Oslo Chamber of Commerce

STEPHEN KNUDTZON

1 Introduction

In 2004, Norway enacted a new arbitration act, hereinafter the 'Arbitration Act' or 'Act', which is called the *Lov om voldgift* (2004/05/14 nr. 25) in Norwegian.

Norway is a party to the Convention on the Recognition and Enforcement of Foreign Arbitral Awards that came in force on 7 June 1959 (the 'New York Convention').

Most of the arbitrations in Norway are conducted as *ad hoc* arbitrations, in accordance with the relevant arbitration clause, and as supplemented by the Arbitration Act.

Institutional arbitration is offered by the Arbitration and Dispute Resolution Institute of the Oslo Chamber of Commerce (the 'Oslo Institute'). In addition, there are so-called standing technical arbitration courts (*Faste Tekniske Voldgiftsretter*) in some of the major cities, but these institutions are used less frequently today than they were previously. Occasionally, an arbitration may be conducted in Norway pursuant to the rules of the ICC Court of Arbitration in Paris.

There are few statistics available on the number of arbitrations conducted in Norway in any given year. The Oslo Institute currently administers between three and five cases per year. Norwegian legislation provides for a copy of arbitration awards to be sent to the local city court. A survey shows that 372 arbitration awards were filed with the Oslo City Court in the period between 1987 and the middle of 2001.

2 The Arbitration Act

The Arbitration Act was passed in Parliament on 14 May 2004 and came into force on 1 January 2005.

The Act applies to all arbitrations that have been initiated since the Act came into force, but certain transitional rules apply according to section 49 of the Act.

The Arbitration Act was prepared by the same commission that proposed a complete reform of the Civil Procedures Act. The commission's report on arbitration and the proposal in respect of the new Act can be found in NOU 2001: 33 'Voldgift'. The proposition from the government to the parliament to pass new legislation, which was prepared by the Ministry of Justice and, in all material respects, followed the proposal from the commission, can be found in Ot.prp. no. 27 (2003–2004). The new Civil Procedures Act was not passed in Parliament until 17 June 2005 and has no specific rules or regulations on arbitration.

The Norwegian Arbitration Act is based on the UNCITRAL Model Law (the 'Model Law') on International Commercial Arbitration (as adopted on 21 June 1985).

The structure of the Arbitration Act very much follows the same structure as that of the Model Law.

The Arbitration Act has 11 chapters.

The first chapter (sections 1–5) contains the 'general provisions'. Chapter 2 (sections 6–8) regulates the relationship between arbitration proceedings and the ordinary courts. These first two chapters of the Act reflect some of the provisions in the Model Law's chapter I.

Chapter 3, about the arbitration agreement (sections 9–13), incorporates, to a large extent, chapter II of the Model Law. Chapter 4, dealing with the composition of the arbitration tribunal (sections 14–17), is almost identical to chapter III of the Model Law. In addition, chapter 5, with provisions on the jurisdiction of the arbitration tribunal (sections 18 and 19) corresponds to chapter IV of the Model Law. Chapter 6, regarding the conduct of arbitral proceedings (sections 20 to 30), is also mostly based on chapter V of the Model Law. Chapter 7, with provisions on the making of the award (sections 31 to 38), is almost identical to chapter VI of the Model Law.

Chapter 8 (sections 39 to 41) of the Act has provisions on costs. Similar provisions are not found in the Model Law. Chapter 9 (sections 42 to 44) has the relevant provisions about recourse against an arbitration award, corresponding to chapter VII in the Model Law. Chapter 10 (on the recognition and enforcement of awards), sections 45 to 47, provides provisions that are similar to chapter VIII of the Model Law.

The most important differences between the Act and the Model Law are the following sections in the Act:

(a) Section 5 provides that the arbitration proceedings and the award of the arbitration tribunal are not subject to confidentiality, unless the parties have agreed otherwise for the case in question.
(b) Section 9 provides that an arbitration tribunal can decide upon the civil law consequences of competition legislation. In this context, it should also be mentioned that the arbitration tribunal, with the assistance of the Norwegian courts, can ask for advice from the European Free Trade Association (EFTA) court when dealing with the construction of matters related to the European Economic Area (EEA) Agreement (see section 30).
(c) Norwegian law no longer requires that arbitration agreements are entered into in writing (section 10) as opposed to the Model Law's article 7(2). It should be borne in mind that a written arbitration agreement will be required to enforce a Norwegian award abroad under the New York Convention.
(d) Section 11 provides that an arbitration agreement is not binding on a consumer, if entered into before the dispute has arisen.
(e) It should also be noted that the Model Law states that each party has the burden of proving its case – section 28 in the Act has a slightly different regulation. Section 28 states that the parties are responsible for providing the evidence in the proceedings, with certain rights for the arbitration tribunal to refuse evidence of no importance to the case or if there is no reasonable proportionality between the importance of the dispute and the evidence that is offered.

Two commentaries to the Arbitration Act have been published in Norway.[1]

Both commentaries have English translations detailing the provisions of the Norwegian Arbitration Act.

The Arbitration Act provides, in section 2, that the Act can be derogated from following agreement between the parties, when this is expressly provided for in the particular section of the Act. In practice,

[1] B. Høgetveit Berg (ed.), *Voldgiftsloven med kommentarer* (Gyldendal, 2006) and H.-J. Kolrud (ed.), *Lov om voldgift – Kommentarutgave* (Universitetsforlaget, 2006).

this means that the Act is applicable in a mandatory fashion, unless otherwise provided for in each section.

3 The Arbitration and Dispute Resolution Institute of the Oslo Chamber of Commerce (the 'Oslo Institute')

3.1 History

The Oslo Institute was founded on 1 January 1983. Originally, it only provided services in respect of ordinary arbitration. In 1997 and 1998, the Oslo Institute extended its services to mediation and changed to its current name. In 2007, the Oslo Institute also included certain rules on expert assistance for the preventing of disputes.

3.2 Services provided by the Oslo Institute and the Rules

The Oslo Institute has adopted rules for arbitration and dispute resolution (the 'Rules'). The Rules were revised and adapted to fall into line with the Arbitration Act when this came into force on 1 January 2005. The Rules can be found on the website of the Oslo Chamber of Commerce.[2]

The board of directors of the Oslo Institute has also established a list consisting of a panel of recommended arbitrators and their specialities. A similar list of a panel containing qualified mediators is also provided by the Institute.

The Oslo Institute administers the arbitration proceedings under its Rules. The secretarial functions are provided by the Oslo Chamber of Commerce. The secretariat can assist with adequate premises, equipment and secretarial staff for the arbitration tribunal, if so required.

The Oslo Institute can also be nominated as the appointing authority under the UNCITRAL Arbitration Rules.

The Oslo Institute has, as one of its main objectives, the promotion of the use of arbitration and alternative dispute resolution ('ADR') and for that purpose, from time to time, it arranges its own seminars about arbitration and provides lecturers for seminars that are held by other institutions.

The Oslo Institute has also prepared brochures and articles about arbitration in order to promote the use of arbitration for dispute resolution.

[2] Visit www.chamber.no for the Oslo Institute's Rules.

Together with the Rules, the Oslo Institute has also drafted certain model clauses, both in respect of arbitration and mediation, which can be found in annex A of this chapter.

The current board of directors of the Oslo Institute comprises representatives from law firms, industrial companies, the ordinary courts, government agencies and the University of Oslo.[3]

The Oslo Institute charges an administration fee for the handling of arbitration cases. This administration fee currently varies from NOK 10,000 to NOK 70,000 depending on the amount in dispute. The relevant administration fees can be found on the website of the Oslo Institute and are adjusted from time to time.

The Oslo Institute does not review the awards that are rendered according to its Rules in advance. The decisions in the arbitration cases are thus the sole responsibility of the arbitrators. However, the Oslo Institute[4] receives a copy of the awards rendered. During the proceedings, it has contact with the arbitrators to ensure that there is progress in the proceedings.

3.3 *The Rules applicable to ordinary arbitrations and fast-track arbitration*

The Oslo Institute provides two sets of Rules applicable to arbitration. The Rules, chapter II (articles 6 to 21), provide regulations applying to ordinary arbitration, while chapter III (articles 22 to 36) provides regulations applicable to 'fast-track' arbitration.

The main differences between the two sets of Rules are the following:

(a) An ordinary arbitration is normally conducted with three arbitrators (article 7) while a fast-track arbitration is normally conducted with one arbitrator (article 23).
(b) While the award in an ordinary arbitration is expected to be rendered no later than one year after the appointment of the tribunal

[3] Advokat (H) Stephen Knudtzon (Advokatfirma Thommessen AS) – Chairman; Wenche Agerup (Norsk Hydro ASA); Advokat (H) Fanny Platou Amble (Attorney General's Office); Judge Thor Henning Auestad (Stavanger City Court); Professor Dr Jurisprudence Knut Kaasen (University of Oslo); Advokat (H) Christian Fr. Michelet (Arntzen de Besche advokatfirma AS); Professor Dr Jurisprudence Giuditta Cordero-Moss (University of Oslo); Advokat (H) Gunnar Sørlie (Advokatfirma BA–HR).

[4] The Oslo Institute, Arbitration and Dispute-resolution Institute of the Oslo Chamber of Commerce, Henrik Ibsens Gate 100, 0255 Oslo, Norway. Telephone: +47 22 12 94 00; fax: +47 22 12 94 01; E-mail: mail@chamber.no

and no later than six weeks after the conclusion of the main hearing, the fast-track arbitration is expected to be concluded no later than six months after the appointment of the arbitrator.

(c) Under both procedures, it is contemplated that a 'main hearing' is held, unless the parties agree that the arbitrators can decide the case based on the documents submitted.

(d) The time frame for the main hearing in a fast-track arbitration is limited and it shall last no more than four days (articles 15 and 31).

4 The Rules and the Arbitration Act

As explained above, the Arbitration Act states, section by section, whether each section is mandatory or not. The Arbitration Act provides that procedural matters, to a large extent, are left to the discretion of the arbitrators.

The Rules are intended to provide a more defined and clearer regime for the conduct of the arbitration proceedings. Articles 6 and 22 provide that the Rules are supplemented with the provisions of the Arbitration Act, unless otherwise agreed between the parties. That means that the Rules will apply where they deviate from the provisions of the Arbitration Act, but that the parties in any relevant case can agree to deviate both from the Rules and from the non-mandatory provisions of the Arbitration Act.

5 The arbitration agreement

As explained above, the arbitration agreement does not need to be in writing. The agreement can be in respect of an existing dispute or for all, or for specific disputes that can arise out of a specific legal relationship (section 10 of the Act).

Sometimes it is difficult to determine whether the arbitration clause applies to the whole agreement between the parties. The Hålogaland Appeal Court held[5] that the arbitration clause in a time-charter party only applied to that agreement and not to a separate option agreement that gave the charterer certain rights to continue the charter party.

It is a requirement under section 9 of the Act that the parties have unrestricted disposition over the legal relationship. Disputes that can be settled by agreement between the parties can normally be the subject of

[5] RG 2008/1179.

arbitration. Matters that are regulated by public rules such as divorce, whether or not a patent exists or whether a decision by a public agency is valid or not, can normally not be the subject of arbitration.

There may also be mandatory legislation that excludes arbitration. Section 11 of the Act is already mentioned and provides that a consumer is only bound by an arbitration agreement if it is entered into after the dispute arises. In a case that was decided on by Borgarting Appeal Court in 2010,[6] it was held that the buyer of a vacation apartment was a consumer and was therefore not bound by the arbitration clause, despite the fact that the apartment could be used by the buyer both for his private use and for rental income.

The Borgarting Appeal Court held[7] that an arbitration clause in a contract entered into between the football club Lyn and the football player Mikel was invalid because it related to the termination of an employment contract that was subject to the jurisdiction of the ordinary courts under mandatory labour law.

The Oslo Institute will apply the Rules to an arbitration when the arbitration clause refers the dispute to the Oslo Institute, but the parties are free to agree on variations from the Rules both in the original arbitration clause or after the arbitration has been initiated. The annex at the end of this chapter contains the model clauses that have been drafted by the Oslo Institute for inclusion in contracts.

When a legal relationship is assigned to another party, it follows from section 10 of the Act that that party becomes bound by the arbitration clause. This was the case in a decision by the Borgarting Appeal Court in 2007,[8] where the court found that a broker agreement had been taken over by another entity, who was then bound by the arbitration clause in the original broker agreement.

6 The involvement of the Norwegian courts

It follows from the Arbitration Act section 6 that the ordinary Norwegian courts only have authority in disputes that are subject to arbitration when the Arbitration Act specifically provides for that. It further follows from section 7 in the Act that the ordinary courts will reject a case that is brought before them where arbitration has been agreed or where arbitration proceedings have been initiated, unless the agreement to arbitrate is invalid or the arbitration agreement cannot be

[6] LB-2010-46071. [7] RG 2006/1324. [8] LB-2007-151969.

conducted as intended. A court case in respect of the same dispute that is also the subject of an arbitration does not prevent the arbitration tribunal from initiating or continuing the arbitration proceedings and even reaching a decision on the arbitration (section 7, third paragraph). This avoids any delays in the arbitration proceedings on the basis of unfounded parallel court cases that are initiated. However, it follows from section 18 that a party can challenge, before the courts, a decision by the arbitration panel that it has jurisdiction in a matter.

In respect of the above provisions in section 7, a decision has to be reached as to whether or not a dispute can be subject to an arbitration and, if so, then the case can be decided on with finality. A decision by the Norwegian Supreme Court[9] illustrates this. The parties had agreed to leave the decision on the valuation of a property to a panel of three appointed persons. The Supreme Court held there was a dispute on a legal matter, since it related to the principles for valuation. Furthermore, it was held that there was an arbitration, since the decision was to be 'final and binding' on the parties. Thus, the valuation could not be tried by the courts, since it was subject to arbitration. A similar decision was rendered by the Agder Appeal Court in 2009,[10] while the Borgarting Appeal Court in 2008[11] came to the conclusion that the determination of the market rent for a property was not an arbitration award, since the agreement did not specifically state that the rent was determined with final effect by the valuator.

If a party wishes to rely on an arbitration clause and is summoned in court proceedings, it follows from section 7 of the Act that it shall object to the jurisdiction of the courts at the latest when it engages in a discussion of the reality of the case before the courts. Accordingly, the Supreme Court[12] held that a party had lost its right to arbitrate, because it did not make the objection in a timely manner.

The courts may also be involved when the impartiality and independence of an arbitrator is challenged or a request is made for removal of an arbitrator (sections 15 and 16).

The competent court will be the court where a case in the relevant dispute could have been commenced if there had been no arbitration agreement. If no such Norwegian court can be determined, the Oslo City Court will be the competent court. Once a court has been involved in a matter, all later applications and matters regarding the same arbitration proceedings will be made to that court.

[9] Rt 2010/748. [10] LA-2009-90969. [11] LB-2008-170748. [12] Rt 2008/1623.

Applications to secure evidence can be made to other courts, for example, for the purpose of taking statements from witnesses at their domicile or for requests to third parties to submit documents, for example, under the Civil Procedures Act chapter 28.

When the courts are involved in matters relating to arbitration, the matter will normally be handled on the basis of written pleadings, but the court may decide on oral deliberations if that is required to ensure proper and fair proceedings.

The arbitration agreement does not exclude the right of the parties to require injunctions or other conservatory measures in accordance with the Civil Procedures Act chapters 32 to 34. That would apply to an arrest and to similar applications. Under the Arbitration Act section 19, the arbitration tribunal is competent, at the request of one of the parties, to order interim measures. As a condition for such measures, the party requesting them may be required by the arbitration tribunal to provide security for any consequences. The arbitration tribunal can also limit and cancel the interim measures. Under section 19 paragraph 3, a party can claim damages in respect of an interim measure if the other parties' claim did not exist at the time when the interim measure was decided. The arbitration panel is competent to decide upon the damages. Article 11, paragraph 2 item (f) in the Rules provides for the same measures. It should be noted, however, that the interim measures decided upon by the arbitration tribunal are not enforceable before the ordinary courts.

Under section 13 of the Arbitration Act, it would be the ordinary courts that would be authorized to appoint arbitrators when the parties fail to do so. Under the Rules, the appointment of arbitrators is made by the Oslo Institute under article 7 paragraph 2. Only where the Oslo Institute fails to appoint an arbitrator in a proper manner are the ordinary courts competent, under section 13, to make such an appointment. The appointment of arbitrators by the courts, in accordance with the Act section 13, is not subject to any appeal.

Section 30 of the Arbitration Act provides that the arbitration tribunal or one of the parties with the consent of the arbitration tribunal can ask the courts to take statements from the party representative or the witnesses, or to take other steps to secure evidence. The arbitration tribunal has the right to be present and to ask questions in these court sessions, after having been given reasonable advanced notice of such sessions.

As mentioned above, the arbitration tribunal may ask for an interpretation of the EEA Agreement from the EFTA court. The application has to be made to a Norwegian court that may then request the EFTA court to give an advisory opinion on the matter.

The ordinary courts also have a function in determining the fees of the arbitrators in accordance with section 39 paragraph 3, if these are challenged by one of the parties.

Finally, recourse cases against the validity of an arbitration award are brought before the ordinary courts in accordance with sections 42 to 44. Objections against the enforcement of an arbitration award are also decided on by the ordinary courts, as provided for in section 46 of the Act.

7 The appointment and dismissal of arbitrators

7.1 The number of arbitrators and the appointment of the same

Article 7 of the Rules leaves it to the parties to agree on the number of arbitrators. If no agreement is made in that respect, the Rules provide that the number of arbitrators shall be three. This corresponds with the Arbitration Act section 12. Both under the Arbitration Act section 13 and the Rules article 7, the parties are given the opportunity to agree on the persons to be appointed as arbitrators. If they do not agree within a certain time frame set by the Oslo Institute, each of the parties will appoint one arbitrator and the Oslo Institute will appoint the chairperson. If it is agreed that the arbitration is to be conducted with a single arbitrator, the Oslo Institute will appoint the single arbitrator when the parties do not agree on a person. The Oslo Institute, before appointing an arbitrator, will always ask for the views of the parties on possible candidates.

The appointment of the arbitrator is made by the board of directors of the Institute, but may be delegated to one or more board members in a specific case. The Rules also provide for the possibility of a deputy arbitrator being appointed. In certain big cases, a need may be identified to have a deputy arbitrator available, to avoid the case being delayed because one of the arbitrators becomes ill or becomes otherwise incapacitated during the proceedings. Normally a deputy arbitrator will not be appointed, unless one party so requests.

In fast-track arbitration it follows from the Rules (article 23) that only one arbitrator is appointed. The Oslo Institute will appoint a person suggested by both parties, but otherwise the Oslo Institute will freely appoint an arbitrator, after having received the views of the parties.

7.2 Replacement and removal of arbitrators

Both under the Rules article 10 and article 23, the Oslo Institute may replace arbitrators who are held to be prejudiced, incompetent or who have mishandled their tasks as arbitrators. This can be done both at the initiative of the Oslo Institute or at the request of a party. The idea is to give the Oslo Institute the right to dismiss an arbitrator who does not follow up a case at the expected rate.

The removal of an arbitrator can also be requested under the Arbitration Act section 15. This provision is mandatory and a decision made by the Oslo Institute could thus be tried by the ordinary courts.

7.3 Impartiality, independence and qualifications of an arbitrator

The Rules are supplemented by sections 13–17 of the Arbitration Act. An arbitrator is required to be impartial and independent of the parties and to be qualified for the task.

It will normally be expected that the arbitrator who is appointed, is 'qualified' for the task. This will normally require some experience in arbitration in general or in the field that the dispute relates to. Consequently, it is difficult to challenge an arbitrator on the basis of a lack of qualifications, except in some clear cases. If an arbitrator is mentally reduced because of illness or does not meet the qualifications that were expressly agreed on (for example, being a practising lawyer), there would be a basis for challenging the appointment. The same would apply if the arbitrator did not understand the agreed language for the arbitration proceeding.

The Act gives little guidance on what 'impartiality' and 'independence' means. The Act reflects the Model Law article 12 on this issue. Foreign jurisprudence on the interpretation of similar provisions incorporated in foreign legislation may therefore provide relevant guidance on issues arising in this respect. The Norwegian Court Act, sections 106 to 108, contains certain rules about the qualifications applying to ordinary judges. These provisions may also give some guidance, but are not necessarily applicable by analogy. Arbitrators are often people who participate in business or who are practising lawyers and they will have larger networks and more extensive business relationships than professional judges normally have.

A decision from the Frostating Appeal Court in 2009[13] may illustrate the issues. The chairperson of an arbitration tribunal discovered during the main hearing that the assistant to the lawyers pleading the matter for one of the parties had accepted a job offer as an associate in the same law firm where the arbitrator was a partner. The partner had not been involved in the appointment of the associate and although the associate started working in the same firm before the award was rendered, the associate did not work in the same department of the firm as the partner. The associate and the partner had no day-to-day contact and had no contact concerning the case before or after the award was rendered. While the Trondheim City Court held that the arbitration award was invalid because there were justifiable grounds against the impartiality or independence of the arbitrator, the Appeal Court came to the opposite conclusion. In its reasons, it was emphasized that it was unlikely that an associate could have influenced a partner in respect of the outcome of the case, that the law firm in question was a big law firm where the people in different departments had little contact and that the law firm, as such, had a very remote interest in the associate being on the winning team of his previous law firm.

In another case before the Oslo City Court,[14] it was held that there were justifiable grounds against the impartiality or independence of an arbitrator. The arbitrator, who was a practising lawyer, represented the law firm that acted for one of the parties in the arbitration, in a case where that law firm was held liable for a considerable amount of damages. The client relationship between the law firm and the arbitrator was therefore sufficient reason to accept the objection against the arbitrator.

Some general observations can be made about what constitutes justifiable grounds against the impartiality or independence of an arbitrator. Close family relations between an arbitrator and a party or its attorney may give rise to objections. Similarly, an arbitrator may not hold positions in corporate bodies (boards of directors etc.) or be employed by one of the parties. An arbitrator cannot have any prior involvement as a legal advisor in the dispute that is being arbitrated or have acted recently as a legal advisor for one of the parties. As demonstrated by the above decision from the Oslo City Court, it is not advisable for the arbitrator to have too close a link with one of the law firms representing a party in an arbitration. An arbitrator who has been appointed frequently by one of the law firms representing a party in an arbitration may, in the

[13] LF-2009-1094. [14] In a decision on 5 April 2006.

circumstances, be considered to have too close a tie to that side. An arbitrator who starts communication with one of the parties without involving the other arbitrators, may also be considered impartial.

A candidate for the appointment as arbitrator has, at his or her own initiative, an obligation to disclose any circumstances that can raise justifiable doubts as to his or her impartiality or independence. The same obligation applies to an appointed arbitrator throughout the entire arbitration proceeding (section 14 of the Act).

Objections against an arbitrator in respect of impartiality or independence can only be made on justifiable grounds or on the basis that the arbitrator does not have the qualifications that were agreed upon between the parties. Only circumstances that become known after the appointment has been made will be taken into account. Under the Arbitration Act, an objection against an arbitrator has to be reasoned and submitted in writing to the arbitration panel within 15 days after a party became aware of the appointment of an arbitrator or of the circumstances on which the objection is based. The arbitration tribunal will then resolve the issue, unless the arbitrator withdraws or the other party agrees to the objection. It should be noted that when an arbitrator withdraws on this basis, that does not imply that the basis for the challenge is accepted (section 15, paragraph 1, cf. section 16, paragraph 2).

If the arbitration tribunal does not accept the objection against an arbitrator, the question may be brought before the courts within one month from the decision of the tribunal. When the court has made its decision, the objection cannot later be used as the basis for recourse against the award or as an objection against the enforcement of the award (see sections 44 and 46 of the Act).

7.4 Removal of the arbitrator for other reasons

If an arbitrator becomes de jure or de facto unable to perform his functions as an arbitrator or if an arbitrator fails to act without undue delay, his mandate terminates if he withdraws from his office or if the parties agree on the termination. Each of the parties can also make an application to the court to have the arbitrator removed for the said reasons as provided in section 16 of the Act. The decision of the court is not subject to appeal.

Under the Rules, the Oslo Institute has similar powers to discharge an arbitrator, as mentioned above in relation to articles 10 and 23 of the Rules; for example, if the arbitration is not making the progress required.

8 Commencement of the arbitration proceedings

8.1 For the purposes of interruption of the prescription period

It follows from section 23 of the Arbitration Act that arbitration proceedings are considered initiated when the respondent receives a request for a dispute to be the subject of arbitration proceedings. The claimant can thus simply notify the respondent of his claim for arbitration. This is decisive for the purposes of determining when proceedings are being initiated in order to avoid prescription of a claim taking place (see the Prescription Act 18 May 1979 no. 18, section 15 no. 3).

8.2 The request for arbitration

Under the Rules article 9, a claimant is required to make a request for arbitration to the Oslo Institute.

In order to identify the dispute, the request should contain the name and addresses of the parties and a brief description of the nature of the dispute, the claim that is made and what it is based on. Depending on whether or not the parties have already agreed on the composition of an arbitration tribunal or whether or not the claimant wishes to try to reach such an agreement, and also depending on what is provided for in the arbitration clause, the suggested arbitrators may be identified in the request or the claimant may have appointed his arbitrator. Alternatively, the claimant may request the Oslo Institute to appoint the whole tribunal or the chairperson. The Oslo Institute also normally requires a copy of the contract on which the claim is based and the evidence of the existence of an arbitration agreement.

Under article 8 of the Rules, the Oslo Institute may ask for payment of its fees and prepayment of its expenses before proceeding after receiving the request (see articles 8 and 10).

8.3 Notification to the respondent

The Oslo Institute notifies the respondent of the claimant's request for arbitration. Together with the notification, the Oslo Institute will set a time limit for the respondent to contribute to the establishment of the arbitration tribunal and a time limit for the respondent to appoint an arbitrator, if applicable.

The respondent will also be required, in brief, and within the same time limit to state its position in respect of the claim and whether it has any counter-claims or set-offs and, if so, to describe their nature and the basis and extent thereof.

8.4 *Dismissal of the case or appointment of arbitrators*

If it is evident that the Oslo Institute lacks jurisdiction, the case will be dismissed. Otherwise, the Oslo Institute will proceed with the appointment of arbitrators as required. When the arbitration tribunal has been established, the handling of the case will be transferred to it and the resulting arbitration proceedings will be administered by the tribunal.

8.5 *The involvement of the Oslo Institute after establishment of the tribunal*

As mentioned above, the Oslo Institute will, at its own initiative or upon the request of a party, discharge arbitrators who are held to be prejudiced, incompetent or to have mishandled their tasks as arbitrators.

8.6 *Replacement of an arbitrator*

The Oslo Institute will also be involved in the appointment of a new arbitrator if an arbitrator dies, resigns or is discharged pursuant to what is stated above. The Oslo Institute will then assist in appointing a new arbitrator under the provisions of article 7 of the Rules.

It follows from section 17 of the Arbitration Act that a new arbitrator is appointed in the same manner as the arbitrator that is being replaced. When an arbitrator is replaced, all proceedings that form part of the decision have to be repeated after the new arbitrator is appointed. If this takes place before the main hearing, this does normally require more than the new arbitrator receiving copies of the pleadings. If the main hearing has been held in full or in part, it has to be repeated in order to allow all the arbitrators to have the same basis for their decision.

8.7 *Fast-track arbitration*

The rules applicable to fast-track arbitration are largely the same as for ordinary arbitrations and can be found in articles 24 to 26. Since a fast-track arbitration has to be agreed upon specifically, it follows from article 26 that the reply from the respondents should state whether the respondents agree to a fast-track arbitration or not.

9 The conduct of the arbitration proceedings

9.1 Equal treatment

The Arbitration Act section 20 provides that the parties shall be treated equally at each stage of the proceedings and shall have the full opportunity to present their case. The corresponding provision is found in the Rules article 13, paragraph 5 and article 26, paragraph 6.

The Rules of procedure must be within the scope of the parties' agreement and are always subject to the Arbitration Act. The arbitration tribunal shall conduct the matter in the manner it finds appropriate (section 21 of the Arbitration Act). Immediately following the appointment of the tribunal, the tribunal as a whole or its chairperson will, after consultation with the parties, draw up a schedule for the further conduct of the case (section 21 of the Arbitration Act and the Rules article 13, paragraph 3).

In order to expedite matters, the Oslo Institute may set dates for the initial pleadings in the form of a statement of claim and a defence (or reply). Normally, the scope of the arbitration and the number of further pleadings cannot be determined with certainty before each of the parties have had an opportunity to plead their case and it will be the responsibility of the arbitration tribunal to provide deadlines for further pleadings.

9.2 Applicable language

The parties shall be free to agree on the language of the pleadings used during the hearings and in the award (the Rules articles 14 and 30, and section 24 of the Arbitration Act).

It follows from the Rules article 14 that if the parties have not agreed on a language, it shall be that of the contract that contains the arbitration clause. The Rules further provide that documents of evidence may be submitted in their original language and that witnesses may be heard and examined in a language of their choice. The Rules thus modify the non-mandatory provisions of the Arbitration Act section 24, which would leave it to the arbitration tribunal to decide upon the language used in the arbitration. The Arbitration Act allows Swedish and Danish to be used in Norwegian-language proceedings. It further requires the chosen language to be used in all communications and gives the arbitration tribunal the right to have documents translated into the relevant language.

9.3 *Oral or written proceedings*

The pleadings exchanged in the proceedings will normally be in writing. All written material that the arbitration tribunal receives from a party should be sent to the other parties in the proceedings. Material that the arbitration tribunal receives directly from third parties should be promptly sent to the parties. This is provided for in section 26 of the Arbitration Act.

Normally, a main hearing is held where each of the parties is given the opportunity to plead their cases orally. In substance, articles 15 and 30 of the Rules are the same as section 26 of the Arbitration Act. Under the Rules, articles 15 and 30, an oral hearing is the main rule, unless the parties agree that the award can be made based on the documents without having a hearing. Under the Act section 26, it is the arbitration tribunal that decides whether an oral hearing should be held, but each of the parties can require an oral hearing if the arbitration tribunal favours a written procedure.

In fast-track arbitrations, the main hearing shall not take more than four days (article 4).

9.4 *The failure to file pleadings without reasonable cause*

If the claimant does not file a statement of claim with the arbitration tribunal, it follows from section 27 of the Arbitration Act that the arbitration tribunal may terminate the proceedings.

If the respondent fails to file a reply brief, the arbitration tribunal will continue with the case and not interpret the failure as an acceptance of the claimant's claim.

If either party does not appear, without reasonable cause, during the main hearing or fails to produce documentary evidence, the arbitration panel can continue the handling of the case and make an award on the basis of the material available.

9.5 *Evidence*

As mentioned above, the parties are responsible for providing the necessary evidence in a case and have the right to present the evidence they wish (section 28 of the Act). However, the arbitration tribunal can refuse evidence to be submitted when it is obvious that it has no relevance for the decision in the dispute. The arbitral tribunal curtail the presentation of evidence if the extent of the evidence presented is not in reasonable proportion to the importance of the dispute (section 28, paragraph 2 of the Act).

9.6 Experts

The arbitration tribunal has the right to appoint one or more experts to give advice on specific issues that will be decided on by the arbitration tribunal. The arbitration tribunal can compel the parties to give the experts all relevant information and make available other evidence. If an expert has given a written statement, the expert, at the request of either party or the arbitration panel, has the obligation to appear in the oral hearing. The parties are there given the opportunity to ask questions and to present their own expert witnesses. These provisions follow from section 29 of the Arbitration Act.

10 The competence of the arbitration tribunal

10.1 Introduction

The provisions about the competence of the arbitration tribunal are found in article 11 of the Rules of the Oslo Institute, which have to be supplemented by chapters 5 and 6 of the Arbitration Act.

The competence to conduct the proceedings in a fair and efficient manner in accordance with the wishes of the parties and the authorization to the chairperson of the tribunal to take any measures necessary for the proper conduct of the proceedings correspond to section 21 of the Act.

Procedural matters may be decided on by the chairperson of the arbitration tribunal alone, if authorized by the parties or the other arbitrators (see section 34 of the Act).

10.2 Validity of the arbitration agreement and competence of the arbitration tribunal

Article 11 of the Rules provides that the arbitration tribunal shall decide on the existence or validity of the arbitration agreement and its own competence. This corresponds to the provisions in section 18 of the Act, which has more detailed provisions. Section 18 states that the arbitration agreement shall be considered as a separate agreement, independent of other parts of the contract. The decision that the contract is invalid does not in itself imply that the arbitration agreement is invalid.

Section 18 paragraph 3 provides that objections against the jurisdiction of the arbitration tribunal have to be made at the latest in the first submissions that deal with the substance of the claim. The arbitration tribunal can allow objections to be made at a later stage if the parties are not significantly to blame for the delay in raising the objection. It is specifically stated that a party is not precluded from raising an objection about the jurisdiction of the arbitration tribunal by participating in establishing the tribunal.

The arbitration tribunal can deal with the objections against its jurisdiction either during the arbitration proceedings or in the award that decides on the dispute. If a separate decision is made during the proceedings to the effect that the tribunal has jurisdiction, each of the parties can have that decision tried by the ordinary courts by starting proceedings within one month from the decision of the tribunal. The arbitration tribunal can continue the proceedings and render an award, even while the ordinary courts are determining the question of its jurisdiction.

10.3 Determination of any question of law arising in the arbitration proceedings

Article 11 (c) of the Rules provides that the tribunal shall determine any question of law arising during the arbitration proceedings, simply reflecting the principle that the arbitration is to resolve disputes concerning legal relations. In addition to making decisions on the applicable law concerning the substance of the dispute, the tribunal is also authorized to make decisions on procedural issues.

10.4 The place of the arbitration

Under article 11 (c) of the Rules, the arbitration tribunal can determine the place of the arbitration, unless otherwise agreed on by the parties. This corresponds to section 22 of the Act, which, however, also states that the arbitration tribunal can hold meetings to deliberate, hear witnesses, experts and parties and consider other evidence at any other convenient place.

10.5 Failure of a party to cooperate

Article 11 (d) of the Rules also provides that the arbitration tribunal can proceed with the arbitration, notwithstanding the failure or refusal of a party to comply with its directions after having given the party due notice. To a large extent, this corresponds with section 27 of the Act, which has been dealt with above in Section 9.4.

10.6 Inclusion of new claims and new parties

Article 11 of the Rules also states that the tribunal can allow the scope of the arbitration to be extended through the inclusion of new claims and have other parties join the arbitration proceedings, unless a party objects. The right to include new claims is somewhat stricter than what follows from section 25 of the Act, which allows the parties to submit new claims, extend the basis for a claim and submit new grounds for the claim as well as provide new evidence. However, the arbitration tribunal is authorized to refuse changes being made when it finds that it would be detrimental to the progress in the matter or where there are other valid concerns.

In the arbitrations conducted under the Rules of the Oslo Institute, it is contemplated that the request for arbitration and the subsequent response from the respondent shall be the basis for the claim and for counter-claims.

10.7 Provisional measures

Article 11 also states that the tribunal can order each party to implement such provisional measures that the tribunal finds necessary based on the nature of the dispute, including requiring that security is furnished in order to secure a party's interests. This provision simply reflects the provisions in section 19 of the Act, which has been dealt with above in Section 6.

10.8 Rendering of the award

Rule 11 finally provides that the arbitration tribunal shall make awards in the matters in dispute between parties. This is dealt with below in Section 11.

11 The award

11.1 Applicable law

The decision of the arbitrators shall be made on the basis of the applicable law. It also follows from section 31 of the Act that the arbitration tribunal shall not decide on the basis of reasonableness only (*amiable compositeur*), unless the parties have explicitly authorized the arbitration tribunal to do so.

In a case decided on by the Borgarting Appeal Court in 2009 (LB-2008–136865), it was held, on the basis of the following wording of the arbitration clause, that the arbitrators were 'relieved from all judicial formalities, and shall interpret the present Agreement from a practical view and from equity' and that the arbitrators were entitled to take into account fairness in their decision (see section 31 paragraph 3 of the Act).

A reference to the law of substance in a contract is not considered as a reference to the conflict-of-law rules of the law of substance. If the parties have not made a choice of law, the arbitrators will apply the Norwegian 'conflict of law rules' (section 31).

11.2 Contentions of the parties

Rule 20 provides that the award must not go beyond the contentions made by the parties. This reflects the principle in section 32 of the Act, which provides that the arbitration tribunal shall only decide on the claims that are raised in the case. The decision of the parties has to lie within the framework of the contentions of the parties and the court can only make its decision on the basis of contentions that have been made. When it comes to assessment of the evidence, the court shall base its decision on a free assessment of the evidence that has been presented to it.

11.3 Separate awards

Article 19 of the Rules provides that a separate issue or part of the matter in dispute may, at the request of a party, be decided on by a separate or interim award. If the other party objects to such a separate award, it may only be made when, in the tribunal's view, there is a special reason for making it. Article 19 limits the powers of the arbitration tribunal pursuant to section 33 of the Act. Section 33 gives the arbitration tribunal broad powers to decide that separate proceedings shall take place in respect of one or more claims in the case.

11.4 Voting

Both article 17 of the Rules and section 34 of the Act provide that decisions are taken by a majority vote among the members of the tribunal. If it is not possible to obtain a majority of votes, the chairperson of the tribunal shall have the casting vote.

11.5 *Amicable settlement*

Both article 16 of the Rules and section 35 of the Act provide for the tribunal to render an award confirming an amicable settlement. Under both provisions, the arbitration tribunal can oppose making such an award if it has reason to do so. An award affirming an amicable settlement has the same effect as any other arbitration award.

11.6 *Time limit for making awards*

The Arbitration Act has no provisions about any time limits for making the award. The Rules in article 18 provide that an award should be rendered no later than six weeks after the conclusion of an oral hearing and not later than one month after the appointment of the tribunal in ordinary arbitrations. In fast-track arbitration, the time limit is six months after the appointment of the arbitrators. In both cases, these time limits may be extended by the board of the Oslo Institute in special cases.

It should be noted that if the tribunal breaches these provisions, the arbitration award will not necessarily become invalid. This was decided in a decision by the Trondheim City Court and affirmed *obiter* in the decision of the Frostating Appeal Court in 2009 (LF-2009–1094) (mentioned in Section 7.3 above).

11.7 *Correction of the award*

The arbitration tribunal, according to section 38 of the Act, can correct miscalculations, clerical errors and similar errors both of its own initiative and at the request of a party. The correction shall be made within one month if done at the initiative of the tribunal, and a party requesting a correction has to make such a request within one month of receiving the award, in which case the correction shall take place within one month. A party can also request a supplemental judgment to decide upon a claim made in the arbitration proceedings that has not been decided on in the award itself. A request for such a supplemental award also has to be made within one month and the arbitration tribunal has to make its decision in the supplemental award at the latest two months after the request is received.

Similar provisions can be found in article 21 of the Rules.

11.8 Termination of the arbitration proceedings

The arbitration proceedings terminate with the award, but can also terminate with a decision to dismiss the proceedings because the claimant gives up his claim and the defendant has no reasonable ground to request an award, because the parties agree to that effect or because the tribunal finds that the continuation of the case has become unnecessary or impossible (section 37 of the Act).

The authority and powers of the arbitrators cease from such termination of the proceedings, except in respect of the correction of errors and when making supplemental awards.

12 Costs

12.1 Security for the costs of the arbitration

It follows from article 8 of the Rules that the Oslo Institute may require a sufficient sum to be deposited to cover its estimated costs. In addition, the arbitration tribunal may decide, before acting in a case, that the parties shall deposit, with the Oslo Institute, an amount sufficient to cover the estimated costs of an arbitration case. Additional deposits may be required if the tribunal considers this necessary. If one party fails to make such a deposit, the tribunal may require the other party to make such a deposit. The tribunal may terminate the proceeding in part or in its entirety if payment of deposits is not made. These provisions in the Rules reflect section 41 of the Act.

12.2 Determination of the costs of the arbitration tribunal

The Rules have no specific provisions on how the costs of the arbitration tribunal are determined. It follows from section 39 of the Act that the arbitration tribunal decides upon its own compensation and settlement of expenses, unless something else has been agreed on between the arbitration tribunal and the parties. A decision is made in the final award or in the decision that concludes the matter. The amount is due for payment one month after the decision is made.

The parties are jointly and severable responsible for the costs of the arbitration tribunal, unless otherwise agreed.

The decision of the arbitrators becomes final and enforceable, unless it is challenged before the ordinary courts within one month from the day when the party received the determination of the costs. If the award has been corrected or a supplemental award is rendered, a new one-month time limit applies.

If the costs of the arbitration tribunal are reduced, this also binds the other party in the arbitration that has not challenged the costs before the courts.

12.3 The costs of the parties

The Rules have no specific provision about awarding costs to a party.

According to section 40 of the Act, the costs of the arbitration are divided between the parties as the tribunal sees fit. At the request of a party, the tribunal can also award the whole or part of that party's costs if it sees fit. The division of the costs has to be included in the award or in the decision that ends the proceedings. The decision of the arbitration tribunal in respect of costs is final.

In proceedings before the ordinary courts, a party is normally awarded costs when it is successful in full in pursuing its claim, although it will not be awarded costs when the losing party had reasonable grounds to bring the dispute before the courts.

Before the new Arbitration Act came into force, it was normal practice to follow the same rules in respect of the division of costs that applied before the ordinary courts. The impression is that since the new Arbitration Act came into force, arbitration tribunals have tended, to a larger extent, to refrain from awarding costs, thus leaving each of the parties with 50% of the costs of the arbitration tribunal and each of the parties having to bear its own costs.

13 Invalid arbitration awards, recognition and enforcement

13.1 The jurisdiction of the ordinary courts

The Rules of the Oslo Institute have no provisions about invalid arbitration awards or about the recognition and enforcement of arbitration awards. This is under the sole jurisdiction of the ordinary courts.

13.2 Proceedings about validity of an arbitration award

It follows from section 42 and 44 of the Act that a recourse claim in legal proceedings to set aside an arbitration award has to be commenced within three months from the day the party received the arbitration award. If a supplemental award is rendered, correcting or supplementing the original award, the three-month period is calculated from the date of the supplemental award. If the court decides that there is a basis for the award being invalid, it can make a decision rendering the award invalid, but it can also defer the handling of the matter before the court and refer the case back to the arbitrators if a new decision from the arbitration tribunal can correct the basis for the invalidity.

13.3 The basis for challenging the validity of an award

The basis for challenging the validity of an award is very limited and has to be on one of the following grounds, namely that:

(a) One of the parties to the arbitration agreement lacks legal capacity, or the arbitration agreement lacks legal capacity, or the arbitration agreement is invalid under the laws to which the parties have agreed to subject it, or, failing such agreement, under Norwegian law or;
(b) The party bringing the action for setting aside was not given sufficient notice of the appointment of an arbitrator or of the arbitration, or was not given an opportunity to present his views on the case or;
(c) The arbitral award falls outside the scope of the jurisdiction of the arbitral tribunal or;
(d) The composition of the arbitral tribunal is incorrect or;
(e) The arbitral procedure was contrary to the law of the place of arbitration or the agreement of the parties, and this has had an impact on the decision.

The most practical grounds for rendering an award as invalid are the reasons mentioned in (d) and (e) above.

In respect of the composition of the arbitration tribunal (ground (d)), it can be challenged that the arbitrator was not independent or impartial if that becomes known after the award is rendered and if it was not challenged and decided on during the proceedings pursuant to section 15.

In respect of ground (e), it is not unusual for a challenge to be brought forward on the basis that one of the parties was not given sufficient opportunity to contradict a contention made by the other party.

In Rt 2008/420, the Supreme Court affirmed that a party may call arbitrators as witnesses to testify about factual circumstances that have taken place during the arbitration proceedings, as opposed to them testifying about the deliberations on the issues, which they cannot do. In the subject case, the issue was whether a contention was or was not presented during the proceedings, and whether the arbitrators had complied with section 32 of the Act in terms of them not deciding on the case beyond the contentions of the parties.

A court shall *ex officio* take into account the following and set aside the award if one of the following applies, when:

(a) The dispute is not capable of being determined by arbitration under Norwegian law or;
(b) The arbitral award would be contrary to public policy (*ordre public*).

If the validity only affects part of the award, only that part shall be deemed invalid.

13.4 Recognition and enforcement

Section 45 of the Act provides that an arbitration award shall be recognized and shall be the subject of enforcement in Norway, irrespective of the country in which it has been rendered.

When enforcement proceedings are initiated, an arbitration award may be challenged on the same basis as a Norwegian arbitration award is rendered invalid pursuant to section 43. In addition, a foreign arbitration award can be challenged on the basis that the arbitration award is not binding on the parties, or it has been set aside, permanently or temporarily, by a court at the place of arbitration or by a court in a jurisdiction the law of which has been applied in determining the subject matter in dispute.

In a case decided on by the Borgarting Appeal Court in 2010 (LB-2010–14069), the court held that a US arbitration award was valid. The party opposing the enforcement contended that it had not been given an adequate opportunity to defend the US proceedings in terms of sections 45 and 46 of the Arbitration Act, but this argument was rejected by the Norwegian court.

14 Alternative dispute resolution at the Oslo Institute

The Oslo Institute provides other services in respect of ADR and these are:

(a) Mediation – whose objective it is to settle disputes without litigation, whereby the parties endeavour to reach an amicable settlement assisted by an appointed mediator (chapter IV of the Rules).

(b) Mini-trial – a dispute resolution method whose objective is to settle disputes without litigation, whereby the parties present the factual and legal issues before a panel consisting of an executive from both parties and where the Oslo Institute has appointed an umpire, assisting the parties in reaching a settlement agreement (chapter V of the Rules).
(c) Expert assistance – where an unbiased third party assists the parties during the period of contract so that early signs of disputes can be discussed and resolved at an early stage (chapter VI of the Rules).

Annex A: Model clauses prepared by the Oslo Institute

1. **Arbitration**
   'Any dispute arising out of this contract, or other contracts resulting from it, shall be finally settled by Arbitration pursuant to the Rules of the Arbitration and Alternative Dispute Resolution Institute of the Oslo Chamber of Commerce in force at any time.'
2. **Fast-track arbitration**
   'Any dispute arising out of this contract, or other contracts resulting from it, shall be finally settled by Fast-track Arbitration pursuant to the Rules of Arbitration and Alternative Dispute Resolution Institute of the Oslo Chamber of Commerce in force at any time.'
3. **Mediation**
   'Any dispute arising out of this contract, or other contracts resulting from it, shall be finally settled by Mediation pursuant to the Rules of the Arbitration Dispute Resolution Institute of the Oslo Chamber of Commerce in force at any time.'
4. **Mini-trial**
   'If a dispute arises out of the contract, the parties shall undertake to seek to settle it by Mini-trial pursuant to the Rules of the Arbitration and Alternative Dispute Resolution Institute of the Oslo Chamber of Commerce in force at any time.'
5. **Mediation and arbitration**
   'If a dispute arises out of the contract, the parties shall undertake to seek to settle it by Mediation pursuant to the Rules of the Arbitration and Alternative Dispute Resolution Institute of the Oslo Chamber of Commerce in force at any time.

   If the dispute has not been settled by such Mediation within 60 days following its Request by one of the parties, and the parties have not agreed to extend that time period, the dispute shall be settled by

Arbitration pursuant to the Rules of the Arbitration and Alternative Dispute Resolution Institute of the Oslo Chamber of Commerce in force at any time.'

6. **Mini-trial and arbitration**

'If a dispute arises out of the contract, the parties shall undertake to seek to settle it by Mini-trial pursuant to the Rules of the Arbitration and Alternative Dispute Resolution Institute of the Oslo Chamber of Commerce in force at any time.

If the dispute has not been settled by such Mini-trial within 60 days following its Request by one of the parties, and the parties have not agreed to extend that time period, the dispute shall be settled by Arbitration pursuant to the Rules of the Arbitration and Alternative Dispute Resolution Institute of the Oslo Chamber of Commerce in force at any time.'

7. **The UNCITRAL Rules**

Parties wishing the Institute's assistance as the appointing authority under the UNCITRAL Rules (United Nations Commission on International Trade Law) may use the following clause:

'Any dispute, disagreement or claim arising out of or relating to this contract, or the breach, termination or invalidity thereof, shall be settled by Arbitration in accordance with the UNCITRAL and Alternative Dispute Resolution Institute of the Oslo Chamber of Commerce.'

If administrative services are also required, the following provision may be added to the above clause: 'The case shall be administered by the Institute in accordance with the rules on administrative assistance under the UNCITRAL Arbitration Rules.'

8. **Expert assistance**

'The parties agree to seek Expert Assistance in the prevention of disputes in connection with this contract pursuant to the Rules of the Arbitration and Alternative Dispute Resolution Institute of the Oslo Chamber of Commerce in force at any time.'

12

Arbitration in Russia: Features of the International Commercial Arbitration Court at the Chamber of Commerce and Industry of the Russian Federation

ALEXANDER S. KOMAROV

1 Introduction

Arbitration as a means of business dispute settlement has always been an important part of the legal environment of foreign trade activities in the Soviet Union. The long-standing tradition of a positive attitude to arbitration has been inherited by the new Russian legal and business community without hesitation, since there was no reason to believe that under the new economic order in the Russian Federation, arbitration would not continue to be the most adequate dispute settlement mechanism in the field of international trade and commerce, including foreign investment.

Today, the development of arbitration and other means of ADR is a part of the general economic and legal policy in Russia. Arbitration, with its flexibility and dynamism, has significant potential for solving economic and social problems connected with creating a sound legal foundation for the new business environment. Besides that, arbitration has been recognized as playing an important role in developing the favourable legal conditions for international economic cooperation, including foreign investment.

Arbitration in domestic business activities has not had a very long history because in the Soviet period this means of dispute settlement had never been used within the centralized economic system to deal with problems arising from economic activities conducted through state companies and agencies that had to resolve their disputes in a special adjudication system: the 'state *arbitrazh*'. As a matter of principle, arbitration was not permitted to develop in respect of disputes between domestic enterprises. Actually, the state took on the role of arbitrator in disputes between state-owned economic operators. However, it is necessary to stress that state *arbitrazh* was supposed not only to solve the disputes between state enterprises but also to exercise regulatory authority in the interests of the national economy.

In the late eighties of the last century the system of state *arbitrazh* had been transformed into a system of special economic courts that, unfortunately, retained the word *arbitrazh* in their official denomination, which was often incorrectly translated into English as 'arbitration courts', leading to confusion between the two different legal institutions.

The introduction of a market economy in Russia led to the extensive development of arbitration in domestic commercial dealings. Immediately after the adoption in 1992 of the regulation of arbitration in domestic economic disputes, arbitration institutions began to appear all over the country. A federal Act providing for the regulation of domestic arbitration was adopted in 2002.[1] It incorporates the generally accepted principles of arbitration but pays more attention to institutional arbitration, leaving the regulation of *ad hoc* arbitration as less effective. Now there are several hundred such institutions, which are attached mainly to regional chambers of commerce and industry, commodity or stock exchanges and various other business and lawyers' organizations. Actually, they now deal predominantly with domestic disputes. International commercial arbitration is expressly excluded from the sphere of application of this Act. It is worth also mentioning that in Russian legal terminology, the expression 'third-party court' (*третейский суд*) is usually used to denominate domestic arbitration in order to distinguish it from international arbitration.

2 Legal framework

The legal regime for international commercial arbitration in Russia is based on the 1985 UNCITRAL Model Law on International Commercial Arbitration. The text of the Law of the Russian Federation on International Commercial Arbitration (the 'Law'), enacted in 1993, is literally very close to the text of the UNCITRAL Model Law.[2] That may be explained not only by the fact that one of the official texts of the

[1] *Федеральный закон от 24 июля 2002 г. N 102-ФЗ 'О третейских судах в Российской Федерации', Собрание законодательства Российской Федерации от 29 июля 2002 г. N 30 ст. 3019.*

[2] See, *Постановление ВС РФ от 7 июля 1993 г. N 5339–1 'О введении в действие Закона РФ О международном коммерческом арбитраже' (Ведомости Съезда народных депутатов Российской Федерации и Верховного Совета Российской Федерации от 12 августа 1993 г., N 32. ст. 1241).*

UNCITRAL Model Law was in Russian but also by previous legal developments, both in the Soviet Union and in the Russian Federation, where there had never been any comprehensive legislation on the subject.

In spite of the fact that there were practically no legal texts that needed to be amended, adjusted or restructured in accordance with the Model Law, some deviations from the UNCITRAL Model Law were introduced. Obviously, they reflect some specific features of past legal development, national legal culture and traditions.

The main international law sources relating to arbitration in Russia include the UN Convention on the Recognition and Enforcement of Foreign Arbitral Awards (New York, 1958) and the European Convention on International Commercial Arbitration (Geneva, 1961). Although the Soviet Union acceded to the New York Convention in 1960, and was one of the first states to become a participant therein, there was no judicial practice whatsoever with regard to the application of New York Convention provisions until the early 1990s. Such a situation can obviously be accounted for by the fact that as the state monopoly on foreign trade dominated in the USSR at that time, the attitude towards the enforcement of arbitration awards acquired a political colouring. No cases of enforcement in the Soviet Union of arbitral awards made by a foreign arbitration court had ever been reported and, indeed, the regulation implementing the New York Convention only appeared in 1988.

When ratifying the New York Convention, the Soviet Union made a reservation that it would apply the Convention with regard to arbitral awards made in the territories of the states that are not the parties to the Convention only on a reciprocal basis. The above reservation has not yet been removed.

The provisions of the Geneva Convention were only rarely applied in the Soviet Union's judicial practice. After the adoption of the Law in 1993, the situations where the Geneva Convention had to be used narrowed substantially.

Apart from the New York and Geneva Conventions, which undoubtedly have played a decisive role in the regulation of international arbitration, especially with regard to the recognition and enforcement of foreign arbitral awards, the Russian Federation has retained its membership in the Convention on the Settlement by Arbitration of Civil Law Disputes Arising from Relations of Economic and Scientific–Technical Cooperation (Moscow, 1972). This international treaty is formally still in force between a few states – former Members of the Council for Mutual Economic Assistance (COMECON). The majority of member states have renounced the Convention. Reform of the fundamental principles behind the national economic and legal systems of member countries that are still formally bound by the Convention led to a substantial limitation in the scope of application of the Moscow Convention. The subject matter of the Convention established the mandatory use of arbitration for settling disputes involving mutual trade, which was conducted in the framework of the state monopoly on foreign trade. Nowadays, foreign trade in Russia is conducted mostly by non-state enterprises. Current arbitration practice indicates that the Moscow Convention usually applies to disputes that arise within state-owned enterprises.

In addition to the above-mentioned specific Russian domestic legislation relating to international commercial arbitration, rules contained in general Russian procedural law also govern relations arising in the context of international commercial arbitration. This regulation ensures the implementation of legislation on international commercial arbitration, including procedures for setting aside and for the enforcement of arbitral awards.

From this point of view, special attention should be paid to the provisions of the Code of *Arbitrazh* Procedure of the Russian Federation ('CAP'), effective as of 1 September 2002.[3] The main contents of CAP are the regulation of procedures in *arbitrazh* courts. This branch of the Russian state judicial system deals with legal questions relating to international commercial arbitration. It is necessary to stress that the courts of general jurisdiction, which had the power to deal with these matters before CAP came into force, have had no jurisdiction with regard to commercial arbitration since CAP's introduction. The rules of CAP relating to arbitration apply to both international arbitration and arbitration of domestic disputes unless there are specific relevant rules in special legislation that are applicable.

With the adoption of CAP, detailed rules regulating the procedure applicable in cases when the state court has to consider issues relating to international arbitration were incorporated into legislation for the first time in Russian legal history. On the whole, the substance of such legal rules meets the standards to be found in both international legal sources and in modern legal doctrine in terms of establishing a balance of power between the administration of justice – vested in the state courts – and

[3] See *Арбитражный процессуальный кодекс Российской Федерации от 24 июля 2002 г. N 95-ФЗ. Собрание законодательства РФ, 29.07.2002, N 30, ст. 3012.*

the freedom granted to the participants in civil and commerce matters to determine dispute resolution procedure.

However, it is worth remembering that, for obvious reasons, the Russian *arbitrazh* courts have, so far, not accumulated sufficient experience and knowledge to allow them to show their expertise in considering disputes relating to enforcing international commercial arbitration. That largely explains the instability of contemporary Russian court practice in matters of international arbitration, especially with regard to the practice of the lower courts, which very often cannot follow internationally established practices in similar situations.

3 Scope of application of the Law

One of the major points of difference between the Law and the UNCITRAL Model text is the scope of its application. Unlike the UNCITRAL Model Law, the 'objective' criteria used for the international character of disputes were not included in the Russian Law as a requirement for its application. In other words, the fact that a substantial part of obligations in a commercial relationship is to be performed outside the Russian Federation is not sufficient to apply the Law. For the dispute to be treated as truly international – that is, covered by the Law – 'subjective' criteria need to be satisfied. The same approach is valid in cases where the place in which the subject matter of the dispute is most closely connected is outside Russia.

The Law expressly states that it only covers the following disputes if the parties have agreed to bring them to arbitration:

(a) Disputes resulting from contractual and other civil law relationships arising in the course of foreign trade and other forms of international economic relations, or provided that a place of business of at least one of the parties in dispute is situated abroad; and
(b) Disputes arising between enterprises with foreign investment, international associations and organizations established in the territory of the Russian Federation; disputes between the participants of such entities; as well as disputes between such entities and other subjects of the Russian Federation law.

At the same time, it is necessary to point out that the Law is applicable to disputes that in other legal orders are usually treated as 'domestic'; that is, disputes where all the parties in a dispute have a place of business in the territory of the Russian Federation. The precondition for the application of the international arbitration regime to such disputes is that at least one of the parties involved in a dispute should have foreign capital (or be fully owned by a foreign person). The Law does not provide for the minimum percentage of foreign capital needed for recognizing a dispute as 'international' in such situations. This question is decided on in each particular case by the arbitral tribunal in the course of dealing with the question of its jurisdiction, often taking into account existing Russian regulations on foreign investments.

This approach adopted by the enactment of the Law with regard to the sphere of regulation on international commercial arbitration in 1993, when social and economic reform in Russia had just started, seemed to be justified and quite reasonable for a country in transition where its national judicial system had not yet adjusted to the new conditions. This solution aimed at meeting certain requirements to create a friendly legal environment for business activity involving foreign partners and investments in Russia.

In the early nineties of the last century, the main form of international cooperation of Russian enterprises, which at that time were predominantly state-owned, with foreign partners was the establishment of joint-venture companies. Subjecting disputes involving joint-venture enterprises to the regulation of international arbitration was necessary because otherwise they would have been subject to the jurisdiction of state *arbitrazh* courts, which at that time lacked international experience. Proceedings in these courts were conducted in accordance with quite rigid rules and the procedure in general, to a great extent, had an inquisitorial character because it was formulated to fit with a dispute settlement procedure for a centralized economic system. Traditionally, the regulation and practice of international commercial arbitration for foreign trade had been more liberal, since it was based on widely recognized international principles and rules of commercial dispute settlement in contrast to the regulation and practice of domestic economic dispute settlement.

4 Institutional and *ad hoc* arbitration

During the previous few decades, the practice of commercial arbitration in the Soviet Union was almost entirely connected with foreign trade activities. Another characteristic feature of arbitration at that time was that it was practised exclusively as institutional arbitration. In the Soviet Union, institutional arbitration had always been considered as a more predictable and reliable method for alternative dispute settlement than *ad hoc* arbitration.

For many decades, the only arbitration institution that had been dealing with foreign trade disputes in the Soviet Union was the Foreign Trade Arbitration Commission at the USSR Chamber of Commerce and Industry (FTAC), which was established in 1932. The activity of FTAC during the years of its existence had been, from time to time, surveyed and analysed in Western legal texts.[4] After the dissolution of the Soviet Union and the discontinuance of the Chamber of Commerce and Industry of the USSR, the name of this internationally reputable institution was changed to the International Commercial Arbitration Court (ICAC) and it continued to function as an institution attached to the Russian Federation Chamber of Commerce and Industry.[5]

At the present time, ICAC continues to be the most experienced and well-known arbitration institution in the territory of the former Soviet Union. In the last few years, it has dealt with more than two hundred international disputes each year. Bearing in mind the recognized authority and experience of ICAC in international commercial arbitration, it seems that this institution will maintain its leading role in the post-Soviet era and into the future.[6]

In addition, it is worth mentioning that in Russia *ad hoc* arbitration is still practised infrequently when resolving international commercial disputes. In such cases, the parties usually prefer to use the UNCITRAL Arbitration Rules than any other set of *ad hoc* rules. The Russian Federation Chamber of Commerce and Industry has adopted a protocol for assistance to the parties if they have agreed on the application of UNCITRAL Arbitration Rules if the place of arbitration is the Russian Federation. The functions of the appointing authority under the UNCITRAL Rules have to be performed in such cases by ICAC.

Ad hoc arbitration in international commercial disputes in Russia in recent years has also been limited by insufficient logistical and infrastructural conditions and the lack of local experience needed for the organization and management of effective arbitration proceedings.

4 See, for example, E. Rushba, 'Settlement of Disputes in Commercial Dealings with Soviet Union', *Col. L. Rev.*, 45(1945); M. Domke, 'Arbitration of State Trading Relations', *Law & Contemp. Prob.*, 24(1959); J. Hazard, 'State Trading and Arbitration', in M. Domke (ed.), *International Trade Arbitration* (New York, 1958).

5 See www.tpprf-mkac.ru

6 Illustrations of current ICAC practice may be found in A. Zhiltsov, 'Recent Arbitration Awards and Supervisory Court Judgment', *Arbitration*, 75(2009), No. 1, p. 131.

However, the situation is improving as a result of the Russian business and legal communities gaining more experience in this respect.

5 Admissibility of arbitration

One of the most significant aspects of regulation relating to the practice of arbitration is the regulation of what disputes may be referred to arbitration. The UNCITRAL Model Law does not provide for the rules determining the admissibility of arbitration. Being a very sensitive issue and one closely connected to the public policy of each state, this problem had been left to be dealt with by national law. That is why there is no formal definition of the term 'commercial' in relation to international arbitration. Article 1 of the UNCITRAL Model Law contains a note calling for 'a wide interpretation so as to cover matters arising from all relationships of a commercial nature, whether contractual or not'.

In modern Russian law, the concept of commercial law as a separate part of private law is not recognized. Generally, it is understood that commercial transactions are those transactions that are concluded between business enterprises in the course of their usual activity. Wide interpretation of the term 'commercial' in Russia with regard to the arbitrability of disputes may be supported by the approach confirmed by the new Russian Civil Code, which regulates relations that might be called 'commercial'. It states that arbitration courts, besides the state courts of general jurisdiction and *arbitrazh* courts, are recognized as a means of protecting civil rights and interests.[7] It means that, in principle, all disputes that can arise from relations of a commercial nature that are regulated by the Civil Code may be subjected to arbitration.

The Law stipulates that it does not affect any other law of the Russian Federation by virtue of which certain disputes may not be submitted to arbitration or may be submitted to arbitration only according to provisions other than those of the Law. Currently there are actually no statutory acts (except for the Federal Law on Insolvency) which expressly exclude the arbitrability of certain disputes. However, sometimes, in current court practice, such an effect has also been attributed to the legal norms stipulating the jurisdiction of *arbitrazh* courts, for example, in cases of exclusive jurisdiction with regard to disputes involving foreign participants. This provision of CAP, in principle, is directed to the agreements on the choice of the court in a foreign country and it

[7] Art. 11, para.1 of the Civil Code of the Russian Federation.

should not apply to arbitration.[8] The main concern of the state in limiting the arbitrability of disputes is based on the idea that a relationship based on public law regulations should not be subjected to non-state adjudication; that is, private arbitration.

In the years following the adoption of the aforementioned rule on the exclusive jurisdiction of Russian *arbitrazh* courts, it had been applied in particular cases with the effect of invalidating arbitration clauses applicable to economic disputes involving Russian public enterprises and agencies, as well as disputes connected with disputed rights relating to real estate situated in the territory of the Russian Federation. Fortunately, just recently, the Supreme *Arbitrazh* Court, which under the Russian Federation Constitution has the right to give the lower courts instructions concerning the interpretation of particular laws, pointed out that the above-mentioned legislative provision would not exclude the arbitrability of international commercial disputes relating to real-estate rights based on the contract concluded between the disputing parties.[9]

6 The making of and the form of the arbitration agreement

The Russian law on international commercial arbitration provides for the validity and the effect of a commitment by the parties to submit to arbitration an existing dispute (*compromis*) or a future dispute (*clause compromissoire*). The latter type of agreement is presently the most widespread in the practice of international commercial arbitration and the arbitral tribunals have to deal mostly with arbitration clauses that are included in contracts and agreements.

Oral arbitration agreements are not recognized by the Russian Law. In court practice, it is now firmly established that traditional written forms of arbitration agreement (that is, a single document signed by both parties) are no longer the only admissible forms of agreement. From that, it follows that an arbitration clause in a contract or a separate arbitration agreement, signed by the parties or contained in an exchange of letters or telegrams, has the same legal force.

The mandatory requirement of the written form is considered to be met by the parties when they conclude an arbitration agreement by any

[8] Art. 248 of CAP.

[9] *Информационное письмо Президиума Высшего Арбитражного Суда РФ от 22 декабря 2005 г. "Вестник Высшего Арбитражного Суда Российской Федерации", 2006 г., N 3,пп.28,29.*

means of telecommunication that provide a record of that agreement. Additionally, an arbitration agreement may be concluded via an exchange of statements of claim and defence in which the existence of an agreement is alleged by one party and not denied by another. The parties are considered to be bound by the arbitration agreement when they have made reference in their contract to a document (e.g., general conditions) containing an arbitration clause.

7 State-court assistance and supervision

The trend to limit court involvement in international commercial arbitration that is characteristic of its present development is reflected nowadays in Russian legislation as an internationally accepted standard. Involvement of *arbitrazh* courts in international commercial arbitration is limited by the Law and it is allowed only where it is expressly provided for by the Law. However, unfortunately, in contemporary practice, Russian courts have seemed to be reluctant to accept this concept in full. The idea that the parties concluding an arbitration agreement have made a conscious decision to exclude court jurisdiction for the sake of expediency and the finality of the proceedings is often treated with rigid criticism by state courts, which in major cases do not seem to trust arbitrators, since they are not professional judges.

The limits of state-court intervention concern the revision of a decision of the arbitral tribunal on its jurisdiction and the setting aside and enforcement of arbitral awards. On the other hand, *arbitrazh* courts may take decisions with regard to interim measures of protection in support of arbitral proceedings.[10] Such decisions have recently been taken by *arbitrazh* courts in respect of arbitration proceedings conducted within Russia or abroad. The request may be brought to the court when arbitration proceedings have already officially started as well as before the claim is filed with an arbitration court.

Like the UNCITRAL Model Law on International Commercial Arbitration, the Russian Law also provides for the possibility of court assistance for an arbitral tribunal or a party with the approval of the arbitral tribunal in terms of taking evidence.[11] The Law also states that the court may execute the request relating to taking evidence within its competence and according to the rules on taking evidence. Yet, so far, in Russia there has been no court decision concerning the application of

[10] Art. 90 of CAP. [11] Art. 27 of the Law.

this rule. The reason for refusing such applications for court assistance in cases where those applications were brought before an *arbitrazh* court was usually that *arbitrazh* courts had no authority to act in this way because there were no corresponding provisions in CAP.

8 The legal effect of the arbitration agreement

The Model Law obliges any state court to refer the parties to arbitration if seized with a claim on the same subject matter unless it finds that the arbitration agreement is null and void, inoperative or incapable of being performed. The referral is dependent on a request, which a party may make no later than when submitting his first statement on the substance of the dispute. A similar provision is included in CAP.[12]

Unlike many national jurisdictions, the authority to exercise certain functions in support of arbitration that takes place on the territory of Russia is vested not in the state courts but in the President of the Russian Federation Chamber of Commerce and Industry. These functions mainly concern the procedure for the constitution of the arbitral tribunal; for instance, the appointment of an arbitrator on behalf of the party that failed to appoint an arbitrator of its choice. According to the Law, the President of the Chamber also has the final say when dealing with the problem that arises when an arbitrator in the proceedings (*ad hoc* or institutional) taking place on the territory of the Russian Federation has been challenged.

In spite of sufficiently clear provisions laid down in current Russian legislation, the relationship between Russian *arbitrazh* courts and arbitration practice, both domestic and international, continues to be rather unpredictable. The attitude of *arbitrazh* courts has sometimes been too rigid when recognizing the validity and effects of arbitration agreements, with a tendency towards narrowly interpreting the arbitrability of commercial disputes. Often, they feel reluctant to accept the jurisdiction of an arbitral tribunal in cases involving even a little uncertainty as regards the contents of the arbitration agreement. A substantial factor in this process is the insufficient expertise of the Russian judges, especially those in the lower courts, in modern international arbitration practice, the shortage of the necessary and appropriate legal materials as well as the inexperience of the judges in terms of adversarial proceedings.

[12] Art. 148 of the CAP.

9 Interim measures

The Law provides, unless otherwise agreed by the parties, that the arbitral tribunal may, at the request of a party order any party to take such interim measures of protection that the arbitral tribunal may consider necessary in respect of the subject matter of the dispute. The arbitral tribunal may require any party to provide appropriate security in connection with such measures.

It may also be of interest to mention that certain interim measures of protection that are equivalent to the court measures may be ordered by the presidents of arbitration institutions attached to the Chamber of Commerce and Industry of the Russian Federation: the ICAC and Maritime Arbitration Commission (MAC). This authority follows from the corresponding provisions of the charters of these arbitration institutions, which are attached to the Law and are considered to be a part of this statute. Such applications are considered only in cases where one of the said arbitration institutions has *prima facie* jurisdiction with regard to the claim to be protected by the corresponding interim measure.

Before the adoption in 2002 of the new text of CAP, which expressly provided for the possibility of applying to the *arbitrazh* court for provisional (interim) measures in support of arbitration proceedings, there were no legal means for the parties participating in arbitration proceedings on the territory of the Russian Federation to apply to the state court for interim measures relating to arbitration proceedings. In this period, the only means for the parties to protect their interests in arbitration proceedings at the preliminary stage – that is, before the tribunal was constituted – was to take advantage of this authority of the presidents of the named institutions. This practice was exercised from time to time. In many instances, the state courts honoured such decisions and enforced them. However, in some cases they refused to recognize decisions of this kind by noting that the current legislation did not contain express rules on enforcement of such interim measures.

Since 2002 the number of such applications have gone down because the parties have given preference to the *arbitrazh* court's jurisdiction, bearing in mind that the enforcement of interim measures taken by state courts would be easier than a similar decision by the arbitration institutions. However, it is worth mentioning that at the present time, due to the unfriendly attitude of the state judiciary towards the practice of arbitration in Russia, and in cases when the application for interim measures was refused by the *arbitrazh* court, the parties apply for provisional measures to the aforementioned arbitration institutions, which are usually more inclined to protect the parties in arbitration proceedings.

10 Appointment of arbitrators

The parties are free to agree on a procedure for appointing the arbitrator or arbitrators. The only formal mandatory requirements for an arbitrator are those that are established by the Law – independence and impartiality – and those that might be agreed by the parties. An arbitrator may be challenged only if the circumstances exist that give rise to justifiable doubts as to their impartiality or independence, or if he/she does not possess qualifications required by the agreement of the parties. A party may challenge an arbitrator appointed by him, or in whose appointment he has participated, only for reasons he becomes aware of after the appointment has been made.

A distinctive feature of the procedure employed by arbitration institutions in the Russian Federation, including ICAC, is that they usually have a list of persons who are able to be appointed as arbitrators under the rules of relevant arbitration institutions. The list of arbitrators is public and it includes well-known Russian and foreign specialists in the field of the legal regulation of international trade and who have experience in law and commercial practice with Russian or other post-Soviet connections. The lists of arbitrators are confirmed regularly by the chambers of commerce and industry or other business organizations, to which particular arbitration institutions are attached.

The ICAC list of arbitrators adopted by the Russian Federation Chamber of Commerce and Industry is not mandatory for the parties in dispute: they are free to appoint as arbitrator any person who meets the requirements provided by the law or by the agreement of the parties. Only when appointments of a sole arbitrator or the chairperson of an arbitral tribunal by the institution in accordance with the Rules are made, must they be from the list.

The parties may agree on a procedure for challenging an arbitrator.

Failing such agreement, a party who intends to challenge an arbitrator shall, within 15 days after becoming aware of the constitution of the arbitral tribunal or after becoming aware of any circumstances disqualifying an arbitrator, communicate the reasons for the challenge in writing to the arbitral tribunal.

Unless the challenged arbitrator withdraws from his office or the other party agrees to the challenge, the arbitral tribunal shall decide on the challenge. If a challenge under any procedure is not successful, the challenging party may request, within 30 days after having received notice of the decision rejecting the challenge, the President of the Russian Federation Chamber of Commerce and Industry to decide on the challenge. This decision is final and cannot be subject to appeal in any state court. While such a request is pending, the arbitral tribunal, including the challenged arbitrator, may continue the arbitral proceedings and make an award. ICAC Rules provide for a different rule for the challenge procedure as compared with the Law. This question is decided not by the other members of the tribunal but by the Presidium of ICAC.

11 Arbitration procedure

The Law guarantees the parties' freedom to agree on the procedure to be followed by the arbitral tribunal in conducting the proceedings. The majority of statutory norms are of a default character. A limited number of mandatory provisions relating to the arbitration procedure ensure that arbitration proceedings will be conducted in accordance with fundamental principles as they are reflected in the text of the Law. The usual manner of exercising this right by the parties is in referring the dispute either to a particular arbitration institution applying its own rules or to widely known *ad hoc* rules such as the UNCITRAL Arbitration Rules.

In case a problem arises with regard to the procedure, which is not settled by agreement of the parties, the arbitral tribunal is empowered to conduct the arbitration in such a manner as it considers appropriate. However, in making any decision relating to the procedure, the arbitral tribunal has to treat the parties with equality and give each party a full opportunity to present their case.

The power conferred upon the arbitral tribunal includes the power to determine the admissibility, relevance, materiality and weight of any evidence. The Rules of ICAC that have been used in the vast majority of international commercial cases in Russia do not provide for any particular rules on evidence. Additionally, current arbitration practice reflects the traditional approach developed in state courts, which is characterized, to a great extent, by formalistic procedures based on predominantly documentary evidence and by (very rarely) using witnesses to find facts or to establish the matter of the applicable law or to deal with the economic aspects of the dispute. Widely recognized international documents relating to these aspects of the arbitration procedure that provide for the possibility of using different types of witness evidence such as the *IBA Rules on Taking Evidence* have hardly been used in international arbitration proceedings in Russia in recent years.

In the absence of the agreement of the parties, the arbitral tribunal has the power to make the determination in respect of the place of arbitration or the language of the proceedings – issues that very often play a vital role in international arbitration.

In order to meet the expectations of the users, arbitration institutions usually expend much effort in keeping their rules in conformity with the state-of-the-art rules in the field. They regularly amend their rules to take into account the latest developments in legislation and arbitration practice. The current ICAC Rules that came into force in 2006 hold to this and their contents, in substance, correspond to modern internationally accepted standards of arbitration procedure in international matters.

12 Applicable material law

Article 28(1) of the Law expressly provides that the arbitral tribunal shall decide the dispute in accordance with 'rules of law' chosen by the parties as applicable to the substance of the dispute. The Law uses the same term as the UNCITRAL Model Law and not the word 'law'. As is generally recognized, the reference to 'rules of law' instead of 'law' in the context of international arbitration gives the parties to international commercial contracts a wider range of options as regards the designation of *lex contractus* applicable to the substance of the dispute. Due to this provision they may, for example, agree on rules of law that have been developed at an international level as international legal instruments but have not come into force and have not become a part of any national legal system or have been drafted to have a non-mandatory legal character.[13] It should also be noted that the ICAC Rules, which deal with the vast majority of international arbitration cases in Russia, reflect the same approach.

UNIDROIT Principles of International Commercial Contracts (UNIDROIT 2010) serve as a good example for the 'rules of law' mentioned in article 28(1). In ICAC practice, there have already been cases

[13] See Explanatory Note by the UNCITRAL Secretariat on the 1985 Model Law on International Commercial Arbitration as amended in 2006, paras. 39–40.

where the arbitral tribunal applied UNIDROIT Principles not only where the parties referred to them in their contract as the applicable law. This has also happened through the arbitrators' initiative, since in the opinion of the tribunal this international document reflected international usages that could supplement the applicable rules of national law or the international instrument in a particular case. Arbitral tribunals acting under ICAC Rules and applying Russian material law use the relevant provisions of the UNIDROIT Principles to supplement Russian civil law when they think that it is appropriate. Such use of the Principles also serves one of the purposes set out in the Preamble.

When the parties have not designated the applicable rules of law, the arbitral tribunal would apply the law – that is, the national law – determined by the conflict of laws rules that it considers applicable. Arbitration courts in Russia usually have no difficulty in applying widely recognized usages and customs of international trade to the dispute, such as INCOTERMS, even in cases when the parties have not made express reference to them in their agreement.

Russian Law on international commercial arbitration does not expressly provide that the parties may authorize the arbitral tribunal to decide the dispute *ex aequo et bono* or as *amiable compositeur*. This approach to arbitration had never been officially recognized in the Soviet Union and, practically, has not been used widely up to now. In the short term, it would be difficult to expect that in contemporary business practice in Russia the parties would agree about the authority of the arbitral tribunal to act in such a capacity. However, one cannot exclude the possibility that in the long run the business community in Russia will become more inclined to avail itself of this opportunity, since the desire to take advantage of an alternative and less formalistic procedure for dispute settlement is noticeable in contemporary business life.

13 Setting aside the arbitral award

The Law provides for the possibility of challenging the arbitral award as an exclusive means of legal recourse and stipulates the grounds for setting it aside.[14] This regulation is in full conformity with the text of the UNCITRAL Model Law. Application for setting aside the arbitral award may be made only to the *arbitrazh* court at the place where arbitration proceedings have taken place. Also, the CAP has provisions to that effect,

[14] Art. 34–35 of the Law.

stating that an award rendered by an international arbitral tribunal may be set aside only on the grounds provided for by international treaties of the Russian Federation and by the federal law on international commercial arbitration.[15] The existence of such grounds shall be proved by the party seeking to set aside an arbitral award. Challenges against arbitral awards on the merits of the dispute are excluded.

The grounds for setting aside are limited and, in the first place, concern procedural irregularities that might occur in the course of arbitration proceedings. Consequently, an arbitral award may be set aside only if the party making the application furnishes proof that:

(a) A party to the arbitration agreement was under some incapacity; or the said agreement is not valid under the law to which the parties have subjected it or, failing any indication thereon, under the law of the Russian Federation; or
(b) The party making the application was not given proper notice of the appointment of an arbitrator or of the arbitral proceedings or was otherwise unable to present his case; or
(c) The award deals with a dispute not contemplated by or not falling within the terms of the submission to arbitration, or contains decisions on matters beyond the scope of the submission to arbitration, provided that, if the decisions on matters submitted to arbitration can be separated from those not so submitted, only that part of the award which contains decisions on matters not submitted to arbitration may be set aside; or
(d) The composition of the arbitral tribunal or the arbitral procedure was not in accordance with the agreement of the parties, unless such agreement was in conflict with a provision of the law regulating international commercial arbitration from which the parties cannot derogate, or, failing such agreement, was not in accordance with this law.

In addition, the award has to be set aside if the court finds on its own initiative that:

(a) The subject matter of the dispute is not capable of settlement by arbitration under the laws of the Russian Federation; or
(b) The award is in contrary to the public policy of the Russian Federation.

[15] Art. 233(4) of CAP.

An application for setting aside must be made within three months after the party has received the award. The present court practice of setting aside arbitral awards in the Russian Federation is still developing and is not yet stable enough. Apart from the fact that such cases are rather novel for the judiciary, their treatment in court practice has been influenced to a great extent by a general reform of the national legal system, which is supposed to serve the national economy in transition. Obviously, it will take considerable time to create an adequate and predictable legal environment for the new economic conditions.

As regards the problem of setting aside arbitral awards, it is also necessary to note that one of the deviations of Russian regulations relating to international commercial arbitration from the regime established by the UNCITRAL Model Law concerns the possibility of challenging a foreign arbitral award in the Russian *arbitrazh* court.[16] The reason for applying such a remedy may be due to the fact that Russian law was applicable to the arbitration proceedings taking place abroad as there were provisions made in an international treaty of the Russian Federation. This provision, in principle, does not appear to follow the modern trend in the regulation of international commercial arbitration, since it would hardly facilitate the development of international arbitration. What is more important is that it might generate situations that are damaging to the practice of international commercial arbitration involving Russian participants. However, it should be mentioned that so far this provision had been applied in practice in very few cases.

14 Recognition and enforcement of arbitral awards

The Law treats all international arbitral awards in a uniform manner irrespective of whether they are made in the Russian Federation or abroad. The borderline is drawn between 'international' and 'non-international' awards (which are not covered by the Law) instead of the traditional division between 'foreign' and 'domestic' awards. Recognition and enforcement of 'international' awards, whether 'foreign' or 'domestic', is governed by the same provisions.

Any arbitral award, irrespective of the country in which it was rendered, shall be recognized according to the Law as binding and enforceable, subject to the provisions that set forth the grounds on which recognition or enforcement may be refused. An application on the

[16] Art. 230(5) of CAP.

recognition and enforcement of a foreign arbitral award should be filed by a party in the arbitral proceedings in whose favour the award was made, in the *arbitrazh* court of a constituent part (federation subject) of the Russian Federation at the place of business or residence of the debtor.[17] If this place is not known, the application should be filed in the court at the place where the property of the debtor is located.

An application to recognize and enforce a foreign arbitral award shall specifically include reference to the name, place of location and the arbitral panel which made the award submitted for recognition and enforcement, the name of the debtor, the place of location thereof, or place of residence and details of the arbitral award. The duly notarized arbitral award and arbitration agreement shall be attached to the application, or to the notarized copies thereof, as well as the duly notarized translation of the above documents into Russian.

A foreign arbitral award should be submitted for enforcement in the territory of the Russian Federation within a time limit not exceeding three years since the day the award entered into legal force.[18] CAP lays down the rules of the procedure in the *arbitrazh* court for examination of the application on the recognition and enforcement of a foreign arbitral award.[19] It should be considered in a court session by a sole judge within a month from the day of its receipt by the arbitration court. The purpose of the application is to decide whether there are grounds that would exclude recognition and enforcement of a foreign arbitral award, as stipulated in the relevant rules contained in the international treaty of the Russian Federation and domestic Russian law relating to international commercial arbitration. The court does this by examining the evidence provided by the parties to the *arbitrazh* court. The grounds for refusing to recognize and enforce international arbitral awards, both foreign and domestic, are stipulated in the Law in full conformity with UNCITRAL Model Law and article V of the New York Convention.

Upon the results of the court examination of the application to recognize and enforce the arbitral award, the court issues a ruling, which should contain a decision either to recognize and enforce the arbitral award, or to refuse to recognize it, in the territory of the Russian Federation.

The decision of the *arbitrazh* court relating to the application for recognition and enforcement of an arbitral award may be appealed only in a cassation (second-instance) procedure in the respective

[17] Art. 242 of CAP. [18] Art. 246(2) of CAP. [19] Art. 243 of CAP.

Federal District *Arbitrazh* court within a month from the day the decision was made by the first-instance *arbitrazh* court.

It is necessary to keep in mind that Russian procedural legislation also provides for a quite unique remedy, which is unknown in the majority of other jurisdictions. It concerns the possible revision of a decision of a lower *arbitrazh* court concerning recognition and enforcement of an arbitral award by the Supreme *Arbitrazh* Court of the Russian Federation after the court decision has entered into legal force.[20]

A right to file such an application arises when a claimant believes that the court decision in question has substantially infringed the claimant's rights and legal interests in an entrepreneurial or other economic-activity sphere, as a result of a violation or wrongful application by the court of the rules of Russian substantive or procedural law. The term for filing such an application shall not exceed three months from the day the judicial act entered into legal force. In modern practice, applications to review a final *arbitrazh* court judgment relating to international arbitral awards have been filed by the parties to the dispute from time to time.

However, the revision of final court decisions in the above-mentioned procedure takes place infrequently. Only if the Supreme *Arbitrazh* Court comes to the conclusion that legal matters touched upon in the court decision that have been brought to its attention are important for establishing a uniform court practice in the country, would it take the case for consideration.

Currently, in the Russian Federation, the court practice relating to the recognition and enforcement of international arbitral awards is at an early stage of its formation. It is characterized by a significant degree of instability and unpredictability. This practice, in recent years, has been influenced by the ongoing reform of the legal system of the Russian Federation both with regard to substantive and procedural law. The major parts of the current Russian law relating to business activity have been substantially amended and expanded.

The achieving of stability in court practice, undoubtedly presupposes the necessity of accumulating experience of the adequate analysis of the problems relating to the recognition and enforcement of arbitral awards. So far, Russian *arbitrazh* courts, which in the past were dealing exclusively with domestic disputes in a centralized economic system, have not gained enough experience to take into account the relevant provisions of international treaties and the corresponding international practices. The

[20] See chapter 36 of CAP.

other important factor in terms of current court practice in relation to international matters that should be taken into account is the fact that the courts are extremely overloaded and disputes concerning international arbitration represent a very small fraction of the caseload.

As mentioned earlier, the Soviet Union was among those states that joined the New York Convention shortly after it was opened for ratification. The Convention was ratified by the Soviet Union in 1960. The Russian Federation has continued, as from 24 December 1991, its membership in the Convention in place of the former Soviet Union. The application of the Convention on the territory of the Russian Federation is conditioned by the reciprocity reservation, which was made by the Soviet Union when it ratified the Convention in 1960. That means that Russia will apply the Convention only to the recognition and enforcement of awards made in the territory of another contracting state. With regard to awards made in the territory of non-contracting states, the Convention will be applied only to the extent to which these states grant reciprocal treatment.

In spite of the early ratification of the New York Convention, the actual practice of its application only started in the early nineties of the last century. In the period before the dissolution of the Soviet Union, there were no cases of the enforcement of foreign arbitral awards either on the basis of the Convention or in terms of non-Convention awards. This fact can probably be explained by the existence at that time of a state monopoly on foreign trade, where all international commercial transactions were made and performed by state foreign trade agencies and voluntary fulfilment of international arbitral awards by Soviet parties was a matter of honour for the state.

The courts in the Russian Federation are steadily gaining the necessary experience in terms of the application of law relating to the enforcement of international arbitral awards under the New York Convention and in accordance with internationally recognized standards of arbitration practice. At the present time, the majority of international awards rendered in Russia and foreign arbitral awards are recognized and enforced in the Russian Federation.

An important aspect, in practice, relating to the recognition and enforcement of international arbitral awards is in determining the limits of interference of the state courts in arbitration proceedings. The idea that an arbitral award is final and is not subject to revision on the merits is generally accepted in the practice of Russian *arbitrazh* courts. However, sometimes the lower courts are inclined to re-examine facts or the legal conclusions of the arbitral tribunal, allying with the position of the party 'attacking' the arbitral award based on the merits. The second-instance (cassation) courts are usually more reluctant to follow this position and usually would not support such an attitude to the finality of international arbitral awards based on the merits of the case.

In principle, the Russian courts are applying in a fairly consistent manner the rules establishing the distribution of the burden of proof in cases where it is alleged that arbitrators have failed to comply with the arbitration procedure or committed other irregularities. The existence of grounds for refusal of recognition and enforcement of the award has to be proved by the party 'attacking' the award.[21]

References to the contradiction of an international arbitral award with the public policy of the Russian Federation with the purpose of blocking its recognition and enforcement on the territory of the Russian Federation has been characterized as a typical feature of Russian practice in relation to international arbitral awards.[22] At the same time, despite quite a considerable number of cases where respondents have attempted to deny the recognition and enforcement of an international arbitral award with reference to a violation of Russian public policy, *arbitrazh* courts have seldom decided to reject an application to recognize and enforce an award because it would violate the public policy of the Russian Federation. For the time being, Russian court practice in this respect remains rather unstable, which brings a certain degree of unpredictability in respect of the successful enforcement of international arbitral awards in Russia.

[21] An example of a court judgment relating to recognition and enforcement of foreign arbitral award in the territory of the Russian Federation is given in Zhiltsov, 'Recent Arbitration Awards', p. 134.

[22] For analysis of current practice see, for example, D. Tapola, 'Enforcement of Foreign Arbitral Awards: Application of the Public Policy Rule in Russia', *Arbitration International*, 22(2006) No. 1, p. 151; E. Kurzinsky-Singer and D. Davydenko, 'Materiellrechtlicher odre public bei der Anerkennung und Vollstreckbarerklärung von schiedsrechtlichen Urteilen in der Russischen Föderation: eine Rechtsprechungsanalyse', *SchiedsVZ (German Arbitration Journal)* (2010), p. 203.

13

Arbitration in Sweden: Features of the Stockholm Rules

HENRIK FIEBER AND EVA STORSKRUBB

1 Introduction

1.1 History and statutory framework

Arbitration has a long history in Sweden. In 1734, the first major Statute Book was published in Sweden. This included the 1734 Enforcement Code, which contained a provision dealing with arbitration to the effect that if the parties had referred a dispute to entrusted persons and agreed to abide by their decision, the resulting decision was enforceable.[1]

The first comprehensive Arbitration Act in Sweden was not adopted until 1887. The Arbitration Act currently in force is the 1999 Swedish Arbitration Act (*Lagen om skiljeförfarande*, SFS 1999: 116) (the 'Arbitration Act'),[2] which governs both domestic and international arbitration. During the decades preceding the enactment of the Arbitration Act, Sweden had become the chosen place of arbitration for an increasing number of international arbitrations. Therefore, the legislator considered that the legitimate expectations and requirements of the users ought to be met by creating an efficient and easily comprehensible legislative framework for the resolution of disputes.[3] The UNCITRAL Model Law on International Commercial Arbitration (the 'Model Law') has served as an important source of inspiration for the Arbitration Act, but does not qualify Sweden as a Model Law country. Certain provisions in the Act deviate from, and even contradict, the approach of the Model Law.[4]

[1] For earlier traces of arbitration in Sweden see, *inter alia*, K. Hobér, *International Commercial Arbitration in Sweden* (Oxford University Press, 2011), pp. 1–2.
[2] See www.chamber.se/?id=23746 for the Act in English.
[3] Government Bill 1998/99: 35, p. 42. [4] Government Bill 1998/99: 35, p. 47.

Specific rules regarding international arbitration and enforcement of foreign arbitral awards are found in sections 46–60 of the Arbitration Act. In general, the same procedure is adopted for international and domestic arbitrations. One notable difference is that commercial parties without any connection to Sweden may agree in advance to limit or exclude certain grounds for challenging an award[5] (see further Section 14 below). In addition, the *travaux préparatoires* to the Arbitration Act confirm that – due also to its applicability to international arbitrations – the Arbitration Act is to be applied independently without direct or indirect reference to Swedish rules on judicial procedures, even though these may have, in some respects, played a role in the formulation of the provisions in the Arbitration Act.[6]

Arbitration is today generally considered as the preferred method to resolve commercial contract disputes in Sweden. This finding was also reflected in the Roschier Disputes Index of 2010 and 2012, a survey on facts and trends in dispute resolution in Sweden and Finland. In the survey, around 71 per cent of all respondents stated a general preference for arbitration.[7] Among the perceived advantages of arbitration are the relative speed and lower costs in comparison to litigation and the fact that arbitrators may be chosen for their experience or particular expertise. In addition, the non-public nature of arbitration proceedings is perceived as a benefit.

1.2 *Institutional framework and international venue*

Although there are no available statistics to support this proposition, the general perception is that most large arbitrations in Sweden today are institutional. The principal arbitration institute in Sweden, the Arbitration Institute of the Stockholm Chamber of Commerce (the 'SCC'), was established in 1917.[8] In the 1970s, the SCC's caseload started to grow significantly. An important factor in this development was the conclusion of an optional clause agreement for Soviet–American Contracts in 1977. The

[5] Section 51 of the Arbitration Act. [6] Government Bill 1998/99: 35, p. 47.

[7] See Roschier Disputes Index 2010 and 2012, available at www.roschier.com. The surveys were based on interviews conducted with the 100 largest companies operating in either Finland or Sweden.

[8] The homepages of the SCC can be found at www.sccinstitute.com/. According to the Roschier Disputes Index 2010, the ICC Arbitration Rules were the second most preferred among Swedish respondents.

agreement designated Sweden as the place of arbitration for disputes between parties from the two countries.[9]

In the past 35 years, Sweden has established itself as an important venue for international arbitration, especially in the field of East–West disputes (predominantly disputes involving parties from the former Soviet Union or China). Sweden has also become increasingly popular for international disputes in general. Today the SCC's caseload involves parties from roughly 30 countries and has, in recent years, seen approximately 200 new arbitrations each year. Among the SCC arbitrations over the past few years, roughly half of them have been international (meaning that at least one party originated in a country other than Sweden).[10]

The SCC is generally recognized as one of the world's leading arbitration institutes. The current Arbitration Rules of the SCC Institute (the 'SCC Rules') entered into force on 1 January 2010.[11] In addition to the SCC Rules, the SCC provides rules for expedited arbitration and mediation. The SCC also administers arbitration proceedings under different rules and, in particular, acts as appointing authority under the UNCITRAL Rules.

1.3 Sources and delimitation

The principal sources of Swedish law on international arbitration are the Arbitration Act, case law from the highest civil courts in Sweden (the Swedish Supreme Court and the Courts of Appeal), the *travaux préparatoires* and legal doctrine.[12]

For Swedish court proceedings, the Code of Judicial Procedure (*Rättegångsbalken* SFS 1942: 740) (the 'Code of Judicial Procedure')[13] is the relevant statute. The Code of Judicial Procedure does not directly apply to arbitral proceedings. However, it may, on a general level,

[9] See, *inter alia*, F. Andersson *et al.*, *Arbitration in Sweden* (Jure, 2011), p. 29.

[10] See www.sccinstitute.com/hem-3/statistik-2.aspx for the statistics of the SCC.

[11] See www.sccinstitute.com/?id=23718 for a link to the SCC Rules in various languages.

[12] Judicial decisions by the highest courts in Sweden are sources of law, although the *stare decisis* doctrine is not strictly applicable. The *travaux préparatoires* – in particular, the relevant Government Bill for a Swedish statute – are considered relevant in order to be able to elucidate ambiguous points. Legal doctrine is not, strictly speaking, a source of law, but is frequently considered and referred to by the courts.

[13] For an English translation of the Code of Judicial Procedure that is unfortunately not up to date see www.sweden.gov.se/content/1/c4/15/40/472970fc.pdf.

influence Swedish lawyers' approach to certain procedural issues (especially in domestic arbitrations).[14] In addition, the Code of Judicial Procedure will apply to any court proceedings that relate to arbitration.

Furthermore, case reports on arbitration proceedings conducted under the auspices of the SCC Rules may serve as examples of how the SCC Rules have been interpreted.[15]

We will deal with the set features and topics from the perspective of the SCC Arbitration Rules 2010 below and, where relevant, from the perspective of the SCC Rules for Expedited Arbitrations 2010. In addition, the Arbitration Act and the other above-mentioned sources will be referred to and taken into account where appropriate.

2 Time frame for the proceeding

The length of an arbitral proceeding varies depending on the size and complexity of the subject matter and the behaviour of the parties. In recent years, arbitrators and institutions have become increasingly aware of the need for speed and efficiency in arbitration proceedings.

In institutional arbitration, there are certain projected time frames. Under the SCC Rules, a six-month time frame applies for rendering the award from the time when the case was referred to the arbitral tribunal.[16] However, in practice, this time requirement is not always adhered to and the secretariat or the board of the SCC may extend this deadline upon reasoned request from the tribunal. However, the parties will be heard and an extension of more than two months is rarely granted unless all parties agree or there are special circumstances that warrant the extension.[17] Under the Expedited Rules, the corresponding time frame is three months.[18]

Typically, arbitration proceedings in Sweden of ordinary complexity may take 12 to 18 months. Once the matter has been referred to the

[14] See note 6 *supra* and our comment above in relation to the independent application of the Arbitration Act.

[15] See L. Bergman and S. Bond (eds.), *SCC Arbitral Awards 2004–2009* (Juris, 2011). See also the *Stockholm International Arbitration Review* and the *Stockholm Arbitration Newsletter* (both published by the SCC). See www.sccinstitute.se/contact-2/nyhetsbrev-5.aspx for a link to the *Newsletters*.

[16] Article 37.

[17] M. Öhrström, *Stockholms Handelskammares Skiljedomsinstitut: en handbok och regelkommentar för skiljeförfaranden* (Norstedts Juridik, 2009), p. 222.

[18] Article 36.

tribunal, the proceedings can be expected to last some 12 months. According to information received from the SCC proceedings under its Rules take on average around ten months and under the Expedited Rules around five and a half months.

3 Cost determination (including security)

In arbitrations under the SCC Rules, the board shall determine an amount to be paid by the parties as an advance on costs corresponding to the estimated fees and expenses of the arbitral tribunal, the administrative fee and the expenses of the SCC. Each party shall pay half of the advance, but if a party fails to make the required payment the other party will be afforded the opportunity to do so. If the requested advance is not posted at all, then the board shall dismiss the case.[19] Under the Arbitration Act, the arbitrators may also request security for their fees and there are rules requiring a party to provide the entire security and termination of proceedings where security is not paid. Note also that – pursuant to the SCC Rules – if a party fails to pay its share of the advance, the tribunal can render an interim award ordering that party to compensate the party that paid its share of the advance.[20]

Unless otherwise agreed by the parties, the arbitral tribunal may – in an arbitration under the SCC Rules – upon request of a party, make an order as to the distribution of the costs of the arbitration.[21] In determining the final distribution of the costs, the tribunal enjoys wide discretion. Generally, costs are allocated on the basis of the outcome of the case and the relative success of the parties on the principal issues. Arbitrators may also typically take into account the other relevant factors such as outcome of procedural issues dealt with by the tribunal, or unnecessary, negligent or obstructive behaviour by the parties that have caused increased costs.[22]

The elements of costs typically include reasonable costs for legal representation, expenses for witnesses and experts as well as the fees

[19] Article 45; the Expedited Rules include similar provisions in Article 44.

[20] Section 38.

[21] Articles 43(5) and 44 and Articles 42(4) and 43 of the Expedited Rules.

[22] See L. Heuman, *Skiljemannarätt* (Nordstedts Juridik, 1999), pp. 582–3 and Hobér, *International Commercial Arbitration in Sweden*, p. 274.

and expenses of the arbitral tribunal. If the arbitration has been institutional, the fees of the arbitral institution are also included.[23]

In arbitrations under the SCC Rules, the board of the SCC will finally determine the fees of the arbitral tribunal, the administrative fee and the expenses of the tribunal and the SCC.[24] There is some level of predictability in terms of the fees of the arbitral tribunal, since the fixed-fee schedule of the SCC includes minimum and maximum amounts for most disputes.[25]

Under the Arbitration Act, the arbitrators decide on the amount to be paid in terms of their own compensation. An action can be brought in the district court against the award on compensation to the arbitrators within three months of the award. A judgment according to which the compensation to an arbitrator is reduced also applies to the party who did not bring the action.[26] According to a recent Supreme Court decision, the right to bring an action against the fees of the arbitrators also applies where the fees have been decided by an arbitral institution.[27]

4 Procedure for the appointment of the tribunal

In SCC arbitration, the parties may agree on the number of arbitrators. Where the parties have not agreed, the default rule is that the tribunal shall consist of three arbitrators unless the board of the SCC decides that the dispute should be decided by a sole arbitrator. When considering the number of arbitrators, the board of the SCC will have regard to the complexity of the case, the amount in dispute and other relevant circumstances.[28] Relevant circumstances that may be taken into account are *inter alia* that the dispute involves parties from different countries, that it is a multi-party or multi-contract arbitration or that the dispute involves a state party.[29]

The parties may also agree on the procedure for appointment. If the tribunal has not been appointed within the time period agreed by the parties or within a time period set by the board of the SCC, the

[23] Article 41(1); see also Appendix III to the SCC Rules that defines, in further detail, the heads of costs.

[24] Article 43(2). [25] See Appendix III to the SCC Rules. [26] Section 41.

[27] *NJA* (2008), p. 1118. [28] Article 12.

[29] Öhrström, *Stockholms Handelskammares Skiljedomsinstitut*, p. 148.

appointment shall be made pursuant to the SCC Rules.[30] According to the SCC Rules, the parties shall make a joint decision on a sole arbitrator within a set timetable of ten days. If they fail to do so, the board will make the appointment.[31] Otherwise, each party shall appoint an equal number of arbitrators and the chairperson shall be appointed by the board. If a party fails to make an appointment of an arbitrator within a set time period, the board will make the appointment.[32]

In arbitration according to the Expedited Rules of the SCC the dispute will be decided on by a sole arbitrator. Unless the parties agree otherwise, the appointment procedure corresponds to what is mentioned above; that is, the board will make the appointment unless the parties can agree within the stipulated time period.[33]

If the parties have not specifically agreed on the appointment process, the default rule under the Arbitration Act is that the arbitral tribunal shall consist of three arbitrators. Moreover, each party shall appoint one arbitrator and the party-appointed arbitrators shall then appoint the chairperson of the tribunal.[34] If a party, the party-appointed arbitrators or any third party fails to appoint an arbitrator pursuant to the parties' agreement or applicable law, the local district court shall appoint this specific arbitrator upon application by the party seeking to progress arbitration.[35] However, this situation very seldom occurs in practice.

Finally, in case an emergency arbitrator (who can be appointed to deal with interim relief before the arbitral tribunal proper is appointed) is to be appointed under the provisions in the SCC Rules, the board will appoint the arbitrator within 24 hours of receipt of the application.[36] See section 9 below for more detail in relation to the emergency arbitrator.

5 Identity and role of the appointing authority

As noted above under section 4, under the SCC Rules the parties may appoint a sole arbitrator or one of three arbitrators. However, if the parties fail to do so, the board of the SCC will make the appointment. In addition, the board will, under the appointment procedure set out in

[30] Article 13(1). [31] Article 13(2). [32] Article 13(3).
[33] Expedited Rules Articles 12 and 13(1)–(2). [34] Section 13. [35] Sections 14 and 44.
[36] Appendix II, Article 4.

the Rules, always appoint the chairperson if there is more than one arbitrator.

The SCC Rules and the Expedited Rules include the following guidance on the appointments to be made by the board. The board should consider the nature and circumstances of the dispute, the applicable law, the seat and language of the arbitration and the nationality of the parties. In addition, it is explicitly stated that if the parties are of different nationalities, the sole arbitrator or the chairperson of the arbitral tribunal should be of a different nationality than the parties, unless the parties have agreed otherwise or unless an arbitrator of the same nationality as one of the parties is deemed appropriate.[37] As examples of other factors that may be taken into account are the nationality of counsel, the relevant field of law and the experience and competence of the candidate.[38]

Appendix I to the SCC Rules outlines the organization of the SCC including stipulations on the composition, appointment, function and decisions of the board. The board may delegate certain matters to the secretariat, but these do not include the appointment of arbitrators. The board includes both Swedish and non-Swedish practicing arbitration specialists.[39]

6 Form of the arbitration agreement

There are no specific form requirements under Swedish law in order for an arbitration agreement to be valid. The written form is of course the most common, but an arbitration agreement may also, in theory, be concluded orally or through conduct.

General contract law rules and principles apply as to the formation and validity of an arbitration agreement. Hence, an arbitration agreement will not be valid and enforceable if the parties had no legal capacity to enter into such an agreement in the first place. In addition, under Swedish contract law, duress, fraud or mistakes can in rare cases nullify an arbitration agreement.

In exceptional circumstances, an arbitration clause may also be adjusted based on section 36 of the Contracts Act due to it being

[37] Article 13(5)–(6); Expedited Rules Article 13(3)–(4).

[38] Öhrström, *Stockholms Handelskammares Skiljedomsinstitut*, p. 150.

[39] See also www.sccinstitute.com/hem-3/styrelsen-21.aspx for the current composition of the board.

objectively perceived as having been unreasonable. However, adjustment of arbitration agreements on this basis is extremely rare in contractual relations between commercial parties.[40]

More relevant perhaps is where an arbitration clause is included in standard terms that are referred to in the main agreement. Generally, the standard terms will be incorporated into the contract as long as the other party has had the opportunity to access and review the standard terms when the main agreement was concluded. The Supreme Court has specifically confirmed that a reference to standard terms, which included an arbitration clause, was sufficient to bind the parties to arbitration.[41]

According to the Arbitration Act, an arbitration agreement may cover existing and future disputes pertaining to a specific legal relationship. A further requirement is that, under Swedish law, the dispute is considered to be arbitrable.[42]

7 Interference/support from the courts (including the tribunal's powers to involve them)

There are several ways in which the arbitral proceedings can be 'supported' or 'interfered with' by the courts.

7.1 Jurisdiction

A valid arbitration agreement constitutes a bar to court proceedings.[43] If a party to an arbitration agreement initiates court proceedings, the

[40] See Hobér, *International Commercial Arbitration in Sweden*, pp. 114–15, noting that adjustment has mainly been applied in situations involving consumer agreements. See further S. Lindskog, *Skiljeförfarande: En kommentar* (Nordsteds Juridik AB, 2005), pp. 131–43, noting that, *inter alia*, a situation where an arbitration agreement would breach due process rules may be considered as unreasonable.

[41] *Tureberg-Sollentuna Lastbilcentral ekonomisk förening yrkade* v. *Byggnadsfirman Rudolf Asplund* reported in the *NJA* (1980), p. 47.

[42] Section 1 of the Arbitration Act, 'Disputes concerning matters in respect of which the parties may reach settlement may, by agreement, be referred to one or several arbitrators for resolution.' The issue of arbitrability under Swedish law is not dealt with here. See, *inter alia*, Hobér, *International Commercial Arbitration in Sweden*, pp. 115–23 and Andersson *et al.*, *Arbitration in Sweden*, pp. 57–65 for a review of arbitrability under Swedish law.

[43] Section 2.

other party can move for a dismissal of the court proceedings. According to the Arbitration Act, an objection to the court's jurisdiction must be raised the first time the objecting party enters a substantive defence.[44] Swedish courts generally favour arbitration and arbitration agreements are interpreted extensively rather than restrictively. The party invoking the arbitration agreement has the burden of proving its existence.

However, related to the fundamental premise mentioned above is the question of who can ultimately decide on the jurisdiction of the tribunal: *compétence-compétence*. According to the Arbitration Act, the arbitrators may rule on their own jurisdiction to decide a dispute.[45] However, this does not prevent a party from raising a separate challenge on jurisdiction in court. In the meantime, the arbitral tribunal need not suspend the arbitral proceedings, but may do so at its discretion.[46] Arbitral tribunals are usually reluctant to suspend the proceedings unless they have reason to believe that the challenge may have merit.

Under the SCC Rules, the board will decide (when necessary) whether the SCC Institute manifestly lacks jurisdiction over the dispute and the Institute may then dismiss the case, in whole or in part, before referring it to an arbitral tribunal (i.e. a *prima facie* assessment).[47] The threshold for the board to accept *prima facie* jurisdiction is fairly low and it will often suffice that the Institute is in some manner mentioned in the arbitration clause, also without its full or correct name, and that some practical connection between the clause and the dispute is at hand.[48]

7.2 Appointment of arbitrators

The courts may, in practice, under certain rare circumstances, be involved in the appointment of arbitrators (see Section 4 above).

7.3 Interim measures

Courts are also involved in issuing interim measures in matters that are pending in arbitration (see Section 9 below). This kind of involvement is

[44] Section 4(2). [45] Section 2. [46] Section 2.

[47] Article 10. See as an example SCC Case 12/2000 referred to in Bergman and Bond (eds.), *SCC Arbitral Awards 2004–2009*, pp. 73–5.

[48] See Öhrström, *Stockholms Handelskammares Skiljedomsinstitut*, p. 139.

more common than that in which the courts are requested to make arbitrator appointments.

7.4 Evidence

Courts may also assist the parties to an arbitration in the process of the taking of evidence. Unlike a state court, an arbitral tribunal cannot impose certain measures in relation to evidence; for example, it can neither administer oaths, nor force the attendance of witnesses or the production of documents. Such measures must be obtained upon application by a party to a court, subject to that party having obtained consent from the arbitral tribunal.[49]

The requirement of obtaining the arbitrators' consent to submit such requests means that the arbitrators will decide whether the request is appropriate in view of the arbitral proceedings. If, for example, in the arbitrators' opinion the evidence will not have any impact on the dispute, a request for a court order will merely serve as an unnecessary delay in the proceedings and may, therefore, be dismissed.

The court may summon a witness to appear before the court but cannot order a witness to appear in the arbitral proceedings. The arbitrators are invited to attend hearings of witnesses before the court and will, if they choose to attend, be given an opportunity to ask the witness questions.

Notably, the court shall grant and execute the application if it is lawfully made.[50] Hence, the court will not evaluate the merits or necessity of the application. However, this also means that to the extent that the evidence requested breaches rules on evidence in the Code of Judicial Procedure, the court is not obliged to grant the request. Examples of situations under which a request for evidence may not be in compliance with the Code of Judicial Procedure include those where the evidence involves trade secrets or issues of witness privilege.[51] The arbitral tribunal shall designate the relevant district court and, in the absence of such designation, the District Court of Stockholm will have jurisdiction to decide on the relevant issue.[52]

[49] Sections 25–26. [50] *NJA* (2012), p. 289.
[51] Chapter 36 section 5 of the Code of Judicial Procedure.
[52] Section 44 of the Arbitration Act. Notably, this rule relates to internal jurisdiction within Sweden and does not determine whether the Swedish courts have international jurisdiction over such a request. There is no settled guidance from the Supreme Court on the issue, but it may not be sufficient that the arbitration is pending in Sweden. See Hobér, *International Commercial Arbitration in Sweden*, p. 240.

7.5 *Challenge of awards*

The courts interact with arbitration indirectly when awards are challenged (see Section 15 below).

7.6 *Enforcement of foreign awards*

Finally, the courts are relevant to the arbitral process when the question of enforcement of awards arises. A domestic award can be enforced in Sweden directly upon application to the execution authority (*Kronofogdemyndigheten*) following the rules in the Enforcement Code (*Utsökningbalken* SFS 1981: 774).[53] However, an application for recognition and enforcement of a foreign award must be lodged with the Svea Court of Appeal. The original award or a certified copy of the award must be appended to the application. As a general rule, a certified translation of the entire award into Swedish must also be submitted.[54] The decision of the Court of Appeal can be appealed to the Supreme Court.[55] The grounds for opposing enforcement are that:[56]

(a) the parties lacked capacity to enter into the agreement or were not properly represented, or the arbitration agreement is otherwise invalid;
(b) a party was not given proper notice of the appointment of the arbitrator, or of the proceedings or was otherwise unable to present its case;
(c) the award deals with a matter not falling within the terms of the submission to arbitration or that is beyond the scope of the arbitration agreement; and
(d) the composition of the arbitral tribunal, or the arbitral procedure, was not in accordance with the agreement of the parties or with the law of the country where the arbitration took place.

[53] See Chapter 3, section 15 of the Enforcement Code. The Enforcement Authority may refuse execution when the award does not meet the form requirements in the Arbitration Act or when the arbitration agreement foresees the possibility of appealing the award based on the merits and the time limit for such an appeal is still running; in addition, the award may be invalid when it concerns a non-arbitrable matter or when it goes against the *ordre public* in Sweden. If the award might be invalid then the Enforcement Authority directs the party seeking enforcement to initiate, within one month, court proceedings regarding the validity.

[54] Section 56. [55] Section 59.

[56] Section 54. The grounds are basically the same as those set out in the New York Convention, which Sweden ratified in 1972.

A party can further claim that the award has not yet become binding between the parties, or that it has been set aside or suspended by a competent authority in the country in which the award was made.[57]

Recognition and enforcement of a foreign award should also be refused when the court finds that the award includes determination of an issue which, under Swedish law, may not be decided on by arbitrators or when it would be clearly incompatible with the basic principles of the Swedish legal system (public policy) if the award were to be recognized or enforced.[58]

Enforcement may, upon request by a party, be stayed by the court. Upon request, the court may also order the opposing party to provide a reasonable security (most often in form of a bank guarantee). The purpose of such security is to cover the other party's loss caused by the stay should the court subsequently decide that the award is, in fact, enforceable. Failure to provide such reasonable security might result in the request for a stay being declined and subsequent enforcement.[59]

It can generally be said that the arbitration-friendly approach of the Swedish courts is also evident with respect to enforcement. The Supreme Court has emphasized the importance of respecting the aims of the New York Convention and noted that the Arbitration Act must, in its relevant parts, be interpreted in light of the purpose behind the Convention.[60] This is evidenced by the very few cases that exist where enforcement is denied.[61]

8 Tribunal's powers *ex officio*

Ultimately, the conduct of the proceedings lies with the parties. In that sense the tribunal has very little power to act *ex officio*. However, to the extent that the parties have not agreed or cannot agree on the procedure, the arbitral tribunal will step in and must decide on the conduct of the proceedings. When that happens, the arbitrators must ensure that the parties will have an equal opportunity to present their respective cases

[57] Section 54. [58] Section 55. [59] Section 58.

[60] *K.B. AB* v. *Société Planavergne S.A.* reported in the *NJA* (2003), p. 379. See also Hobér, *International Commercial Arbitration in Sweden*, p. 359. In particular, see note 8.

[61] See though, *inter alia*, *Lenmorniiprojekt OAO St Petersburg* v. *A.L. & Partner Leasing AB* reported in *NJA* (2010), p. 219 on refusal to recognize based on due process and lack of notice of the proceedings and *R. G.* v. *J. L.* reported in the *NJA* (2002), Note C45 on refusal to recognize based on *ordre public* due to attempts to circumvent insolvency proceedings, and Andersson *et al.*, *Arbitration in Sweden*, pp. 184–7.

and the arbitrators are obliged to handle the dispute in an impartial, practical and speedy manner (see Section 11 below).[62]

In relation to the subject matter of the dispute, the arbitrators, as a general rule, do not have any powers *ex officio*. Under Swedish law, they are limited by the scope of the arbitration agreement as well as by the prayers for relief that define the remit of the specific dispute. Otherwise, they may risk going outside their mandate and the award may potentially be set aside as either being *ultra vires* or *ultra petita*. However, notably, the question of the scope and remit of the specific dispute may be a complex question.

In relation to the applicable law of the arbitral proceedings, the issue has arisen in the recent international debate over whether the principle of *jura novit curia* applies in arbitration or not, similar to what would be the case under the procedural laws of many countries, including Sweden. The Svea Court of Appeal has found the principle of *jura novit curia* applicable *in dubio* in an arbitral proceeding between two Swedish parties and in relation to domestic law.[63] However, it is still the prevalent position among commentators that the principle is not, or should not be, applicable to international arbitrations in Sweden.[64]

Another more subtle issue is how active the arbitrators are in managing and conducting the proceedings. The case management of the tribunal may depend on the culture and style of the arbitrators. However, the main and overriding principle is that the arbitrators must always treat the parties equally (see also Section 11.2 below).[65]

9 The possibility of interim measures and their enforceability

Under the SCC Rules, the tribunal may, at the request of a party, grant any interim measure it considers appropriate and may order the party requesting such a measure to provide security.[66] There are similar provisions in the Arbitration Act.[67] Hence, the arbitral tribunal has considerable freedom to decide on what type of provisional measures

62 SCC Rules Article 19(2) and Sections 21 and 24 of the Arbitration Act.

63 Svea Court of Appeal Case T 8090–99, *Rolf Gustafson* v. *Länsförsäkringar Bergslagen*.

64 See, *inter alia*, G. Calissendorff, 'Jura novit curia i internationalla skikjeförfaranden i Sverige', *Juridisk Tidskrift*, 1(1995/1996), 147–9, and Andersson *et al.*, *Arbitration in Sweden*, p. 119.

65 On the issue or case managament ('processledning' in Swedish) see, *inter alia*, Heuman, *Skiljemannarätt*, pp. 384–7 and Öhrström, *Stockholms Handelskammares Skiljedomsinstitut*, pp. 172–4.

66 Article 32. 67 Section 25.

to order. The purpose of the interim measure may be to prevent irreparable harm, to preserve evidence or to preserve the future enforcement of the award. The action should aim to safeguard the claim to be heard by the arbitral tribunal.

The SCC Rules also include particular rules on the appointment of an emergency arbitrator for the purpose of granting interim measures before the arbitration has commenced or before the case has been referred to the arbitral tribunal.[68] Once the application for an emergency arbitrator has been received by the SCC, the other party shall be notified. Once the emergency arbitrator has been appointed, he/she must endeavour to give both parties the opportunity to present their case.[69] The emergency arbitrator, who cannot be appointed as a regular arbitrator in the same matter, shall make his/her decision within five days unless given an extension by the board.[70] The emergency arbitrator's decision is immediately binding on the parties. However, it can be amended, or revoked by the emergency arbitrator upon request and it ceases to be binding under certain circumstances, such as where the arbitral tribunal so orders upon its formation or where arbitration is not commenced within 30 days.[71]

The possibility of applying for an emergency arbitrator was a new tool introduced in the SCC Rules that entered into force in 2010.[72] In 2010, there were four cases of emergency arbitration under the SCC Rules. Only one request was successful. The case report shows that the emergency arbitrators all applied similar criteria for determining the matter: (a) a *prima facie* reasonable possibility of success on the merits and (b) an urgent need due to risk of irreparable harm. The basis for denying the application in two cases was a lack of imminent and irreparable harm. In addition, in one case the relevant measures were sought against third parties, which the emergency arbitrator found that he could not order.[73]

Based on the consensual nature of arbitration, the powers of the arbitrators to order provisional measures is limited to the parties to the arbitration. In addition, arbitrators will invariably – unless the parties have

68 Appendix II. 69 Appendix II Article 7. 70 Appendix II Article 8(1).

71 Appendix II Article 9.

72 Note that when the 2010 SCC Rules entered into force the new emergency rules became applicable to all arbitrations that were instituted. Hence, in cases where the parties do not wish such rules to be applicable, they must explicitly exclude them: the so-called opt-out.

73 See J. Lundstedt, *SCC Practice: Emergency Arbitrator, Decisions Rendered in 2010*, available at: www.sccinstitute.se/filearchive/4/41504/Emergency%20arbitration%20final.pdf.

agreed otherwise – hear both parties. Hence, the procedure will be *inter partes*. Finally, the decision of arbitrators on interim measures is not enforceable under law in Sweden, regardless of whether it is called a decision or an award. Notwithstanding, parties generally tend to abide by the interim decisions of arbitral tribunals. In addition, it is not excluded that non-compliance may, depending on the circumstances, come to affect the tribunal's evaluation of the case or cause the tribunal to draw adverse inferences.[74] However, it may nevertheless under certain circumstances be more effective to resort to the courts for interim protection.[75]

A party may apply to the district court for interim measures before, as well as at any time during the arbitral proceedings. Such court orders are enforceable in Sweden but may be appealed to the superior courts. The interim measure will remain in force for as long as the court has decided and often for the duration of the arbitral proceedings. The types of interim measures that the courts may order and the conditions for such measures are set forth in the Code of Judicial Procedure.[76] Examples of such measures are attachment of property or orders for specific performance. The purpose of the interim measures may be to protect the substantive interests of the applicant or to preserve evidence.

10 Multiparty arbitration (including joinder and consolidation)

The SCC Rules specifically include a rule on consolidation. According to this rule, if arbitration is commenced concerning a legal relationship in respect of which an arbitration between the same parties is already pending under the rules, the board may, at the request of a party, decide to consolidate the new claims with the pending proceedings. The board can only make such a decision subsequent to consulting with the parties and the arbitral tribunal. Hence, the specific requirements for consolidation are that the parties are the same, that both proceedings have been commenced and that they both concern the same legal relationship.[77]

[74] See, *inter alia*, Lindskog, *Skiljeförfarande: En kommentar*, pp. 741–2 and Öhrström, *Stockholms Handelskammares Skiljedomsinstitut*, p. 207.

[75] Section 4 of the Arbitration Act confirms that the arbitration agreement does not bar the parties from applying to court for interim relief.

[76] See Chapter 15 of the Code of Judicial Procedure. Note that Swedish courts are not empowered to grant anti-suit injunctions.

[77] Article 11.

Other than for consolidation, the SCC Rules do not include any specific provisions to streamline proceedings in multiparty situations.[78] There are also no provisions in the Arbitration Act or precedent case law that address multiparty scenarios. Therefore, in such situations, it is unlikely that joinder or consolidations can take place without the consent of all parties.

The SCC Rules nevertheless clarify and assist the proceedings in such situations in that the rule on appointment of arbitrators specifically deals with the situation of multiple claimants or respondents.[79]

11 Conduct of arbitration (terms of reference, number of briefs, disclosure, written or oral evidence, modality of hearings, applicable law)

11.1 General

According to the SCC Rules, unless the parties have agreed otherwise, the board will determine the seat of arbitration.[80] Factors that the board may come to take into account are, amongst other, the domicile of the parties, the domicile of the arbitrators, which country the relevant contract has a connection to, practical and costs aspects, as well as what expectations the parties are presumed to have.[81] The parties may often be presumed to expect Stockholm as the seat, but not always, and where a foreign seat is chosen the board strives to ensure that it is an arbitration-friendly jurisdiction.[82]

When Sweden has been settled on as the seat of arbitration, the Swedish arbitration law is the *lex arbitri*.[83] In accordance with the principle of party autonomy, the Arbitration Act only stipulates a few rules for the conduct of the proceedings and most provisions are non-mandatory. In practice, the parties are free to agree on the procedural rules that they find appropriate. Similarly, the starting point of the SCC Rules is that, subject to any agreement by the parties, the arbitral tribunal may conduct the arbitration in the manner it considers appropriate.[84]

[78] The SCC Rules do however take into account multi-party arbitration in the procedure for appointment of arbitrators.

[79] Article 13(4).

[80] SCC Rules Article 20(1). Note that the arbitral tribunal may after consultation with the parties conduct hearings elsewhere without impacting on the determination of the seat of arbitration: Article 20(2).

[81] Öhrström, *Stockholms Handelskammares Skiljedomsinstitut*, p. 180.

[82] Ibid.

[83] Section 46 of the Arbitration Act.

[84] SCC Rules Article 19(1).

In practice, the parties seldom make very detailed agreements on the procedure in advance of arbitral proceedings being commenced. Usually the parties subsequently manage to agree on procedural issues before or at an initial case-management conference. Otherwise, the arbitral tribunal will have to decide on the conduct of the proceedings.

11.2 Right to be heard and the right to equal treatment

A general guideline to the arbitral tribunal that is enshrined in both the SCC Rules and the Arbitration Act is that the arbitrators shall afford the parties an equal opportunity to present their case.[85]

According to the Arbitration Act, a party shall be given the chance to review all documents and other materials pertaining to the dispute that are supplied to the arbitrators by the opposing party or another person. If the parties have not agreed otherwise, an oral hearing will be held, if requested by a party. These fundamental requirements relate to a party's right to be heard and are founded on principles of legal certainty and the right to a fair trial in Article 6 of the European Convention on Human Rights.[86] These requirements set out in the Arbitration Act are mandatory and the parties may not deviate from them by agreement. If these requirements are not fulfilled, they may form grounds for setting aside an award (see Section 15 below).

Both the SCC Rules and the Arbitration Act require the arbitrators to handle the dispute in an impartial, practical and speedy manner.[87] The requirement on impartiality is strict. The practical implication is that no decision by the arbitrators shall be unduly influenced by a party affected by the decision and that both parties should, at all times, be treated equally. The requirement of impartiality binds all the arbitrators, including those nominated by parties.[88]

11.3 Efficiency of proceedings

In relation to expeditious handling of the proceedings, see, in general, Section 2 above. The SCC Rules further require the arbitral tribunal to promptly consult with the parties with a view to establishing a provisional

[85] SCC Rules Article 19(2) and Section 24 of the Arbitration Act.
[86] Government Bill 1998/99: 35, pp. 228–9 and p. 112.
[87] SCC Rules Article 19(2) and section 21 of the Arbitration Act.
[88] Government Bill 1998/99: 35, p. 83.

timetable, a copy of which shall be sent to the Secretariat of the SCC.[89] The provisional timetable may thus support the efficiency of the proceedings.

Notably, there is no general practice of 'terms of reference' in Swedish arbitration and no similar cut-off function in relation to adding new claims as the signed terms of reference have under the ICC Rules.[90] In particular, both the SCC Rules and the Arbitration Act state that the parties are free to amend or supplement their claims, counterclaims and defences at any time prior to the close of proceedings, unless the arbitral tribunal considers that it is inappropriate to allow an amendment with regard to the delay caused thereby and the prejudice to the other party.[91] However, it must be noted that a very late amendment may have costs consequences for the party introducing the amendment.[92]

11.4 Outline of proceedings

If the parties have not agreed on the conduct of the proceedings, the SCC Rules envisage the submittal of statements of claim and defence and potential additional written submissions as well as an oral hearing if either party so requests or if this is deemed appropriate by the tribunal.[93] When the tribunal is satisfied that the parties have had a reasonable opportunity to present their case, it shall declare the proceedings closed and proceed to render the award.[94] The Arbitration Act envisages a similar general progression of the proceedings.[95]

The Expedited Rules include particular rules on the conduct of the proceedings, in particular in order to streamline the proceedings. For example, the statements of claim and defence specifically have a requirement of brevity and it is stated that these documents shall be submitted within ten working days from each other.

11.5 Specifically on evidence

As a general principle, it is for the parties to present the evidence that they rely upon. If the parties have not agreed on a procedure for the taking of evidence, the SCC Rules provide that the arbitrators may order the parties to identify the documentary evidence, and the witnesses to be relied upon and

[89] SCC Rules Article 23. [90] ICC Rules of Arbitration.
[91] SCC Rules Article 25 and Section 23 of the Arbitration Act.
[92] Öhrström, *Stockholms Handelskammares Skiljedomsinstitut*, p. 194.
[93] Articles 24 and 27. [94] Articles 34 and 36. [95] Sections 23 and 27.

the circumstances that are to be proven by that evidence. The arbitrators may, upon request, order a party to produce documents that are relevant to the outcome of the case.[96] Testimony of witnesses and experts may be submitted in the form of signed witness statements, but such persons that a party intends to rely on shall also attend the hearing for oral examination unless the parties agree otherwise.[97] The SCC Rules make clear that it is for the arbitrators to determine the admissibility, relevance, materiality and weight of the evidence presented.[98]

The Arbitration Act also clarifies that it is the parties, and not the arbitrators, that identify and present the evidence they rely upon. However, the arbitrators may call expert witnesses, unless both parties object. In addition, the arbitrators may refuse to admit evidence if they find it manifestly irrelevant or if it is presented in an untimely manner. In practice, arbitrators rarely refuse new evidence.[99]

It is not uncommon in international arbitrations that the parties refer to and the arbitrators use as guidance the IBA Rules on the Taking of Evidence when dealing with particular evidence issues.[100]

11.6 Applicable law

According to the SCC Rules, the tribunal shall decide the merits of the dispute on the basis of the laws or rules of law agreed upon by the parties or, in the absence of such agreement, the laws or rules of law that it considers to be most appropriate. Hence, the Rules adopt the so-called *voie directe* method.[101]

The Arbitration Act is silent on the issue of applicable law and there is no explicit rule as to what the arbitrators should do in the absence of party choice.

12 Confidentiality

Commercial parties often assume that arbitration proceedings entail confidentiality due to their non-public nature. However, the Arbitration Act does not contain any provisions on confidentiality.

[96] Articles 26(2)–(3) and 28(1). [97] Article 28(2)–(3). [98] Article 26(1).

[99] Section 25, see also C. Lundblad, *Arbitration World 3rd edition. Sweden* (2010), available at: www.europeanlawyer.co.uk/referencebooks_20_321.html.

[100] See www.ibanet.org/Publications/publications_IBA_guides_and_free_materials.aspx.

[101] Article 22.

The issue of whether a party is obliged to keep arbitration confidential has been dealt with by the Supreme Court in the well-known *Bulbank* case. A company that was a party in an arbitral proceeding had disclosed a separate award issued by the arbitral tribunal to a legal journal for publication. Confronted with the question as to whether a party should be deemed to be bound by confidentiality, the Supreme Court ruled that the parties – as long as they have not agreed otherwise – do not incur any duty of confidentiality sanctioned by liability for damages.[102] Thus, confidentiality is not an implied term of an arbitration agreement under Swedish law and party autonomy entails that the parties must agree specifically on confidentiality.

Arbitrators are deemed to be bound by a duty of confidentiality due to the nature of the mandate that they have undertaken. According to the SCC Rules, the SCC and the arbitral tribunal are bound to maintain the confidentiality of the arbitration and the subsequent award unless otherwise agreed by the parties.[103] Counsel who are members of the Swedish Bar Association are, in addition, bound by the deontological rules of confidentiality.[104]

13 The role of the institution

The SCC plays a vital role as a facilitative support structure for arbitration under its auspices. The SCC can, according to the Rules, assist in deciding on the number and appointment of the arbitrators, on the consolidation of arbitrations and in monitoring the time limit for the rendering of the award.[105] In addition, it can decide on whether or not it manifestly lacks jurisdiction.[106] Significantly, the Institute also determines the costs of the arbitration and has a Schedule of Costs to which it adheres.[107] The SCC finally plays a significant role in shaping the arbitration climate and debate in Sweden and has continued in recent years to take a proactive role in the discussion on current themes in arbitration.

[102] *Bulgarian Foreign Trade Bank Ltd (Bulbank)* v. *A.I. Trade Finance Inc (AIT)*, reported in the *NJA* (2000), p. 538.

[103] SCC Rules Article 46, Expedited Rules Article 46.

[104] See www.advokatsamfundet.se/Advokatsamfundet-engelska/Rules-and-regulations/.

[105] See, *inter alia*, Articles 9 and 37. [106] Articles 9–10. [107] Article 43 and Schedule III.

14 The possibility of excluding the courts' review of the award's validity

If neither party is domiciled or has its place of business in Sweden, they may, under certain conditions, exclude or limit the right to apply for setting aside an award but not the right to apply for invalidity of the award (see Section 15 below for the distinction between the types of challenges). For such an exclusion agreement to be valid, the law requires that neither party is domiciled in Sweden, that the parties' relationship is of a commercial nature and that the exclusion agreement is made in writing in addition to being clear and explicit.[108] See Section 15 regarding challenges to awards.

15 Grounds for invalidity of the award

There are two main types of challenges against arbitral awards under Swedish law: (a) a challenge on grounds for invalidity and (b) a challenge on grounds for setting aside.

An award may be challenged on grounds of invalidity if:[109]

(a) the subject matter of the dispute was not arbitrable;
(b) the award is clearly incompatible with public policy; or
(c) the award is not made in writing or has not been signed by the majority of the arbitrators.

The right to apply for invalidity cannot be waived by agreement. A challenge based on the grounds for invalidity has no time limit.

An award given in Sweden can also be challenged by a party and set aside by the court if:[110]

(a) the arbitration agreement is invalid;
(b) the arbitrators have exceeded their mandate;
(c) the arbitral proceedings should not have taken place in Sweden;
(d) there were irregularities in the appointment of an arbitrator;
(e) there is a lack of capacity or impartiality of an arbitrator; or
(f) there are other procedural irregularities that may be presumed to have influenced the outcome of the case.

A challenge based on the grounds for setting aside must be brought within three months from the date upon which the party received the award.

[108] Section 51. [109] Section 33. [110] Section 34.

A challenge shall be submitted to the Court of Appeal within the jurisdiction of the seat of arbitration and, where the place is not stated in the award, the action may be heard by the Svea Court of Appeal.[111]

The issue of international jurisdiction of the Swedish courts to deal with challenge applications became the topic of some controversy following a decision by the Svea Court of Appeal in 2009. The Svea Court of Appeal found that it did not have jurisdiction on the grounds that the case did not show a sufficiently strong connection to Sweden. None of the parties in the arbitration were Swedish. The award indicated that Stockholm was the place of arbitration and that Swedish arbitration law was the *lex arbitri*, but the main hearing had been held in Paris by a sole arbitrator from England.[112] The much-criticized judgment has been addressed and dealt with fairly recently by the Supreme Court in its reasoning in another case. In the *RosInvest* case, the Supreme Court confirmed that if the parties have agreed on the place of arbitration, it is irrelevant if hearings are conducted elsewhere, whether the arbitrators are foreign or whether or not the contract in dispute has any connection to Sweden.[113]

In addition to invalidity and setting aside, where the arbitrators have closed the proceedings without having ruled on the substantive issues submitted to them – but instead made a negative jurisdiction decision – the award may be reviewed by a court upon application by a party within three months from the date upon which the party received the award.[114] This separate type of challenge is considered as an ordinary appeal.

The other party will be heard on a challenge application for invalidity, setting aside or review of a negative jurisdiction decision mentioned above. The length of the proceedings varies depending on the circumstances of the case and the capacity of the particular court. A court may, under certain circumstances, stay its proceedings for a certain period of time in order to provide the arbitrators with an opportunity to resume the arbitral proceedings or to take some other measure which, in the opinion of the arbitrators, will eliminate the ground for the invalidity or setting aside.

As a general principle, the Swedish Courts observe the finality of an arbitral award and apply the rules on the challenge of arbitral awards

[111] Section 43.
[112] Svea Court of Appeal, Case T 1038–05, *Titan Corporation* v. *Alcatel CIT S.A.*
[113] *Russian Federation* v. *RosInvest Co UK Ltd* reported in the *NJA* (2010), p. 508.
[114] Section 36 of the Arbitration Act.

restrictively.[115] Based on various sources, it appears that the perception of the users is supported by findings in relation to the relatively low number of successful challenges.[116]

If a party is successful in obtaining leave to appeal to the Supreme Court over the Court of Appeal's decision, the length of the proceedings will be extended. Leave to appeal can only be granted by the Court of Appeal itself on the single ground that the case is important as a matter of precedent.[117]

16 Conclusion

Based on the history and tradition of international arbitration in Sweden, in particular under the auspices of the SCC, Sweden has a solid standing as a neutral and popular venue for international arbitration. In addition, the fairly recent reforms of the SCC Rules and the various initiatives among the Swedish arbitration community show that it meets the demands of modern arbitration practice. Finally, having a procedural culture that in many respects can be seen as a hybrid between the classic common and civil law traditions Sweden can be considered particularly well suited for international arbitration.

[115] This concords with the aims of the Arbitration Act; 1998/99: 35, pp. 142, 148 and 234.

[116] There have been roughly one hundred challenges of arbitral awards in Sweden, with a rough success rate of some 6 to 10 per cent during the past ten years according to research by N. Elofsson, 'Klandrade skiljedomar mellan 1999 och 2009 – särskilt om skiljemäns uppdragsöverskridande och handläggningsfel', *Juridisk Tidskrift*, 3 (2010/11), pp. 732–46 and C. Cederberg and O. Ljungholm, 'Challenge of Swedish Arbitral Awards' (forthcoming). See also Hobér, *International Commercial Arbitration in Sweden*, pp. 456–66, for a list of cases.

[117] Section 43 of the Arbitration Act.

14

Arbitration under the Swiss Rules

DANIEL WEHRLI AND MARCO STACHER

1 Introduction

Switzerland enjoys a long tradition of hosting international arbitrations. Arbitration, in turn, is recognized as a preferred way for dispute resolution in Swiss legal culture: the Swiss legal community strives to set up an effective environment to conduct and host arbitrations – this has led to enacting a new flexible *lex arbitri* for international arbitrations[1] and to the Swiss Rules of International Arbitration; that is, the unified institutional arbitration rules of the Chambers of Commerce and Industry of Basel, Berne, Geneva, Lausanne, Lugano, Neuenburg and Zurich (the 'Swiss Rules' and 'Chambers', respectively).

The Chambers have provided arbitration services from as early as 1868, 1871 and 1911 in the cases of the Basel, Geneva and Zurich Chambers and have based the Swiss Rules on the UNCITRAL Arbitration Rules of 1976 ('UNCITRAL Rules 1976'). The drafters were in a position to both benefit from the experience of the Chambers as well as to rely on the well-tested UNCITRAL Rules 1976. Due to the importance that these rules had for the Swiss Rules, the Chambers closely monitored the revision of the UNCITRAL Rules 1976, which has led to the new rules of 2010 ('UNCITRAL Rules 2010'). Since the Swiss Rules had proved to work well, the Chambers, however, revised the Swiss Rules by aligning them to the UNCITRAL Rules 2010 only insofar as was appropriate and necessary to ensure that they remain easily accessible for users all over the world. The revised Swiss Rules entered into effect on 1 June 2012 and apply to all arbitral proceedings initiated thereafter unless otherwise agreed by the parties. Therefore, this contribution focuses on the revised version and does not intend to compare the revised to the old version.

[1] See Section 2 below.

Despite their name, the Swiss Rules apply on a global level: (a) the parties may choose to have the seat of their arbitration outside Switzerland, thus embedding it in another legal framework than that of the Swiss *lex arbitri*. The drafters did not amend the UNCITRAL Rules 1976 in a way that would create conflicts between the Swiss Rules and the different *leges arbitri*. They limited themselves to the changes that were necessary to transform the UNCITRAL Rules 1976, which are designed for *ad hoc* arbitrations, into a set of institutional rules, and to refining and aligning them to modern practice. The Swiss Rules are, in particular, well compatible with *leges arbitri* that are based on the UNCITRAL Model Law. (b) The parties are not required to appoint Swiss nationals as arbitrators or to choose Swiss law to govern their dispute. Rather, the framework provided by the Swiss Rules leaves the parties with the leeway to be able to structure their arbitration as they deem fit, and the administration by the Swiss Chambers is soft, non-bureaucratic and independent. The Chambers are, in particular, not related to the ASA (the Swiss Arbitration Association), which is an association that aims to promote arbitration and one that does not administrate arbitrations.

The Swiss Rules have so far stood the test of practice: between 2009 and 2011, an average of approximately 100 new cases was initiated per year with over 75% of the parties coming from outside Switzerland.[2]

Certain special features of the Swiss Rules – for example, the availability of an expedited procedure and non-bureaucratic administration – are perceived as particular benefits. The Chambers' motto for administration is 'as much as necessary, as little as possible'. The Chambers, for example, assist in appointing the arbitral tribunal, if necessary; they thus ensure that the arbitration takes place as agreed between the parties. The Chambers, however, do not restrict the parties' freedom in choosing their arbitrators by way of a list of arbitrators. Likewise, the power of the Chambers to interfere with and thus delay an arbitration is limited. The arbitrators and the parties are in charge of the time frame of their arbitration and the way in which they conduct it. The Swiss Rules, for example, allow the parties and the arbitral tribunal to define the mandatory provisional timetable (article 15(3) Swiss Rules) as they deem fit and do not require the drawing up of terms of reference, as in an ICC arbitration (but of course, the Swiss Rules do allow for this). Likewise, the scrutiny of the award focuses on the assessment and apportionment of the costs. This logically increases the

[2] See www.swissarbitration.org, subsection '*News*', '*Statistics*'.

efficiency of the process and results in shorter proceedings than under other sets of institutional rules.[3]

The special features that distinguish the Swiss Rules from other sets of arbitration rules will be discussed below. Before turning to these special features, it is, however, worthwhile briefly addressing the Swiss *lex arbitri*. While the parties are perfectly free to seat a Swiss Rules arbitration outside Switzerland, practice suggests that Switzerland is the preferred host state. It is therefore appropriate first to provide an overview of the most basic cornerstones of the Swiss *lex arbitri* and its interaction with the Swiss Rules.

2 The Swiss *lex arbitri* and its interaction with the Swiss Rules

2.1 *Introduction*

The Swiss Rules and the applicable *lex arbitri* interact in three ways: (a) the Swiss Rules (like the UNCITRAL Rules 1976) do not contain provisions on issues which are, as a rule, addressed by the *leges arbitri* in a mandatory way (e.g., formal and substantive validity of the arbitration agreement, arbitrability, support of the arbitration by state courts), thus minimizing the risk of conflicts with the applicable *lex arbitri*; (b) for issues where *leges arbitri*, as a rule, afford discretion to the parties (e.g., for the mechanism of appointing the arbitrators), the Swiss Rules contain specific rules, which supersede the non-mandatory provisions of the *lex arbitri*; and (c) the Swiss Rules repeat certain provisions that *leges arbitri*, as a rule, contain, since they are deemed fundamentally important and are undisputed (e.g., the independence and impartiality of arbitrators).

Switzerland distinguishes between a *lex arbitri* for international arbitrations (Chapter 12 of the Federal Private International Law Statute: 'PILS')[4] and a *lex arbitri* for domestic arbitrations in effect since 1 January 2011 (Part 3 of the Federal Code of Civil Procedure: 'CCP').[5]

3 The average length of a Swiss Rules arbitration is a little less than one year, while an average ICC arbitration is around 16 to 24 months (Gabrielle Nater-Bass, 'How to Work with the Swiss Rules: The Counsel's Perspective', in Rainer Füeg (ed.), *The Swiss Rules of International Arbitration: Five Years of Experience* (Basel: Swiss Chambers' Court of Arbitration and Mediation, 2009), p. 57; Michael W. Bühler and Fabian von Schlabrendorff, '10 Jahre ICC-Schiedsordnung 1998: Ein Blick zurück, zwei Blicke nach vorne', *Schieds VZ* (1/2009), 26 *et seq.* at 34.

4 An English translation is available at www.swissarbitration.org

5 An English translation is available in Bernhard Berger and Franz Kellerhals, *International and Domestic Arbitration in Switzerland*, 2nd edn (Berne: Stämpfli Verlag AG, 2010), pp. 559 *et seq.* The CCP, a federal law, replaces the Concordat on Arbitration, which had been concluded

The PILS applies if the seat of the arbitration is in Switzerland and if at least one of the parties to the arbitration did not have its domicile or habitual residence in Switzerland when signing the arbitration agreement.[6] If the latter condition is not met, the CCP will apply. Since the CCP is only relevant in purely domestic settings, the rest of this contribution focuses on the PILS.

The Swiss Rules and the PILS are both easily accessible.[7] The controlling language of the Swiss Rules is English and they are translated into various other languages;[8] moreover, the commentaries of the Swiss Rules are in English.[9] The PILS is also translated into English and the case law of the Swiss Supreme Court on the PILS (and any other statute) is available online.[10] Since 2007, most decisions on the PILS have been translated into English by Michele Patocchi/Matthias Scherer in the *Swiss International Arbitration Law Reports* (Juris Publishing).

2.2 Main features of the Swiss lex arbitri

2.2.1 Spirit of the Swiss *lex arbitri*

Various provisions of the PILS show a spirit favourable to arbitration: the PILS provides for a wide definition of arbitrability, only sets minimal standards for the formal validity of arbitration agreements, generally favours substantive validity[11] and affords the parties with discretion as to how they wish to conduct their arbitration and appoint the arbitral tribunal. The PILS, in essence, limits itself to providing for certain safeguards.

First, the PILS ensures that freedom does not entail inequity; the arbitrators are required to be independent from the parties and the tribunal must afford

between all Swiss Cantons and which was applicable to domestic arbitrations only, after the enactment of the PILS and until the end of 2010.

6 Article 176 PILS; Article 353 CCP.

7 A list of articles and books on the Swiss Rules is published on www.sccam.org/sa/en/publications.php

8 Namely, into the three Swiss official languages of French, German and Italian and also into Russian, Spanish, Chinese, Croatian, Arabic, Turkish, Portuguese and Czech. These translations are – like the English text – available at www.swissarbitration.org.

9 See Tobias Zuberbühler, Christoph Müller and Philipp Habegger (eds.), *Swiss Rules of International Arbitration, Commentary* (Zurich: Schulthess Juristische Medien AG, 2005; second edition to be published in 2013) and the *Handbook on Arbitration in Switzerland* edited by Manuel Arroyo to be published in 2013.

10 www.bger.ch. The decisions of the Swiss Supreme Court are referred to as 'DFT' below.

11 By providing that it is sufficient if the requirements under one out of three jurisdictions are met (article 178(2) PILS).

due process to them (equal protection, right to be heard).[12] Second, the PILS ensures that valid arbitration agreements are implemented and that the lack of coercive powers of an arbitral tribunal does not hinder the proper conduct of an arbitration.[13] Third, the PILS provides for fall-back solutions, which apply in case the parties fail to make use of the discretion afforded by the PILS. If the parties, for example, (a) are unable to agree on how to structure the arbitration, the arbitral tribunal is empowered to take the necessary decisions in their stead;[14] and (b) if the parties did not choose the law governing their dispute, the tribunal is instructed to apply the law having the closest connection to the dispute.[15]

The underlying pattern of the PILS thus is (a) to leave discretion to the parties and (b) to only interfere when required, either in the interest of justice or to ensure the smooth conduct of an arbitration.[16]

2.2.2 Validity of the arbitration agreement

A valid arbitration agreement is the basis of any arbitration.[17] If the arbitration is seated in Switzerland, the arbitration agreement must satisfy three conditions.

First, there needs to be a meeting of minds under (a) Swiss law, or (b) the law governing the dispute between the parties, or (c) the law chosen by the parties to (specifically) apply to the arbitration agreement. By referring to the validity under any of these three national laws, article 178(2) PILS plainly favours the validity of arbitration agreements. The limit to this *favor arbitri* lies in the rule that the prerequisites of one of the three jurisdictions listed in article 178(2) PILS must be complied with in full: the parties cannot cherry-pick, by, for example, referring to the rules of representation under one jurisdiction and the rules on unconsciousness under another.[18]

Second, the meeting of minds must be to bindingly submit certain disputes to arbitration.[19] The arbitration agreement must, in other

[12] Articles 180 and 182 PILS.

[13] To this effect, a party may resort to Swiss state courts to appoint the tribunal in case its counter-party refuses to cooperate (article 179 PILS), and the arbitral tribunal may, if necessary, request the Swiss state courts to assist them in the taking of evidence (article 184 PILS).

[14] Article 182 PILS. [15] Article 187 PILS.

[16] For the role of state courts see Sections 2.2.5 and 2.2.7 below.

[17] See, e.g., article V(1)(a) of the New York Convention of 1958.

[18] Berger and Kellerhals, *International and Domestic Arbitration in Switzerland*, N 372.

[19] DFT 130 III 66 E.3.1; Jean-François Poudret and Sébastien Besson, *Comparative Law of International Arbitration*, 2nd edn (Zurich: Schulthess Juristische Medien AG, 2007), N 155; see also Werner Wenger and Christoph Müller, in Heinrich Honsell *et al.* (eds.),

words, define its scope; that is, the parties bound by it and the disputes covered by it. A wording defining 'any and all disputes arising out of or in connection with the present agreement'[20] as the scope of the arbitration agreement is perfectly valid, whereas a reference to all disputes 'arising out of the business transaction between the parties' is considered overly broad and invalid by part of the doctrine.[21]

Third, article 178(1) PILS provides that the arbitration agreement[22] must be made in writing, by telegram, telex, telecopier or any other means of communication that permits it to be evidenced by text. This form requirement is mandatory in that the parties cannot replace it with standards that are more liberal;[23] the parties are, however, free to set up a more strict form requirement.[24] The prerequisites of article 178(1) PILS are met if the claimant is in a position to prove that both parties, in writing, agreed to arbitrate.[25] This

Basler Kommentar, Internationales Privatrecht, 2nd edn (Basel: Helbing Lichtenhahn Verlag, 2007), N 30 to Art. 178.

20 Non-contractual claims (torts, unjust enrichment) are within the scope of such an arbitration agreement (a) if the factual bases of the contractual and the non-contractual claims are the same, and (b) if the facts of the case also give rise to a contractual claim (Berger and Kellerhals, *International and Domestic Arbitration in Switzerland*, N 473). Two reasonable parties must, in such circumstances, be presumed to wish to submit both types of disputes to the same tribunal, rather than to split their case and so incur additional costs. The case law of the Swiss Supreme Court indeed endorses that the scope of disputes covered by an arbitration agreement is construed in a wide manner (DFT 116 Ia 56 E.3b).

21 Wenger and Müller, *Basler Kommentar*, N 34 to Art. 178; the better view, however, is to hold such language valid, too, as it does enable one to define the scope of the arbitration agreement and does not prejudice either party (see also Berger and Kellerhals, *International and Domestic Arbitration in Switzerland*, N 286).

22 If the form requirement was met when the arbitration agreement was initially agreed upon, it is, as a rule, binding on a successor of one of the parties, even if the successor does itself not satisfy the form requirement (DFT 4C.40/2003 E.4; 4P.115/2003 E.5; see also Philipp Habegger, 'Extension of Arbitration Agreements to Non-signatories and Requirements of Form', *ASA Bulletin* (22/2004), 410; *contra* Jean-François Poudret, 'Un statut privilegié pour l'extension de l'arbitrage aux tiers?', *ASA Bulletin*, 22 (2004), passim). Likewise, if the arbitration agreement is extended to a third party by means of piercing the corporate veil, the party whose veil is pierced is bound, without itself satisfying the form requirement (i.e. it is met if the party with which it is grouped agreed to arbitration in writing; DFT 134 III 565 E.3.2; 129 III 727; 4P.48/2005 E.3.4.1).

23 Berger and Kellerhals, *International and Domestic Arbitration in Switzerland*, N 394; Poudret and Besson, *Comparative Law of International Arbitration*, N 193.

24 Since the arbitration agreement is a stand-alone agreement and separable from the contract containing the arbitration agreement, stricter form requirements for that contract do not apply to the arbitration agreement (Wenger and Müller, *Basler Kommentar*, N 12 to Art. 178), unless evidence shows that this was intended.

25 The form requirement of article 178(1) PILS is limited to (a) the *essentialia* of an arbitration agreement, i.e. that an arbitral tribunal shall bindingly decide certain disputes. Other agreements between the Parties, e.g., on the seat of the arbitration or procedural issues, such as the

does not require that the parties express their agreement in the same document or that the declarations they exchange[26] are signed; it solely requires a showing of written communications (be it by e-mail or in any other way).

2.2.3 Arbitrability

Any dispute of a financial nature may be brought to arbitration.[27] Such a 'financial nature' does not only exist in the case where the claimant requests that the defendant be ordered to pay money; rather, the criterion of article 177(1) PILS is satisfied in any case where the claimant has some sort of financial interest; such interest, for example, exists when a claimant shareholder requests to hold and declare a resolution taken at the occasion of a general assembly to be null and void – the award of the tribunal may impact the value of the company and, indirectly, that of the claimant's shareholding.

The parties may, if the criterion is met, also submit sports matters (including doping), which are generally considered as being financial in nature,[28] to arbitration, as well as patent, employment and tenancy law disputes. There are, however, certain limits – the parties can, in particular, not submit disputes to arbitration that are, from a Swiss perspective, not to be dealt with by the judiciary, but by administrative authorities. The cases in which this may be an issue are rare, and, for example,[29] would encompass an arbitration on the transfer of Swiss real estate: while the arbitral tribunal is perfectly competent to be able to decide which party holds a valid title and to order that a transfer must be made, it

language of proceedings, need not comply with article 178(1) PILS and are binding even if made orally. The form requirement is, moreover, limited to (b) the agreement between the initial parties: if one of the parties assigns a claim to which the arbitration agreement applies, the party acquiring this claim is bound by the arbitration agreement even if the transaction does not satisfy the form requirement under article 178(1) PILS (DFT 119 II 394 E.3a; Wenger and Müller, *Basler Kommentar*, N 16 to Art. 178).

26 See, however, Poudret and Besson, *Comparative Law of International Arbitration*, N 193, according to whom an '*exchange of documents*' is not required.

27 Article 177 PILS.

28 The best-known sport arbitrations taking place in Switzerland are those conducted by the Tribunal Arbitral du Sport, known as 'TAS' or 'CAS', with its seat in Lausanne, Switzerland (see www.tas-cas.org).

29 Likewise, the parties cannot request an arbitral tribunal to hold and declare that a certain contract does not violate applicable antitrust laws; the parties cannot circumvent competent antitrust authorities to request a declaration that would not only bind the parties, but anyone else potentially affected by the contract at stake. This does not, of course, bar the tribunal from assessing antitrust matters as preliminary issues; for example, when the claimant requests money under a contract and the defendant alleges that the contract is null and void as it violates applicable antitrust laws.

cannot itself effect this transfer because entering it into the real-estate registry is reserved for state authorities. As a rule, however, article 177(1) PILS defines the scope of arbitrable matters in a broad manner and the issue hardly ever gives rise to dispute.

2.2.4 Interim measures and their enforceability

An arbitral tribunal is, by law, authorized to order provisional or conservatory measures unless the parties have otherwise agreed (article 183(1) PILS). The power of an arbitral tribunal is not exclusive, but complementary to those of a state court:[30] if a state court judge is, under applicable laws, competent to order interim measures, the parties have the choice of applying either to the arbitral tribunal or to the state court.[31] In the latter case, it is well settled and undisputed that the party requesting interim relief in a state court does not forgo its right to bring the dispute to arbitration.[32]

Article 183 PILS does not limit an arbitral tribunal to ordering interim measures that are available to a Swiss state court judge; the rules of civil procedure have no bearing on international arbitration. A recent landmark decision of the Swiss Supreme Court[33] suggests that the interim relief available under article 183 PILS is not limited to (a) orders defining how the parties are to conduct their business in relation to the matter in dispute during the arbitration and (b) orders securing enforcement of a future award,[34] but (c) that

30 See also article 10 PILS.

31 This raises two questions; namely, (a) whether a party requesting interim measures may turn both to the state court judge and the arbitral tribunal, and (b) whether the applicant is entitled to apply to the arbitral tribunal after the state court judge has denied its request (and vice versa). We submit that neither should be the case: the parallel jurisdiction aims to enable the applicant to choose in which forum he wishes to lodge his request, the state court being particularly attractive in case the arbitral tribunal is not yet constituted (Berger and Kellerhals, *International and Domestic Arbitration in Switzerland*, N 1125). Allowing the applicant to file the same request twice (and thus to have two bites at the apple), however, would go beyond that purpose. The right view is, therefore, to only allow a second application after the circumstances have materially changed as compared to the basis on which the first decision was taken.

32 Sébastien Besson, *Arbitrage international et mesures provisoires* (Zurich: Schulthess Polygraphischer Verlag Zürich, 1998), N 228.

33 DFT 4A_582/2009.

34 While this appears to provide unfettered authority to the arbitral tribunal as to how it ensures enforcement, we submit that an arbitral tribunal cannot freeze assets, the exception being specific goods, e.g., the objects of a sales agreement, whose transfer is requested and which therefore form part of the matter in dispute (Gerhard Walter,

they may potentially include orders that preliminarily grant the relief requested.[35]

The arbitral tribunal will – as a rule – hear the opposing party before issuing interim measures. In case of extreme urgency, *ex parte* proceedings are, however, admissible. It goes without saying that the opposing party in such a case must be heard as soon as possible and that the order must be quashed if that party's submission demonstrates it is unwarranted.

The PILS does not detail what conditions must be met for interim relief to be ordered. Failing an agreement of the parties, an arbitral tribunal may, in particular, take into account whether the following criteria are met: (a) *prima facie* competence;[36] (b) connection between the matter in dispute and the interim measure requested;[37] (c) likelihood of success; that is, whether a summary assessment of the case shows that the applicant is likely to succeed on the matter in dispute; (d) urgency; that is, whether the applicant would suffer irreparable harm if it were not awarded interim relief;[38] and (e) if the interests of the applicant outweigh the interests of the opposing party.

Wolfgang Bosch and Jürgen Brönnimann, *Internationale Schiedsgerichtsbarkeit in der Schweiz: Kommentar zu Kapitel 12 des IPR-Gesetzes* (Berne: Verlag Stämpfli & Cie AG, 1991), pp. 130 *et seq.*; Andreas Bucher, *Die neue internationale Schiedsgerichtsbarkeit in der Schweiz* (Basel: Helbing & Lichtenhahn, 1989), p. 81; *contra* Stephen V. Berti, in Heinrich Honsell, *et al.* (eds.), *Basler Kommentar, Internationales Privatrecht*, 2nd edn (Basel: Helbing Lichtenhahn Verlag, 2007), N 7 to Art. 183).

35 Certain legal writers submit that an arbitral tribunal may, in addition to the types of interim measures described above, take evidence in an expedited manner as a special form of interim relief if there is a risk that the means of evidence in question is no longer available when evidence taking is scheduled to take place (Berger and Kellerhals, *International and Domestic Arbitration in Switzerland*, N 1140; Besson, *Arbitrage international*, N 444; Pierre Lalive, Jean-François Poudret and Claude Reymond, *Le droit de l'arbitrage interne et international en Suisse* (Lausanne: Editions Payot Lausanne, 1989), N 6 to Art. 183; Thomas Rüede and Reimer Hadenfeldt, *Schweizerisches Schiedsgerichtsrecht*, 2nd edn (Zurich: Schulthess Polygraphischer Verlag Zürich, 1993), p. 253). While an arbitral tribunal is certainly entitled to do so, the basis is not its power to issue interim measures, but to define the conduct of the arbitration failing an agreement of the parties (article 182 PILS).

36 Given the time pressure inherent when an application for interim relief is filed, the arbitral tribunal is not required to fully review whether it has jurisdiction for the case submitted to it, but should assess this issue in a preliminary manner (Georg von Segesser, 'Vorsorgliche Massnahmen in Internationalen Schiedsprozess', *ASA Bulletin* (25/2007), 477).

37 Walter, Bosch and Brönnimann, *Internationale Schiedsgerichtsbarkeit*, p. 131.

38 Berti, *Basler Kommentar*, N 7 and 8 to Art. 183; Walther Habscheid, 'Einstweiliger Rechtsschutz durch Schiedsgerichte nach dem schweizerischen Gesetz über das Internationale Privatrecht (IPRG)', *IPRax* (1989), 135. Additionally, the arbitral tribunal may require the applicant party to deposit security in cases where the opposing party suffers damage from the interim measure (article 183(3) PILS).

An arbitral tribunal has no coercive powers and, therefore, cannot enforce the interim relief it issues. Yet, if the opposing party should not comply, the arbitral tribunal and the applicant party[39] may request assistance of the state courts at the seat of the arbitration or at the Swiss place where the interim measure is to be enforced.[40] Additionally, the Swiss state courts will ask foreign state courts for judicial assistance, if required.

2.2.5 Support of state courts

Arbitral tribunals seated in Switzerland cannot hold a party in contempt of court when it does not comply with the arbitral tribunal's orders. The PILS balances this lack of coercive power by providing for judicial assistance by state courts. This assistance is set up as 'support', not as 'interference'; there is no basis for a Swiss state court to interfere with the conduct of an on-going arbitration, be it *sua sponte* or upon the request of one of the parties.

The state courts at the seat of the arbitration are generally competent to render any support that may be required for the proper conduct of the arbitration.[41] They may, for example, impose contempt-of-court measures if a party refuses to comply with a procedural order of the arbitral tribunal. Most importantly, an arbitral tribunal and/or one of the parties with its consent may petition for their support in taking evidence.[42]

If the state courts at the seat of the arbitration are unable to render assistance – for example, because a witness who refuses to testify lives outside Switzerland – they will request judicial assistance on behalf of the arbitral tribunal. The PILS thus provides the arbitral tribunal with a contact point that will, upon a proper request, redirect requests for assistance to the state courts best suited to provide assistance. This

[39] Berti, *Basler Kommentar*, N 16 to Art. 183; Poudret and Besson, *Comparative Law of International Arbitration*, N 637; *contra* Berger and Kellerhals, *International and Domestic Arbitration in Switzerland*, 7, N 1161.

[40] Berger and Kellerhals, *International and Domestic Arbitration in Switzerland*, N 1161.

[41] Article 185 PILS.

[42] Article 184(2) PILS. The state courts are, in such a case, required to render assistance without assessing whether the arbitral tribunal is competent or whether the evidence at issue is relevant for the future award. They may only refuse assistance if (a) the petition is made by one of the parties without the consent of the tribunal, or in cases where (b) the arbitral tribunal would be in a position to take the evidence at issue and petitions assistance for another reason, e.g., to save costs.

service does, of course, not bar the arbitral tribunal from lodging petitions for assistance directly with a foreign court.

2.2.6 *Ex officio* powers in the event of bribery, money laundering and fraud

Arbitration is adversarial and not inquisitorial: in principle, an arbitral tribunal has no *ex officio* power to examine severe illegalities amounting to a violation of public policy; that is, it can only do so if one of the parties invokes illegality and sufficiently substantiates its factual basis. Nevertheless, while recognizing that an arbitral tribunal is primarily a body adjudicating a civil dispute and not a body with investigatory powers of a public prosecutor,[43] an arbitral tribunal must confer with the parties if it becomes aware of possible bribery, money laundering or misappropriation of state funds. It must, 'to the extent possible obtain the necessary evidence'[44] by inviting the parties to further address the factual background and legal aspects of the possibly illegal act or transaction.[45]

[43] See Bernardo M. Cremades and David J. A. Cairns, 'Transnational Public Policy in International Arbitral Decision-making: The cases of Bribery, Money Laundering and Fraud', in Kristine Karsten and Andrew Berkely (eds.), *ICC Dossiers, Arbitration, Money Laundering, Corruption and Fraud* (Paris: ICC Publishing S.A., 2003), pp. 65 *et seq.*

[44] See Allan Philip, 'Arbitration – Money Laundering, Corruption and Fraud: The Role of the Tribunals', in Kristine Karsten and Andrew Berkely (eds.), *ICC Dossiers, Arbitration, Money Laundering, Corruption and Fraud* (Paris: ICC Publishing S.A., 2003), p. 153; Anne-Catherine Hahn, 'Schweizer Schiedsgerichte und der internationale Kampf gegen Korruption' (5/2010), *SZW/RSDA*, 388 at fn. 47 with reference to FT 132 III 389, published also in *ASA Bulletin* (2009), pp. 501 *et seq.* and commented on by François Knöpfler in 'Jurisprudence suisse en matière d'arbitrage international', *SZIER*, 1 (2007), 89; Matthias Scherer, 'Beweisfragen bei Korruptionsfällen vor internationalen Schiedsgerichten', *ASA Bulletin* (4/2001), 689–90; Pierre Tercier, 'La corruption et le droit des contrats', *Sem Jud*, II (1999), 279.

[45] On the subject in general, see the ICC publication referred to above in fn. 43; Hahn, 'Schweizer Schiedsgerichte'; Richard Kreindler, 'Die internationale Investitionsschiedsgerichtsbarkeit und die Korruption: Eine alte Herausforderung mit neuen Antworten', *Schieds VZ*, 1 (2010), 2 *et seq.*; Antonio Rigozzi and Elisabeth Leimbacher, 'The Swiss Supreme Court Refits the Frigates: ICC Award Set Aside After More than Thirteen Years', *Journal of International Arbitration*, 27(2010), 307 *et seq.*; Richard H. Kreindler, 'Schiedsgerichte und Rechtsverstösse der Vertragsparteien: Das für die Beurteilung von Rechtsverletzungen anzuwendende Recht', in Birgit Bachmann *et al.* (eds.), *Grenzüberschreitungen, Beiträge zum Internationalen Verfahrensrecht und zur Schiedsgerichtsbarkeit, Festschrift für Peter Schlosser zum 70. Geburtstag* (Tübingen: Mohr Siebeck, 2005), pp. 429 *et seq.*; Noradèle Radjai, 'Switzerland, Where There's Smoke, There's Fire? Proving Illegality in International Arbitration', *Arbitration*

If the respondent invokes illegality and requests that the claim be dismissed based on this argument, the arbitral tribunal may do so without infringing the general rule that its decision should be within the parties' prayers for relief.[46] If, however, the parties conspire in order to get an enforceable award for money laundering or other illegal purposes, the arbitral tribunal should not render support and may have to step down.[47]

A prime example of disputes where a possible violation of public policy is invoked is service agreements. When assessing the evidence, the arbitral tribunal may conclude that the absence of plausible evidence establishing that relevant services have been provided is an indication that the agreement is a scam and/or that the fee paid thereunder is designed for bribery or for laundering illegal funds.[48]

If there is suspicion of illegality, the allocation of the burden of proof is difficult. In our view, it may, for example, be justified to hold that the burden of proof for the genuineness of services is with the party alleging that proper services have been rendered.

The Swiss Supreme Court has confirmed the basics of the above-described principles and stated that an arbitral tribunal may also decide, as a preliminary issue, on violations of foreign public or criminal law.[49] The Swiss Supreme Court may further remand an arbitral award to the arbitral tribunal, if a party in a petition for revision submits new evidence supporting the illegality of the nature described.[50]

2.2.7 Annulment and revision of awards

The Swiss *lex arbitri* provides for two types of recourses against an arbitral award, which are both lodged with the Swiss Supreme Court as a sole instance: (a) an action to annul an arbitral award, which must be lodged within 30 days after the award is rendered; and (b) a petition for

Newsletter (March, 2010), 137 *et seq*; Berger and Kellerhals, *International and Domestic Arbitration in Switzerland*, N 230 to 233 and 1602.

46 See Hahn, 'Schweizer Schiedsgerichte', p. 389 with detailed further references in fn. 48 to 50.

47 Whether the approach suggested by Kreindler, 'Die internationale Investitionsschiedsgerichtsbarkeit', p. 11, to declare the claim as inadmissible in a procedural decision (*Prozessurteil*), i.e. without examining the merits of the claim, is available under the Swiss *lex arbitri* needs to be further examined.

48 With regard to bribery, see Hahn, 'Schweizer Schiedsgerichte', pp. 389–90 with further references in fn. 55.

49 Ibid., p. 387 at fn. 37 with reference to DFT 118 II 193, 195 *et seq*. E. 5c; 118 II 353, 356 *et seq*. E. 3c; 133 III 139, 141–142 E. 5.

50 See the decisions referred to in fn. 61 below.

revision, which must be lodged within a short period (30/90 days) after the reason to file the petition has been detected (e.g., that the award was impacted by criminal action). Both types of recourses only provide for a limited power of review.

2.2.7.1 Action for annulment

a) *Grounds for annulment* The Swiss Supreme Court does not have unfettered powers of review, but may only annul an award if one of the five narrow grounds of article 190(2) PILS is met: (a) if the arbitral tribunal was not properly appointed, in particular, if one of the arbitrators was biased; (b) if the tribunal wrongly accepted or declined jurisdiction;[51] (c) if the award went beyond the claims submitted to it or if the tribunal failed to decide one of the items of the claim; (d) if the tribunal violated the parties' due-process rights (equal protection, right to be heard); or (e) if the award is incompatible with international public policy.[52]

The Swiss Supreme Court will not assess whether the arbitral tribunal arguably or even manifestly disregarded the law when deciding the merits[53] of the case. The Swiss Supreme Court only verifies whether the arbitral

[51] That is, if the arbitral tribunal's decision as to whether there is a valid arbitration agreement for the matter in dispute or on the arbitrability of the matter in dispute is mistaken.

[52] These rules include the prohibitions of abuse of rights, discrimination and expropriation without indemnity (DFT 132 III 392; 117 II 606), the prohibition to protect and implement promises of bribery, kickbacks and transactions designed for money laundering purposes (DFT 119 II 380 E.4b, 4P.208/2004) as well as the violation of the principle of *pacta sunt servanda*; that is, cases where the arbitral tribunal holds that there is a contract between the parties but fails to take the existence of the contract into account in the award (and vice versa; DFT 4A_260/2009 E.3.1; 4A_42/2007 E.6.2; 116 II 637; Berger and Kellerhals, *International and Domestic Arbitration in Switzerland*, N 1601; Stephen V. Berti and Anton K. Schnyder, in Heinrich Honsell *et al.* (eds.), *Basler Kommentar, Internationales Privatrecht*, 2nd edn (Basel: Helbing Lichtenhahn Verlag, 2007), N 74 to Art. 190). Case law and doctrine also hold that a violation of most crucial procedural rules (other than equal protection and the right to be heard, which are specifically listed in article 190(2) PILS) may qualify as a violation of procedural public policy and may entail vacation of the award (DFT 4A_490/2009 E.2.1; 132 III 389 E.2.2.1). This may exceptionally be the case, for example, when the tribunal does not respect the *res iudicata* barrier of an earlier decision or if it renders an interim award on a certain issue (e.g., liability), but a later stage renders a decision that is incompatible with its interim award (DFT 4A_490/2009 E.2.1; 128 III 194–195). The way in which the arbitral tribunal weighs the evidence and establishes the facts of the case, however, does not violate procedural public policy even in cases where it is manifestly wrong or contradicts the documents on file (DFT 120 II 155 E.6a).

[53] A different rule applies if the applicant does not challenge the decision on the merits, but the decision on jurisdiction: the Swiss Supreme Court will then fully review whether the arbitral tribunal properly applied the law on this issue.

tribunal complied with the few rules perceived to pertain to public policy. Neither will the Supreme Court double-check whether the tribunal properly weighed the evidence submitted by the parties.[54]

An annulment action is not only an uphill battle, given the limited power of review of the Swiss Supreme Court; it may, additionally, only succeed if the applicant used procedural caution during the arbitration and in its motion to set aside: (a) an award is only set aside for partiality of an arbitrator, violation of due-process rights or a wrong decision on jurisdiction if the applicant objected in due time during the arbitration. A party cannot, for example, challenge an award for lack of jurisdiction if it did not raise the plea of lack of jurisdiction before starting to plead on the merits; likewise, it cannot request annulment for failure to provide due process if it did not protest immediately after its procedural rights were allegedly violated; (b) the annulment action needs to carefully explain which basis applies to set the award aside for which reason; the Swiss Federal Supreme Court will not *ex officio* scrutinize the award or the conduct of the arbitration; and (c) a motion to set aside must be lodged against the first (partial or interim) award that suffers from the defect on which the applicant bases its annulment action. A party cannot, for example, only invoke a wrong decision on jurisdiction to challenge the final award when the tribunal has issued an interim award on jurisdiction in an earlier stage of the arbitration.

Given these prerequisites and the limited power of review, it comes as no surprise that annulment actions are, in most cases, rejected. Surveys conducted over the past few years suggest that an average of only slightly more than five per cent of all actions was successful.[55]

b) *Option to exclude actions for annulment* The parties may waive their right to apply to the Swiss Supreme Court to annul the award if none of them has its domicile, its habitual residence or a business establishment in Switzerland.[56] They may, in other words, exclude the very limited annulment review.[57] Further to the lack of any relevant

[54] Rather, the Swiss Supreme Court is bound by the facts established by the arbitral tribunal unless the applicant is able to show that the tribunal violated its due-process rights when taking evidence.

[55] See Felix Dasser, 'International Arbitration and Setting Aside Proceedings in Switzerland – An Updated Statistical Analysis', *ASA Bulletin* (1/2010), 82 *et seq.*

[56] Article 192 PILS.

[57] Article 192 PILS, which entitles the parties to waive their right to file a motion to set the award aside, does not apply to petitions for revision. The parties may, however, do so

connection of either party to the Swiss legal system, an exclusion of a court review requires an express written agreement; that is, an agreement that is unambiguous in excluding a future motion to annul an award.[58] While it is not necessary that the agreement expressly refers to the statutory provision allowing for such waiver (article 192 PILS), the condition is not met if the agreement merely states that an award will be 'final' and/or 'binding' upon the parties.[59] Rather, the agreement should include wording that the award is 'not subject to review by state courts' or that 'any remedies to seek annulment of the award with state courts is excluded'.

2.2.7.2 Petition for revision Petitions for revision of arbitral awards[60] are rare in Switzerland. Revision is only available if (a) the decision of the arbitral tribunal was impacted by a criminal action to the detriment of the applicant; (b) an arbitrator did not surrender his office despite his or her lack of independence; or (c) the applicant discovers new facts or evidence that would have been relevant for the decision on the merits. A petition for revision, however, is no device to escape procedural mistakes made during the arbitration. The petitioner may, for example, only rely on new evidence and/or facts that are discovered after the award is rendered if it is able to show that it diligently aimed to establish the facts and was nevertheless unable to locate them.[61]

In contrast to a motion to set aside, a petition for revision is available until 10 years after the award is rendered or, in cases where the award was impacted by a criminal action, for an unlimited period of time. This balances the need to vacate awards that suffer from the most serious defects and the need to provide judicial certainty in that awards are otherwise final unless annulled shortly after the award is rendered.

based on general principles of law (see also Berger and Kellerhals, *International and Domestic Arbitration in Switzerland*, N 1814 and 1815).

58 DFT 4A_500/2007, E.3.1; 4A_18/2007, E.3.1; 133 III 235 E. 4 (see, however E. 4.3.2.1. for sports arbitration); 131 III 173 E.4.2.3.2.

59 DFT 4A_464/2009 E.3.1.1; 4A_194/2008 E.2.1; 131 III 173 E.4.2.1; 116 II 639 E.2c.

60 The PILS does not contain rules on petitions for revision. Case law and doctrine are, however, unanimous in that the provisions on revision of the Federal Law on the Swiss Supreme Court ('BGG') apply by analogy and that certain of the grounds for revision listed in the BGG also apply to arbitral awards.

61 Article 123 Abs. 2 lit. a BGG; DFT 4A_42/2008 E.4.2; 4A_528/2007 E.2.5.2.2; 4P.102/2006 E.2.1.

3 Institutional structures

The Chambers decided to adopt the Swiss Rules and to apply this joint set of rules instead of the individual rules that each Chamber had applied before.

To provide arbitration services, the Chambers founded the Swiss Chambers' Arbitration Institution as an arbitral institution. In order to administer arbitrations under the Swiss Rules, the Swiss Chambers' Arbitration Institution has established the Arbitration Court (hereinafter the 'Court'),[62] which is comprised of experienced international arbitration practitioners. It may delegate to one or more members or committees the power to take certain decisions pursuant to its Internal Rules. The Chambers publish these Internal Rules on their website.

The Court is assisted in its work by the Secretariat at the Chamber in charge of the file (hereinafter the 'Secretariat'). The Court and the Secretariat, in essence, guarantee the proper conduct of a Swiss Rules arbitration. The Court, for example, is charged with confirming the arbitrators appointed by the parties, and the Secretariat, for example, forwards a copy of the request for arbitration to the respondent.

The institutional administration focuses on an efficient and proper constitution of the arbitral tribunal and thereafter focuses on the assurance of the efficiency of the process. Otherwise, the Swiss Rules entrust the conduct of the arbitration to the arbitral tribunal and the parties once the file is transmitted to them (article 3(12) Swiss Rules). The Swiss Rules, in particular, afford the arbitral tribunal and the parties discretion in terms of how to organize the arbitral proceedings and ensure efficiency through the mandatory tool of the provisional timetable (article 15(3) Swiss Rules).

In practice, arbitral tribunals constituted under the Swiss Rules align with the parties and hold an organizational hearing or an organizational telephone conference[63] at the outset of the arbitration and do not only draft the provisional timetable, but also issue an organizational

[62] This is the institutional structure provided for by the 2012 version of the Swiss Rules, which entered into effect on 1 June 2012. The 2004 version provided for an 'arbitration committee' and a 'special committee'. The two committees assisted and guided the Chambers in administering arbitrations conducted under the Swiss Rules. The members of both committees worked on a pro bono basis.

[63] On the initial organization of proceedings, and the further management of proceedings as well as the assurance of quality control, see Daniel Wehrli, B. Gino Koenig and Claudius Triebold, 'Management of the Proceedings and Quality Control under the Swiss Rules', in Gabrielle Kaufmann-Kohler and Blaise Stucki (eds.), *The Swiss Rules of International Arbitration, ASA Special Series No. 22* (Zurich: ASA, 2004), pp. 97–102.

document, which may take the form of a constituting order and/or of a set of separate and detailed procedural rules that are tailor-made for the specific proceeding.[64]

4 Special features of the Swiss Rules

4.1 The appointment of the arbitral tribunal

4.1.1 Number of arbitrators and manner of appointment

The role of the parties in designating the arbitrators is paramount: first, they may choose the number of arbitrators; that is, whether they wish to submit their dispute to a sole arbitrator or to a three-member tribunal.[65] While the Court may invite the parties to reconsider their agreement for a three-member tribunal in case this appears inappropriate given the amount in dispute or other circumstances, the parties have the final say.[66] Second, the parties may define the mechanism with which to designate their sole arbitrator or three-member tribunal.[67]

The Swiss Rules provide for fall-back solutions if the parties do not address the number of arbitrators or the way in which they are designated (particularly also for multi-party arbitrations[68]): as a rule, the Court will refer the case to a sole arbitrator unless the complexity of the subject matter and/or the amount in dispute justifies referral to a three-member tribunal.[69]

Depending on the number of arbitrators determined by the Court, the parties are to jointly appoint the sole arbitrator or, unless they have otherwise agreed, to designate one arbitrator each (with the two party-appointed arbitrators designating the Chairman).[70] As a fall-back solution, the Court will appoint the arbitrators in the parties' stead if they are unable to agree on a sole arbitrator or if a party fails to designate its arbitrator within the time limit set by the Court.[71]

[64] For a list of matters to be addressed in such an organizational document, ibid., pp. 98–100.

[65] Article 6(1) Swiss Rules.

[66] Article 6(3) Swiss Rules.

[67] Articles 7(1) and 8(1) Swiss Rules.

[68] See section 4.3 below.

[69] Article 6(2) Swiss Rules.

[70] Article 7(1), (2) and 8(1) Swiss Rules.

[71] Articles 7(3) and 8(2) Swiss Rules. The Court will also appoint the Chairperson of a three-member tribunal in case the two party-appointed arbitrators are unable to agree (article 8(2) Swiss Rules).

4.1.2 Confirmation of arbitrators by the Court

In all cases, it is foremost for the parties to choose the arbitrators, while the prospective arbitrator's disclosure obligation and their confirmation by the Court ensure that the arbitration is in good hands.[72]

Article 5(1) Swiss Rules provides that both a designation by the parties (sole arbitrator or party-appointed arbitrators of a three-member arbitral tribunal) and the designation of the presiding arbitrator by the party-appointed arbitrators only become effective after confirmation by the Court.[73] This confirmation will only be made after the arbitrator has complied with his disclosure obligations under article 9(2) Swiss Rules, which require him to sign a form similar to the one used in ICC arbitrations. Articles 5(1) and 9(2) Swiss Rules thus provide the Court with a tool to control the overall qualification of any given designated arbitrator and the compliance of his curriculum with the specific qualifications possibly required by the arbitration agreement (e.g., nationality, language skills and experience in a specific (field of) law).[74]

After the non-confirmation of a party-designated arbitrator and in lieu of inviting the concerned party to make a new designation, the Court may proceed with the appointment of the respective arbitrator (article 5(2)(b) Swiss Rules). This tool of quality control will, of course, be applied as an *ultima ratio* measure. It can, however, be a proper remedy if a party, after its designated arbitrator has been successfully challenged under articles 10 and 11 Swiss Rules, again designates an arbitrator who appears to lack impartiality or independence and cannot, therefore, be confirmed.

[72] See section 4.2 below.

[73] The Secretariat transmits the file to the arbitrators once all arbitrators have been confirmed by the Court, and the registration fee, as well as any provisional advance, have been paid (article 5(5) Swiss Rules). They will, however, send a copy of the Notice of Arbitration and/or the Answer (without exhibits) to the arbitrators designated by the parties or appointed by the Chambers to enable them to appoint a presiding arbitrator as well as to verify their independence.

[74] See Wolfgang Peter, 'Some Observations on the New Swiss Rules of International Arbitration', in Gabrielle Kaufmann-Kohler and Blaise Stucki (eds.), *The Swiss Rules of International Arbitration, ASA Special Series No. 22* (Zurich: ASA, 2004), p. 6; on the requirement of the arbitrator's neutrality see Pierre Lalive, 'On the Neutrality of the Arbitrator and of the Place of Arbitration', in Claude Reymond and Eugène Bucher (eds.), *Swiss Essays on International Arbitration* (Zurich: Schulthess Polygraphischer Verlag Zürich, 1984), pp. 23–28.

4.2 *Disclosure obligations of designated arbitrators*

Article 9(2) Swiss Rules adopted article 9 UNCITRAL Rules 1976 on the duty to disclose circumstances which could likely 'give rise to justifiable doubts' as to an arbitrator's 'impartiality or independence'; article 9(1) Swiss Rules additionally requires the arbitrators to 'be and remain at all times impartial and independent of the parties'. Article 9 Swiss Rules thus establishes a test that is both subjective (impartial) and objective (independent).[75] In contrast, the wording of the PILS suggests it does not require impartiality, but only independence.[76]

The Court implements article 9 Swiss Rules by requiring prospective arbitrators to sign a form entitled *Consent to Appointment and Statement of Independence*, in which they additionally undertake to disclose 'any circumstances arising in the future [i.e. after their designation and confirmation] which are likely to give rise to justifiable doubts as to my impartiality or independence, until the arbitration is concluded'.[77]

4.3 *Multi-party arbitration*

While the UNCITRAL Rules 1976[78] are silent, the Swiss Rules contain state-of-the-art provisions on multi-party arbitration in articles 8(3) to (5). These provisions apply if there is a group of parties on the claimant's and/or respondent's side. In our view, they also apply if a respondent files both a counter-claim and a claim against a co-respondent.

[75] See Marc Blessing, 'Comparison of the Swiss Rules With the UNCITRAL Arbitration Rules and Others', in Gabrielle Kaufmann-Kohler and Blaise Stucki (eds.), *The Swiss Rules of International Arbitration, ASA Special Series No. 22* (Zurich: ASA, 2004), p. 35; Jean Marguerat, in Tobias Zuberbühler, Christoph Müller and Philipp Habegger (eds.), *Swiss Rules of International Arbitration: Commentary* (Zurich: Schulthess Juristische Medien AG, 2005), N 10 and 28 to Art. 9.

[76] Doctrine and case law, however, confirm that article 180(1)(c) PILS, despite its wording, also requires impartiality (DFT 4A_234/2010; Wolfgang Peter and Sébastien Besson, in Heinrich Honsell *et al.* (eds.), *Basler Kommentar, Internationales Privatrecht*, 2nd edn (Basel: Helbing Lichtenhahn Verlag, 2007), N 15 to Art. 180; see also Peter, 'Some Observations', p. 7. On the meaning of the terms '*independence*' and '*impartiality*' see also Marguerat, *Swiss Rules of International Arbitration*, N 4 *et seq.* to Art. 9).

[77] Article 11 UNCITRAL Rules 2010 modified article 9 of the UNCITRAL Rules 1976 by stating that the disclosure obligation applies '*throughout the arbitral proceedings*' and by introducing a model statement of independence in Annex A, which includes a declaration of the arbitrator that he or she will '*devote the time necessary to conduct this arbitration diligently, efficiently and in accordance with the time limits in the Rules*'.

[78] The UNCITRAL Rules 2010 were inspired by article 8(3) to (5) Swiss Rules and provide in article 4(1) and (3) in different words the same solution.

The provisions in the Swiss Rules (as with other modern provisions on multi-party arbitration) attempt to avoid the *Dutco* issue.[79] They provide that a group of claimants or a group of respondents must jointly designate an arbitrator (article 8(4) Swiss Rules) and state that the Court 'may' appoint the arbitrator on behalf of a non-complying group of parties or even 'all of the arbitrators' and 'specify the presiding arbitrator' (articles 8(4) and (5) Swiss Rules), thus depriving all of them of the possibility of designating their own arbitrator and thus rendering any previous designation by the parties ineffective.[80] The word 'may' in article 8(5) Swiss Rules, affords the Court discretion and mandates them to decide on a case-by-case basis.

4.4 *Consolidation of arbitral proceedings*

Article 4(1) Swiss Rules contains a detailed provision on the consolidation of arbitral proceedings, which has no counterpart in the UNCITRAL Rules 1976. The provision gives the Court (not the arbitral tribunal) the power to decide on a consolidation of two arbitrations[81] when the Notice of Arbitration (in the second arbitration) is submitted. The Court may consolidate a new case with a pending arbitration, if both cases are between the same parties, but also if the parties to the second arbitration are 'not identical to the parties in the existing arbitral proceedings'.[82]

[79] In *Dutco*, the French Cour de cassation (7 January 1992, *Rev.arb.* (1992), 470) annulled an award as it deemed the way the arbitral tribunal had been appointed violated the right of equal treatment. The underlying facts were as follows: Dutco initiated ICC arbitration against Siemens and BKMI and nominated its arbitrator. The ICC requested Siemens and BKMI to nominate a joint arbitrator, which they did under protest (claiming they should not be forced to make a joint nomination while Dutco was free to appoint an arbitrator of its own). The French Cour de cassation shared the view of Siemens and BKMI and annulled the award of the arbitral tribunal, which had deemed itself properly constituted.

[80] See Micha Bühler, in Tobias Zuberbühler, Christoph Müller and Philipp Habegger (eds.), *Swiss Rules of International Arbitration: Commentary* (Zurich: Schulthess Juristische Medien AG, 2005), N 37–39 to Art. 8.

[81] The Chambers discussed whether the revised Swiss Rules should contain a provision also allowing the arbitral tribunal to consolidate two arbitration proceedings; they, however, decided not to amend the provision to this effect (see, however, Nathalie Voser, 'Multi-party Disputes and Joinder of Third Parties', Congress series no. 14 (2009), *50 Years of the New York Convention, ICCA International Arbitration Conference, ICCA Congress*, pp. 343 *et seq.* at 388, seems to submit that this approach is (already) admissible under article 4(1) Swiss Rules.

[82] See Franz Kellerhals, 'Highlights from the Arbitration Committee', in Rainer Füeg (ed.), *The Swiss Rules of International Arbitration: Five Years of Experience* (Basel: Swiss

In any event, the parties to the two arbitral proceedings must have concluded arbitration agreements referring to the Swiss Rules,[83] while it is not necessary that the dispute arises out of the same contract. When deciding on a consolidation, the Court must (a) consult with 'the parties to all proceedings and any confirmed arbitrator', and (b) 'take into account all relevant circumstances, including the links between the cases and the progress already made in the pending arbitral proceedings'.

Unlike a joinder under article 4(2) Swiss Rules, consolidation does not require a request of a party; the Court can start the consolidation process on their own motion. The Court is, however, reluctant to order consolidation when the parties do not agree.[84]

If the Court approves of the consolidation, 'the parties to all proceedings shall be deemed to have waived their right to designate an arbitrator'.[85] This implies that consolidation may also be ordered if one arbitration would be referred to a panel of three arbitrators and the other to a sole arbitrator. Likewise, the Chambers may consolidate two arbitrations which would take place at different seats within[86]

Chambers' Court of Arbitration and Mediation, 2009), pp. 25, 30; Peter, 'Some Observations', p. 5 and Torsten Lörcher, 'The Swiss Rules of International Arbitration Seen from Abroad', in Rainer Füeg (ed.), *The Swiss Rules of International Arbitration – Five Years of Experience* (Basel: Swiss Chambers' Court of Arbitration and Mediation, 2009), p. 68, suggesting a cautious application of article 4(1) Swiss Rules in cases 'involving one or more third parties'.

83 This is not stated in article 4(1) Swiss Rules but results from the fact that article 4(1) Swiss Rules requires a Notice of Arbitration to be submitted to the second arbitration, which is only possible if the second arbitration also provides for an arbitration under the Swiss Rules (see Christoph Brunner, 'The Swiss Rules of International Arbitration: An Overview for Prospective Users', *Schieds VZ*, 5 (2010), 243 *et seq.* at 250).

84 The Zurich Chamber rejected consolidation in a case (a) in which one party, which in the first case was the respondent and in the second the claimant, was opposed to consolidation, and (b) in which the constitution of both arbitral tribunals had already been completed (decision of 27 June 2007). In that case, the Zurich Chamber refused to consolidate the two proceedings based on article 4(1) Swiss Rules and stated that the circumstances did not mandate formal consolidation in such a case. Franz Kellerhals and Bernhard Berger, 'Widerklage und Verrechnung nach den Swiss Rules of International Arbitration', in François Bohnet and Pierre Wessner, *Mélanges en l'honneur de François Knoepfler* (Basel: Helbing & Lichtenhahn, 2005), p. 218 at fn. 46, also seem to submit that there are good reasons not to consolidate two proceedings in such a situation. However, since the two arbitral tribunals were composed of the same arbitrators, it might have furthered efficiency and would certainly have been less costly for the parties if the arbitral tribunal had had the power to consolidate the two proceedings.

85 See article 4(1) Swiss Rules. Under the previous version of this article, such a waiver merely applied to the 'parties of the new case'.

86 If the seat of an arbitration is outside Switzerland, the fact that two different *leges arbitri* would apply prevents consolidation without the consent of all parties.

Switzerland if the 'language of the different proceedings is the same'.[87] However, if one arbitration is to be submitted to an expedited procedure while the other is not, this will, as a rule, be a reason to refuse consolidation.[88]

A first draft of the UNCITRAL Rules 2010 contained a provision on the 'consolidation of arbitral proceedings'.[89] The final text, however, does not include such provision, because the draft provision did not go beyond the scope of possible amendments to the claim or defence under article 20 UNCITRAL Rules 1976; a (narrow) rule on consolidation thus would not have had any effect, given article 20 UNCITRAL Rules 1976,[90] which remained essentially unchanged and is now in article 22 UNCITRAL Rules 2010.[91]

4.5 *Participation (joinder) of third parties*

The UNCITRAL Rules 1976 contained no provision on the joinder of third parties. Article 4(2) Swiss Rules allows for such joinder and uses the following wording:

[87] See Philippe Gilliéron and Luc Pittet, in Tobias Zuberbühler, Christoph Müller and Philipp Habegger (eds.), *Swiss Rules of International Arbitration: Commentary* (Zurich: Schulthess Juristische Medien AG, 2005), N 8 to Art. 4.

[88] See also the example used by Kellerhals, 'Highlights from the Arbitration Committee', pp. 30–1.

[89] Draft article 15(4) stated that the arbitral tribunal may, on the application of any party, 'assume jurisdiction over any claim involving the same parties and arising out of the same legal relationship, provided that such claims are subject to arbitration under these Rules and that the arbitration proceedings in relation to those claims have not yet commenced' (see document of the working group A/CN.9/WG.II/WP.145/Add.1, p. 2, para. 2, available at www.uncitral.org/uncitral/en/commission/working_groups/2Arbitration.html).

[90] See document of the working group A/CN.9/619, p. 23 para. 119 on the website referred to in fn. 89 above stating that 'either the provision was intended to deal with new claims under the same contract, and that situation would be better dealt with under provisions on amendment of the statement of claim, or that provision was intended to cover several distinct disputes arising between the same parties under separate contracts containing separate arbitration clauses'. This decision was confirmed in the document of the working group A/CN.9/WG.II/WP.147/Add.1, p. 4, para. 7.

[91] Article 22 of the UNCITRAL Rules 2010 clarifies that the provision applies also for defences, including counter-claims or claims 'for the purpose of a set-off' and replaces the words 'outside the scope of the arbitration clause or separate arbitration agreement' with 'outside the jurisdiction of the arbitral tribunal'.

> Where one or more third parties requests to participate in arbitral proceedings already pending under these Rules or where a party to pending arbitral proceedings under these Rules requests that one or more third persons participate in the arbitration, the arbitral tribunal shall decide on such request, after consulting with all of the parties, including the person or persons to be joined, taking into account all relevant circumstances.

The provision is, as Gabrielle Nater-Bass states, an 'important innovation' and a 'distinctive advantage compared to other institutional rules'.[92] The provision grants an arbitral tribunal broad discretion and permits a joinder even if the third person is not a party to the arbitration agreement[93] or if the non-requesting party does not consent to the joinder.[94]

The UNCITRAL Rules 2010 took inspiration from article 4(2) Swiss Rules and introduced a provision on joinder, which – contrary to the Swiss Rules – requires that the third person be a 'party to the arbitration agreement' (article 17(5) UNCITRAL Rules 2010). Moreover, even if this condition is met, the arbitral tribunal may not permit the joinder if the participation of the third person could cause 'prejudice' to a party or to the person(s) to be joined.

If the arbitral tribunal accepts the joinder of a third person based on article 17(5) of the UNCITRAL Rules 2010, it may render awards 'in respect of all parties so involved in the arbitration' and therefore also against or in favour of the joining party. As the Swiss Rules do not require that the joining person is a party to the arbitration agreement, the wording of article 4(2) Swiss Rules does not provide for such a possibility. However, if the joining person is a party to the arbitration agreement or if all parties agree to a request of the third party to accede to

[92] See Nater-Bass, 'How to Work with the Swiss Rules', pp. 61–2.

[93] Andrea Meier analyses article 4(2) Swiss Rules in detail in her thesis on, *Einbezug Dritter vor Internationalen Schiedsgerichten* (Zurich: Schulthess Juristische Medien AG, 2007), pp. 104–8 and 151–2. See also Voser, 'Multi-party Disputes', pp. 395–397. On the joinder in general see also Nathalie Voser and Andrea Meier, 'Joinder of Parties or the Need to (Sometimes) Be Inefficient', *Austrian Arbitration Year Book* 2008, 115 *et seq.*

[94] See Gilliéron/Pittet, *Swiss Rules of International Arbitration*, N 11 to Art. 4 at the end; Voser, 'Multi-party Disputes', p. 396 and Meier, *Einbezug Dritter*, p. 148. On this '*no agreement approach*' see also Cristián Conejero Roos, 'Multi-party Arbitration and Rule-making: Same Issues, Contrasting Approaches', Congress series no. 14 (2009), *50 Years of the New York Convention, ICCA International Arbitration Conference, ICCA Congress*, p. 424.

the arbitration agreement, there is no reason for an arbitral tribunal not to render an award against or in favour of the joining party.

By not requiring the participating person to be a party to the arbitration agreement, article 4(2) Swiss Rules permits the joined/joining person not to become a 'formal party' to the arbitration and instead to be a mere 'side party'.[95] This is namely in the event of:

(a) A 'third-party notice' (in German *einfache Streitverkündung*, in French *dénonciation d'instance*), intending 'to cause a third party to participate in the arbitration'; and
(b) A so-called accessory or side intervention (in German *Nebenintervention*, in French *intervention accessoire*), when the third person itself intends to participate.

In both of these cases, the joined/joining party is permitted to support a formal party to the arbitration or to only play a passive role by not exercising its right to participate, but merely receiving the submissions of the parties to the arbitration.

As stated above, if the joining party is a mere 'side party', the joinder does not require that it consents to the arbitration agreement. However, permitting a side party that is not a party to the arbitration agreement to participate, in our view, requires in most cases that the parties to the arbitration consent to the participation and so 'waive their right to confidentiality and private proceedings'.[96] Such consent can, for example, be implied in the fact that one party, with the knowledge of the other party, concluded a subcontract or other related contracts with the 'side party'.

The possible application of article 4(2) Swiss Rules to side parties demonstrates that there is 'little difference . . . between a debate' under article 4(2) Swiss Rules 'on the participation of a third party against the objections of that party or of an existing party . . . and a debate on jurisdiction over a non-signatory that was named as a defendant from the outset'.[97]

[95] See the terminology used by Voser, 'Multi-party Disputes', pp. 381–2.
[96] Ibid., pp. 381–2 with reference to a decision in ICC case number 12171 in fn. 205, published in the *ASA Bulletin* (2/2005), pp. 270 *et seq*., in which the participation of a side intervener was denied because one of the parties did not consent, which was deemed to bar participation by side intervention given the intention of the parties reflected in the arbitration to be 'subject to private and confidential proceedings' (at p. 273).
[97] See Elliott Geisinger, 'How to Work with the Swiss Rules: The Arbitrator's View', in Rainer Füeg (ed.), *The Swiss Rules of International Arbitration – Five Years of Experience* (Basel: Swiss Chambers' Court of Arbitration and Mediation, 2009), p. 46 at the end of para. 3.4. See also Voser, 'Multi-party Disputes', p. 387 at fn. 2.

Overall, article 4(2) Swiss Rules provides for a more flexible provision on the joinder of third parties than the UNCITRAL Rules 2010 and so permits an arbitral tribunal to find an adequate solution. However, as Elliot Geisinger rightly states, the fact that article 4(2) Swiss Rules grants an arbitral tribunal 'broad powers does not mean that' it 'will necessarily exercise them'.[98] Arbitrators use these powers with caution and the Chambers have, therefore, not yet noted problems in the application of article 4(2) Swiss Rules.

4.6 Set-off defences

There are differing opinions on whether an arbitral tribunal may hear a set-off claim that a respondent holds against the claimant, but which is not covered by the scope of the arbitration agreement.[99] Such set-off defences often lead to time-consuming discussions and sometimes – depending on the applicable substantive law – even to a suspension of the arbitration on the main claim if the applicable *lex arbitri* and arbitration rules (such as, for example, the ICC Rules) do not address the arbitral tribunal's jurisdiction to decide set-off claims. In order to avoid these discussions[100] and a suspension of arbitral proceedings until the competent court or arbitral tribunal has decided on the set-off claim,[101] some of the former arbitration rules of the Chambers addressed set-off claims.[102] The essence of these provisions was taken over into article 21(5) Swiss Rules. This provision grants an arbitral tribunal jurisdiction to hear set-off defences even if the set-off claim is 'not within

[98] See Geisinger, 'How to Work with the Swiss Rules', p. 39 at para. 2.1 and p. 45 at para. 3.4.

[99] See, for example, Werner Wenger and Markus Schott, in Heinrich Honsell *et al.* (eds.), *Basler Kommentar, Internationales Privatrecht*, 2nd edn (Basel: Helbing Lichtenhahn Verlag, 2007), N 38 *et seq.* to Art. 186 (N 23 *et seq.* in the English edition 2000).

[100] See Daniel Wehrli, 'Die Schiedsgerichtsbarkeit', in Thomas Sutter-Somm and Franz Hasenböhler (eds.), *Die künftige schweizerische Zivilprozessordnung* (Zurich: Schulthess, 2003), Chapter IV/9 at p. 123.

[101] Until the end of 2010, suspension was, for example, necessary pursuant to article 29 of the Concordat applicable for domestic arbitration, which provided that 'proceedings shall be stayed and a reasonable time shall be allowed to the party making the claim to establish it before the court with jurisdiction' (English translation by Payot, *Concordat suisse sur l'arbitrage, Edition quadrilingue et annotée* (Lausanne: Éditions Payot Lausanne, 1974)).

[102] See, for example, article 27 of the former International Arbitration Rules of the Zurich Chamber of Commerce, article 29(1) of the former Arbitration Rules of the Basel Chamber of Commerce and article 12.1 of the former Lugano Arbitration and Conciliation Rules of the Chamber of Commerce, Industry and Handicraft of the cantone Ticino (the latter two still applied for domestic arbitrations until the end of 2010).

the scope of the arbitration clause' or is the 'object of another arbitration agreement or forum-selection clause'.[103]

Since the PILS (as with other *leges arbitri*) does not address set-off claims, the Swiss Rules do so in article 21(5). For main claims that are subject to Swiss substantive law it was not pertinent to do so, since set-off defences are a matter of a substantive and not of a procedural nature and, if successful, extinguish the main claim. Due to such a substantive consequence of valid set-off defences, the view supported by many leading scholars is that an arbitral tribunal is competent to decide on the merits of the set-off defence as a preliminary issue to the question as to whether or not the main claim exists or has been extinguished as a result of set-off.[104] However, since the qualification of set-off claims is not universal and to make the Swiss Rules fit for global use, the drafters included a provision specifically dealing with this issue.

The approach of article 21(5) Swiss Rules, which has been taken over by article 377 CCP, is a pragmatic solution for civil-law countries such as Switzerland with a substantive law providing that a valid set-off defence results in the extinction of the main claim and that the set-off defence can be raised even if the set-off claim is contested.[105] The approach, however, is not compatible with other legal systems with different set-off concepts and thus could not be a model for the UNCITRAL Rules 2010. The working group revising the UNCITRAL Rules 1976 discussed various alternative solutions, including a proposal from the Swiss Government.[106] As a result of these discussions, article 21(3) of the UNCITRAL Rules 2010 merely permits a respondent to 'rely on a claim for the purpose of a set-off provided that the arbitral tribunal has

[103] For a detailed analysis of article 21(5) Swiss Rules see Kellerhals and Berger, 'Widerklage und Verrechnung nach den Swiss Rules of International Arbitration', pp. 207–26.

[104] See Wenger and Schott, *Basler Kommentar*, N 45 to Art. 186 with further references (N 28 in the English edition 2000).

[105] See, e.g., article 120(2) Swiss Code of Obligation ('CO').

[106] The text proposed by the Swiss Government on 8 September 2008 had the following wording: 'The arbitral tribunal shall have jurisdiction to hear a set-off defence even if the claim on which the set-off is based does not fall within the scope of the arbitration agreement, and even if such claim is the object of a different arbitration agreement or of a forum selection clause, provided that the requirements for a set-off under the substantive law applicable to the main claim are fulfilled' (see the document of the working group A/CH.9/WG.II/WP.152, p. 2 at the website referred to in fn. 89 above; in this context see also Daniel Wehrli, 'The Swiss Rules of International Arbitration and the Revision of the UNCITRAL Arbitration Rules', in Rainer Füeg (ed.), *The Swiss Rules of International Arbitration: Five Years of Experience* (Basel: Swiss Chambers' Court of Arbitration and Mediation, 2009), pp. 90–1.

jurisdiction over it'.[107] This wording encompasses 'a wide range of circumstances', does not 'require substantive definitions of the notions of claims for set-off' and takes 'account of the situation where the claim had been extinguished by the set-off'. Article 21(3) UNCITRAL Rules 2010 thus permits reliance on the practice in the country at the seat of arbitration and, therefore, does not require a specific provision in the *lex arbitri*.

It may be efficient to hear set-off defences out of a legal relationship, which is outside of the scope of application of the arbitration clause. If a party nevertheless wishes that this should not be the case and that the arbitral tribunal, despite article 21(5) Swiss Rules, does not have the authority to address a set-off defence, this party may try and make its counterparty agree to a provision of substantive law in their contract that excludes set-off defences out of other contracts. However, even in such a case, the arbitral tribunal remains competent to decide on the validity and the scope of such waiver of set-off claims.[108]

4.7 *Counter-claims*

Article 21(3) Swiss Rules states that the plea of lack of jurisdiction with respect to a counter-claim must be raised at the latest in the 'reply to the counter-claim'. The Swiss Rules, however, do not expressly address the more important issue of under what circumstances an arbitral tribunal has jurisdiction to hear a counter-claim.[109] Accordingly, the general principle applies that an arbitral tribunal has jurisdiction over a counter-claim only if (a) it is based on the same contractual relationship as the main claim[110] or if (b) the counter-respondent has agreed

[107] This softer provision is the result of the concern of some delegates of the UNCITRAL working group that 'the proposal might invite challenges under the New York Convention with respect to the scope of the arbitration agreement even if the parties would have accepted such extension by agreeing on the application of the Rules' (see document of the working group A/CN.9.669, p. 8, para. 29 at the website referred to in fn. 89 above).

[108] See Daniel Wehrli, 'Die Schiedsgerichtsbarkeit', Chapter IV/9 at p. 124.

[109] Article 19(3) of the UNCITRAL Rules 1976 address the subject by stating the obvious; that is, that counterclaims 'arising of the same contract' may be raised.

[110] See Wenger and Schott, *Basler Kommentar*, N 38 to Art. 186 and N 21 in the English edition 2000. See also Daniel Girsberger and Nathalie Voser, *International Arbitration in Switzerland* (Zurich: Schulthess Juristische Medien AG, 2008), p. 62 referring to more liberal opinions at fn. 60, which are, for example, expressed by Jean-François Poudret and Sébastien Besson in *Droit comparé de l'arbitrage international* (Zurich: Schulthess Médias Juridiques SA, 2002), N 574 at pp. 524–5, by Berger and Kellerhals, *International and Domestic Arbitration in*

to hear the counter-claim or failed to object in a timely fashion (article 21(3) Swiss Rules).[111] Therefore, it does not suffice – as under article 377(2) CCP for domestic arbitrations – that the counter-claim relates to a dispute covered by a concurring arbitration agreement (*übereinstimmende Schiedsvereinbarung, convention d'arbitrage concordante*).

Kellerhals and Berger suggest, in their detailed analysis on the relationship between counter-claims and set-off defences, that, if both sides allege monetary claims, an arbitral tribunal sitting under the Swiss Rules may – as an exception – affirm its jurisdiction for the full counter-claim that is subject to a separate dispute resolution mechanism (a so-called *klauselfremde Gegenforderung*) if the arbitral tribunal must anyway decide on part of the counter-claim, since it is also brought as a set-off defence (article 21(5) Swiss Rules). They argue that it would, in such a case, be inadequate that the exceeding amount must be decided on in a separate proceeding.[112]

The UNCITRAL Rules 2010 pay tribute to the fact that not all jurisdictions distinguish between counter-claims and set-off claims; they therefore jointly address the jurisdiction on counter-claims and set-off defences in article 21(3), to the effect that the criteria for set-off claims (that 'the arbitral tribunal has jurisdiction over it') also applies to counter-claims. It is therefore for the *lex arbitri* to decide whether an arbitral tribunal can hear a counter-claim or not.

4.8 Applicable substantive law

Article 33(1) Swiss Rules provides that the governing law is established as follows (emphasis added):

Switzerland – with reference to the intention of the parties – N 486–490 as well as by Kellerhals and Berger, 'Widerklage und Verrechnung', p. 220 with further references; Pierre Karrer, 'Verrechnung und Widerklage vor Schiedsgericht', in Monique Jametti Greiner, Bernhard Berger and Andreas Güngerich (eds.), *Rechtssetzung und Rechtsdurchsetzung: Zivil- und schiedsverfahrensrechtliche Aspekte, Festschrift für Franz Kellerhals zum 65. Geburtstag* (Berne: Stämpfli Verlag AG, 2005), pp. 49–54.

111 See e.g. Brunner, 'The Swiss Rules of International Arbitration: An Overview', Chapter VI/3 at p. 251 and Nater-Bass, 'How to work with the Swiss Rules', p. 62 at fn. 37.

112 See Kellerhals/Berger, 'Widerklage und Verrechnung', pp. 225–6 referring to an older Federal Supreme Court decision, i.e. DFT 23 I 774, 779 *et seq*. (confirmed in an *obiter dictum* in DFT 63 II 133, 142, addressing the opposite situation, in which a state court refused to decide on a counter-claim subject to an arbitration clause, and suggesting that this jurisprudence should not be maintained).

> The arbitral tribunal shall decide the case in accordance with the *rules of law* agreed upon by the parties or, in the absence of a choice of law, by applying the *rules of law* with which the dispute has the closest connection.

The wording of article 33(1) Swiss Rules is virtually identical with the provision on the applicable law in article 187(1) PILS.[113] The UNCITRAL Rules 1976 used the term 'law' in article 33(1), rather than 'rules of law', both for the designation by the parties as well as the determination by the arbitral tribunal, while article 35(1) of the UNCITRAL Rules 2010 as well as article 381 CCP applicable to Swiss domestic arbitration now refer to 'rules of law' for the purposes of a designation by the parties, but not for the determination by the arbitral tribunal. The consequence of this difference is that under the Swiss Rules not only the parties, but also the arbitral tribunal can provide for the application of 'rules of law' (e.g., such as the UNIDROIT Principles[114] or the European Principles[115]) in lieu of specific national laws.[116]

As to the criterion that the arbitral tribunal has to apply when choosing the governing national law, article 33(1) Swiss Rules, like article 187(1) PILS, refers to the law with which the dispute has the 'closest connection'. The Swiss Rules thus deviate from (a) article 33(1) of the UNCITRAL Rules 1976, which referred to the law determined by 'the conflict of law rules which it considers applicable' as well as from (b) article 35 of the UNCITRAL Rules 2010, which refers to the law that the arbitral tribunal 'determines to be appropriate'. The 'closest connection' rule under article 33(1) Swiss Rules and article 187(1) PILS thus has not found its way into the UNCITRAL Rules 2010 as a majority of the working group found

113 *Nota bene* that the English translation of the PILS published as an appendix to the Swiss Rules mirrors the French wording of article 187(1) PILS, which twice uses the term *'règle de doit'* and does not, as the German and Italian text (twice), use the term *'Recht'* and *'diritto'*. Despite the differing wordings under the three languages, it is undisputed in Swiss doctrine that the French wording prevails (see Berger and Kellerhals, *International and Domestic Arbitration in Switzerland*, N 1265).

114 For the UNIDROIT Principles see www.unidroit.org/english/principles/contracts/main.htm

115 For the European Principles see www.jus.uio.no/lm/eu.contract.principles.part1.1995/

116 It was highly debated in the working group as to whether the UNCITRAL Rules 2010 should – like the Swiss Rules – twice refer to 'rules of law'. For reasons on which the document of the working group elaborates (A/CN.9/641, pp. 21–22, paras. 106–112), the Swiss solution did not find a majority.

the criterion of the 'appropriate' law to be the more flexible and modern solution.[117]

4.9 *Decision making of the arbitral tribunal*

Much debated in international arbitration is the question of whether an arbitral tribunal that cannot reach a unanimous decision can decide by a majority of arbitrators or whether the presiding arbitrator has the authority to decide alone. The Swiss Rules did not adopt the majority requirement of article 31(1) of the UNCITRAL Rules 1976 and provide for the latter solution in article 31(1):

> If the arbitral tribunal is composed of more than one arbitrator, any award or other decision of the arbitral tribunal shall be made by a majority of the arbitrators. If there is no majority, the award shall be made by the presiding arbitrator alone.

The working group intensely debated whether the Swiss solution should be taken over by the UNCITRAL 2010 Rules. Some delegates expressed the fear that this would prompt dominant presiding arbitrators to decide on their own rather than to attempt to find a majority. This view prevailed and the more liberal solution of the Swiss Rules was not adopted; article 31(1) of the UNCITRAL Rules 1976, therefore, remained unchanged in this respect.[118]

Article 31(2) Swiss Rules, article 33(2) UNCITRAL Rules 1976 and article 33(2) UNCITRAL Rules 2010 take a liberal approach on questions of procedure and permit arbitral tribunals to authorize the presiding arbitrator to 'decide on his own,[119] subject to revision, if any, by the arbitral tribunal'.

4.10 *Approval of the cost decision by the Court*

The Swiss Rules do not provide for an ICC-like scrutiny of the award,[120] but merely require the arbitral tribunal to submit a draft award to the

[117] See document of the working group A/CN.9/WG.II/LI/CRP.1/Add.4, p. 2, para. 10 and Wehrli, 'The Swiss Rules of International Arbitration', p. 94.

[118] Ibid., p. 93.

[119] Article 35(2) of the UNCITRAL Rules 2010 replaced the words 'on his own' with 'alone'.

[120] For scrutiny by the ICC, see W. Laurence Craig, William Park and Jan Paulsson, *International Chamber of Commerce Arbitration*, 3rd edn (Dobbs Ferry, New York: Oceana Publications, 2001), pp. 24, 41–2, 375–83.

Secretariat for approval or adjustment of the decision on certain cost items (article 40(4) Swiss Rules). Since the arbitrators themselves propose their fees for the arbitral tribunal, such approval is appropriate to ensure that the cost decision is in line with the Schedule of Costs of Arbitration in appendix B of the Swiss Rules and the standards generally applied by arbitral tribunals in Swiss Rules arbitrations. The draft award is the proper basis for this approval by the Court, as it will allow for the understanding both of the complexity of the dispute and of the procedural history.[121]

The Court will also assess whether the arbitral tribunal correctly computed the administrative costs payable to the Chambers (article 38(g) Swiss Rules and sections 2.2 and 2.3 appendix B) and, to a lesser degree, whether its decision on the reimbursement of the costs of legal representation and assistance of the successful party is appropriate.[122]

Needless to say, the Court will, in the interest of the reputation of the Swiss Rules, use their right to adjust the cost decision to discretely advise an arbitral tribunal if it finds that a draft award obviously does not meet an acceptable quality standard.

The review of the cost decision was discussed in the working group revising the UNCITRAL Arbitration Rules. After long discussions, the working group decided that the revised rules should not provide for a mere consultation on cost issues, as foreseen in article 39(4) of the UNCITRAL Rules 1976, but for a system permitting the parties to refer for review by the appointing authority both (a) a proposal for the determination of the arbitral tribunal made at the outset of the proceedings as well as (b) the arbitral tribunal's ultimate determination of its fees and expenses in the final award or other decisions.[123]

121 See Wehrli, Koenig and Triebold, 'Management of the Proceedings and Quality Control', p. 104.

122 See Markus Wirth, 'Financial Aspects: The Costs of Arbitration', in Gabrielle Kaufmann-Kohler and Blaise Stucki (eds.), *The Swiss Rules of International Arbitration, ASA Special Series No. 22* (Zurich: ASA, 2004), pp. 112–13.

123 This authority will, if necessary, adjust the arbitral tribunal's determination (article 40(1) and article 41(3) to (6) of the UNCITRAL Rules 2010). If no appointing authority has been designated by the time the award is rendered, the final determination of the arbitral tribunal's fees and expenses is for the Secretary General of the Permanent Court of Arbitration (the 'PCA') at The Hague to decide upon (article 41(4)(b) of the UNCITRAL Rules 2010).

4.11 *Emergency arbitrator*

The 2012 version of the Swiss Rules introduces emergency relief proceedings (article 43). This procedure is designed for cases where a party urgently requires interim relief but does not yet have access to an arbitral tribunal. Article 43 Swiss Rules thus provides that party with a venue for interim relief in cases where the arbitral procedure has not yet been started and where the tribunal is not yet appointed. The applicant party, however, subsequently needs to link the emergency relief proceedings to a regular arbitration proceeding: the Court terminates the emergency relief proceedings if the Notice of Arbitration is not submitted within ten days from the receipt of the Application (article 43(3) Swiss Rules).

The claimant starts emergency relief proceedings by submitting a request to the Secretariat. The Court then appoints the emergency arbitrator (subsequent to payment of the registration fee and of the deposit) and the emergency arbitrator is to render his decision within fifteen days after transmission of the file to him.

The emergency relief proceedings are akin to interim relief in an ongoing arbitration and, therefore, do not exclude an initial *ex parte* decision.

The emergency arbitrator must be independent and impartial and he must ensure that both parties have a reasonable opportunity to present their case. The emergency relief proceedings thus both guarantee a swift decision in an urgent matter and due process. Unless otherwise agreed by all parties, an emergency arbitrator may not serve as arbitrator in any arbitration relating to the dispute for which he has acted (article 41(1) Swiss Rules).

5 Expedited procedure

The Swiss Rules offer specific rules on expedited procedure, which apply if the amount in dispute is below one million Swiss francs[124] or if the

[124] For the determination as to whether the expedited procedure shall apply (because the amount in dispute does not exceed one million Swiss francs), the Court relies on the aggregate of the claim and the counterclaim (or any set-off defence) known upon receipt of the Answer (article 3(11) Swiss Rules). Accordingly, later amendments of the claim, a later set-off defence or counter-claim (or an increase thereof) or a later decrease of the amounts in dispute do not require an expedited procedure to be transformed into an ordinary procedure or vice versa. Although articles 6(4) and 42(2) Swiss Rules do not explicitly state so, this seems to be the logical consequence

parties agree that an expedited procedure shall take place irrespective of the amount in dispute.[125] Vice versa, the parties may opt out in cases where the amount in dispute is below one million Swiss francs. The Swiss Rules aim to provide a special service, but do not intend to impose it on the parties and limit their autonomy.[126]

If the rules on expedited procedure apply, the tribunal must render the award within six months from the transmission of the file.[127] The procedure as such is 'expedited' (or simplified when compared to the ordinary procedure) in that the parties are limited to one exchange of briefs and one hearing, and that the arbitral tribunal is only required to provide the reasons for its decision in summary form.[128] Likewise, cases are usually referred to a sole arbitrator, unless the arbitration agreement provides otherwise, and the parties are unwilling to amend their agreement,[129] all of which is designed to accelerate dispute resolution.

The Court may extend the six-month time limit in exceptional circumstances (article 42(1)(d) Swiss Rules). The Swiss Rules do not detail what would qualify as 'exceptional circumstances'; conceivably, a joint application to stay the proceedings during settlement discussions, or even the submission of new and unexpected arguments and/or exhibits at a rather late stage may meet the criterion of article 42(1)(d) Swiss Rules.[130] The expedited procedure should not endanger the due-process rights of either party or prevent procedural agreements of the parties.

If the Chambers do not extend the six-month deadline and the arbitral tribunal does not render its award in a timely fashion, this may expose the award to the risk of annulment or non-enforcement. This risk does, however, not exist in Switzerland, where the Supreme Court decided that

of article 3(11) Swiss Rules (see the contribution of Elliott Geisinger, 'The Expedited Procedure under the Swiss Rules of International Arbitration', in Gabrielle Kaufmann-Kohler and Blaise Stucki (eds.), *The Swiss Rules of International Arbitration, ASA Special Series No. 22* (Zurich: ASA, 2004), sections 4.2 and 4.3).

125 Article 42(2) Swiss Rules.

126 On the expedited procedure in general, see also Lörcher, 'The Swiss Rules of Arbitration Seen from Abroad', pp. 72–5.

127 This deadline may be extended in exceptional circumstances only (article 42(1)(d) Swiss Rules).

128 Article 42(1) Swiss Rules.

129 Article 42(2)(c) Swiss Rules. In the event that the parties do not agree on a sole arbitrator, the fee of an arbitral tribunal of three members shall be at least CHF 350 per hour and arbitrator (section 2.8 of appendix B).

130 Matthias Scherrer, 'Acceleration of Arbitration Proceedings – The Swiss Way: The Expedited Procedure under the Swiss Rules of International Arbitration', *Schieds VZ* (5/2005), 233 *et seq.*

an arbitral tribunal does not forgo jurisdiction by failure to respect a time limit set for rendering the award.[131]

The expedited procedure under the Swiss Rules has been well received and accounted for more than 30% of the new proceedings initiated in the years 2009 to 2011.

[131] DFT 127 III 576; the risk, however, is inherent if the arbitration is seated in other states, such as France (see Brunner, 'The Swiss Rules of Arbitration: An Overview', p. 249).

PART IV

New trends in international arbitration

15

'Domesticating' the New York Convention: The impact of the US Federal Arbitration Act

GEORGE A. BERMANN

1 Introduction

Much as one may try to universalize and even 'de-nationalize' international commercial arbitration – whether through Conventions, uniform or model laws or soft law – the phenomenon remains profoundly affected by national law and policy. That is indeed very much one of the leitmotifs of this book.

The incongruities – big and small – between domestic and international arbitration regimes typically present themselves on a purely *ad hoc* basis; that is to say, in specific and often isolated contexts, as when a particular case in a national court produces a result that looks anomalous from the point of view of a major international instrument such as the New York Convention.[1] The current American Law Institute's Restatement of the US Law of International Commercial Arbitration[2] provides a very different and, indeed, unprecedented context for observing the discontinuities that may affect the application of the New York Convention in national law.

This is so for three basic reasons. First, few commercially significant countries can compete with the United States for the World Title in International Law Exceptionalism. If any state were poised to disrupt the simple and sleek view of international arbitration held dear in many international arbitration circles, it would be the USA.

Second, a Restatement of US law in any given field comes around only rarely and it has only just now come around for international commercial arbitration. By its very nature, a Restatement re-examines a field in a fashion

[1] United Nations Convention on the Recognition and Enforcement of Foreign Arbitral Awards, reprinted at 9 USC sec. 201.

[2] American Law Institute, Restatement of the Law (Third) of the US Law of International Commercial Arbitration, Council Draft No. 2, approved, Oct. 20, 2010 (hereinafter 'Restatement').

that is both comprehensive, on the one hand, and detailed and focused, on the other. A Restatement of the US Law of International Commercial Arbitration can thus reveal on a large scale, but at the same time with great specificity, the tensions between international arbitration as viewed both nationally and internationally. It is helpful to recall that Restatements began over 80 years ago in the USA for the purpose of fostering clarity, consistency and coherence in the fields of law most apparently in need of them.[3] Unsurprisingly, the initial fields subject to Restatement were ones not only of state rather than federal law, but also ones characteristically taking common law rather than statutory form. Against that background, when a federal law subject (such as international commercial arbitration) that is governed by federal statute (again, such as international commercial arbitration) becomes the subject of a Restatement, it is a sure sign that something is not entirely right with it.

This circumstance may, in turn, be explained by the combination of legal sources – a domestic statute that long predates the New York Convention and a vast case law interpreting the Convention chiefly on the basis of interstate, rather than on international cases – on which a US Restatement draws. The USA stands in a position that is very different from the many jurisdictions having modern international commercial arbitration legislation, particularly those that have adopted UNCITRAL's own Model Law on International Commercial Arbitration,[4] among whose purposes was precisely to reduce to a minimum, if not to vanishing point, contradictions between the New York Convention and the local *lex arbitri*.

Third, this moment is further apt for gauging the 'fit' between US and international models of international commercial arbitration; since the New York Convention is itself the subject both of proposals for comprehensive reform[5] and of what may fairly be called 'Restatement'-type activity. As regards the latter, UNCITRAL has recently commissioned an 'UNCITRAL Guide to the New York Convention', whose purpose is to expose and, hopefully, mitigate the divergent interpretations that the

[3] George A. Bermann, 'Restating The US Law of International Commercial Arbitration', *NYU J Int'l L. & Pol.* 42(2009), 175; George A. Bermann, *The American Law Institute Goes Global: The Restatement of International Commercial Arbitration* (2008), p. 300.

[4] UNCITRAL Model Law on International Commercial Arbitration (adopted by the United Nations Commission on International Trade Law, June 21, 1985, as amended).

[5] Albert Jan van den Berg, 'Hypothetical Draft Convention on the International Enforcement of Arbitral Agreements and Awards', available at www.arbitration-icca.org (29 May 2008); Albert Jan van den Berg, *Fifty Years of the New York Convention* (Kluwer, 2009).

Convention has received in the hands of national courts around the world.[6] Anyone who takes the Convention's ambitions seriously will be sensitive to its vulnerability to, at best, idiosyncratic and, at worst, destructive national interpretations. This is a risk that all international treaty regimes run when they lack their own designated international tribunal charged with establishing the treaty's authoritative interpretation – and it is a risk that UNCITRAL is seeking to mitigate.

2 A taxonomy of tensions

It would ordinarily be too early in the Restatement process to reach conclusions about the nature of, and reasons for, the tensions that exist between the US law of international commercial arbitration, on the one hand, and the New York Convention and UNCITRAL Model Law, on the other. However, for completely unrelated reasons, the Restatement work began with the chapter on recognition and enforcement of international arbitral awards, the Convention's own subject.[7] This made it possible – much earlier in the life of the project than one might have thought – to identify the discontinuities.

A review of the tensions that have emerged in the course of this still quite young project, shows that they fall within four main categories: (1) tensions due to the age and character of the Federal Arbitration Act (FAA) as such; (2) tensions created by certain procedural features of US law that affect international commercial arbitration, much as they do any other US law field; (3) tensions generated by an effort by US courts – consciously or unconsciously – to promote international arbitration's efficiency and economy; and (4) tensions traceable, quite simply, to aspects of American federalism.

2.1 *The Federal Arbitration Act*

A first set of tensions stem from peculiarities embedded in the now quite old FAA, even as amended pursuant to the New York Convention.[8]

[6] See www.uncitral.org/uncitral/en/uncitral_texts/arbitration/NYConvention.html.

[7] The Restatement chapter titles, as currently contemplated are: Ch. 1 Scope and definitions; Ch. 2 The agreement to arbitrate and its enforcement; Ch. 3 Judicial involvement in the international arbitral process; Ch. 4 Post-award relief; Ch. 5 Investor–state arbitration.

[8] Federal Arbitration Act, 9 USC secs. 1ff.

The Convention, it will be recalled, permits states, upon ratification, to declare that they will consider themselves bound to recognize and enforce only those foreign awards rendered on the territory of another contracting state.[9] Like many other states, the USA has made such a declaration.[10] The result, however, is that awards made on the territory of states (such as Taiwan or Liechtenstein) that have not become parties to the Convention – i.e. 'foreign non-Convention awards' – are not entitled to the presumptive recognition and enforcement in the USA that is guaranteed by the Convention.

Unfortunately, these awards – admittedly few in number – do not fall within the scope of any of the three current chapters of the FAA. FAA Chapter One – the original chapter – contemplates awards in interstate commerce, which could possibly, by extension, include foreign commerce, except for the fact that the chapter is suffused with references to the *vacatur* of such awards by US courts.[11] Clearly, when Congress enacted FAA Chapter One, it had in mind only awards made on the territory of the USA. By definition, FAA Chapters Two and Three do not cover such awards either, as those chapters apply specifically and exclusively to Convention awards. It would not be acceptable to apply the FAA chapters governing Convention awards analogically to those awards from which the USA has expressly withheld the promise of recognition and enforcement under the Conventions.

The Restatement eventually determined that, while recognition and enforcement of foreign non-Convention awards could plausibly be governed by some judge-made, general federal common law rule or by the law of award recognition and enforcement of the relevant US state, both solutions presented severe drawbacks. On the one hand, the subject does not present the evident overriding federal interest – such as sovereign immunity in the pre-FSIA days and the act of state doctrine today – that is required in order to justify the creation of a federal common law. On the other hand, subjecting the recognition and enforcement of any class of foreign awards to state statutory or common law, which can and

[9] New York Convention, *supra* note 1, art. I (3): 'When signing, ratifying or acceding to this Convention, . . . any State may on the basis of reciprocity declare that it will apply the Convention to the recognition and Enforcement of awards made only in the territory of another Contracting State.'

[10] United States Reservation, reprinted at 9 USC sec. 201.

[11] See Federal Arbitration Act, 9 USC sec. 10(a): 'In any of the following cases the United States court in and for *the district wherein the award was made* may make an order vacating the award upon application of any party to the arbitration' (emphasis added).

does vary from state to state, would thwart the fundamental purpose of the FAA, which was to adopt a single broadly pro-arbitration set of principles at the federal level. In the end, the Restatement favours application to foreign non-Convention awards of the principles of FAA Chapter One governing arbitral awards in interstate commerce, while also allowing resort to state arbitration law to the extent not inconsistent with FAA Chapter One.[12]

The USA not only imposed the reciprocity requirement that generated the problem just discussed, it also – and here it acted very much alone – accepted the invitation in the Convention to ratifying states to declare unilaterally that they will consider as foreign Convention awards, within the meaning of the Convention, awards that, while rendered on national territory, bear some reasonable relationship with a foreign country and could therefore be deemed as 'non-domestic'.[13] The FAA accordingly states that the Convention shall govern recognition and enforcement of awards arising out of a relationship that involves a party that is not a citizen of the USA or that 'involves property located abroad, envisages performance or enforcement abroad, or has some other reasonable relation with one or more foreign States'.[14] This seemingly harmless, even generous, act of the United States has caused substantial problems of its own. On the one hand, since by most accounts, the Convention does not govern the *vacatur* or annulment of awards made locally, these 'Convention awards made in the US' should be subject to purely domestic grounds for annulment. On the other hand, since the USA has declared by statute that these awards are to be treated as if 'foreign', they logically should be subject to annulment only on the Convention's grounds for denying recognition and enforcement to foreign Convention awards.

The situation would be unproblematic if the US grounds for annulling domestic awards perfectly paralleled the US grounds for denying recognition and enforcement to foreign awards. But they do not. Controversially, domestic awards may apparently be vacated on grounds

[12] Restatement, sec. 5–3(d): 'A party may seek recognition or enforcement of a non-Convention award by proceeding under Chapter One of the Federal Arbitration Act or under applicable state law to the extent that it does not conflict with Chapter One of the Federal Arbitration Act.'

[13] New York Convention, *supra* note 1, art. I(1): 'This Convention . . . shall also apply to arbitral awards not considered as domestic awards in the State where their recognition and enforcement are sought.'

[14] Federal Arbitration Act, 9 USC sec. 202.

of 'manifest disregard of the law'[15] – a concept whose contours remain unclear and which seems at variance, in letter and spirit, with the notion that international arbitral awards are not subject to review by national courts based on their merits. The lower federal courts remain divided on this issue.[16]

Clearly, the language and structure of the FAA are inapt for purposes of dealing convincingly with two of the Convention's most basic categories of awards: awards rendered on the territory of non-Convention states and Convention awards made on domestic territory.

2.2 *Procedural aspects of US law*

A second and larger category of tensions between US law and the New York Convention stems from the straightforward application to the recognition and enforcement of Convention awards of a variety of traditional US law assumptions of a procedural character. The research conducted in connection with the Restatement has revealed a significant number of such tensions.

By way of example, US law is generally tolerant of alternative avenues of relief. In that spirit, the Restatement – like the case law before it[17] – gives prevailing parties in international arbitration the option of either (1) bringing a foreign award, as such, directly to the US for enforcement or (b) seeking confirmation of the award in the courts of the place of rendition and then bringing that judgment to the USA for enforcement. This is widely known as 'parallel entitlement'.[18] Although parties almost invariably prefer the award enforcement over the judgment enforcement route, they have the choice. This approach may well offend those in arbitration circles who believe that making the Convention merely an option (albeit an option that parties will practically always elect), rather than the exclusive means, diminishes the Convention and unduly

[15] See, e.g., *Marcy Lee Mfg. Co* v. *Cortley Fabrics Co.*, 354 F.2d 42 (2d Cir. 1965).

[16] See generally, *I/S Stavborg* v. *National Metal Converters, Inc.*, 500 F.2d 424 (2d Cir. 1974).

[17] See, e.g., *Seetransport Wiking Trader Schifffahrtsgesellschaft mbH & Co.* v. *Navimpez Centrala Navala*, 29 F.3d 79 (2d Cir. 1994).

[18] Restatement, sec. 4–3(c): 'If a foreign award has been reduced to judgment by a court in the arbitral seat, a party may seek either (1) recognition or enforcement of the award in accordance with the provisions of this Chapter; or (2) recognition or enforcement of the judgment in accordance with the foreign judgment recognition and enforcement standards of the forum in which such relief is sought.'

complicates the enforcement of foreign awards. However, it ultimately broadens the avenues for award enforcement in the USA.

Second, US law typically gives wide scope to the notion of 'waiver', so that, under absent compelling circumstances, parties are free to waive the rights that they otherwise enjoy, and may do so either expressly or impliedly, as through conduct. Courts are accordingly quick to find that parties have waived their procedural objections to the way an arbitration is conducted by failing to raise the objection on a timely basis before the arbitral tribunal.[19] More specifically, in the context of litigation, parties waive most of the Convention grounds for non-recognition and non-enforcement by failing to raise them by way of defence on a timely basis in an enforcement action.[20] This is not to say that waiver knows no limits under US law. For example, the Restatement does not consider that a party has waived the Convention's grounds for defeating recognition or enforcement on account of its failure – deliberate or otherwise – to bring a local annulment action against the award. On the other hand, if a party does bring an annulment action and fails to raise a particular ground in support of its action to annul, it may be barred from raising that ground in the context of later enforcement action.[21]

Third, and more generally, US law recognizes that many objections to the recognition or enforcement of awards may plausibly be raised at various stages in the lifecycle of an arbitration. For example, a party may, early on, resist an order of a court to compel arbitration, on the ground that the dispute at hand falls outside the scope of the agreement to arbitrate.[22] If it is unsuccessful, and the arbitration occurs and an award is rendered, that same party may seek to have the award annulled,

[19] See, e.g., *International Standard Elec. Corp.* v. *Bridas Sociedad Anonima Petrolera*, 745 F. Supp. 172 (SDNY 1990).

[20] Restatement, sec. 5–17(a): 'Except as provided in secs. 5–13 and 5–14, a party may waive its right to invoke an objection that would justify a court denying recognition or enforcement of a Convention award at any time after the basis for such objection is known or should have been known. Such waiver may be the result of either express consent or failure to raise an objection in a clear and timely manner.' The only unwaivable grounds are those found in Articles V(2)(a) (non-arbitrability) and V(2)(b) (violation of public policy).

[21] Restatement, sec. 4–25 (f): 'A party ordinarily does not waive a particular objection merely by failing to bring a timely action to stay the arbitration or by failing to seek to have the award set aside. However, a party waives an objection to the extent that it: (1) participated in judicial proceedings to enforce the arbitration agreement, to stay the arbitration, or to set aside the award; (2) knew or should have known the relevant facts underlying an objection; and (3) failed to raise the objection in any such proceedings'.

[22] See, e.g., *Mediterranean Enterprises, Inc.* v. *Singsong Corp.*, 708 F.2d 1458 (9th Cir. 1983).

again on the ground that the dispute at hand falls outside the scope of the agreement to arbitrate.[23] This attempt will, in principle, be made before a court of the place of arbitration, often a court other than the one that compelled arbitration in the first place. If that attempt too is unsuccessful, the award may then be brought for enforcement to a court of yet another jurisdiction (a jurisdiction where assets of the respondent may be found) and the respondent may seek to defeat enforcement once again on the ground that the dispute at hand falls outside the scope of the agreement to arbitrate.[24]

Should a court's judgment on the 'scope of arbitration' issue be deemed binding on another court before which essentially the same question is raised at a later date in time? Or is the issue of 'scope' so fundamental to the legitimacy of the arbitration and the award that each of these courts should determine the question independently? The same situation may arise in connection with other grounds for non-recognition and non-enforcement under the Convention.[25]

Strong arguments may be made in favour of entitling, and even obligating, the court at every one of these stages to undertake an independent examination of the issue. Certainly, the effectiveness of the Convention's grounds for denying recognition and enforcement would be enhanced by authorizing *de novo* consideration of the issue at each stage. However, preclusion is deeply embedded in the practice of US litigation. The Restatement accordingly takes the position that judgments on these issues – whether local or foreign – should be given the same preclusive effect that prior judgments enjoy generally under the forum's judgment-recognition policies. This practice illustrates not only the kind of domestic procedural 'overlay' that this section evokes, but also an emphasis on economy in litigation that marks the third category of tensions described below.

[23] 9 USC sec. 10(a) authorizing *vacatur* '(4) where the arbitrators exceeded their powers . . .': UNCITRAL Model Law, *supra* note 4, art. 34(2)(a)(iii), authorizing set aside if '[t]he award deals with a dispute not contemplated by or not falling within the terms of the submission to arbitration, or contains decisions on matters beyond the scope of the submission to arbitration'.

[24] New York Convention, *supra* note 1, art. V(1)(c), authorizing denial of recognition or enforcement if '[t]he award deals with a difference not contemplated by or not falling within the terms of the submission to arbitration, or it contains decisions on matters beyond the scope of the submission to arbitration'.

[25] For example, a person may deny being a party to the arbitration agreement at the time a court is asked to compel arbitration, to annul an award or deny the award recognition or enforcement.

Fourth, and more problematic in the New York Convention context, is the common law's traditional embrace not only of 'claim preclusion' (or, broadly, *res judicata*), but also of 'issue preclusion' (or collateral estoppel). Claim preclusion goes, of course, to the heart of 'recognition', within the meaning of the New York Convention. If recognition of an award means anything, it means that a party to an arbitration is not permitted to re-litigate a legal claim finally adjudicated in the arbitration.[26] Issue preclusion, or collateral estoppel, is a well-established principle of the law of judgments in common law countries, but not elsewhere. And there is nothing in the negotiating history of the Convention to suggest that the drafters intended by recognition to make awards binding not only as to the claims actually arbitrated, but also as to issues actually determined by the arbitral tribunal in the course of deciding the case.

The question then arises as to whether the Convention, even if it cannot be said to *compel* issue preclusion, nevertheless *permits* US courts to give issue preclusive effect to Convention awards. Although it would be possible to deny awards any preclusive effect whatsoever, the Restatement leaves open that possibility. It provides that, in order for a Convention award to exert issue preclusive effect in a US court, three sets of conditions must be met: first, the award must be entitled to recognition (i.e. claim preclusion) under the terms of the Restatement; second, the award must meet all the requirements that forum law imposes before judgments may be given issue preclusive effect. Third, application of issue preclusion must not in any event cause unfair surprise to the party against whom issue preclusion is sought.[27] The latter requirement that must be met before issue preclusion is accorded to a judgment,[28] and the same should, *a fortiori*, apply to awards. Taken together, these conditions seek to ensure that a party's reasonable expectations concerning the binding effect of awards in other cases will be met and that there will not be, for any reason, unfair surprise.[29] It is difficult to think of a matter on

[26] See, e.g., *Rudell* v. *Comprehensive Accounting Corp.*, 802 F.2d 926 (7th Cir. 1986).
[27] Restatement, sec. 4–10: 'A court grants preclusive effect to the determination of a specific issue made by an international arbitral award if (a) the award is entitled to recognition under this Chapter; (b) the award satisfies the requirements for issue preclusion prescribed for an arbitral award by the law of the forum in which such recognition is sought; and (c) barring relitigation of the issue will not cause unfair surprise to the party against whom issue preclusion is sought.'
[28] See generally Restatement of (Second) Judgments, sec. 84(1).
[29] Restatement, sec. 4–10, *b(ii), (iii)*.

which the task of accommodating the Convention to peculiarities of US procedure is as challenging as issue preclusion.

Fifth, and finally, we come to a bundle of purely procedural features that have the potential of adversely affecting, or at the very least complicating, enforcement of foreign awards in the USA under the Convention. The problem arises from Article III of the Convention, which directs states to accord recognition and enforcement 'in accordance with the rules of procedure of the territory where the award is relied upon'.

For some procedural issues, the difficulties are easily overcome. It seems uncontroversial, for example, that a legal system should be able to apply to recognition and enforcement actions in its courts the same hearing and evidentiary regimes as govern the conduct of civil and commercial litigation generally. So too, states may themselves determine the limitations period applicable to actions for the enforcement of awards, at least if it is not unreasonably short.[30]

Slightly more problematic is the effect on the recognition and enforcement of awards of domestic law rules on personal jurisdiction. Virtually all jurisdictions place general limitations on the right of its courts to exercise personal jurisdiction over non-domiciliaries. Unless one reads the Convention as impliedly doing away with any such discipline on the exercise of personal jurisdiction by domestic courts over non-domiciliaries, the personal jurisdiction rules of the place where recognition or enforcement is sought should continue to apply as usual. That seems to be a common assumption.

The real test arises when contracting states invoke domestic law limitations on the *exercise* of jurisdiction to bar the maintenance of a recognition or enforcement action in its courts. These limitations may take the form of *lis pendens* or *forum non conveniens*. The former will rarely present a problem in the USA, since US courts, unlike courts in the European Union,[31] do not regard themselves as obligated to decline jurisdiction on *lis pendens* grounds. By contrast, dismissals or stays on *forum non conveniens* grounds are common in international litigation in US courts. Although actions to enforce foreign arbitral awards will not generally present the degree of inconvenience required for application of

[30] The Federal Arbitration Act, sec. 207, prescribes a three-year statute of limitations running from the date of issuance of the award.

[31] Council Regulation 44/2001 of 22 December 2000 on 'Jurisdiction and the Recognition and Enforcement of Judgments in Civil and Commercial Matters', *OJ L*, 12 (Jan. 16, 2001), art. 27.

the doctrine, US courts do entertain such motions[32] and have, admittedly rarely, granted them.[33]

While it may be argued that *forum non conveniens* is just another domestic procedural rule that Article III of the Convention invites courts to apply in enforcement actions, its application entitles a court in its discretion to refuse to hear a case it is competent to hear. To stay or dismiss an action to recognize or enforce a foreign arbitral award on convenience grounds stands in obvious tension with states' international obligation under the New York Convention to recognize and enforce qualifying awards. The Restatement accordingly excludes all application of *forum non conveniens* to arbitral awards subject to the Convention.[34]

2.3 *Economy and efficacy interests*

Several of the broadly procedural examples given above – such as waiver and preclusion – share the characteristic of promoting economy and efficiency in international arbitration. To that extent, they represent more than mere procedural 'overlays'. They could just as easily be placed in a third category of litigation features; namely, features driven by economy and efficiency concerns. The Restatement contains a significant number of such provisions.

Among the most controversial is the Restatement's tentative decision to treat the grant of interim measures by arbitral tribunals as arbitral awards for recognition and enforcement purposes.[35] (Reference here is made to interim *measures*, not interim or partial *awards*.[36]) This decision, which may seem counterintuitive inasmuch as interim measures are in a sense by their nature non-final, was taken essentially to

[32] See Restatement, secs. 4–29, 5–21, reporters' notes *a*, *b* and *c*, and cases cited therein.

[33] See, e.g., *Monegasque de Reassurances S.A.M.* v. *Nak Naftogaz of Ukraine*, 311 F.3d 488 (2d Cir. 2002); *CHS Europe S.A.* v. *El Attal*, 2010 US Dist. LEXIS 76619 (SDNY, July 22, 2010).

[34] Restatement, sec. 4–29(a): 'An action to confirm a US Convention award or enforce a foreign Convention award is not subject to a stay or dismissal in favour of a foreign court on forum non conveniens grounds.' However, the Restatement leaves open the possibility, rare in practice, of a *forum non conveniens* stay or dismissal of an action to enforce a non-Convention award. See *supra* notes 9–12 and accompanying text.

[35] Restatement, sec. 1–1(a): 'An "arbitral award" is a decision in writing by an arbitral tribunal that sets forth the final and binding determination on the merits of a claim, defense, or issue, whether or not that decision resolves the entire controversy before the tribunal. Such a decision may consist of a grant of interim relief.'

[36] To avoid terminological confusion, the Restatement avoids use of the term 'interim award', recognizing only 'interim measures' and 'partial awards'.

strengthen the enforceability of arbitral interim measures and, thereby, the efficacy of arbitration. Treating arbitral orders of interim relief as awards will of course impose costs. At a minimum, it will require drawing a line between procedural orders (which are not awards) and interim orders (which are).[37] It will also enable parties to seek their annulment, occasioning some delay. Yet the benefits of rendering interim measures immediately enforceable – hence more reliably effective – have prevailed thus far in the Restatement deliberations.

Discussion in the course of preparing the Restatement chapter on recognition and enforcement also concerned the weight to be given to arbitral findings of fact when those findings relate directly to the presence or absence of a ground for denying recognition or enforcement of an award under the Convention. The ordinary assumption is that courts determine independently whether such a ground is established. But might occasions not arise in which the presence or absence of a ground depends on a pure finding of fact that the arbitral tribunal had occasion to make and may have been better placed to make? For example, if, in deciding whether a party received adequate notice of proceedings, a court must determine the moment at which notice was given, the court may consider it appropriate to give weight to an arbitral finding on that issue, particularly if the tribunal heard conflicting witness testimony on the matter. The availability or unavailability of a defence to recognition and enforcement will not frequently depend on such testimony-based factual conclusions. But if and when it does, it may serve economy and efficiency for the arbitral finding of fact to be shown a measure of deference.

Relatedly, the parties may, in their agreement, have expressly given the arbitrators final authority to determine whether a given dispute falls within the scope of a pre-dispute arbitration agreement. Again, US courts, in principle, determine independently whether a party seeking to defeat recognition or enforcement of an award has established the circumstances necessary for such a defence.[38] However, this particular ground for non-recognition or non-enforcement squarely entails contract interpretation, an exercise on which arbitral tribunals are generally

[37] Restatement, sec. 1-1, comment q: 'Interim measures are to be distinguished from routine scheduling, procedural, or evidentiary rulings relating to the proceedings. Such rulings serve organizational as opposed to remedial purposes, and for that reason do not ordinarily warrant judicial enforcement.'

[38] Restatement, sec. 4-7.

meant to have the final word, and it may be more efficient for courts to give weight to the arbitrators' determination of the breadth of the agreement to arbitrate. Consequently, the Restatement, much like the case law generally,[39] permits the parties to shift ultimate authority on the 'scope' question to the arbitral tribunal, provided the parties have clearly and unmistakably delegated that authority to the tribunal.[40]

Considerations of economy and efficiency will undoubtedly figure more prominently in the chapters of the Restatement that lie ahead. For example, and without prejudging the matter, serious consideration is sure to be given to the availability of anti-suit injunctions in support of orders referring the parties to arbitration. Such considerations are likewise likely to influence Restatement positions concerning legal aspects of the conduct of the arbitration. However, as the examples here given illustrate, economy and efficiency concerns have surfaced already in regard to the recognition and enforcement of awards.

2.4 *American federalism*

We come finally to the quintessentially US law problem of federalism – unsurprisingly so, given the extent to which state law in the USA can have an impact on matters of apparent federal concern. The federalism dimension arises in various guises.

In some respects, state law affects jurisdiction and procedure only. For example, in the US judicial system, state courts have jurisdiction over many, indeed most, claims arising under federal law. Odd as it may appear, in some instances, federal courts lack subject-matter jurisdiction to entertain claims even though they arise under federal law; such is the case with actions arising under Chapter One of the FAA.[41] Such claims may be brought in federal court only if some independent basis for federal court jurisdiction exists.[42] In other cases, federal courts may enjoy subject-matter jurisdiction, but not exclusively so, so that such actions may be brought in state court[43] – though even then, they are

[39] *Corp.* v. *WAK Orient Power & Light, Ltd.*, 168 F. Supp. 2d 403, 411 (E.D. Pa. 2001). See also *Rent-a-Center, W., Inc.* v. *Jackson*, 130 S.Ct. 2772, 177 L.Ed. 2d 403, 2010 US LEXIS 4981 (June 21, 2010).

[40] Restatement, sec. 4–14(c): 'A court determines de novo whether a Convention award deals with matters that were not submitted to arbitration, unless the parties clearly and unmistakably submitted that issue to arbitration.'

[41] *Moses H. Cone Mem. Hosp.* v. *Mercury Constr. Corp.*, 460 US 1, 24 (1983).

[42] Restatement, sec. 4–26(b). [43] *Southland Corp.* v. *Keating*, 465 US 1 (1984).

subject to removal to federal court. Such is the case with actions arising under Chapters Two and Three of the FAA.[44] In short, cases arising under the FAA may well proceed in state court.

One may ask, in these circumstances, whether the state court is entirely free to follow its usual practices on matters of procedure. Surely the presumption must be that actions in state court are subject to state court procedural norms. But are there situations in which application of state procedural law would be inconsistent with the FAA or otherwise harmful to the achievement of federal policy in the matter of interstate and international arbitration? Although the latter question generated debate in the context of the Restatement, it was ultimately determined that the statute of limitations provided for in the FAA should be regarded as so closely intertwined with the substantive rights and claims created by the statute that it should apply even to actions under the FAA brought in state rather than federal court.[45] By contrast, rights of appeal from state court decisions granting or denying enforcement of awards remain governed by state law,[46] as does the decision whether to follow summary or expedited, rather than ordinary procedures in the enforcement action.[47]

State law may, however, have a more substantial impact on the enforcement of international awards. Although the FAA is commonly said to establish the federal government's paramount interest in arbitration in interstate and foreign commerce[48] and to exert a powerful pro-arbitration bias,[49] the fact remains that many US states have enacted legislation governing arbitration in both interstate and foreign commerce and that this legislation differs in many important respects both from the FAA and indeed from state to state.[50] It is clear that the FAA

[44] Restatement, sec. 4–26(d): 'A post-award action may also be brought in any competent state court.'

[45] Restatement, sec. 4–32(a): 'The limitations period applicable to a post-award action under federal law and the rules pertaining to its application are governed by federal law, irrespective of whether the action is brought in federal or state court.'

[46] Restatement, sec. 4–34(b): 'A party to a post-award action has a right of appeal from the final disposition of the action in a state court to the extent that it is permitted by the law of the forum and is not pre-empted by federal law.'

[47] Restatement, sec. 4–33, reporters' note a (ii).

[48] See, e.g., *Prima Paint Corp.* v. *Floor & Conklin Mfg. Co.*, 388 US 395 (1967).

[49] See, e.g. *Parsons & Whittemore Overseas Co.* v. *Société Générale de l'Industrie du Papier*, 508 F.2d 969 (2d Cir. 1974).

[50] For a discussion, see Gary B. Born, *International Commercial Arbitration*, 2nd edn (Kluwer, 2001), p. 39.

enjoys supremacy over state arbitration law, but it is equally clear that the FAA does not pre-empt the field.[51] It remains unclear – and will for some time – when exactly state law that is *different from* federal law is also *in conflict with* federal law.

The question is not an idle one. The US Supreme Court recently ruled that the FAA does not permit parties to heighten the scrutiny to be exercised by courts in actions to vacate local awards.[52] In other words, parties are not permitted by contract to add grounds for *vacatur* to those provided for in the FAA. It would seem that a state arbitration law that enables the parties to do so is not only different from, but also in conflict with federal law. Yet in that same decision, the Court – admittedly in pure dictum – raised the possibility that parties may be able, by subjecting their arbitration and award to a state arbitration law that permits contractual enhancement of the judicial review of awards, to achieve the very result that the FAA forbids.[53] This position is quite unconvincing on the merits, but what is significant for present purposes is its depiction of the tolerance that US law has, even in a federal statutory field such as arbitration, for federalism complications in the form of discrepant state law. Since the New York Convention does not govern *vacatur* of awards as such, the differences in grounds for *vacatur* among state laws should not adversely affect application of the Convention in the USA, except as regards enforcement of Convention awards made in the USA.[54]

However, US federalism can have a more direct impact on recognition and enforcement claims under the New York Convention. The Convention permits courts of contracting states to deny recognition or enforcement of a Convention award insofar as giving effect to the award would violate the public policy of the place where recognition or enforcement is sought.[55] Yet public policy within the USA is not exclusively federal; states are entitled to have and enforce their own public policy

51 *Volt Information Sciences, Inc.* v. *Board of Trustees*, 489 US 468, 477 (1989).

52 *Hall Street Associates, L.L.C.* v. *Mattel, Inc.*, 552 US 576, 586 (2008).

53 *Hall Street Associates*, *supra* note 52, at 590: 'In holding that [FAA sections 9 and 10] provide exclusive regimes for the review provided by the statute, we do not purport to say that they exclude more searching review based on authority outside the statute as well. The FAA is not the only way into court for parties wanting review of arbitration awards: they may contemplate enforcement under state statutory or common law, for example, where judicial review of different scope is arguable. But here we speak only to the scope of the expeditious judicial review under [the FAA], deciding nothing about other possible avenues for judicial enforcement of arbitration awards.'

54 See notes 9–13 *supra* and accompanying text.

55 New York Convention, *supra* note 1, art, V(2)(b).

insofar as it is compatible with federal law. Admittedly, confining public policy within the meaning of the Convention to federal, as distinct from state, public policy would enhance uniformity and predictability in the recognition and enforcement of awards in the USA, but that benefit would be purchased at a significant cost to the careful balance between policymaking at the federal and state levels. In the interest of maintaining that balance, the Restatement recognizes a place for state public policy within the meaning of the exception,[56] but narrows substantially the circumstances in which it can be invoked.[57]

3 Conclusion

The fact that international agreements do not translate perfectly into the national legal orders of countries that subscribe to them is nothing new, and agreements on inherently international law subjects such as international commercial arbitration are no exception. What is exceptional is the opportunity that the current elaboration of a Restatement of the US Law of International Commercial Arbitration provides for observing the discontinuities comprehensively and in detail. These discontinuities stem from a number of national peculiarities that the Restatement has furnished the occasion to observe.

A factor of fundamental importance in understanding the tensions between US law, even as restated, and the New York Convention is the central role that the FAA plays in establishing the legal framework of international commercial arbitration in the USA. It is not surprising that national legislation that precedes the international instrument by some 45 years would give rise to divergences between them, and that those

[56] Restatement, sec. 4–18(c): 'A court generally determines whether a grant of post-award relief violates public policy in accordance with federal law. However, in exceptional circumstances, a court may vacate or deny confirmation of a U.S. Convention award or deny recognition or enforcement of a foreign Convention award based on repugnance to the public policy of a state if that state has a sufficiently compelling and predominant interest in the matter, and provided that the state policy is not inconsistent with federal policy.'

[57] Restatement, sec. 4–18, comment e: 'Courts look principally to federal law to determine the existence and application of public policy. However, their judgments in this regard are legitimately informed by the policies of the several states and, in a rare case, may be determined largely by reference to the policy of a single state. The offense caused to a single state's policy will not properly justify vacatur, or a denial of confirmation, recognition, or enforcement unless that state has a compelling and paramount interest in the matter that is not inconsistent with federal policy.'

divergences might be heightened by the discrepant ways in which that legislation has been interpreted by courts over the years. However, the divergences are themselves substantial.

Moreover, to one degree or another, every legal system translates international law through its own complex of procedural rules and assumptions. As the examples in this chapter show, procedures and assumptions of US law have shaped, in ways large and small, the operation of the New York Convention in the US legal order. Although the importation of the *forum non conveniens* device into the enforcement of foreign arbitral awards may be the best known of these, it is only one among many.

Procedures do not develop in a vacuum. Rather, they reflect priorities and orientations of the legal systems in which they develop. Although US legal practice surely entails costs and inefficiencies, economy and efficiency remain the stated goals of the system. US law pursues these goals in a variety of ways, from treating interim measures as awards to embracing issue preclusion in international arbitration. It thereby leaves its distinctive imprint on the New York Convention regime in practice.

Finally, notwithstanding the presence of a federal statute and the inherently international character of international commercial arbitration, US federalism is leaving its mark on the subject. This is due, in part, to the dual court structure in the USA, whereby state courts are available even for the vindication of federal, including treaty-based, claims. However, it is also due to the belief that, in a federal system such as that of the USA, public policy is not the exclusive province of the federal government.

Few, if any, of the divergences identified in this chapter can be said to seriously impair the functioning of the New York Convention, much less place the USA in breach of its international treaty obligations. That, however, is not the point. The point, rather, is to recognize how much room there is for differential application even of a treaty that is deemed to be as successful and nearly as universal as the New York Convention.

16

New trends in international commercial arbitration in Latin America

DIEGO P. FERNÁNDEZ ARROYO

1 The mantra of the Latin-American hostility towards arbitration

The word 'hostility' usually appears in different kinds of contributions about the vast field of Latin-American arbitration. In the best-case scenario, this word is used to indicate that the hostile attitude towards arbitration is becoming less aggressive.[1] However, a common assumption seems to remain, according to which some rather generalized negative feeling against arbitration either existed or still exists in Latin America. It is true that sometimes the use of the expression is probably due to a simple repetition of clichés, yet even the most conspicuous specialists, in accurate works, often refer to it.[2] It makes it obvious that there is something that does not work perfectly in regard to arbitration in Latin America.

In this succinct contribution, aimed only at offering a survey of Latin-American international commercial arbitration, I will try to show that, if no nuances are introduced, the mentioned common assumption can be totally misunderstood. As a general statement, it must be underlined that there is a certain preoccupation with the concept of the state submitting to foreign (or 'heteronymous') jurisdictions and, in a broader sense, with any possibility that state sovereignty is conditioned by external powers or decisions. Needless to say, such a preoccupation, on the one hand, has

[1] H. A. Grigera Naón, 'Arbitration in Latin America: Overcoming Traditional Hostility (An Update)', *Univ. Miami Inter-Am. L. Rev.*, 22(1991), 203.

[2] P. Lalive, 'On the Reasoning of International Arbitral Awards', *Journ. of Int'l Dispute Settlement*, 1(2010) 55, 57; J. Kleinheisterkamp, *International Commercial Arbitration in Latin America. Regulation and Practice in the MERCOSUR and the Associated Countries* (Dobbs Ferry: Oceana, 2005), p. 465.

never been a peculiarity of Latin-American countries[3] or, on the other hand, of Latin-American history – in particular, but not only, during the last decades of the nineteenth and the first decades of the twentieth centuries – yet it generates suspicion about the neutrality and fairness of these powers and decisions.

Many authors reiterate that the root of the Latin-American hostile attitude towards arbitration can be found in the strength of the Calvo Doctrine,[4] which was adopted as a principle by most legal systems of this region. According to this widespread opinion, the Calvo Doctrine – sometimes considered together with the Drago Doctrine and often confused with the Calvo Clause – would have blocked the development of arbitration by affirming that foreign investors must submit to the courts of the host state. However, the reality is that the Calvo Doctrine appeared as an answer to the abuse of diplomatic protection and the Drago Doctrine as an answer to the use of the reimbursement by force of state debts. That is to say that the matters directly affected by these doctrines were state contracts and public interest issues involved therein. Therefore, they should not be, in principle, the direct cause of some sort of reluctance vis-à-vis commercial arbitration or arbitration in general.

A significant amount of data confirms that, insofar as neutrality and fairness seemed to be respected, the prevailing attitude has not been significantly hostile towards arbitration from a political perspective.[5] It has been, at least, not less favourable than the general attitude of other countries from outside the region. Most Latin-American states have chosen to submit their disputes either to international tribunals or courts

[3] Even in a country such as France, unanimously recognized as being arbitration friendly, the participation of public persons in arbitration may generate controversial judicial decisions. For example, *Tribunal des conflits*, 17 May 2010, case no. 3754, *Inserm* v. *Fondation Letten F. Saugstad*; see the strong critique of T. Clay, 'Les contorsions byzantines du Tribunal des conflits en matière d'arbitrage', *La Semaine Juridique* (21/2010), 1045–49. See also M. Laazouzi, 'L'impérativité, l'arbitrage international des contrats administratifs et le conflit de lois. A propos de l'arrêt du Tribunal des conflits du 17 mai 2010, *Inserm c/ Fondation Saugstad*', *Rev. crit. DIP*, (2010), 653. An English translation is available in *Mealey's International Arbitration Report*, 25/6(2010), with comments of D. Bensaude and J. Kirby.

[4] For two recent articles, see N. Blackaby and S. Noury, 'International Arbitration in Latin America', in B. Fauvarque-Cosson and A. Wald (eds.), *L'arbitrage en France et en Amérique latine à l'aube du XXIe siècle* (Paris: Société de législation comparée, 2008), pp. 283, 284, 295; J. Astigarraga, 'A Glimpse into the Cristal Ball: Latin American Arbitration Ten Years Hence', *Revista latinoamericana de mediación y arbitraje*, 10(2010), XXIII.

[5] See H. A. Grigera Naón, 'Arbitration and Latin America: Progress and Setbacks (2004 Freshfields Lecture)', *Arb. Int.*, 21(2) (2005), 127.

whenever they have felt confident about the latter.[6] Lack of confidence has always occurred when a state or state-owned company has been involved in a dispute, for the reasons mentioned above. Additionally, when the ICSID dispute settlement mechanism really started to operate, the old ghosts raised their heads. It was at that moment – only a few years ago – when some scepticism regarding arbitration in general regained notoriety. In other words, traditionally general and diffused worries regarding the activities of the states and the foreign pressures that were placed upon them started to create real discomfort about investment arbitration and, later, spread a degree of mistrust over arbitration as a way of solving disputes.

A completely different issue is that the existence of the closed link between arbitration and procedural law, borrowed from some old European concepts, still provokes practical difficulties when trying to solve legal disputes in several Latin-American countries (as well as in other countries around the world).[7] It is indeed clear that modern arbitration is at odds with (traditional) procedural law, even if, in several countries, arbitration rules are still located in general procedural legal bodies. Since modern arbitration proceedings are essentially flexible, while procedural law in many legal systems tends to be rigid and formalistic, coincidences between both systems are often little more than mere exceptions. Several legal systems have had problems in finding the right niche for arbitration within their own framework. For some, arbitration has been seen as an exception to the 'natural judge' (or to the 'ordinary jurisdiction') and, for that reason, the scope of arbitration agreements has had to be constructed in a restrictive manner. For others, arbitration is included in local jurisdiction and, therefore, the general rules applicable to judicial procedure (such as those dealing with available remedies) should, in principle, be applicable to arbitral procedure. There have also been some older technical elements that have impeded the normal development of arbitration. Among them, one can mention the requirement of a 'compromise' between the parties in order to validate a previous arbitral agreement and the requirement of judicial

[6] Ibid., in particular, when solving inter-state disputes such as those concerning border demarcations.

[7] To some authors, rather than the hostility towards arbitration, the problems concern the strong tradition of local procedural rules and the lawmakers' lack of experience of practical arbitration issues. See, F. Montilla Serrano, 'Le traitement législatif de l'arbitrage en Amérique Latine (quelques réformes récentes)', *Revue de l'arbitrage*, 3(2005), 561, 600–2.

recognition of the award in the country of the seat of arbitration in order to get enforcement abroad. This kind of 'conceptual' hostility has shown itself to be more difficult to overcome than the previously mentioned 'political' one. Perhaps the main reason for this is that the (missing) development of arbitration was traditionally under the control of civil-procedure scholarship.

I should also raise another preliminary consideration. Although this chapter deals with Latin America as a whole, it is obvious that in the matter of arbitration – as is true of many other legal and non-legal fields – Latin America is anything but a homogenous concept. Even if the concept is taken in its strictest sense, relating to the twenty independent states that are the former colonies of Spain, Portugal and France,[8] attitudes towards arbitration differ from country to country in the same way that attitudes related to, for example, politics, the economy or international relations differ. Consequently, any generalizations made concerning the matter of arbitration in the region generate the unavoidable risk of mistakes and misunderstandings.

2 Current legal framework

2.1 International instruments

To state that Latin-American countries have kept themselves outside of the wave of international codification of the international arbitration law is unjustified. All Latin-American states are contracting parties to the 1958 New York Convention on the Recognition and Enforcement of Foreign Arbitral Awards – the most important multilateral legal instrument in matters of arbitration.[9] Furthermore, only two states, Cuba and Haiti, are outside the framework of the main regional legal instrument – the 1975 Inter American Convention on International Commercial

[8] Namely Argentina, Bolivia, Brazil, Chile, Colombia, Costa Rica, Cuba, the Dominican Republic, Ecuador, El Salvador, Guatemala, Haiti, Honduras, Mexico, Nicaragua, Panama, Paraguay, Peru, Uruguay and Venezuela. Often, in scholastic contributions, Caribbean states that are former British or Dutch colonies are added to this list. However, in the usual language of international organizations, whenever a common list is made, the more precise expression of 'Latin-American and Caribbean' countries is used. In any case, it is well known that the concept of 'Latin America' is based on historical and political considerations that justify its use and has its roots in several other points of view.

[9] Honduras (2000), Brazil and the Dominican Republic (2002) and Nicaragua (2003) have been the last to join it. See www.uncitral.org/uncitral/en/uncitral_texts/arbitration/NYConvention_status.html.

Arbitration (better known as the Panama Convention) – that is elaborated within the framework of the Organization of American States (OAS).[10]

Individually, all Latin-American states have noted their agreement with the basic general assumptions shared by the international community about arbitration and, collectively, their attitude is not so different when developing regional economic-integration organizations or when aiming to form free-trade agreements. In particular, the promotion of arbitration as a dispute settlement mechanism has been officially sought by the Southern Common Market (MERCOSUR),[11] the Andean Community (CAN)[12] and the Central American Integration System (SICA).[13] Yet, neither the undoubted interest in promoting arbitration nor the adoption of some regional legal instruments concerning the

[10] In addition, more precisely, by its Inter-American Specialized Conference on Private International Law, designated under the Spanish acronym of CIDIP. See www.oas.org/juridico/english/sigs/b-35.html. Nevertheless, it is worth mentioning that Cuba and Haiti are the only Latin-American countries that have not ratified any CIDIP instrument. That is particularly understandable in the case of Cuba, whose OAS membership was suspended in 1962. Although the General Assembly reversed that decision in 2009, the Cuban Government has stated that Cuba is not interested in recovering its full membership to the body. There is another instrument of CIDIP applicable to arbitration (the 1979 Inter-American Convention on Extraterritorial Validity of Judgments and Arbitral Awards, in force in ten Latin-American states, www.oas.org/juridico/english/sigs/b-41.html), although its application to arbitration is avoided because of its character of *lex generalis* in respect of the other conventions (the New York and Panama Conventions).

[11] In spite of the availability of other international legal instruments – namely, the New York and Panama Conventions – Mercosouthern authorities decided in 1998 to elaborate a legal text – developed in an amazingly short time frame – the Agreement on International Commercial Arbitration. The Agreement, in force in the four member states, was adopted together with another identical instrument, which was developed in order to produce a common legal text for the Mercosouthern member states of Bolivia and Chile. This has not yet entered into force. Previously, in 1992, MERCOSUR had adopted the Las Leñas Protocol on the Judicial Co-operation in Civil, Commercial, Labor and Administrative Matters, which also includes rules on the recognition and enforcement of foreign judicial decisions and arbitral awards. Fortunately, both texts do not seem to be taken into account in matters of arbitration.

[12] The Treaty of the Court of Justice of the Andean Community contains two specific provisions (articles 38 and 39) on the 'arbitral function' that may be developed in both the Andean Court of Justice and by the General Secretary of the Andean Community. Those provisions have not yet been implemented, although the Andean Community, with the support of the European Union, has been trying to make them work (www.comunidadandina.org/ATRC/arbitral_1.html).

[13] SICA has introduced arbitration as a 'modern, supple, effective' means for the settlement of disputes between member states within the text of its constitutive treaty, known as the Tegucigalpa Protocol (article 35).

matter assure, in themselves, the improvement of the conditions for arbitration development. On the contrary, notwithstanding these efforts, whenever concrete decisions and the specific instruments are not appropriate, the outcome has proven itself to be either futile or directly negative in nature.[14]

In addition to the institutional features that have arisen from the framework of the regional economic-integration organizations, several other specific initiatives related to arbitration are ongoing. One of them is the creation of an organization called OHADAC, its main purpose seemingly based on the adoption of common rules on arbitration for several countries of the Caribbean region including Latin-American and non-Latin-American states.[15]

2.2 *Domestic rules*

At a domestic level, Latin-American countries have also experienced an intense modernizing impulse during the last two decades.[16] Almost all the countries in the region have adopted new legal arbitration texts,[17] most of them under the direct or indirect influence of the UNCITRAL Model Law on International Commercial Arbitration. Indeed, UNCITRAL recognizes, from among the states whose arbitration law is based on the Model Law,

[14] Perhaps the clearest example of a work characterized by total futility is the 1998 Mercosouthern Agreement mentioned above. In this sense, see J. R. Albornoz, 'El arbitraje en el derecho internacional privado y el MERCOSUR (con especial referencia a los acuerdos de arbitraje de 23 de julio de 1998)', *Anuario Argentino de Derecho Internacional*, IX(1999), 51–92; J. Kleinheisterkamp, 'Conflict of Treaties on International Arbitration in the Southern Cone', in *Liber Amicorum Jürgen Samtleben* (Montevideo: Max-Planck-Institut/FCU, 2002), pp. 695–7. Cf A. M. Perugini, 'Arbitraje comercial internacional en el MERCOSUR', in *Liber Amicorum Jürgen Samtleben*, pp. 633–7.

[15] Moreover, even the French territories. OHADAC is the acronym of the *Organisation pour l'Harmonisation du Droit des Affaires dans le Caraïbe* and, as its name suggests, it intends to follow the experience of its African model (OHADA), notwithstanding that the latter is an inter-governmental organization. See www.ohadac.com.

[16] According to certain authors, however, this degree of modernization would clearly not be sufficient. See, for instance, F. Cantuarias Salaverry, '¿Qué tanto ha avanzado Latinoamérica en el establecimiento de una normativa amigable a la práctica del arbitraje internacional?' *Revista latinoamericana de mediación y arbitraje*, 10(2) (2010), 59.

[17] The most significant exceptions are Argentina and Uruguay, although in both countries, several drafts on the matter have been elaborated on and the adoption of a new legislation on arbitration is expected. The UNCITRAL Model Law is nevertheless invoked in Argentinian judgments such as Supreme Court, 5 April 2005, *Bear Service SA* v. *Cervecería Modelo SA de CV*. See below note 44.

Chile (2004), the Dominican Republic (2008), Guatemala (1995), Honduras (2000), Mexico (1993), Nicaragua (2005), Paraguay (2002), Peru (1996, 2008) and Venezuela (1998).[18] Even most of the Latin-American arbitration laws that have not 'deserved' the UNCITRAL label have received a strong, though heterogeneous, influence from Model Law solutions. It means, at least from a formal perspective concerning the very domestic legal frameworks involved, that Latin-American arbitration should not be so different from the laws of Norway, Australia, California, Zambia or Azerbaijan.

In such a context, two particular national experiences have to be underlined. The first one is that of Brazil, which embodies the greatest change in the region. If there is a legal system that is deserving of the epithets generally applied in matters of arbitration to Latin America as a whole, it is that of Brazil. Actually, based on sovereignty arguments, this country and especially its judges and courts were traditionally reluctant to take on developments in arbitration, which explains the fact that the 1996 Arbitration Act[19] was frozen for five years before its practical implementation.[20] Nevertheless, once this legal obstacle was removed, the development of arbitration in Brazil has not ceased to astonish both local actors and foreign observers. The number of institutions, academic programmes, publications and international events related to arbitration has been growing since then.[21] The confidence in – and the familiarity with – arbitration in Brazilian businesses is today much broader than it used to be. The Brazilian judiciary has had to learn to cope with international arbitration because the real levels of activity in this field experienced strong growth. Nevertheless, it has been doing well. An important catalyst for the change of attitude was the shift, by means of Constitutional Amendment 45/2005, in terms of competence, to the

[18] See www.uncitral.org/uncitral/en/uncitral_texts/arbitration/1985Model_arbitration_status.html. Probably the recent Arbitration Act of Costa Rica (2011) will be incorporated into this list.

[19] Act no. 9.307, 23 September 1996.

[20] The concrete reason was the alleged contradiction between certain provisions of the Arbitration Act with the constitutional rule that grants the right of access to the judicial courts. The constitutional question was submitted to the *Suprêmo Tribunal Federal* in a case dealing with the enforcement of an award issued in Spain. After a long discussion, the court, in a majority decision, upheld the constitutionality of contested provisions, in SEC (*Sentença Estrangeira Contestada*) no. 5.206, 12 December 2001. See M. A. Muriel, 'A arbitragem frente ao judiciário brasileiro', *Revista Brasileira de Arbitragem* (2004), 27.

[21] A. Wald, 'L'évolution récente de l'arbitrage en Amérique latine', in B. Fauvarque-Cosson and A. Wald (eds.), *L'arbitrage en France et en Amérique latine à l'aube du XXIe siècle* (Paris: Société de législation comparée, 2008), pp. 217, 226.

recognition of foreign decisions from the *Suprêmo Tribunal Federal* (the STF, the highest Brazilian court, charged with the constitutional control of the rules) to the *Superior Tribunal de Justiça* (the STJ). The case law has confirmed the initial impression of scholars, according to which, since the STJ is both more specialized and more progressive than the STF, its case law could improve international cooperation in Brazil.[22] Judicial decisions both at federal[23] and state level[24] clearly show strong support for arbitration.[25]

The other relevant national feature is the emergence of a Peruvian *avantgardisme*. In 1996, Peru had adopted an Arbitration Act inspired by the 1985 Model Law and its functioning was generally recognized by practitioners and scholars as quite satisfactory. However, in 2008, Peru enacted a new Arbitration Act,[26] which, besides taking into account the amendments introduced into the UNCITRAL Model Law in 2006, contains interesting forward-looking provisions, several of them already

[22] See L. Gama Jr., 'La reconnaissance des sentences arbitrales étrangères au Brésil: évolutions récentes', *Bull. CCI*, 16(1) (2005), 72–3 ('the STJ is better suited to civil and commercial matters than the Supreme Court (whose chief role is to ensure that the Federal Constitution is respected) and more progressive in its decision-making'). See also R. A. Gaspar, *Reconhecimiento de Sentenças Arbitrais Estrangeiras no Brasil* (São Paulo: Atlas, 2009), pp. 59, 266–7. Nonetheless, it seems that the reform would have been even more important if the shift had not been from the STF to the STJ, but to the judges in the first instance. See P. Loula, 'Breves reflexões sobre repercussão da Reforma do Judiciário (Emenda Constitucional no 45/04) no Direito Internacional Privado', in *O Direito Internacional Contemporâneo. Estudos em homenagem ao Professor Jacob Dolinger* (Rio de Janeiro: Renovar, 2006), p. 793 ('it would have been a great service to the country, and helped to make its international relations easier').

[23] See, early after the shift, STJ, *Bouvery International S/A* v. *Irmãos Pereira – Comercial e Exportadora Ltda*, Case no. SEC 887/EX, 15 February 2006; STJ, *Union Europeénne de Gymnastique – UEG* v. *Multipole Distribuidora de Filmes Ltda*, Case no. SEC 874/EX, 19 April 2006.

[24] See, among many others, the recent decisions of the *Tribunais de Justiça* (State appeals courts) of Bahia, 4th Civil Chamber, *FAT Ferroâtlantica SL* v. *Zeus Mineração Ltda*, no 0002546-67.2010.805.0000-0, 6 April 2010; Rio de Janeiro, Civil Appeal, *Durval Biancalana da Silva e outros* v. *DTP Participações e Investimentos S/A e outros*, no. 0063229-77.2010.8.19.0001, 12 May 2010; São Paulo, 5th Public Law Chamber (anti-arbitration measure demanded by Companhia do Metropolitano de São Paulo – Metrô regarding an ICC Arbitral Tribunal no. 15.283/JRF), no. 990.10.284191-0, 28 July 2010; Rio de Janeiro, 20th Civil Chamber, *Litel Participações SA* v. *Eletron SA*, no. 0029077-06.2010.8.19.0000, 4 August 2010.

[25] A similar impression may be found in A. Wald, 'Brazil', *The Arbitration Review of the Americas* (2011) (www.globalarbitrationreview.com/reviews/32/sections/115/chapters/1203/brazil/).

[26] Legislative Decree no. 1071, 28 June 2008.

present in the former Act.[27] The treatment of the application for setting aside the award adopted by the arbitral tribunal is perhaps the one that best summarizes the spirit of Peruvian arbitration law since the Act of 1996. Firstly, the right to apply for setting aside may be excluded or limited by the parties, provided that none of them has a direct connection with Peru.[28] Secondly, the application does not suspend the enforcement of the award; however, under request from one of the parties, the court may suspend the enforcement by ordering the provision of an appropriate bank security.[29] It may be said that the main characteristic of this Act is the clear restriction to the intervention of judicial courts in arbitral proceedings, as a general assumption, except when such intervention is established by the Act[30] and, in particular, when one of the parties submits an application for setting aside the award (and this with the restriction mentioned above).[31] Consistently, according to the Act, all legal references to judges in their role of settling a dispute or taking a decision are deemed to be referred also to arbitrators, provided that an arbitral agreement has been concluded and that the matter is 'arbitrable'.[32] What particularly needs to be pointed out regarding the 2006 Peruvian Arbitration Act, is its clear call for localizing arbitration proceedings in Peru.

2.3 *Latin-American case law on arbitration*

By enacting new arbitration acts and ratifying standard instruments, states are sending out clear and favourable signals regarding arbitration. However, the reception of these signals is not homogeneous and their implementation often provokes contradictions. In countries with a separation of powers, it is common that the judicial power does not keep pace with the legislative or the executive powers. In some cases, it creates bolder solutions but, in other cases, it slows the developments achieved through the approval of new legal texts or the incorporation of international agreements. The paradigmatic

[27] F. Cantuarias Salaverry and R. Caivano, 'La Nueva Ley de Arbitraje Peruana: Un nuevo salto a la modernidad', *Revista Peruana de Arbitraje*, 7(2008), 3.

[28] Art. 63(8) expressly mentions, as a possible connection to Peru: nationality, domicile, habitual residence or principal activity. The other Latin-American legislation that had adopted this solution was the 1999 Panamanian Arbitration Act, art. 36. Nevertheless, the Supreme Court of Justice declared the unconstitutionality of this provision.

[29] Art. 66. [30] Art. 3(1). [31] Art. 3(4).

[32] Fourth complementary provision. In other words, generally speaking, arbitrators' competences are put on the same level as judges' competences, including that of the enforcement of the award (Art. 66).

example of this may be considered as the Brazilian Arbitration Act of 1996, which was delayed for five long years in the Supreme Federal Court because of a troublesome discussion relating to its constitutionality.[33] Another kind of dichotomy between arbitration rules and judicial practice related to arbitration may be found in the experiences of other Latin-American countries.[34] Without any doubt, both contradictions and paradoxical decisions are linked to the proliferation of arbitral controversies on investment issues and state contracts – a matter prone to attracting political, rather than legal arguments. In fact, almost all 'famous' cases considered as anti-arbitration ones (*Termorío*[35] in Colombia, *Copel*[36] in Brazil, *Cartellone*[37] and *Yaciretá*[38] in Argentina) dealt with state contracts.

Having said that, a glance at the recent case law of state courts in Latin America shows, on the one hand, that arbitration has become a real – and, in many cases, the preferred – way to solve legal disputes and, on the other hand, that judicial courts are increasingly supporting its development, sometimes in contradiction to legal reforms aimed at establishing more control over arbitration.[39] Even without doing an exhaustive

[33] See above notes 18–19 and accompanying text.

[34] See C. L. Uribe-Bernate, 'La práctica del arbitraje internacional en Colombia', in *Liber Amicorum Jürgen Samtleben* (Montevideo: FCU/Max-Planck-Institut, 2002), pp. 701, 717 ('it is really worrying ... to realize that the traditional territorialism of judicial authorities is not avoidable by means of legislation or the ratification of international treaties').

[35] Consejo de Estado, Administrative Ch., 3rd section, 1 August 2002, *Electrificadora del Atlántico SAESP* v. *Termorío SAESP*.

[36] Tribunal of Justice of Parana State, 15 March 2004, *Companhia Paranaense de Energia (Copel)* v. *UEG Araucária Ltda.*

[37] Supreme Court of Justice, 1 June 2004, *José Cartellone Construcciones Civiles SA* v. *Hidronor SA*, (see D. A. Casella, 'El control judicial de los laudos arbitrales en el derecho argentino', *DeCITA*, 3(2005), 462). It was a case concerning internal arbitration.

[38] National Judge of First Instance in Administrative Federal Matters no. 3, 27 September 2004, *Entidad Binacional Yaciretá (EBY)* v. *Eriday y otros*, (2005-A) *La Ley* 27, note by A. Bianchi (even more controversial was another decision in the same dispute adopted by the Judge no. 1 of the same jurisdiction, on 18 April 2005, (2005-C) *La Ley* 651, note by A. H. M. Corti).

[39] It is the case in El Salvador, where Art. 66-A of the 2002 Mediation, Conciliation and Arbitration Act, introduced by Legislative Decree no. 141 of 1 October 2009, according to which either party has the right to appeal the arbitral award on the merits before a court of appeals, was disqualified as unconstitutional by the First Court of Appeals of the First Section of the Center (Civil Ch. 20 July 2010, 1-APL-2010). The ground of this decision was article 23 of the Salvadorian Constitution, which establishes the right to settle civil or commercial disputes by arbitration. The same court (26 July 2010, 2-APL-2010) said that by means of that provision the constitution recognizes the right to settle disputes without state intervention. Both decisions have been submitted to the Supreme Court for the final say on the matter.

analysis of court decisions, it is easy to see the clear pro-arbitration trend in the region. Of course, bad, wrong and even unintelligible judicial decisions on arbitral matters arise from time to time and not only in cases concerning states or state-owned companies. Nevertheless, those types of decisions are not an exclusive oddity of Latin-American courts.

It can be said that the case law in Argentina, globally considered and insofar as only private parties are involved, is nowadays fairly favourable to arbitration. This impression is not affected by the fact that there have been some judicial decisions in matters of arbitration in which the courts misapply the relevant rules, namely those of the New York and Panama Conventions. Thus, without even mentioning these conventions, in *Reef Exploration*, the National Commercial Court of Appeal admitted the enforcement of an award that originated in the United States despite the previous existence of an anti-arbitration injunction issued by an Argentinian court.[40] On several occasions, Argentinian courts have dismissed applications for setting aside that invoked mistakes in the reasoning of the award, because such an incursion would jeopardize the very nature of arbitration.[41] The Supreme Court has also showed its support for arbitration. Even in 2004, the year in which two well-known controversial decisions were adopted,[42] the Supreme Court accepted in *Goijman* v. *Gomer*,[43] the validity of an arbitration agreement that was included in a labour contract that had been 'internationalized' due to the entry of new partners in the defendant company. Actually, provisions that were freely chosen by the parties have long been respected in Argentina; in particular, those agreements that derogate Argentinian jurisdiction in favour of courts or arbitral tribunals seated abroad.[44] Any restrictions to these agreements shall be applied cautiously.

[40] National Commercial Court of Appeals, Ch. D, 5 November 2002, *Reef Exploration Inc.* v. *Compañía General de Combustibles*, (2003-E) *La Ley* 937; (2003-III) *Jurisprudencia Argentina* 90, note by R. J. Caivano and R. A. Bianchi; (2004–1) *DeCITA* 344, note by M. B. Noodt Taquela. Both conventions are in force in both Argentina and the United States.

[41] See, for example, National Commercial Court of Appeals, Ch. E., 19 April 2005, *Patrón Costas, Marcelo D. y otros* v. *International Outdoor Advertising Holdings Co y otro s/ queja*, LexisNexis 35001884.

[42] See above, notes 37 and 38 (both cases related to state-owned companies).

[43] Supreme Court, 11 May 2004, *Goijman, Mario Daniel* v. *Gomer SACI*.

[44] For instance, Supreme Court, 5 April 2005, *Bear Service SA* v. *Cerveceria Modelo SA de CV*. See (2006) 5/6 *DeCITA* 431 (note by J. C. Rivera, 422). A paragraph of this judgment is particularly relevant because it expressly invokes article 16 of the UNCITRAL Model Law on International Commercial Arbitration as an 'internationally recognized rule' even in a country that has not followed the Model Law.

In Colombia, there is also a general attitude of respect towards foreign decisions. Thus, the Supreme Court of Justice[45] has elaborated on the notion of public policy as an obstacle to the enforcement of foreign decisions, underlining its exceptional character and stating that: not all Colombian mandatory provisions must be applied, but only those representing fundamental principles; the recognition of foreign judgments does not imply the revision of their merit; the notion of *ordre public* must be defined in reference to international principles, as a requirement of a globalized world; the *ordre public* notion must not be defensive, nor destructive, but dynamic, tolerant and constructive; and that Colombian citizens should not use this subterfuge to escape from the fulfilment of obligations that they accepted abroad.[46] This decision was challenged on due-process grounds, and the Constitutional Court, by refusing this pretension, has confirmed the notion elaborated on by the Supreme Court, adding that: 'it is obvious to the Court that the Supreme Court . . . cannot extend its competence in order to review whether the substantive rules of Colombian private law are identical to the rules of another state'.[47] In the particular matter of arbitration, the strict attitude of judicial courts concerning requests for setting aside deserves to be mentioned.[48]

A similar line of reasoning may be found in an interesting Chilean judgment delivered by the Court of Appeals of Santiago.[49] The court refused the application for setting aside an award, affirming, on the one hand, that the intervention of judicial courts whenever an arbitral agreement exists shall be exceptional and, on the other hand, that the notion of public policy shall be construed in a narrow manner. Shortly afterwards, the Chilean Supreme Court[50] accepted the *exequatur* of an

[45] Supreme Court of Justice, Civil Ch., 6 August 2004, no. 77, *García Fernandes Internacional Importaçâo e Exportaçâo SA* v. *Prodeco – Productos de Colombia* (application for the enforcement of a Portuguese judgment).

[46] See the comment of J. A. Silva, 'Revista mexicana de derecho internacional privado', (2005), 81.

[47] Colombian Constitutional Court, no. T-557, 26 May 2005. The Constitutional Court points out that the sole relevant difference between foreign and national law is that which essentially affects the national legal order.

[48] See recently the Superior District Court of Bogotá, 10 March 2010, *Industria y Distribuidora Indistri SA* v. *SAP Andina y Del Caribe CA*, no. 20100015000.

[49] *Corte de Apelaciones de Santiago*, 27 December 2007, *Publicis Groupe Holdings B.V.* v. *Árbitro Manuel José Vial Vial.* In its decision of 23 July 2010 (*Rol* 2363/2010), the same court stated that an award can only be attacked by an application for setting aside.

[50] Corte Suprema, 8 September 2009, *Comverse Inc.* v. *American Telecommunication Inc. Chile SA* (ATI Chile).

arbitral award issued in New York, pointing out that, in spite of the defendant's opposition, the purpose of the *exequatur* does not include a review of the merits. According to the court, although the defendant was invoking the violation of due process, the very aim of the defendant's application was a review of the merits and the weight to be given to the evidence, which are both excluded from the procedure of *exequatur*.[51]

In Mexico, the favourable attitude of judicial courts vis-à-vis arbitration has been underlined for many years.[52] This trend has been confirmed by their most recent decisions. In particular, some decisions of high Mexican courts[53] as well as *tesis* issued by the Supreme Court[54] have limited the scope of the application for setting aside and clarified its very definition.

Last but not least, Venezuelan tribunals have also merged into the same stream. Even if some differences remain between the two main chambers of the *Tribunal Supremo de Justicia*, the support for arbitration has been strongly confirmed by the Constitutional Chamber, which has, in addition, the last word on the matter.[55] Indeed, while the Political-Administrative Chamber has occasionally showed some reluctance to validate arbitral agreements by taking advantage of flaws or of a lack of precision in their drafting,[56] the Constitutional Chamber has insisted on the total legitimacy of arbitration as a mechanism for dispute resolution. Thus, this Chamber has refocused on the existence of the fundamental right to arbitration implicit in a practical notion of the right of access to

[51] On these decisions, see D. Jiménez Figueres and J. Klein Kranenberg, 'Recent International Arbitration Developments in the Chilean Courts', *Arbitration News*, 15(1) (2010), 161.

[52] See J. A. Silva, 'Algunas resoluciones judiciales de los tribunales mexicanos en torno al reconocimiento de un laudo arbitral', *DeCITA*, 2 (2004), 375, 394 ('in Mexico, for a long time, judicial courts have correctly admitted international commercial awards . . . judicial decisions have been not only favourable to arbitration; they have also fulfilled international commitments').

[53] Tribunal Colegiado, 11 June 2008, *Infored, SA de CV y José Elías Gutiérrez Vivó* v. *Grupo Radio Centro, SA*.

[54] *Tesis* no. CLXXIII/2009, *Amparo en revisión* 131/2009, 27 May 2009; no. I.7°.C.126, *Amparo en revisión* 23/2009, 12 March 2009; no. I.3°.C.729, *Amparo en revisión* 274/2008, 4 December 2008.

[55] The Constitutional Chamber of the Supreme Court has the power to review, due to violation of the Constitution, not only the final decisions of inferior courts but also of the other chambers of the Supreme Court (cf. art. 355 Constitution and art. 25 of *Ley Orgánica del Tribunal Supremo de Justicia*). This last-instance notion was expressly noted by the Constitutional Court in its decision of 17 October 2008, no. 1.541/08.

[56] E.g., 28 April 2010, *DIMAPECA* v. *Servicios Halliburton de Venezuela SA*, no. 331/2010.

justice[57] and holds that any legal rule or judicial interpretation that goes against the constitutional mandate of the promotion and development of arbitration (and other non-judicial means to solve disputes: article 258 of the Venezuelan Constitution) shall be deemed as unconstitutional.[58] Quite recently, the Constitutional Chamber, in a remarkable and erudite decision, has supported the *compétence-compétence* principle and strongly rebutted the arguments previously given in the case by the Political-Administrative Chamber.[59]

3 The impact of investment arbitration

3.1 *The singularities of arbitration with state participation*

States and public powers have been realizing for many years that arbitration does not have a negligible catalytic effect on commercial activity. As a result, the promotion of this dispute settlement mechanism has become a suitable policy. Companies feel more and more comfortable within arbitration (and, therefore, allegedly outside the scope of the jurisdiction) and the states seem to offer them a favourable framework for arbitration development. At the same time, though it may appear as contradictory, states establish the conditions and parameters to control the regularity of arbitral proceedings and decisions. In fact, there is no contradiction: the promotion of a mechanism that is, by definition, fast, specialized and efficient, does not necessarily lead to the total withdrawal of the state functions related to the promotion of justice.

This is the reason behind the observation that states continue to be firmly attached to their double role as both promoters of arbitration and the guardians of its smooth running. However, what has notably changed in a short period of time is the consideration of the role of the state in the governance of international private relationships[60] and, in a broader sense, the scope of the state-law-making power to deal with

[57] *Tribunal Supremo de Justicia*, Constitutional Ch., 28 February 2008, no. 192/2008.

[58] *Tribunal Supremo de Justicia*, Constitutional Ch., 17 October 2008, no. 1.541/08.

[59] *Tribunal Supremo de Justicia*, Constitutional Ch., 3 November 2010, no. 1067/2010, reversing the judgment of the Political-Administrative Chamber, 21 May 2009, no. 687. It is worth mentioning the Constitutional Chamber's order to publish its decision in the *Gaceta Oficial*, stating that this judgment 'fixes the binding interpretation about the arbitration system and the lack of jurisdiction of the organs of the [Venezuelan] judiciary power'.

[60] Ver Ph. Leboulanger, 'Rapport introductif (Les Etats dans le contentieux économique international)', *Rev. arb.*, 3(2003), 618.

the operation of the market, given the fact that states have entered into the dense jungle of international treaties on trade and commerce. Privatization and liberalization, as the component phenomena of globalization, have reached not only into the economy, but also into the law and, regarding some matters, in an astonishing way. The reflection of these phenomena in private law is the enlargement of the margins of party autonomy. In other words, states' powers are supra-limited by international commitments and infra-limited by the freedom recognized as belonging to individuals and legal entities.

In that context, the above-mentioned common state attitudes have been present in Latin America for decades. The first one – the broad promotion of arbitration – is clearly perceptible when examining the legal framework created by Latin-American states at both the international and domestic level, as we have already seen. The second one – some kind of reticence concerning arbitration with state participation – can be analysed through the emergence of investment arbitration and the problems that are associated with it. Even though we know that not all state participation in the field of arbitration concerns cases of investment arbitration, from the point of view of the state attitude in Latin America, the distinction becomes generally superfluous.

Whenever a state takes part in arbitral proceedings, several aspects of the arbitration change or trends are modified. The very idea that a state may withdraw the submission of its own judicial apparatus seemed practically unacceptable not so long ago.[61] Today, when that withdrawal has become the rule and arbitration with state participation is multiplying exponentially, hand in hand with the multitude of bilateral and multilateral investment treaties and the massive acceptance of the ICSID system,[62] there is no room for doubt. Even states that stepped away from the ICSID system are looking for alternative arbitral institutions. This is the case in Ecuador, a country that is trying to lay down an investment arbitration system within the framework of UNASUR (The Union of South American Nations).[63] That means that there is distrust in ICSID, but not in arbitration.

[61] According to B. Oppetit, 'Les Etats et l'arbitrage international: esquisse de systématisation', *Rev. arb.*, 4(1985) 493–4, that idea was traditionally deemed to be in principle 'unusual' and even 'inconceivable and unlawful'.

[62] We talk about 'acceptance' in terms of the number of contracting states (146 nowadays), without prejudice to the criticisms that have been made in regard to its functioning.

[63] See below, at Section 3.3.

However, despite such an overwhelming acceptance of state submission to arbitration, relationships between states and private legal entities still constitute a controversial matter for many legal systems.[64] That is particularly true for relationships based on investment treaties, but the situation is often not less controversial when a state initially enters into a simple commercial contract with a foreign company. When a dispute arises within a mixed relationship, can the dispute-settlement mechanism – in most cases arbitration – be identical to arbitration between private parties? Apparently, it cannot.[65] Theoretically, the traditional distinction – well developed in relation to state immunity[66] – between state activities *iure imperii* and *iure gestionis*[67] could lead to the assumption that whenever the state steps down to the level of private parties by developing any activity *iure gestionis* it should pay the price and lose its prerogatives. In practice, however, the essential differences between the state and private entities remain untouchable. Thus, the state may always have its *imperium* at hand, specifically by invoking immunity,[68] by applying its law-making power[69] or by realizing procedural acts aimed at interfering in the normal development of arbitral proceedings.[70]

[64] On the impossibility for the state in Colombia to submit to arbitration certain acts concerning state contracts, see E. Silva-Romero, 'La distinción entre "Estado" y "Administración" y el arbitraje resultante de "contratos de Estado"', *Revista Brasileira de Arbitragem*, 1 (2004), 53–6. See also, in Brazil, the contradictions concerning this matter in J. B. Lee and C. M. Valença Filho, 'Brazil's New Public-Private Partnership Law: One Step Forward, Two Steps Back', *Journal of International Arbitration*, 22(5) (2005), 419.

[65] In particular, it is obvious that investment disputes are different to any other commercial disputes, notwithstanding the application of the same rules in some cases. Concerning some reasons for this statement, see J. D. M. Lew, L. A. Mistelis and S. M. Kröll, *Comparative International Commercial Arbitration* (The Hague: Kluwer, 2003), pp. 763 ff.

[66] See P. Trooboff, 'Foreign State Immunity: Emerging Consensus on Principles', *Recueil des Cours*, 200(5) (1986), 298.

[67] H. A. Grigera Naón, 'Les contrats d'Etat: quelques réflexions', *Rev. arb.*, 3 (2003), 667, explains how this distinction, well grounded in Latin-American countries, is distorted by the strong irruption of the investment arbitration.

[68] See D. P. Fernández Arroyo, 'La ejecución del laudo arbitral proferido contra el Estado', *DeCITA*, 2(2004), 164.

[69] See I. Hautot, 'Les difficultés spécifiques dues à l'intervention d'Etats ou de personnes publiques dans l'arbitrage commercial international', in *L'intervention de l'Etat ou d'une firme étatique dans l'arbitrage commercial international* (Bruxelles: Kluwer and Story Scientia, 1993), pp. 3–5. Cf. P. Mayer, 'La neutralisation du pouvoir normatif de l'Etat en matière de contrats d'Etat', *Journ. dr. int.* (1986), 5.

[70] See B. Hanotiau, 'Quand l'arbitrage s'en va-t-en guerre: les perturbations par l'État de la procédure arbitrale', *Rev. arb.*, 3(2003), 805; E. Kleiman, 'Les incidences politiques de la souveraineté sur l'arbitrage: les perturbations de la procédure arbitrale', *Rev. arb.*, 3(2003), 827.

3.2 The rapid growth in investment arbitration: early cases and problematic issues

Investment arbitration has experienced a singular evolution during the last few years. A large number of the relevant components of this evolution have arisen from cases dealing with Latin-American countries, with more than a half of ICSID pending cases involving countries of this region as defendants.[71] In consequence, most objections against both investment law and its implementation by means of investment dispute resolution systems have been raised either in those countries or in respect of these cases.[72] The same can be said for the refutations of these objections.

Within this general objective situation, it is not very difficult to identify some particular questions that have had a clear influence on the development of the discussions about the current investment regulations. Thus, cases such as *Santa Elena* in Costa Rica (1996/2000),[73] *Metalclad* in Mexico (1997/2000),[74] *Aguas del Tunari* in Bolivia (2002/2006),[75] the deep Argentinian crisis (2001–) – which made this state become a kind of universal defendant in international-investment dispute resolution systems – or the latest developments in the *Ecuador* v. *Chevron* saga, have provided some of the most significant subject areas for use in the analysis concerning investment regulations. Consequently, the discussions that have arisen all over the world about investment law are more the consequence of the pro and contra points of the functioning of existing rules, rather than a mere theoretical exercise based on ideological prejudices.

Latin-American case law has made its contribution to the framing of some practical issues, such as:

(a) *Scope of the state's consent to arbitration.* The attitude of different states in Latin America to include in the investment contract a clause referring to the jurisdiction of their national tribunal,[76] where these states were parties to an investment treaty providing for an arbitration

[71] Argentina is still the leader in terms of the number of cases put before the ICSID, yet Venezuela seems to be working hard to dispute this 'honour'.

[72] For example, the well-known Philippe Sands' criticism on current investment law is mainly constructed in respect of Latin-American cases. See P. Sands, 'A Safer World, for Investors', in *Lawless World* (London: Penguin, 2006), pp. 117–42.

[73] *Compañía del Desarrollo de Santa Elena SA* v. *Republic of Costa Rica*, ICSID Case no. ARB/96/1.

[74] *Metalclad Corporation* v. *Estados Unidos Mexicanos*, ICSID Case no. ARB(AF)/97/01.

[75] *Aguas del Tunari SA* v. *Republic of Bolivia*, ICSID Case no. ARB/03/2.

[76] For instance, *Azurix Corp.* v. *Argentina Republic*, ICSID no ARB/01/12.

agreement, has originated theoretical discussions concerning the distinction between a treaty claim and a contract claim.[77]

(b) *Affecting public interest.* The influence of public interest on issues such as those involved in public health or environmental protection has provoked discussions. On the one hand, these questions have raised the problem of transparency in international arbitration, which has gained enormous significance.[78] On the other hand, foreign investments are also seen as concerning the very delicate issue of the state's sovereignty, particularly the power of the state to enact rules that can have an impact on the current investments in the state and the effects of the exercise of the law-making power of the state on the investor's assets.

(c) *Nomination and challenge of arbitrators.* Founded or unfounded suspicions based on the recurrence of certain names in different arbitral tribunals, as well as the ability of these actors to change roles (as that some people who act every now and then as arbitrators have done), where they are counsel (or experts) for quite similar cases or for cases involving the same parties, have provoked a number of discussions related to conflicts of interest, and to the impartiality and/or independence of arbitrators.[79]

(d) *Problems caused by indirect expropriation measures (regulatory takings).* Since *Metalclad*, the discussion about the scope of the notion of expropriation has been a permanent issue in arbitral proceedings as well as in the drafting of new bilateral investment treaties.[80]

77 B. M. Cremades and D. J. A. Cairns, 'La seguridad jurídica de las inversiones extranjeras: la protección contractual y de los tratados', *DeCITA*, 2(2004), 231; F. Orrego Vicuña, 'De los contratos y tratados en el mercado global', *DeCITA*, 3(2005), 18; J. Crawford, 'Treaty and Contract in Investment Arbitration', *Arbitration International*, 24(3) (2008), 351.

78 See notes 92–94 below and accompanying text.

79 See N. M. Perrone, 'La recusación de los árbitros en casos de inversiones extranjeras. A propósito de la solicitud argentina interpuesta ante tribunales nacionales respecto de Rigo Sureda', *DeCITA*, 9(2008), 342. Among several examples in ICSID arbitration, see the recent decision of the *Ad hoc* Committee on the second annulment proceeding of *Compañía de Aguas del Aconquija SA and Vivendi Universal SA* v. *Argentine Republic*, ICSID Case no. ARB/97/3.

80 According to the definition of expropriation given by the arbitral tribunal in *Metalclad* (para. 103), the concept includes 'not only open, deliberate and acknowledged takings of property, such as outright seizure or formal or obligatory transfer of title in favor of the host State, but also covert or incidental interference with the use of property which has the effect of depriving the owner, in whole or in significant part, of the use or reasonably-to-be-expected economic benefit of property even if not necessarily to the obvious benefit of the host state'.

(e) *The very concept of investor*. The notion of the investor has also been raised several times; in particular, in cases in which the claims were presented by minority shareholders, while the main shareholders entered into negotiations with the host state.[81]

(f) *Contradictory arbitral awards*. The disparity of conclusions about identical facts reached by different arbitral tribunals,[82] in addition to sharp criticism, has contributed significantly to the rekindling of the debate on whether or not precedents are necessary in investment arbitration.[83]

3.3 *Reactions and current evolution*

Notwithstanding the significance of all these practical issues, perhaps a more fundamental question concerns the relevance of the investment protective rules for the attraction of foreign investors. In other words, is the adoption by states of a high standard of protection of foreign investments attractive for foreign investors? Alternatively, and more concretely, this fundamental question asked by the current law on foreign investment might be expressed in the following way: is the need (or the will) to attract foreign investors a direct cause of the participation of host states in the Washington Convention, and in bilateral or multilateral investment treaties?

First of all, it seems quite obvious that states sign investment treaties in order to attract investors. One of their most important aspects is the waiver by states of their national courts' jurisdiction. Nevertheless, the example of Brazil, which hosts most foreign investments in Latin America, in spite of its reluctance to make investment-arbitration

[81] That was the situation in several actions brought against Argentina by, for example, CMS (case no. ARB/01/8; Techint and TGN, main shareholders), Enron (case no. ARB/01/3; Petrobras and TGS, main shareholders) and LG&E (case no. ARB/02/01; Gas BAN and Gas Natural SDG, main shareholders).

[82] Perhaps the more mentioned situation is that of the state of necessity invoked by Argentina in several cases. Where some tribunals (CMS, Enron, Sempra – case no. ARB/02/16) did not find enough arguments to accept the justification of the state of necessity, others clearly found them (LG&E, Continental – case no. ARB/03/9 – annulment of Sempra). See A. Alvarez-Jiménez, 'Foreign Investment Protection and Regulatory Failures as States' Contribution to the State of Necessity under Customary International Law: A New Approach Based on the Complexity of Argentina's 2001 Crisis', *Journal of International Arbitration*, 27(2010), 141.

[83] See, in general, E. Gaillard and Y. Banifatemi, *Precedent in Arbitration* (New York: Juris, 2008).

commitments,[84] tends to prove the contrary. In reality, the contradiction is only apparent. It is true that states tend to think that the conclusion of an investment treaty will give it an image of security and trust. However, to be part of an investment treaty does not mean that the state has gone the whole mile. Treaties are not the only reason why foreign companies invest. If a state has good opportunities for investors to be able to make profitable deals, it is likely that it will attract investors, even though it is not a party to an investment treaty, or even if that state has shown restrictive behaviour to foreign investors. If we view the problem from the alternate angle, the existence of a treaty does not guarantee investments and the absence of a treaty does not eliminate any possibility of receiving them.[85]

Criticism against the so-called new investment arbitration law has been disseminated all over Latin America. At the root of this criticism are the dozens of investment arbitration proceedings against Latin-American countries that have been initiated since 1996, as well as the large percentage of awards that have been favourable to investors, in particular, during the early years of the current century. Nevertheless, the attitudes of the states are heterogeneous. For some, there is no particular criticism, but rather an expression of traditional mistrust. It was shown in the above-mentioned case of Brazil.[86] However, quite similar rules that were refused by Brazil in the framework of FTTA/ ALCA negotiations have been accepted by other Latin-American states

[84] Brazil has neither ratified the 1965 Washington Convention creating the ICSID nor any of the bilateral investment treaties (BITs) it concluded, and has strongly refused the investment chapter of the Draft Treaty of the Free Trade Area of the Americas (FTAA/ ALCA). However, given the growing relevance of Brazilian investments in other countries, the business sector is asking if such a politic is fully convenient for Brazil. J. Kalicki and S. Medeiros, 'Investment Arbitration in Brazil: Revisiting Brazil's Traditional Reluctance Towards ICSID, BITs and Investor-State Arbitration', *Arbitration International*, 24(3) (2008), 423.

[85] That having been said, one must recognise that states do not always act in a coherent way. Some sign and ratify treaties but refuse them as soon as they could serve as a legal basis for a claim from an investor. In this sense, one might think that it is more coherent and preferable for a state not to sign any treaties and to remain outside of the system of investment protection, or for a state to denounce the treaties that it has concluded, instead of being a party to one treaty and not complying with it.

[86] The other Latin-American state that has shown similar reluctance is Cuba. Conversely, Mexico and the Dominican Republic (the other two Latin-American countries that have never ratified the ICSID Convention) are parties in many BITs and in FTAs containing investment arbitration provisions.

in the context of their free-trade agreements concluded with developed countries – more particularly, the United States.[87] A clearly different attitude is held by both Bolivia and Ecuador, countries that have decided to denounce the ICSID Convention,[88] adopting specific constitutional provisions to limit or prohibit arbitration over disputes with state participation[89] and opening the door to denouncing or renegotiating bilateral investment treaties that are in force.[90] Finally, the vast majority of Latin-American states continue to participate in the international investment system even though some of them openly criticize its functioning. In a parallel way, member states of UNASUR, under an Ecuadorian initiative, are looking for the creation of a sub-regional arbitral investment system as a way to escape from the worldwide (or *worldbankwide*) system.

Actions and reactions within the field of mixed arbitration are not surprising, taking into consideration the sensitive interests that are at stake whenever a state takes part in an international dispute against a foreign private individual or entity. One can agree with or be critical of the state's actions, but generally speaking, the attitudes of states tend to be predictable. The considerable impact that these features of arbitration with the involvement of Latin-American states have had on the arbitration

[87] Among the most recent, it is worth mentioning those between the United States and Peru and between the United States and the Central American states and the Dominican Republic (CAFTA–DR).

[88] Both denunciations were made in accordance with article 71 of the ICSID Convention; they took effect, for Bolivia, on 3 November 2007 and, for Ecuador, on 7 January 2010.

[89] Art. 422 of the Ecuadorean Constitution (2008) avoids the conclusion of treaties, submitting that state to international arbitration institutions dealing with any 'contractual or commercial' dispute in which the state participates, except for arbitrations conducted in Latin-American arbitral institutions and for disputes related to the external debt; nevertheless, article 190, paragraph 2 admits the submission to arbitration in the law of state contracts under the authorization of the public attorney and the legal conditions required (see Judgment of Constitutional Court of 13 March 2009, no. 0001–09-SIC-CC, which upheld an arbitration-in-equity clause in a contract between Ecuador and the Inter-American Development Bank, notwithstanding the opposition of the public attorney; the Court considers that the restriction of article 190, paragraph 2 does not apply to a case exclusively governed by article 422, paragraph 3, dealing with the external debt). The restriction to arbitration made by article 366 of the Bolivian Constitution (2009) refers specifically to foreign companies operating in Bolivia in the hydrocarbon sector.

[90] The last option was also envisaged by Venezuela. E. Gaillard, 'Trends in Anti-arbitration in Latin America', *New York Law Journal*, 239(2008), 108 (also published in Spanish: 'Tendencias anti-arbitraje en América Latina', *DeCITA*, 10(2009), 311).

between private parties, in particular in those countries that have been involved in rather bitter situations, is (not unexpectedly) regrettable. Perhaps some of these negative consequences are due to a feeling of powerlessness in the relevant states (or, more precisely, of some civil servants) that have tried to justify their mistakes and misconduct by covering them up with a supposed plot by arbitrators and arbitral institutions. Nevertheless, it is fair to recognize, at the same time, that some decisions and attitudes of arbitral tribunals and of the ICSID itself could have given the impression (for more than a decade) of underestimating states' rights and powers.[91] That impression (and everybody knows that appearances, deceptive as they can be, are highly significant in arbitration) has provoked a sort of distrust effect vis-à-vis arbitration in general, which has been manifested in non-specialized legal scholarship and – which is far worse – in some judicial decisions.

All in all, that pervasive effect is not as strong as it was at the beginning of the present century. At that time, the avalanche of investment arbitration proceedings brought against Argentina seemed close to bringing about the complete collapse of the arbitration system.[92] Some years later, it can be said that – as a general rule – the distrust towards arbitration and the correlative reinforcing of state powers were somehow confined within the framework of arbitration involving state participation. Even in this field, the movement towards transparency should lead to the elimination of suspicions as well as to an improvement in the systems for adjudicating investor–state disputes. In line with this, the reform of the ICSID Arbitration Rules in 2006,[93] the drafts adopted by new investment arbitration rules in free-trade agreements[94] and the current work on this matter accomplished by the UNCITRAL Working

[91] See G. K. Foster, 'Recent Setbacks for Foreign Investors in Latin America and What They Mean for the Future of Investment Treaty Arbitration in the Region', *Latin American Arbitration Review*, 1(2006), 15, 17.

[92] However, it must be underlined that, notwithstanding the intention of some members of the Argentinean Government in that critical moment (see H. D. Rosatti, 'Los tratados bilaterales de inversión, el arbitraje internacional obligatorio y el sistema constitucional argentino', *La Ley*, (2003-F), 1283), this country sidestepped the temptation to denunciate the Washington Convention.

[93] The core of the reform dealt, on the one hand, with transparency issues (*amicus curiae* participation – Rule 37, open hearings – Rule 32, and the publication of the awards – Rule 48) and, on the other hand, with the reinforcing of arbitrator independence (Rule 6).

[94] Among new free-trade agreements with a high standard of transparency, the CAFTA–DR (Art. 10(21)) deserves to be mentioned.

Group on Arbitration[95] are all sending good signals in terms of avoiding any negative impact on private arbitration. Conversely, the issuing of several arbitral decisions favourable to states in the last few years (a consequence of the transparency wave?) could help to mitigate the reluctance still maintained by some of them in terms of arbitration.[96]

4 Some particular issues

In order to complete this survey about current trends in arbitration in Latin America, at least three singular issues should be pointed out: the growth of Latin-American participation in the 'market' of international commercial arbitration, the constitutionalization of arbitration and the place attributed to arbitration by domestic legal orders.

4.1 Increasing Latin-American participation in international commercial arbitration

The adoption of – broadly speaking – good arbitration acts[97] and the ratification of international instruments on the matter,[98] on the one hand, and the above-mentioned judicial trends,[99] on the other, reflect the current legal status of arbitration in Latin America. However, it does not necessarily indicate the real perception of this status by the business community. The question then is whether the deep modification of the legal framework has stimulated more confidence in arbitration and,

[95] The Working Group on Arbitration and Conciliation (WG II) of UNCITRAL, after finishing the reform of the UNCITRAL Arbitration Rules is elaborating on a legal standard on transparency in treaty-based investor–state arbitration. See www.uncitral.org/uncitral/en/commission/working_groups/2Arbitration.html. Although neither the form nor the content of the instrument have yet been defined, the work in progress has drawn the attention of states, arbitral institutions, businesses and academics, who participate hugely in the discussions. Latin-American states, that usually are not very active in UNCITRAL working groups, are now showing a strong interest in this matter.

[96] According to the UNCTAD's report on investor–state dispute settlement reported cases, published on 1 March 2011, in 2010 it rendered twenty awards, five decisions on liability, and 11 decisions on jurisdiction, as well as 11 other decisions on interim measures, discontinuance of proceedings and costs. Of the 20 awards, 14 were in favour of the state and five were in favour of the investor, and in one case, the parties adopted a settlement agreement. See, in particular, *Sempra* v. *Argentina*, Decision on Annulment, 29 June 2010, and *Enron* v. *Argentina*, Ad hoc Committee, Decision on Annulment, 30 July 2010.

[97] See above, 3.2. [98] See above, 3.1. [99] See above, 3.3.

more particularly, an increasing number of arbitration proceedings in the region.

The answer is a resounding 'yes'. In several Latin-American countries, the number of cases submitted to arbitration has experienced a remarkable increase. Thus, the main Peruvian arbitral institution, according to the statistics shown on its website, has gone from just two cases in 1993 to 1,798 cases in 2010.[100] The increase in the number of arbitration proceedings is also substantial in other countries such as Brazil, Chile and Mexico. Equally, the multiplication of arbitral institutions[101] would indicate the existence of a favourable ambiance in professional and academic circles. Books dealing with 'Latin-American arbitration'[102] and specialized periodicals devoted to arbitration seem to multiply. As a matter of fact, arbitration is becoming a real option for Latin-American parties, as reflected in the statistics of the ICC. It is interesting to note that during the last decade, more than 10% of all cases registered in the Arbitration Court of the ICC involve parties from Latin America and the Caribbean. It is equally astonishing that Argentina, Mexico and Brazil are among the twelve states that offer most arbitrators within that Court.[103] It is true that in most of the cases submitted to ICC arbitration in which a party is from Latin America the seat of the arbitration has been located out of the region. However, the location of these cases in some Latin-American countries is no longer a rare exception. On the contrary, nowadays several 'big' disputes between Latin-American parties are being solved by arbitral tribunals seated in Latin-American towns, often under the auspices of worldwide arbitral institutions.[104]

[100] http://200.37.9.27/CCL/ccl_arbitraje/es/ccl_estadisticas.aspx. The amounts involved in these disputes are also experiencing similar growth, from US$ 232,000 in 1993 to 2,287,000,000 in 2010.

[101] In part, owing to the sponsoring of international agencies such as the Inter-American Development Bank. See, P. E. Mason and M. G. F. dos Santos, 'New Keys to Arbitration in Latin-America', *Journal of International Arbitration*, 25(1) (2008), 31, 41–2.

[102] The fact that sometimes those books are not written by specialists but rather by opportunists shows the expectations generated by arbitration in this region.

[103] See 'Statistical Report', *ICC International Court of Arbitration Bulletin*, 22(1) (2011).

[104] Several years ago, a prominent Latin-American arbitrator based in Paris was already proposing the location of commercial arbitrations without state participation in towns such as Mexico DF, Bogota, São Paulo and Montevideo. E. Silva Romero, 'América Latina como sede de arbitrajes comerciales internacionales. La experiencia de la Corte Internacional de Arbitraje de la CCI', *DeCITA*, 2(2004), 217.

4.2 Constitutionalization of arbitration

The comprehension of the word 'constitutionalization' within the framework of Latin-American arbitration is twofold. At first, given the fact that some contemporaneous constitutions have expressly included a sort of fundamental right to arbitration that goes hand in hand with the duty of public power to promote arbitration,[105] one might think that arbitration is fully supported.[106] However, in the end, this very characterization opens doors to a particular kind of attack against arbitral awards founded in the supposed violation of constitutional principles.[107] Indeed, it is on this stream of constitutionalization that awards adopted by arbitral tribunals seated in Latin-American countries have been challenged by means of different kinds of extraordinary judicial remedies. It is interesting to examine whether these remedies were directly raised against the award or only against the judicial decision related to the setting aside or to the enforcement of the award. In Mexico, for instance, the singular remedy known as *amparo* can be used to challenge judicial decisions related to the award, but not against the award itself.[108] In Peru, although the Constitutional Court had authorized the *amparo* for use against arbitral awards, the Superior Court of Justice of Lima, by applying a notion introduced in the Arbitration Act of 2008, affirmed that this remedy may not serve to review the same arguments previously

[105] See article 258 of the Venezuelan Constitution and Judgment of the Supreme Tribunal of Justice, Constitutional Chamber, no. 1541, 17 October 2008; and article 116 of the Colombian Constitution.

[106] Thus, in El Salvador, article 23 of the Constitution, which establishes the right to settle civil or commercial disputes by arbitration, has been invoked by the First Court of Appeals of the First Section of the Center (Civil Ch. 20 July 2010, 1-APL-2010; 26 July 2010, 2-APL-2010) to declare unconstitutional the rule that authorizes an appeal against arbitral awards. See above note 38.

[107] E. Silva Romero, 'A propos de l'inexorable collision de philosophies dans la constitutionnalisation de l'arbitrage internationale en Amérique latine', in B. Fauvarque-Cosson and A. Wald (eds.), *L'arbitrage en France et en Amérique latine à l'aube du XXIe siècle* (Paris: Société de législation comparée, 2008), p. 269 (underlining the contradiction between the distributive justice of constitutional courts and the corrective justice of arbitral tribunals as well as between the parochial character of constitutions and the typical universalism of international arbitration).

[108] L. Pereznieto Castro and J. A. Graham, *Tratado de arbitraje comercial internacional mexicano* (Mexico: Limusa, 2008), pp. 191–5, 212–15, 223–7. In *Banamex* v. *Corporación Transnacional de Inversiones SA de CV*, 17 February 2004, the court (Décimo Tribunal Colegiado en Materia Civil del Primer Circuito) refused the application of *amparo* made by the arbitrators against the judgment that had annulled the award, due to the arbitrators' lack of *locus standi* (the losing party had sued the arbitrators at the same time that it applied for setting aside the award).

invoked in a set-aside proceeding.[109] In Venezuela, the Supreme Tribunal of Justice has admitted the *amparo constitucional* even against foreign awards.[110] Of course, we can reduce all these issues to a discussion between old conceptions about the legal order and a 'new' legal pluralism and say that international commercial arbitration cannot be subjected to any national constitution.[111] The problem will be to convince some courts of such sophisticated arguments.[112]

4.3 *The place of arbitration in the jurisdictional context*

Legislative and judicial progress in matters that strictly concern arbitration can barely overcome some traditional procedural conceptions. In fact, perhaps the most important issue within the Latin-American domestic legal systems is the generalized conception of the arbitrator as a component of the local judiciary. The meaning of this fundamental assumption is that by selecting the seat of arbitration the parties are not only choosing a geographical place, but also the jurisdictional framework in which the activity of the arbitral tribunal will be developed. As a result, that activity will be submitted to the control of the highest judicial authorities of the state of the seat and the arbitral tribunal will have to apply some procedural (and even substantial) rules of this state. Certainly, this conception is not a particularity of Latin-American states.[113]

[109] The Superior Court of Justice of Lima, *Peru Holding de Turismo SAA*, 30 December 2008. In this case, the *amparo* was brought against the arbitrators and the Center of Conciliation and National and International Arbitration of the Chamber of Commerce of Lima.

[110] See judgments of the Supreme Tribunal of Justice, Constitutional Ch., of 16 October 2001 (*VTV*) and 14 February 2007 (*Todo Sabor CA*). R. Escobar Alvarado, 'Recursos contra laudos arbitrales dictados en el extranjero', in *Derecho procesal civil internacional. In memoriam Tatiana B. de Maekelt* (Caracas: Academia de Ciencias Políticas y Sociales, 2010), p. 783, pp. 800–803.

[111] A. de Jesús O., 'La autonomía del arbitraje comercial internacional a la hora de la constitucionalización del arbitraje en América Latina', *Lima Arbitration*, 3(2008/2009), 151.

[112] A totally different matter concerns the possibility of an arbitral tribunal solving a question of constitutionality (of course, in a country where there is a non-concentrated system of constitutional review). In Argentina, some courts – misapplying the very precedents of the Supreme Court of Justice – have denied this possibility. See the critique by J. C. Rivera, 'Cuestiones constitucionales en el arbitraje', *DeCITA*, 11(2009), 296.

[113] See E. Gaillard, *Aspects philosophiques du droit de l'arbitrage international* (Leiden: Académie de droit international de La Haye, 2008), pp. 34–46.

To a certain extent, such a conception would be an obstacle to the normal application of the *compétence–compétence* principle. Indeed, the consideration of the arbitral tribunal as an organ of the judicial body of the state highlights (for instance) that whenever the competence of an arbitral tribunal is challenged before a judicial court that is deemed to be competent by the applicant, the 'conflict' between that court and the arbitral tribunal can only be solved by a superior judicial court.[114] The procedure for deciding upon that conflict may be long and tortuous and it is likely to encourage procedural strategies aimed at prolonging arbitral proceedings.[115] The result can be even worse for the arbitration if it is taken as a mere exception to the judicial jurisdiction (which would appear as the *ordinary* or *natural* jurisdiction). Of course, this would not be possible where the notion of the arbitration as an autonomous mechanism to settle disputes is deeply rooted and where a simple rule such as that contained in article 16(3) of the UNCITRAL Model Law[116] is in force, provided that that rule is correctly applied by the courts.[117]

5 Concluding remarks

Having presented a general view of the features and trends in Latin-American international commercial arbitration, three key points should be emphasized.

5.1 Strong diversity

In spite of several common features, it is hard to find a single attitude, even a single trend, in Latin-American commercial arbitration. As often happens with the definition of political and economic positions at a national level, the development of the legal systems depends on many

114 Thus, in Argentina, the Supreme Court of Justice, 1 November 1988, *La Nación SA* v. *La Razón SA*, and 10 November 1988, *Nidera SA* v. *Rodríguez Alvarez de Canale, Elena* (note by R. Caivano, (1990-A), *La Ley*, 419); in Brazil, the Superior Tribunal of Justice, Competence conflict no. 111.230, 1 July 2010.

115 Grigera Naón, 'Arbitration and Latin America: Progress and Setbacks', pp. 155–6.

116 According to this rule, if the arbitral tribunal affirms its own competence as a preliminary question, either party may challenge that decision before a court but 'the arbitral tribunal may continue the arbitral proceedings and make an award'.

117 Which seems not to always be the case in Mexico, for example. See F. González Cossío, '*Kompetenz-kompetenz* a la mexicana: crónica de una muerte anunciada' (www.camex.com.mx/fgc.pdf), and Supreme Court of Justice, 1st Ch., *Contradiction of thesis* 51/2005ps, 1 September 2006.

specific factors that are rarely combined in the same way in two different countries. As far as international commercial arbitration is concerned, if any trend is to be identified from the legislative activity of Latin-American states, from the political decisions of their governments and from judicial decisions, it is that arbitration has become a generally accepted method of settlement for international commercial disputes. That is perhaps the single common trend in the current field of commercial arbitration in Latin America. This general acceptance of arbitration does not exclude the existence of exceptions and contradictions, even in the bosom of the same court. Furthermore, the rate of implementation of this common assumption varies both from country to country and, within each country, according to the prevailing economic and social circumstances.

5.2 *Need for a pedagogical effort*

The expansion of arbitration in Latin America has generated a significant critical mass of professionals who are highly educated and often well trained in the matter as well as a diffusion of the advantages of arbitration among the business community. Good arbitral institutions have been created and are functioning throughout Latin America; in some countries, the number of cases (more domestic than international) has considerably increased. The big issue continues to be the education of judges in the interpretation and the application of international instruments and new domestic mechanisms.[118] Every official programme to promote and develop arbitration in the region should make this element its top priority.

5.3 *Isolation and management of the impact on investment arbitration*

The debate (and the backlash) originated within the context of investment arbitration – for instance, around the legitimacy of arbitrators in coping with some public interest issues – and when considered as a whole, it has been rather positive. It has stimulated improvements in investment law, the balancing of the rights and duties of investors and states and the professionalization of the states' attorneys. The negative aspect is related to the impact of the first decade of investment-arbitration cases involving

[118] J. A. Moreno Rodríguez, *Contratación y arbitraje* (Asunción: CEDEP, 2010), p. 280.

Latin-American states on international commercial arbitration in general. Perhaps the original sin was the generalization of the application of rules and mechanisms that had been developed for commercial cases to a substantially different reality. Now, the pendulum seems to be closer to the centre in terms of investment arbitration – in particular, because of the proliferation of transparency standards. Commercial arbitration is differentiating from its complicated cousin. Accordingly, on balance – excluding mixed arbitration – attitudes against arbitration, in general, are today fewer and less influential than legislative, judicial and private pro-arbitration manifestations.[119]

[119] This chapter is updated as of June 2011.

INDEX